I0189483

# Commentary on Romans

## Philip Melanchthon

Translated by Fred Kramer

Second English Edition

CONCORDIA PUBLISHING HOUSE • SAINT LOUIS

Copyright © 2010 Concordia Publishing House
3558 S. Jefferson Ave., St. Louis, MO 63118-3968
1-800-325-3040 • www.cph.org

All rights reserved. No part of this publication may be reproduced, stored in a retrieval system, or transmitted, in any form or by any means, electronic, mechanical, photo-copying, recording, or otherwise, without the prior written permission of Concordia Publishing House.

Manufactured in the United States of America

Library of Congress Cataloging-in-Publication Data

Melanchthon, Philipp, 1497–1560.
    Commentary on Romans / by Philip Melanchthon ; translated by Fred Kramer.
        p. cm.
    Translation based on the revised 1540 ed., which was published as v. 15 of Corpus reformatorum.
    Includes bibliographical references.
    ISBN 978-0-7586-2686-8
    1. Bible. N.T. Romans—Commentaries—Early works to 1800. I. Kramer, Fred. II. Title.
BS2665.M429 1992
227'.107—dc20                                                                    91-39381

4  5  6  7  8  9  10  11  12  13                    27  26  25  24  23  22  21  20  19  18

# CONTENTS

# FOREWORD TO THE SECOND EDITION

## Melanchthon the Exegete

It is necessary that minds be fortified against all snares of this kind [confidence in one's own good works] by sure and firm knowledge of the Word of God. As Peter says in 2 Pet. 1[:19], "You will do well to pay attention to the prophetic message as to a lamp shining in a dark place until the day dawns and the morning star rises in your hearts."[1]

With these words Philip Melanchthon ended his 1540 commentary on Paul's Epistle to the Romans, an admonition to be heeded by 21st-century readers of his insights into the text of what he considered to be the crown jewel of Scripture.

Why Philip Melanchthon and his Romans commentary? As with any movement that shapes society and church for generations, Martin Luther's Reformation would not have taken place apart from the team that supported and extended Luther's work. Luther's many God-given abilities needed support and supplement from a number of others, most in Wittenberg, some in other places, who could translate his ideas into a variety of forms of communication and into the institutions of both church and society. In addition to colleagues such as Justus Jonas and Johannes Bugenhagen, and disciples not in Wittenberg, such as Nikolaus von Amsdorf and Georg Spalatin, Luther found his strongest undergirding in the intellectually most gifted of the team, Philip Melanchthon. Neither Melanchthon nor Luther thought of the younger colleague as a clone of the older. Therefore, they never shared in the later public breast-beating about Melanchthon's divergences from Luther's theological formulations. Instead, they continued mutual conversation and experimentation in delivering the message of forgiveness of sins, life, and salvation in Christ to their contemporaries.

Melanchthon's contributions changed European education: through his textbooks giving elementary instruction in communication and other subjects; through his plans for reform of education in primary, secondary, and higher education; through his actual teaching at Wittenberg. He functioned as an ecclesiastical diplomat for the rulers of Saxony and their Lutheran colleagues,

---

[1] See the end of this translation, pp. 296–97.

and he served as Elector John's ghostwriter for the Saxon prince's answer to Emperor Charles V justifying his introduction of Lutheran reform, in the confession which the elector and his Lutheran colleagues delivered to their overlord at Augsburg on June 25, 1530.

But among the most significant contributions Melanchthon made to the life of the church were his biblical commentaries. As a part of the movement called "Biblical Humanism," a program for reforming education at the end of the fifteenth and early sixteenth centuries, Melanchthon had a burning interest in rhetoric, the discipline devoted to cultivating good communication skills, and he used these principles of communication, which he regarded as gifts of God, for interpreting Scripture and applying its insights. He made best use of the dictionaries and other aids to biblical study that other humanists of his time had developed. But he subjected the work of Jacques Lefevre d'Etaples, Johannes Reuchlin, his own patron, and Erasmus to the service of conveying the Wittenberg understanding of justification by grace through faith in Christ.

In 1519 he began lecturing on Romans, taking up the Epistle again two years later. From these lectures he developed a textbook, an introduction to the edifying and proper reading of Paul's longest letter. He entitled this reader's guide *Theological Commonplaces* [or *Topics*: Loci communes]. After his arrival in Wittenberg in 1518 he had first treated Matthew in the Latin text. He had been called, however, as an instructor in Greek, and he soon turned to the Greek texts of the two Corinthian Epistles and John's Gospel. Pirated editions of his notes as well as his lecture manuscripts that Luther commandeered and sent to a printer brought his exegetical insights to the public before he took control of the publication of his exegetical work. Over the four decades of his teaching career he treated many parts of both Testaments, often briefly, some books only in part. Often these lectures found their way into print as commentaries. Proverbs and Colossians were among his favorite books, but his four distinct commentaries on Romans reinforce his own claims that Romans provided readers of Scripture the key to its message.[2]

John Thompson, a contemporary American Reformation historian, has noted the advantages of "reading the Bible with the dead." Thompson argues that there is much to be learned for preaching and teaching from the history

---

[2] For an overview of his exegetical activity, see Timothy J. Wengert, "The Biblical Commentaries of Philip Melanchthon," pp. 106–48 in *Philip Melanchthon (1497–1560) and the Commentary*, edited by Timothy J. Wengert and M. Patrick Graham (Sheffield: Sheffield Academic Press, 1997). See also on Melanchthon's earliest exegetical work, Timothy J. Wengert, *Philip Melanchthon's* Annotationes in Johannem *in Relation to Its Predecessors and Contemporaries* (Geneva: Droz, 1987).

of exegesis that simple examination of the biblical text does not convey.[3] We profit from the conversation that has gone on through the ages over the texts of Scripture. This volume from Melanchthon's hand offered a model for the proclamation of the Gospel and a vital help for understanding the whole body of biblical teaching to Wittenberg students in the sixteenth century. It continues to be of value to preachers and other students of Scripture today.

Robert Kolb
Missions Professor of Systematic Theology Emeritus
Concordia Seminary, St. Louis, MO

# FOREWORD TO THE FIRST EDITION

This translation of Philip Melanchthon's *Commentary on Romans* is a final bequest to the church from Dr. Fred Kramer (1902–91). It takes its place next to Dr. Kramer's monumental translation of Martin Chemnitz's *Examination of the Council of Trent* as a reminder to the contemporary church of the rich theological heritage we have received from those who have gone before, which we must consider to be God's gift also to future generations. In offering Melanchthon's *Romans* to the church, Dr. Kramer noted, "It is a masterful work, full of sound biblical theology. Especially fine are Melanchthon's excursus on the distinction between Law and Gospel, his excursus on the doctrine of the church, and his genuine moderation in tone, which some of us sorely need."

Dr. Kramer was born in Frohna, Missouri, and graduated from Concordia Seminary, St. Louis, in 1927. He entered the parish ministry in Alsace-Lorraine, followed by pastorates in the towns of Clay Center and Ellenwood, Kansas. In 1947 he joined the faculty of St. John's College in Winfield, Kansas. In 1951 he began teaching at Concordia Theological Seminary in Springfield, Illinois (now located in Fort Wayne, Indiana). Here he served as registrar and academic dean and was instrumental in a curriculum revision which led to a raising of the seminary's academic standards. In 1950 he earned the Master of Sacred Theology degree from his *alma mater* and was awarded the Doctor of Divinity degree by her in 1960. Besides matriculating at the University of Kansas and the University of Nebraska at Lincoln, he earned the Master of Arts Degree from the University of Michigan at Ann Arbor in 1950. His translation of

---

[3] John L. Thompson, *Reading the Bible with the Dead: What You Can Learn from the History of Exegesis That You Cannot Learn from Exegesis Alone* (Grand Rapids: Eerdmans, 2007).

Chemnitz's *Examination of the Council of Trent* was published by Concordia Publishing House in four volumes (1971–86). In 1991 Concordia Seminary, St. Louis, recognized his service to the church by awarding him the seminary's *Christus Vivit* award.

## Melanchthon's *Commentary on Romans*

Philip Melanchthon, Master of Arts, came to Wittenberg in 1518 with a commission to teach language and literature. At Luther's urging, he presented his baccalaureate theses to the Wittenberg faculty of theology and received his Bachelor of Bible degree. This degree authorized him to teach theology, which he did for the rest of his life.

As part of his duties as a member of the theological faculty, Melanchthon began in 1519 to lecture on St. Paul's letter to the Romans—the course which Luther had taught from 1515–16. It is possible that Melanchthon even used Luther's notes as a basis for his own work.[4] Melanchthon's first writing on Romans was "A Theological Introduction to Paul's Letter to the Romans" (*Theologica Institutio in Epistulam Pauli ad Romanos*), published in 1519. In 1520 some of his students published his preliminary study of the contents of Romans arranged topically under the title "Themes or Topics of Theological Matters" (*Rerum Theologicorum Capita seu Loci*). Unsatisfied with this publication, Melanchthon reworked these topics into his highly acclaimed *Loci Communes Theologici* of 1521. Then, in 1522, Luther obtained a copy of Melanchthon's Romans lectures and lectures on Corinthians and had them published under the title of "Annotations" (*Annotationes Phil. Melanchthonis in Epistolas Pauli ad Romanos et ad Corinthios*).

Melanchthon himself did not publish a commentary on Romans edited by his own hand until 1532. The 1532 commentary is published in a modern edition in *Melanchthons Werke*, edited by Robert Stupperich.[5] Melanchthon revised and expanded this commentary, then published his revised work in 1540. This 1540 commentary, as found in *Corpus Reformatorum*, volume 15—and compared to an original edition in the library of Concordia Seminary, St. Louis—is the basis for the translation presented here. (We have in a number of places indicated significant differences between the *Corpus Reformatorum* edition and the Concordia Seminary volume.)

Melanchthon's 1532 commentary has come under severe criticism. Friedrich Bente contended that Melanchthon is "the father of synergism" among Lutherans, pointing to statements such as the following (on Rom. 9:6): "divine

---

[4]  See Luther's Works, American Edition (St. Louis: Concordia, 1972), 25:xii.

[5]  *Melanchthons Werke in Auswahl*, 5. Band (Gütersloh: Gerd Mohn, 1965).

compassion is truly the cause of election, but . . . there is also some cause in him who accepts, namely, in as far as he does not repudiate the grace offered."[6] This "cause in him who accepts" is omitted from the 1540 commentary. One hesitates to say that Melanchthon changed his mind, because in his editions of the *Loci Communes* of 1543 and following he speaks openly about the "three causes of conversion," namely, "the Holy Spirit, the Word of God, and the will of man," and also asserts the human "ability to apply oneself to grace."[7] With these words, Melanchthon opened up a controversy that would rage for forty years, until peace was obtained—at least among the Lutherans—by Article II, "Free Will," and Article XI, "Predestination," of the 1580 Formula of Concord.

The controversial statements of 1532, however, are absent from the 1540 commentary presented here. Melanchthon speaks of the elect in words that the authors of the Formula of Concord could readily affirm: "those who believe are righteous, so the elect do not resist the calling, but believe the Gospel and do not in the end reject it. Nevertheless, it must be held in the meantime that to believe and not to reject are results [!] which come about when the Holy Spirit impels."

What comes through in this commentary is the careful work of an evangelical Lutheran scholar and a master teacher. Melanchthon was not called the Preceptor of Germany without cause. In this book, he provides outlines and analysis for the student of Romans so that the student may not only understand but also be prepared to teach others. The excursus after chapter 14 on the strengths and weaknesses of the church fathers shows the breadth of Melanchthon's learning, as well as his discernment and affirmation of the principles of *sola scriptura* and *sola gratia*. In some detail, he shows his evaluation of and his appreciation for the works of those who have gone before. In a like manner, four and half centuries later, we are pleased to provide English-speaking students and pastors with the translation of this work of Philip Melanchthon, for contemporary evaluation and appreciation.

The Publishers

---

[6] *Historical Introductions to the Book of Concord* (St. Louis: Concordia, 1921; repr., 1965), p. 197; see *Melanchthons Werke* V, p. 254.

[7] See Melanchthon's *Loci Communes*, trans. by J. A. O. Preus (St. Louis: Concordia, 1992), *passim*.

# Introduction

## The *Argumentum* or Subject Matter
## of the Epistle of Paul to the Romans

There are two parts to the epistle. The first contains a long disputation. In the latter part there are precepts about morals. Many people judge that only the latter about morals is now worthy to be read, and they read it like a poem of Hesiod or Phocylides. They think it contains only quarrels regarding Jewish ceremonies about which nobody now fights. But one ought to think far otherwise. The first part contains an examination (*disputationem*) which is most necessary for every age and for the entire church. It contains the foremost and enduring topics of Christian doctrine, distinguishes the Gospel from the Law and from philosophy, shows the benefits of Christ, the gratuitous remission of sins, liberation from eternal death, the imputation of righteousness, the gift of the Holy Spirit, and eternal life. It proclaims these great things; it does not quarrel only about ceremonies.

I am not bringing forth either an absurd or a new interpretation. The very course of Paul's argument brings about this meaning which I give. The meaning must be taken from the apostolic speech itself, not another imagined sense invented against the proper sense of the speech. Then our interpretation will agree most fittingly with the perpetual doctrine passed down in the Prophets and the Gospel. Traces are found also in Ambrose, Basil, Augustine, Gregory, and Bernard.

Finally, the judgment of the church approves of our interpretation. Pious and experienced consciences acknowledge that it must be maintained in all true disputes, that we receive remission of sins and the imputation of righteousness not on account of our good deeds, but *gratis,* on account of Christ, by faith, i.e., by trust in the promised mercy on account of Christ. What darkness follows when this meaning is wiped out in the church? Then the benefits of Christ cannot be understood, then the distinction between Law and Gospel cannot be discerned, firm consolation of consciences and true prayer cannot be retained. What Paul is proclaiming about this very understanding is clear from the speech itself. Therefore we hold fast to what is said, because with it agrees the constant consensus of the rest of the prophetic and apostolic Scripture also the more learned fathers, and the judgment of the experienced and pious consciences in the church.

11

Since all these are in agreement, we have sufficiently firm testimonies for our interpretation and are not afraid of the chicaneries of Mensinger, Mustela, Campanus, and others who loudly proclaim that we are inventing for Paul a new and absurd meaning. Meanwhile they themselves bend the sayings of Paul to civil and human opinions about righteousness and morals, and think that it is a great praise of prudence to think up an elegant interpretation which agrees with philosophy and the common understanding of all the godless. They imagine that what Paul wants is this: men should have forgiveness of sins and be pronounced righteous on account of faith, i.e., profession of the history about Christ, and honorable morals. And that righteousness before God is this discipline, such as people furnish, and that this satisfies the law of God. They reject these seemingly contradictory statements, that the nature of man has been corrupted, and is not able to satisfy the law of God, and that this infirmity of nature, doubt about God, and other spiritual illnesses which original sin embraces, are truly sins in the sight of God. They proudly deride what we say about original sin and recall us to philosophy. In sum, they imagine that righteousness in the sight of God or what the law of God demands is nothing else than the discipline with which philosophy is satisfied. Pelagius professed this opinion, but the seeds are scattered in the commentaries of Origen. And since this opinion is in agreement with the judgment of human reason, which has not truly experienced fear and true comfort in repentance, people easily embrace these reasonings.

The prophets always had controversies with hypocrites, with priests who taught that people were righteous through works of the Law, and who with this opinion heaped up ceremonies and other exercises. Therefore the Psalms constantly inculcate the conviction that no one is without sin, as in Psalm 142 [Ps. 143:2] "No man living is righteous before you."[1] And Ps. 129 [130:3] "If you, O Lord, kept track of iniquities, Lord, who could stand?" And Ps. 31 [32:5] "I said, I will confess my transgressions to the Lord." And Daniel [9:7]: "To you, O Lord, belongs righteousness, but to us confusion of face." After they have shown the judgment of God against sin and hypocrisy, then they again raise us up, command us to acknowledge the promised mercy, and testify that forgiveness is given by faith in mercy, that we are received into grace, as he [Ps. 119:25] says: "My soul was sustained by his Word," that is, by the promise. "My soul hoped in the Lord, because with God there is mercy" [Dan. 9:9], that is, because he truly wants to have pity, according to his promise.

---

[1] Scriptural quotations are Melanchthon's own translations. The chapter references are according to the Septuagint. The corresponding English Bible references have been added in brackets.

And in such pronouncements mention is frequently made of faith, as in 2 Chron. 20[:17]: "Believe in the Lord your God and you will be safe." There they do not want merely the knowledge of the history to be understood, but they call faith confidence in the promised mercy, and without this confidence reject prayer and all worship. As therefore all the prophets inculcate this doctrine, so Paul presses the same cause. He does not urge simply that ceremonies are to be omitted. The error of retaining ceremonies arises from this source: the hypocrites imagined that people are righteous through the Law and so they abandoned the doctrine about gratuitous imputation, and contended that righteousness is to be sought through works of the Law. Therefore Paul recalls the question to the source, as also the prophets do, and shows what is the use of the Law, and speaks not only about ceremonies, but about the entire Law, and most of all about the Decalog. The Decalog is satisfied least of all, so these sayings should be accepted as concerning it chiefly: The Law works wrath [Rom. 4:15]; through the Law is the knowledge of sin [Rom. 3:20]. Therefore he teaches that sin is revealed and condemned by the Law, not taken away.

Thereafter he adds that the proper benefit of Christ is to take away sins, as Isaiah [53:12] says: "And he bore the sins of many, and made intercession for the transgressors." And John [1:29]: "Behold the Lamb of God, which takes away the sins of the world." For he indicates that this one is the Lamb, that is, the victim destined to placate the wrath of God. Therefore people obtain forgiveness of sins, not on account of the Law or of any other sacrificial victims, but *gratis,* by faith in this sacrificial victim, namely, the Son of God, who by his death satisfied the Law for us and abolished the curse. Therefore he says [Rom. 3:21]: "Now however the righteousness of God was revealed without Law," that is, the imputation of righteousness is given on account of Christ, not on account of the Law. The Law was there before, and has not now been taken away by Christ, but he brings a far greater benefit, as John [1:17] says: "The Law was given through Moses. However grace and truth came about through Jesus Christ." Christ gives us grace, that is, remission of sins, *gratis,* and brings about in us true knowledge of God, true love, true faith, true prayer. Thus our interpretation agrees with the perpetual consensus of the prophetic and apostolic Scripture, and the parts of the disposition are in harmony according to our interpretation.

The interpretation of Origen tears Paul's speech shamefully apart, and it does not retain the original meaning of the words. What Paul says, "We are justified by faith [Rom. 3:28]," means nothing to our adversaries. They excuse it by way of a synecdoche, and invent for it an entirely alien interpretation: "By faith," i.e., we are justified by a knowledge of history; we are prepared so that we may learn the commandments by which we may afterward merit the imputation of righteousness. Much more absurd is the interpretation of this saying: "The righteousness of God was revealed without Law" [Rom. 3:21], i.e., without the natural law, but Christ brought in certain new laws, such as this one: "Let not your left hand know what your right hand does" [Matt. 6:3]. Error, it is said, is fruitful. Otherwise so childish and foolish an interpretation could not have entered any sane mind. But I desist from following inept interpretations.

A comparison of our interpretation with its opposite shows sufficiently in which one of the two the parts are in harmony, in which one the particular nature of the speech is preserved, whether it agrees with the Prophets and the Gospel. In order that the leaders may consider this diligently, I admonish all again and again. For I do not want one lone statement to be victorious. Let studious persons compare the interpretations; let them compare them with the other sacred books, but in such a way that they judge piously, not slanderously. If they do this, I have no doubt that they will support us. In this matter there is need also for this diligence, that they give heed to what in the sacred writings these words truly and properly mean: faith, justification, righteousness, sin, Law, Gospel.

The church unlearned its language among monks and other unlearned persons and positively, as Tyndar says to Menelaus in Euripides [*Orestes,* line 485]: "You have become barbarous, being a long time among barbarians." Thus the long servitude of the church with the monks changed the language. Nor is it easy to restore the true meanings, for the power of custom is great. The deceivers, Mensinger and Cochlaeus, scourge me about the word *faith,* likewise about the word *justification,* and they have gone completely astray. And some other person, whose authority in the state is great, argues with me whether faith signifies trust in mercy. Who would not deplore the darkness in the church? So great has been the carelessness and thoughtlessness of the bishops and teachers that they have forgotten the meaning of the words which they have in their mouths daily. When the meanings have been changed, also the things themselves have been lost, and many kinds of insane ideas have followed. I see that also now many depraved minds have arisen which, either because of curiosity or because of ambition, are eager again to disturb and destroy with new deceptions the things which are now being rightly taught in our churches and have been explained most faithfully and simply.

Therefore I pray Christ and call to witness all pious persons who are versed in studies that they love the simple truth revealed in our churches and guard it, which I desire to illustrate and fortify as far as I am able, that it may be propagated to those who come after us. Although I have set forth the argument of the epistle to the Romans as well as I could, and have urged that the meaning of the words be observed, it seemed good to add the interpretation of certain terms and to set forth the entire controversy concerning justification. For these prolegomena add a certain amount of light to the argument. And when the reader has once embraced the entire matter in his mind, he will notice more correctly how the parts of the disputation harmonize in Paul since he had first conceived it in his mind as if it were the plan of a building.

## The Sum of the Doctrine Taught in the Prophetic and Apostolic Writings about Justification before God

I tried elsewhere, in my *Loci Communes Theologici*, to explain as simply and clearly as I could the doctrine of justification taught in the prophetic and apostolic writings. Neither am I going to say anything different here. But since these materials are the particular subject of this Pauline Epistle, I shall repeat these same things, and perhaps somewhere I may say something in plainer words.

The philosophers call universal righteousness obedience according to all virtues, i.e., honorable outward discipline which a person can bring about by his own powers. This Paul also calls righteousness of the Law, or righteousness by works. We have often said God demands that all men be compelled by means of outward discipline, as Paul says: The Law was given for the unrighteous [cf. 1 Tim. 1:8], and God punishes those who violate discipline, such as men who swear falsely, who speak shamefully about God, seditious persons, murderers, adulterers, thieves, and liars [cf. 1 Cor.6:9–10]. What Aristotle says is true: "Neither the evening star nor the morning star is more beautiful than righteousness," i.e., honorable discipline. For it is an outstanding ornament of man, nor is this weak nature of man able to bring about a more outstanding ornament. Nevertheless, one must know that this discipline by no means satisfies the Law, but is a kind of faint shadow of the Law, as St. Paul learnedly teaches in 2 Cor. 3[:7], when he says: "The Jews looked upon Moses with a veiled face," i.e., they were not overwhelmed by the lightning of the Law; the knowledge of God did not shine forth in them, and did not bring forth perfect obedience but only outward works.

But the Law of God demands not merely outward works, but perfect obedience. Therefore it is easily understood that no one is able to be righteous before God, that is, accepted because of outward discipline, as Paul clearly says: "By the works of the Law no flesh shall be justified" [Rom 3:20]. This statement takes away the praise of righteousness not only from ceremonies, but also from moral works, and speaks about the entire discipline.

Furthermore, philosophy and human laws speak about this external discipline, about the veiled face of Moses. They do not ask how we are to be righteous before God, i.e., accepted. Neither are the pronouncements of the philosophers to be confused with the statement of Paul. Let this carnal righteousness be given its place, that is, let the wicked be compelled by this discipline; let the philosophers wander about in the assembly of the people and look upon the veiled face of Moses; let them not ascend the mountain of God. Let Origen and those who follow him remain in this crowd, since they teach no other righteousness except the carnal.

Although reason may not see how we may be accounted righteous before God, the Gospel proclaims another righteousness, not known to reason, but revealed to the patriarchs by God, and afterward revealed more and more through the prophets, and finally disseminated in the world through Christ and the apostles. Therefore John [1:18] says: "No one has seen God at any time: however the Son of God, who is in the bosom of the Father, he has declared him to us." It is as if he said: This will of God—that God wants to forgive us *gratis,* and to give eternal life on account of his Son—no creature, no human reason was able to grasp; but this will has been revealed only through the Son. This wonderful benefit Paul proclaims, as I shall show briefly.

And Christ, as befits a master, most aptly embraced the sum and method of the Gospel when he commands to preach repentance and remission of sins in his name. Therefore the ministry of the Gospel first accuses sins, as Christ says: "The Holy Spirit will accuse the world because of sin . . . " [John 16:8]. Here, once the mind acknowledges sin and the wrath of God and experiences true terrors, the Gospel sets forth consolation. That word, which is the Gospel's very own—the promise of the benefit of Christ—shows the Mediator, the Son of God, as John pointed him out, saying: "Behold the Lamb of God which takes away the sin of the world" [John 1:29]. It must establish that on account of this Mediator, the Son of God, our Lord Jesus Christ, remission of sins is freely given to us. Righteousness is also imputed, not on account of any works or merits of ours, but *gratis,* by faith, that is, when we believe that these things are truly and certainly given us on account of Christ. When we raise ourselves up and sustain ourselves by this faith, looking to Christ, we truly receive remission of sins and are accounted righteous, i.e., accepted before God, and are given the Holy Spirit and made children of God and heirs of eternal life, as is written John 1[:12]: "He gave them power to become sons of God, to those who believe in his name."

These things are plain and clear, and suited for the use of consciences, and can be seen in examples. David, guilty of adultery and murder, was oppressed by immense fears when he was accused by the prophet. Afterward he is raised up by the word of absolution, when the prophet says: "The Lord has taken away your sin: you will not die" [2 Sam. 12:13]. Hearing this word, he believes that his sin is forgiven, not on account of his worthiness or merits, but *gratis,* through mercy, and knows that liberation from sin and death is promised on account of the Liberator who will come. He knows that Christ will be the sacrificial victim for the sins of the human race, as he says in a Psalm [110:4]: "You are a priest forever . . . " Sustaining himself by this faith he is made righteous, i.e., accepted before God to eternal life.

Thus Luke 7[:50]: A woman came weeping to Christ, acknowledging her sins. Afterward Christ said to her: "Go in peace; your faith has saved you." Thus these two emotions in conversion are described: fear and faith. The common people call the fear contrition, but one must know that fear does not merit forgiveness of sins. Yes, unless faith comes to it, a mind oppressed by terrors rushes into eternal death, as Saul and Judas perished, since they did not raise themselves up by faith and by acknowledging mercy in the midst of terrors. That is what this saying of Paul about the Law intends: "The Law works wrath" [Rom. 4:15], i.e., it arouses horrible terrors, which are frequently described in the Psalms. And Ezechias [Isaiah 38:13] says: "Like a lion he has broken all my bones." Therefore these terrors bring on the end— eternal death—unless faith comes to them, lifting up the minds little by little, looking at the promises of Christ, and thus laying hold of Christ.

The Psalms tell us how many such struggles there are. We see David wrestling with himself when he exclaims: "Lord, do not accuse me in your wrath. Have mercy on me, Lord. For in death there is no one who remembers you, nor in hell who praises you. Cast me not among the damned, who are burnt by your dreadful and eternal wrath and curse you. Let me not be cast away into this assembly of your enemies" [Ps. 6:1–5]. And Ps. 41 [Ps. 42:11]: "Why are you cast down, O my soul, and why are you disquieted within me? Hope in God; for I shall again praise him."

Here also Paul is preaching about these great struggles. He is not talking only about eating swine's meat or similar rites. He shouts that all are under sin; this statement is preached about the terrors. Thereafter he shows Christ and says we are justified by faith, etc. And in order that we may know that he is not speaking about idle cogitations, but about faith struggling with fears, he says: "Being justified by faith we have peace with God, likewise access to God" etc. [Rom. 5:1–2]. Likewise: By faith we know that we are loved by God [cf. Rom. 5:5]. Since therefore these sayings of Paul agree so aptly with the rest of the prophetic Scripture, what perversity is it to invent a different sense for Paul?

But I continue. This proposition which I have described about the conversion and justification of a person is clear and plain, useful in life, the firm and immutable sense of the Gospel, and was revealed to the fathers. Therefore the blindness of the adversaries who condemn our interpretation is generally to be deplored and their stubbornness to be detested. In the name of Christ I implore all pious persons to weigh what is said on each side. The adversaries admit that terrors are necessary, but they speak differently about faith. They want a knowledge of the history, but command men to doubt the remission of sins, and if someone should happen to be forgiven, they say it is on account of his merits. Thus they simply do away with the Gospel, which teaches that this benefit happens to us on account of Christ. In order that it may be certain, the promise was sent out, and God commands that we believe and assent to the promise and declare that it pertains to us. It is necessary to confess that this is the true and perpetual meaning of the Gospel. Paul also refutes the error about doubting when he teaches that the promise must be accepted by faith. Rom. 4[:16]: "It is by faith, *gratis,* in order that the promise may be firm." And he commands that we give God the praise that he is truthful, even as Abraham did not doubt through mistrust. Also 1 John 5[:10]: "Whoever believes in the Son of God has the testimony in himself; whoever does not believe God makes him a liar . . . "

Therefore when we say that faith lays hold of the benefits of Christ, it is necessary to understand that people lay hold of them because of Christ, and they must assent to the divine promise and believe that the promises are truly given for us. Faith does not signify merely a knowledge of history, but trust in the promised mercy because of Christ, giving assent to the divine promise. Paul calls for the kind of faith which believes all the articles of the Creed, particularly that because Christ suffered and rose again remission of sins is given to us. For to this article, as to the ultimate cause, the earlier articles are to be referred. When in their prayers the adversaries recite this article, "I believe the remission of sins," they fight with themselves. They command to doubt, and nevertheless dare to say that they should believe the forgiveness of sins. And I know certain persons whom this very article has admonished, who should accept consolation, assent to the promise of God, and cast off the doctrine of the monks about doubting and merits.

## The Particle *Gratis*

Why is the little word *gratis* added? Not on account of our works, but on account of Christ. Consciences (also the prophets and apostles) struggle particularly about this little word *gratis.* It embraces two things: it excludes our works, and sets forth the merits of Christ. Here can be seen first of all the wrath of God against sin, because no sacrificial victim was able to placate God except the death of his Son. Second, there shines forth the greatness of his love, because he gave his Son for us. It is necessary for the conscience to struggle to hold fast to both. The merits of Christ must be set before God. We must ask and expect grace on account of Christ, not on account of our merits.

The great violence of that struggle is this: A terrified mind does not ask whether God wants to be favorable on account of other deserving and worthy works. It agrees that God is good and merciful, but only toward those who are worthy, who have no sins, or who have greater merits. The knowledge of the Law with which we are born teaches that God is good, but only toward those who are worthy. It asks whether God wants to be favorable toward me, the unworthy one.

Here the little word *gratis* must be examined so we may declare that God truly remits sins *gratis*, because of Christ, not on account of any of our works or merits. This little word *gratis* also shows the distinction between Gospel and Law. The Law also proclaims that God is good and merciful, but it adds the condition of worthiness or merit. It says that God is favorable toward those who are without sin. But the Gospel removes the condition of our worthiness or merits. It testifies that God is reconciled to us *gratis*, on account of the merits of Christ, not on account of any of our merits, since this faith, i.e., trust in mercy, rests on Christ.

Instead of exclusively using the formula, "We are justified *gratis* by faith," we are accustomed to use this formula, "We are justified solely by faith," where this little word does not exclude other virtues so that they are not present, but excludes the opinion of merit or the condition of worthiness, or excludes them from the cause of justification, that is, of acceptance, as I shall later say at greater length. In fact, it is precisely the same thing to say, "We are righteous by faith," "We are righteous *gratis* by faith," and "We are righteous by faith alone [*sola fide*]." For faith cannot exist if confidence must rest on our worthiness or merits, or partly on Christ and partly on merits, as some imagine.

Faith is driven out if one must think God will be propitious when you have enough merits. Faith can rest on nothing except the promise of God which points to Christ, on account of whom the Father has promised that he will certainly be propitious to us. And when Paul asks whether we are justified by faith or by works, he understands faith to be trust in the mercy promised because of Christ. This he opposes everywhere to our worthiness, as though he were asking, "Ought you to say that sins are remitted to you and that you are a child of God on account of your worthiness, on account of any virtues or actions of yours, or ought you indeed to say that sins are remitted to you and that you are a child of God through mercy alone, because of Christ?" Therefore the thing itself is exclusive when he says, "We are justified by faith," i.e., not on account of our worthiness.

Therefore if anyone wants to judge truly, let him acknowledge that it actually means one and the same thing: We are justified by faith, and we are justified *gratis* by faith, and we are justified solely by faith [*sola fide*]. In passing, I have added these comments about the form of the language so that the meaning may be diligently noted. As for the rest, in whatever way we speak, this must be noticed, lest the matter itself be forgotten.

The exclusive meaning must be retained about gratuitous acceptance, for this brings about the distinction between the Law and the Gospel, as has been said. I have spoken about the little word *gratis*. Concerning it, pious persons should also consider that merits are taken away and rejected not because we are to do nothing, but in order that the promise should be sure—it would become uncertain if it hung on the condition of merits—and also in order that due honor be given Christ, and because even if we do something, nevertheless we fall far short of the perfection of the Law. Faith arises from the Word of God, from the Gospel, which is that Word in which the benefits of Christ are both promised to us and then conferred. For the human mind could establish nothing about the remission of sins if God had not revealed his will in a sure word or with a sure promise.

One must know that this Gospel promise is universal. The godly must be reminded of this because uneasy minds argue most of all about these two questions: worthiness and election. We ask first whether God receives the unworthy. Then, even if we were worthy, we think that God nevertheless elected certain of his friends, to whom he wants to impart these benefits. We are in doubt whether it also pertains to us; we are afraid we are not in their number. Thus human reason wavers about the will of God. For also the philosophers agree that God favors a certain few, namely, heroic men, and that he governs their fate, but they believe that the rest of men are neglected by God. Precisely in this way the mind thinks about predestination, as they call it. However, the heavenly voice criticizes this human opinion. This distinguishes the Gospel from philosophical opinions and from the Law, for it shows that the will of God is otherwise. It shows that God truly wants to accept also the unworthy, and that he offers grace to all, asking only that they believe the promise.

Therefore pious persons should learn that the promise is universal, as innumerable statements testify, such as: "Come to me, all who labor and are burdened" [Matt. 11:28]. Rom. 3[:22]: "The righteousness of God through faith in Christ is for all and upon all who believe." Likewise Rom. 10[:12]: "The same Lord of all is rich toward all . . ." Let us include ourselves individually in these universal statements, and declare that the promised benefits truly pertain to us.

Therefore in the question concerning justification, disputes about predestination are to be laid aside for quite a while. We must begin with the Gospel, because it both accuses all, and offers the promised grace to all on account of Christ. Indeed it offers it to all, but they must accept it by faith. Let us look upon the Word, which is universal, and not permit ourselves to be turned aside from the promise by speculations about predestination. For one must not determine the will of God apart from his Word. As the promises are universal, so I understand this statement: "God wants all men to be saved" [1 Tim. 2:4], even as in his promises he offers salvation to all. But the human will in those who are unwilling to believe fights against the promise. Those who sustain themselves by means of the promise declare that the benefits of Christ are truly given to them, lest they accuse God of lying. And when they accept the voice of the Gospel and sustain themselves, the Holy Spirit is efficacious at the same time through the voice of the Gospel, according to this statement: "Faith comes by hearing" [Rom. 10:17]. And Gal. 3[:14]: "That we may accept the promise of the Spirit by faith." Thus when terrified minds are raised up by faith, they receive the Holy Spirit.

This is the conversion which in the Gospel is called regeneration. It embraces these three things: remission of sins, justification or imputation of righteousness, and the gift of the Holy Spirit and eternal life. I am speaking about impulses which can be understood by the godly, about terrors, and about consolation, which results from faith. Therefore this Pauline statement is neither absurd nor intricate; neither does it contain useless sophistries, but is clear and in agreement with the other proclamations of the prophets and apostles. It sets forth the greatest things which the godly experience in life, and the knowledge which is necessary for the church. Now I shall add a brief explanation of the terms *Law, Gospel, sin, justification, grace,* and *faith.*

## The Distinction between Law and Gospel

There is a great difference between Law and Gospel. The Law is a doctrine in which God prescribes what manner of persons we should be, and what things are to be done and what things avoided. And although the Mosaic [civil] state has been destroyed, the moral law nevertheless remains, which is one and the same at all times since we are born with the knowledge of it. God wanted some knowledge to be in man which would judge sin. Sin has always been accused at all times by the voices of the Law in the preaching of repentance. Therefore Paul says: "By the law is the knowledge of sin" [Rom. 3:20]. He is not talking only about ceremonies, as certain persons imagine, but chiefly about the Decalog or the moral law. It always accuses, and accuses all persons. One must think far differently about the divine Law than about the morals of civil life. In civil life only outward discipline is demanded, but the Law requires perfect obedience, inward and outward, as the commandment testifies: "You shall love the Lord your God with all your heart . . ." [Deut. 6:5]. In Matthew 5, Christ interprets the Law in this way. However, since human nature, vitiated by original sin, is not able to furnish perfect obedience, the Law shows the wrath of God against sin. It accuses

and condemns all men except Christ, who, as Paul says, has set us free from
the curse of the Law. He set free not only the Jews, and others who were
saved after the Mosaic law was given and abolished, but also the patriarchs
before Moses. Therefore they also were under the Law, i.e., they were accused
and terrified by the judgment of the natural law, and they would have perished
if they had not held fast to the promises concerning Christ, on account of
whom they knew that liberation from sin and death had been promised.

Perhaps persons in political positions will ridicule these things, when we
say that the Law demands perfect obedience, and that no one is able to satisfy
the divine Law because ignorance and contempt for God cling to the nature
of man. These things seem foolish to philosophers and those who judge in
human fashion. But the prophets and apostles do this very thing. They want
men to acknowledge the greatness of sin—that they do not truly know and
glorify God. They teach that this sin is the cause of the greatest miseries and
calamities by which this weak nature is oppressed, and to seek the true righteousness and deliverance from sin and death which is given through Christ.
Students (who will read these things in the interest of learning) will find more
about the Law in the *Loci Communes,* which I have published.

The Gospel proclaims repentance and the promise of grace and eternal
life. The promise should be diligently distinguished from the Law. And although the Law has certain promises of its own, nevertheless, these differ
from the unique promise of the Gospel. Moreover, the promises of the Law
require the condition of perfect obedience as is said in the first commandment:
"I will do good to those who love me" [cf. Deut. 5:10]. But the evangelical
promise—about remission of sins, justification, and the gift of eternal life—
is gratuitous, offered on account of Christ, without a condition of our merits
or our worthiness.

No human language is able to express the greatness of this benefit, which
God imparts to us through His Son, our Lord Jesus Christ: with sin wiped
out and death destroyed, we may enjoy the vision of God in eternal life,
righteousness, and joy. The promise of this benefit is only divinely revealed,
as John [1:18] says: "The Son, who is in the bosom of the Father, he has
declared it to us." For although we are born with some knowledge of the
Law, we certainly are not born with knowledge of the Gospel. Human reason
by itself by no means sees this will of God—that God would send His Son
that he might become a sacrificial victim for the church, that God wants to
remit sins *gratis.* These things lie far beyond the scope of human reason.
Therefore dicta of the Law ought to be carefully distinguished from the evangelical promise. In the works of Phocylides, Hesiod, and similar authors some
dicta of the law are collected.

The evangelical promise of gratuitous forgiveness, or about the Son of

God, is nowhere read in those who only followed the judgment of reason or the light of nature. Although we are born with some knowledge of the Law, the mind itself in us accuses sins, nor considers anything except that God punishes and rejects the unrighteous. That is the judgment of the Law, and according to the Law it is true. In the immense struggle in repentance, the gratuitous promise of mercy ought to be set in opposition to what the Law says and to our natural judgment, and preferred to the Law, because Christ has set us free from the Law.

When Adam had fallen and was accused, he could think nothing except what the Law showed—that he would perish because he had not obeyed God. But God comes forward, and although he subjects the human race to death of the body and other ills, he nevertheless sets forth a consolation: he promises liberation from sin and death, and restoration of the human race. He says that it would come to pass that the seed of the woman would crush the head of the serpent [Gen. 3:15]. When this had been said, the Son of God moved the heart of Adam and poured new light and life into him. When the Son of God was made guardian, governor, and preserver of the church, he began to wage war with the devil. As the devil goes about with fearful savagery among humankind, he destroys very many. In his hatred for God he seeks chiefly to destroy the church, and sinks his poisonous teeth in our heel, as we frequently experience. The Son of God is again efficacious in believers as he represses the fury of the devil, restores the saints, and sets them free.

The world does not see this struggle, but the dreadful falls of very many people and the most sad and tragic calamities, and thereafter the glorious liberations (such as that of David and others) shows what kind of struggle this is. The words in Genesis [3:15]: "The Seed will crush the head of the serpent," signify nothing other than the same thing which John says: "For this the Son of God was revealed, that he might destroy the works of the devil" [1 John 3:8]. Adam understood the promise in this way, and thereafter all the patriarchs believed that on account of this promised seed their sins were forgiven them, and that they would be set free from sin and from eternal death. Through this faith they were righteous, not through fulfillment of the Law. By this faith they were raised up in all dangers and terrors. Indeed they knew that this Lord was present with them, as Jacob plainly says, in Gen. 48[:16]: "The Angel who set me free from all evil bless these boys"; for he proclaims him Lord who had set him free from all evils, and asks of him that he would bless his descendants. These things can be understood in no other way except as pertaining to the Son of God. Paul also says that the Son of God accompanied the camp of the people of Israel [1 Cor. 10:4]. John [1:5] also says that all things were made through this Son, and that the Light shines on the darkness. All triumphs against our adversary, the devil, are imparted through this Son. Noah was preserved, Abraham defended, Joseph brought out of prison, the people freed from Egypt, and Daniel also spoke with him. Thus the Gospel of the apostles preaches Christ, and testifies that He is the sacrificial victim, liberator, and Savior, and commands us to trust this leader and liberator, as also many statements of the prophets teach, as Ps. 2[:12] says: "Kiss the Son . . . blessed are all who trust in him." And without this faith, i.e. trust in the mercy promised because of the Son, there is no true invocation of God, no true worship. For through this Priest we have access to the Father, as we often find written.

Therefore we must renounce the blindness of those who imagine that the Gospel is a law which contains certain precepts about loving one another, however requiring faith, i.e., knowledge of the history about Christ, and that Christ is to be regarded as teacher, even as Socrates and Phocylides handed down good precepts, and that people should be considered righteous on account of these services of love, but that one must nevertheless doubt whether God forgives us or answers our prayers, or whether he has anything to do with us. Thus the monks and now also certain would-be philosophers transform the Gospel into school-philosophy, i.e., a doctrine about works. They command us to doubt the divine promises. Neither do they teach that it is necessary to have faith, i.e., trust which rests on Christ, the liberator, and which seeks and expects the promised benefits because of him.

Therefore I ask all pious readers, if they love Christ, that they consider this distinction between Law and Gospel, between Moses and Christ, and that they diligently consider what glory should be given to the Son of God, and what true honors the fathers—Adam, Jacob, the prophets, and apostles—have given Him. From these let us learn that Christ is present with his church as leader, ruler, liberator, savior, and defender against the devil. Let us learn also that the benefits of Christ must be accepted by faith, and let us remind ourselves that the Gospel is a Word which promises and imparts these benefits, as Paul says [Rom. 1:16]: "[The Gospel] is the power of God for salvation to everyone who believes," i.e., the Gospel offers to us grace and eternal life *gratis,* on account of Christ, not on account of the Law. And through this Gospel God is truly efficacious, gives the Holy Spirit, and begins in us a new light and eternal life.

### Sin

Sin signifies not only evil actions, as the philosophers indicate about the term, but embraces also the immense weakness with which we are born, which is called original sin. Although carnally secure persons judge this to be a small evil, and philosophers do not even consider it to be an evil, it must be judged quite differently. For darkness and doubting whether God cares about human affairs, whether he punishes, whether he nourishes, whether he aids, and whether he grants people's prayers, are not trivial evils. Likewise, to lack fear and love for God; to love ourselves while neglecting the love of God; to admire our own wisdom; to play with opinions which flee from God—with Epicurean or superstitious opinions; to have impulses that wander about here and there, turned away from God, and fighting against the Law of God; these things are very great evils, as shown by the punishments. For on account of these evils God subjected the human race to death, and punishes and coerces them with immense calamities. Since God was not willing to be placated by any sacrificial victim, only by the death of his Son, it must be an immense evil which had to be redeemed at so great a price. It is strange that there is such a great stupidity in human minds that they do not recognize this sickness. Therefore God wanted to make it known by means of His Word and teaching. To this let us assent, and not listen to the quibbles of the sophists, who laugh sardonically and minimize the sickness, and lightly esteem the sacrificial victim, Christ, or totally despise him. We must shrink back with minds and ears from this godless philosophy.

## Justification

According to the Hebrew usage of the term, to justify is to pronounce or to consider as just, as is said in Hebrew: "The Roman people justified Scipio when he was accused by the tribunes," that is, absolved him or pronounced him just. Thus we know for certain that in these disputations of Paul justification signifies the remission of sins and acceptance to eternal life, as the fourth chapter of Romans testifies in a sufficiently clear manner, where it defines justification as the forgiveness of sins. Therefore when we say we are justified by faith it is the same thing as saying that we are accounted just by God on account of Christ when we believe. And the word *iustitia* does not signify the righteousness of the Law, or universal obedience, or our qualities, when it is said, "By faith there is given us *iustitia*." It signifies the imputation of *iustitia*, or acceptance. And *iustus* is in this way understood relationally as acceptance to eternal life. But one must know that in the forgiveness of sins there is given at the same time the Holy Spirit, as I have said above, when we raise ourselves up by faith.

Thus the gift of the Holy Spirit is connected with justification, which begins not only one virtue—faith—but also others: fear and love of God, love of the truth, chastity, patience, justice toward the neighbor, as I shall say later about works. But these virtues do not merit forgiveness of sins, nor are they the righteousness on account of which a person is accepted though still afflicted with much infirmity. Rather, when a terrified conscience asks how we may be justified, it does not ask what virtues we possess, but how we can receive forgiveness and reconciliation with God. It is worried about the will of God toward us; it does not contemplate its own virtues, and does not oppose them to the judgment of God. Therefore those who interpret justification as infusion of virtues do not notice that the question here is about the forgiveness of sins, and about peace of conscience in the sight of God, or about reconciliation. We are asking how we may be justified, i.e., when we may have remission of sins, and why it can be said that God is favorable toward us. Therefore it is necessary to understand justification as forgiveness of sins and divine acceptance, or imputation of righteousness.

## Grace

*Gratia* signifies gratuitous acceptance, or the mercy promised because of Christ, with which there is connected the gift of the Holy Spirit, as Paul says Rom. 5[:15]: "How much more the grace of God, and the gift in grace." When he mentions grace there he means gratuitous reconciliation, and the gift in grace he understands to be the gift of the Holy Spirit and the beginning of eternal life. For in the remission of sins, as I have said, the Holy Spirit is given. And the profane philosophy of Pelagius, who contended that people become children of God and heirs of eternal life without the action of the Holy Spirit, is to be execrated. The term grace often signifies the help and activity of the Holy Spirit. However, the chief significance is gratuitous acceptance, as when we say, "Paul received forgiveness of sins by grace," that is, "Paul received forgiveness of sins *gratis*, on account of Christ." To be repudiated is the explanation of the monks, who invented an interpretation which is directly opposed to Paul: We receive remission through grace, that is, we receive it on account of our virtues.

### Testimonies of Scripture Where Grace Signifies Gracious Acceptance

There are many sayings which testify that grace chiefly signifies acceptance promised on account of Christ, such as: "You are not under the Law, but under grace" [Rom. 6:14]. For God judges that the righteous, although they have sins, are nevertheless not accused because they are under grace, that is, they are already accepted as pleasing because of Christ. He does not want them to think they are pleasing because of their character.

**1.** Rom. 4[:16]: "Therefore it is of faith, and according to grace, in order that the promise may be firm." Furthermore, the conscience is not certain on account of our character or our virtues, but on account of the gratuitous mercy which has been promised. Therefore the interpretation of the monks, who interpret grace only in regard to our virtues, by no means agrees with this passage.

**2.** Rom. 5[:20]: "Where sin has abounded, grace abounded much more.'' This means that the gratuitous mercy is perceived much more when the greatness of our sin is viewed, and we understand that we receive forgiveness of sins *gratis*, not on account of our merits.

**3.** To the Ephesians, 1[:5] ''Predestinating us through Jesus Christ, according to the good pleasure of his will, to the praise of the glory of his grace.'' Here he certainly does not want our virtues to be praised, but the gratuitous mercy of God.

**4.** To the Galatians, 2[:21] ''I do not despise the grace of God, for if righteousness is by the Law, then Christ died in vain.'' He does not say: ''I magnify my virtues,'' but, ''I magnify the gratuitous mercy by which I state that God is rendered favorable to me on account of the death of Christ.''

**5.** 2 Thess. 2[:16]: ''He has given us good hope in grace.'' He does not command us to hope on account of our virtues, but on account of the gratuitous mercy promised on account of Christ.

**6.** To the Hebrews, 4[:16] ''Let us approach with confidence to the throne of grace,'' that is, of promised mercy. For it is quite clear that grace cannot here be understood of our virtues.

**7.** Finally there is known to the learned the nature of Hebrew speech. When this is observed it will be easy to decide the meaning of the word. Consequently there is no one who does not know that Paul emphasizes this word *grace* for the very reason that we should declare that we are pleasing to God on account of Christ, not on account of our virtues. This is the interpretation the monks simply turn upside down when they command us to think that we are justified by grace, that is, on account of our virtues.

There is in the Greek term for *grace* something exclusive which, as I have said above, must be diligently noted. For the difference between the Law and the Gospel is shown chiefly by the exclusive particle *gratis*, because of Christ. However, there is not excluded, as I have said, repentance or the other virtues, but the condition of worthiness or merit, in order that terrified minds may have firm comfort. Neither do the promises become sweet for minds unless we always include for them the little word *gratis*. ''Everyone who shall call on the name of the Lord shall be saved'' [Rom. 10:13]. If I add: ''If he is worthy,'' the mind will be scared off. Therefore the Gospel proclaims about the little word *gratis:* Call on God even if you are unworthy, because all who call upon the Lord will be saved *gratis*. Thus it is said in the Psalm [Ps. 130:7]: ''For with the Lord there is mercy.'' If I add: ''toward the worthy,'' the conscience shrinks back. But the Gospel commands that it be understood that gratuitous mercy is certainly promised because of Christ, as if it said: Do not shrink back, but approach God and accept the gift offered to you by faith, for on account of Christ God wants to forgive you *gratis*. Therefore the decree is sure and immutable. If anyone thinks it is uncertain, he inflicts shame on the Son of God, who is the pledge of this promise. It is necessary that the gift be accepted by faith.

I have repeated these things because it is very important that this exclusive word be diligently explained, so that the distinction between Law and Gospel will be clearly seen, and so pious minds may think that a firm comfort has been set before them and may be aroused to faith and prayer in all troubles and dangers. For this faith must be exercised in daily difficulties. Neither can the Gospel be understood without these exercises, nor is there true invocation of God without this faith, of which we have already spoken so often, as Christ says: "Whatsoever you shall ask the Father in my name," that is, in faith in my name, "that I will do" [John 15:16]. This distinction is necessary between heathen and Christian invocation. The heathen pray doubting whether God heeds human prayers, whether he is affected by our troubles. To pray in this way is to bring shame on God. Yet such are the clamors of the ungodly in their temples, and the monks command us to doubt when we pray.

To these errors there must be opposed the following statements: Rom. 5[:2]: "Through him we have access in faith." Eph. 3[:12]: "Through whom we dare to approach confidently, through faith in him." And Rom. 8[:34]: "Who sits at the right hand of God that he may make intercession for us." Therefore no one is able to approach God except with this Mediator and Priest bringing our prayers to God. As it is also said in Rom. 10[:14]: "How shall they call on him in whom they do not believe?" James [1:6] says: "Let him ask in faith, without wavering." Matt. 21[:22]: "Whatsoever you shall ask in prayer, believing, you will receive." Therefore in order that we may render God the highest, true, and pleasing worship—invocation—it is necessary that this doctrine about faith and gratuitous mercy be held to and known.

### Faith

I come to the term *faith*. Many are quarreling with us chiefly concerning it. It is strange that there is so great a fog in the church that the genuine significance of this term—which has always been in the mouth of all and which resounds in the ears of everyone—should almost have been lost. To this evil there comes now another even worse one. It is difficult to tear an old error out of the minds of men, and certain deceivers, such as Cochlaeus and others, seek to preserve it. Since the deceivers are not seeking the truth but are serving their own sickness, I did not think that I should enter into a quarrel with them. However, I do not shun the judgment of the pious and learned. The prophetic and apostolic statements show so clearly what the term *faith* signifies that no sane person is able to contradict it. Therefore faith signifies not only knowledge of history, but trust in the mercy promised because of Christ, or assent to the promise of grace.

This is assent in the intellect: both to want this divine consolation, and to acquiesce in it when we hear that God is propitious on account of his Son, Jesus Christ. Therefore, when it is said, "We are justified by faith," one must not imagine that we are just by faith on account of the worthiness of this virtue. These words must be understood correlatively: "We are justified by faith," that is, we are pleasing to God through mercy, on account of Christ. But we accept or acknowledge this mercy by faith, and apply it to ourselves. Although I fully agree that faith and trust are qualities, they nevertheless become, like the names of the other desires, relational, as love behaves itself in a way relative to that which we love, fear to the object which is feared, and trust to its object on which it rests.

These points in the art of disputing are known even to boys, but Mensinger, an ignorant and foul joker, has slandered them with the ugliest impudence. But I appeal to the judgment of saner and more learned persons, who understand what it means that something is said relationally, as it is called, and notice what is the use of these childish pre-judgments in more serious controversies. This speech therefore is understood correlatively: through trust in his treasure a rich man is tranquil in mind when there is a poor harvest; that is, a rich man is tranquil in mind on account of his treasure. Thus when you hear, "We are justified by faith," there at once comes to mind the correlative: "We are accounted just through mercy on account of Christ." Therefore we are said to be righteous "by faith", that is, by trust in Christ, or by trust in the mercy promised because of Christ.

And I remember that I have sometimes been asked why one must say, "We are just by faith," if we want a person to be just through mercy. To this I answer that these expressions are correlatives: "We are justified by faith," and, "We are just through mercy." But it is necessary that mention be made of faith because it is necessary that there be some impulse by which we accept the gift and apply it to ourselves. And when we mention faith, let the mind look upon Christ and think of the gratuitous mercy promised because of him. You are to say that you are accounted just not on account of any virtues or actions of yours, but on account of something outside of ourselves, namely, on account of Christ, the Mediator, who sits at the right hand of the Father, making intercession for us. This impulse of faith in our minds is not an idle cogitation, but it wrestles with the terrors of sin and death. It fights with the devil, who attacks weak minds in dreadful ways in order to drive them either to contempt of God or to despair, like Cain, Saul, Judas and innumerable others who decided that they had been rejected by God and so hated God furiously. Others become atheists or Epicureans when they despise the Word of God and divine comfort in great troubles. They do not sustain themselves by faith, but broken in mind they yield to the devil, as wicked people clamor when things are against them: "Surely there are no gods, since the world is being ruined by blind chance." But those who hear the Gospel— who know that the works of God are to lead into hell and to lead back out— sustain themselves in such a struggle by faith. They flee to their leader, Christ. They know that he is the victor, who crushes the head of the serpent [Gen. 3:15], or, as is said elsewhere, who destroys the works of the devil [1 John 3:8], and who has always been with his own from the beginning. Therefore, helped by the Son of God, they overcome the devil and do not depart from God.

For that is what the fight is about. The devil urges minds to fall away from God. Faith, on the contrary, fights lest it lose God, lest it be torn away from God. It declares that there is a God who, although he punishes, nevertheless adds the gratuitous promise of mercy on account of his Son. He gave his Son as our advocate and promised eternal salvation. God is seen in his Word, and when the mind looks upon the Word, its faith is strengthened. It does not fall away from God, but acknowledging his mercy, it calls upon him, expects liberation, and submits to the will of God. It does not permit itself to be torn away from him. And praise for the victory belongs to Christ, who helps his own, as he himself says: "Without me you can do nothing" [John 15:5].

Those who experience these things in life and in invocation [worship] are able to understand the doctrine of faith, and at the same time to make the distinction that though we are just, i.e. accepted because of Christ, faith meanwhile must nevertheless be increased in us, which is true acknowledgment of God, and cannot be retained without a very sharp struggle.

### Testimonies Where Faith Signifies Trust in Mercy

I shall now add testimonies which show that faith does not signify mere knowledge of history but trust in mercy, which fights against despair and contempt of God.

**1.** Rom. 4: Paul puts together the promise and faith, so as to relate them, teaching that the promise must be accepted by faith. Therefore faith signifies trust, which rests on the divine promise. This testimony is so clear that it cannot be shaken by any sophistries. Therefore "by faith, and according to grace," that is, "I demand faith, by which the promise of reconciliation is accepted."

**2.** Eph. 3[:12]: "Through whom we dare to approach confidently through faith in him." Reader, what clearer testimony do you ask for? For I am now no longer fighting with the deceivers, but am addressing the glory of Christ, that they diligently weigh these testimonies. Paul is here explaining the nature of faith by means of three meaningful words. He says that by faith we have παρρησία (boldness), προσαγωγή (access) and πεποίθησις (confidence). These do not correspond to a knowledge of history, which rather deters, if one must think that we shall have access to Christ when we shall be worthy. Therefore it is necessary that faith be understood as confidence in mercy. This interpretation cannot be shaken by the sophistry of Cochlaeus, who says, "If faith and confidence were one and the same thing, he would not have added, as though it were an effect, confidence through faith." O, the sophistry of those who follow Carneades! One impulse in the heart is described in many words. When faith is this impulse by which we approach God, it certainly cannot be merely a knowledge of history, which rather deters the minds, as I have said. Thus also Paul says in Rom. 5[:12]: "Through whom we have access by faith."

3. Rom. 5[:1]: "Being justified by faith we have peace with God." Knowledge of history by no means brings peace of conscience, but rather increases fears, when the *opinio legis* [the opinion that we are justified by the Law] is retained. For it is a sign of the terrible wrath of God against sin, since God was not willing to be placated with respect to it by any other sacrificial victim except by the death of his Son. When we consider this, it increases fears since we think that the benefit of Christ pertains only to those who bring with them enough merits. Since faith raises up terrified minds and comforts them, it is necessary that it be understood as trust in mercy. Since Paul shows sufficiently that he is speaking about faith wrestling with fears, his statements cannot be understood to refer to the mere knowledge of history.

4. Col. 2[:12]: "In which you also were raised through faith by the working of God." He says that we have been sanctified by faith, i.e., by the confidence that God is working in us.

5. [1] John 5[:10]: "Whoever does not believe God makes him a liar, because he does not believe the testimony that God would give eternal life . . ." He joins faith to the promise, and demands that the promise be believed. If anyone does not assent to the promise, he accuses God of lying, as though he did not keep his promises. Furthermore, assent to the promise is confidence in mercy.

6. Rom. 4[:18]: "Who against hope believed in hope." I ask you, Christian reader, whether it is not necessary in this passage that the word, "he believed," be interpreted of confidence. There is no need to seek the meaning far off. Abraham is praised because he believed that God would bring his promises to pass, although nature was against it. In this way the godly should be instructed about faith, that when we are devoid of all human support, we nevertheless expect help from God and do not let go of God. And somewhat later in the same chapter he opposes faith to doubt. Abraham did not doubt

because of mistrust. He is speaking about faith wrestling with doubt in a promise which must be accepted.

**7.** Mark 9[:24]: "I believe, Lord; help my unbelief." This passage does not speak of a knowledge of history, but of trust by which the father expected the liberation of his son. In the gospels faith often signifies confidence which seeks and expects benefits, as in the story of the woman of Canaan, Matthew 15[:21–28], who, having been repulsed twice by Christ, and indeed insultingly, nevertheless did not cease her prayers, and with wonderful wisdom refutes the saying of Christ, confesses that she is unworthy of the benefit, but still expects a gift on account of the goodness of the Lord. Christ adorns this faith of the heathen woman with a weighty testimony when he says: "O woman, great is your faith; be it done to you as you ask" [Matt. 15:28]. How can we doubt here and in similar stories that by faith there is signified confidence which seeks and expects benefits. Since this ought to shine forth in invocation [worship], it is necessary that the godly be rightly instructed concerning it. But the monks command to remember history, and then say one should doubt whether God is propitious to us or regards our prayers. This teaching militates totally against the example of this highly praised woman and similar examples, and abolishes true worship of God, true invocation.

**8.** The description of faith in Hebrews 11[:1] shows that also there faith signifies confidence, because he says, "Faith is the ὑπόστασις, that is, the expectation of the things hoped for." This is truly the grammatical explanation of the word, as all learned persons know. Furthermore, that expectation is trust in the promise.

**9.** Acts 15[:9]: "Purifying their hearts by faith." It is clear that hearts are not purified by a knowledge of history. Shortly aftward in that passage the saying is explained: he says that neither the fathers nor anyone else had a pure heart on account of the righteousness of the Law. He says that hearts are purified if they believe that they are purified through the grace of the Lord Jesus Christ. Therefore he shows that the term *faith* signifies confidence which rests upon the mercy promised because of Christ.

**10.** Rom. 10[:11]: "Every one who believes in him will not be confounded." Here Paul himself distinguishes the benefit of the Gospel from the Law, and he is speaking not about mere knowledge of history but about the confidence by which we declare that God is certainly propitious to us on account of Christ, not on account of the Law. The same thought is often repeated in the Prophets. Ps. 2[:12]: "Kiss the Son. . . . Blessed are all who trust in him." Here it is necessary that trust be understood. For he commands that the Son of God be acknowledged; he commands that we should trust this Lord. Since it is not possible that the condition of the Law be patched on— for faith is not to rest partly on Christ and partly on the Law—it is necessary that faith be understood as confidence, which establishes that we are freed from sin and from the tyranny of the devil by the Son of God.

**11.** 2 Chron. 20[:20]: "Believe in the Lord your God, and you will be secure." The army stood prepared, and was commanded to seek and confidently expect help from God. There he is not discussing a knowledge of history; rather, confidence which seeks help from God is commanded.

These testimonies show sufficiently clearly that the word *faith* signifies confidence. Studious persons will find many examples when they read the Prophets. I am not ignorant of the fact that deceitful tricks can be found to escape these testimonies. There is now a remarkable frivolousness of intellects; some criticize these things from ambition, others from ill will, and others from hatred of true piety. But I beg and beseech pious readers to diligently weigh this interpretation and consider that if this is wiped out, great harm will follow. Firm comfort will be snatched away from consciences, true invocation [worship] will be destroyed, and the benefit of Christ will be obscured. Sophistry must be removed from every life, but most of all must it be kept out of the church. Neither should the mind games be tolerated which imagine, like painters, whatever they please. Let the simple truth necessary for the church be retained, and let us take care that this is transmitted uncorrupted to posterity. God requires this service of all, and most of all of those who govern doctrine, or the state, and this service is owed to the church. Neither is any worship more pleasing to God.

The statements quoted from Paul [Rom. 4:3; cf. Gen. 15:6] should be understood in this way: "Abraham believed God, and it was counted to him for righteousness," that is, Abraham acknowledged that he was not righteous because of the Law, or because of his virtues. He acknowledged the infirmity of nature, which gives birth to many vices, doubt concerning God, and lusts wandering about in different directions. He also remembered the errors he had committed among the Chaldaeans, where he was contaminated by godless worship. But because he afterward heard the promise of the Seed, and God had said to him: "I will be your protector" [cf. Gen. 15:1], he concluded that remission of sins had been given him through mercy, and that he had a propitious God, a defender and Savior. Thus he was pronounced just by faith, that is, by trust in divine mercy, although he sees that his nature is infirm and evil. Frequently faith fights not only about the remission of sins or about acceptance, but also is concerned with external objects, as the faith of David in his single-handed combat with Goliath. These examples also belong here, for the faith which accepts the forgiveness of sins always precedes this faith which expects help for the body. The mind does not conclude that God will help us unless it had first concluded that God is propitious. This rule shows that Paul is correctly quoting the testimonies about faith, and instructs us about invocation [true worship].

## Dicta of the Ancient Writers

I shall add also the dicta of ancient writers. Augustine says: "As a result of the Law we fear God; by faith we flee to mercy." Augustine speaks correctly, and this cannot be understood of the mere knowledge of history.

Chrysostom, in his commentary on the Epistle to the Romans, ch. 4, says: "By faith we not only love God, but also believe that we are loved by him— although we are many times guilty—and that our sins are forgiven. This worship is superior to other kinds of worship and glorifies God more than the other worship of works, such as not to steal and not to kill." Although Chrysostom frequently drives off the road, nevertheless this saying is rightly praised. He explains the nature of faith clearly, and as I may say, in living colors when he says that we must believe that we are loved by God although we are guilty, and that we receive remission of sins: "The believer on his part boasts, not that he has loved God only and genuinely, but that although he has withheld much honor and love from God, for as soon as he loved him, telling great things about him, for this is the proof of love, and God loved him so much, although he was guilty of a thousand sins, that he not only set him free from punishment, but also made him righteous."

Worthy of praise are also the words of Bernard, who says in a sermon on the Annunciation: "First of all it is necessary to believe that you could not have remission of sins except by the forgiveness of God [. . .] But add further that you believe this also: your sins are forgiven *you* through him. That is the testimony which the Holy Spirit works in your heart when he says, 'Your sins are forgiven you' [1 John 2:12]. For the apostle declares that a man is justified *gratis*, by faith." A number of similar statements by this man may also be found, although he is a more recent writer, but not one inexperienced in spiritual exercises, through which he learned that the conscience cannot be set at rest unless it is convinced by faith that sins are remitted *gratis* on account of Christ. Therefore he understands faith as trust, just, as we do.

I have said above that we value a knowledge of history and all the articles of faith, and when faith looks upon this article: I believe a remission of sins, it is necessary that we adopt confidence so we can truly receive this benefit. The others who understand faith only as knowledge of history do not believe this article—the forgiveness of sins—even as they publicly command to be in doubt about the remission of sins.

I think I have said enough about this word, which I hope will be satisfactory to pious, honest persons and to all who love the truth. Now I must reprove the sophistry of Origen, of the monks, and of many others who think that "We are justified by faith" is spoken according to the figure of speech called synecdoche, that is, on account of our knowledge of the history of Christ, or on account of professing [the faith] and other virtues or that we are righteous on account of general obedience. This is how they understand faith, and they think that professing is praised by Paul because, although the profession is made also by criminal persons, nevertheless, without it the other virtues, as is the case with Turks, would not please God. Thus this synecdoche transforms the Gospel into Law, transfers the glory of Christ to our virtues, destroys the comfort of consciences, and does away with the true doctrine about faith, that is, trust in mercy. Yes, the monks even command us to doubt concerning the remission of sins. For they see that doubts about the will of God inhere naturally in human minds. Therefore they confirm these doubts and do not consider them vices, darkness born with us, entirely like the school philosophers or Pyrrhonians. Therefore I shall refute this synecdoche, which militates against the entire disputation of Paul, more fully below in the commentary.

We hold fast to what is said by Paul: "We are justified *gratis, by faith*" [cf. Rom. 3:24, 28, etc.], that is, we receive remission of sins and imputation of righteousness before God, not on account of any merits of our own, but by faith, that is, by trust in the mercy promised because of Christ. Therefore we do not invent a synecdoche for Paul, neither do we change what he says, but we learn from him, we hold fast to his statement which both the character of the language and the course of the disputation call for.

I hope that when the words have been explained, the proposition will be understood: "We are saved by faith, *gratis.*" It is of the greatest benefit to pious persons to keep in mind the sure testimonies and confirmations of this proposition, both for teaching the minds and to incite to faith and invocation [worship]. Elsewhere I have brought together many statements of Paul concerning this proposition. Here let it suffice to have shown the chief passages. At the close of the third chapter to the Romans Paul clearly and with many words teaches this proposition; thereafter he applies to the proposition (as the chain of the disputation demanded) the most weighty and most learned confirmations, which must be fixed in the minds so they may kindle faith and light the way before us in all dangers.

### Concerning Good Works

I have spoken about justification and about faith. Now I shall briefly add the doctrine about good works or about the new obedience, which ought to follow faith. These four things are being asked: What works are to be done? How can they be done? How do they please God—are the regenerate righteous on account of the new obedience, that is, accepted by God to eternal life, or are they without sin and worthy of eternal life on account of their purity? In the fourth place the question is asked about the distinction between sins. What sins cast out grace, faith, and the Holy Spirit? Which sins are called venial?

Concerning the first question—what works are to be done: It is right to lead the minds to the Word of God so they may know that their whole life— in the midst of the struggle of the conscience and in actions—is to be ruled by the Word of God, as the prophet says, "Your Word is a lamp to my feet" [Ps 119:105]. Therefore I answer that the works taught to us by God are to be done. Moreover, a sure Word should be set before us, namely, the Decalog, as it is repeated and explained in the New Testament, although certain other precepts about morals are found in the preaching of Christ and of the apostles. This must be said, lest people think it is permitted to invent acts of worship and works by our own will without a command from God, as the Enthusiasts do at all times. Some time ago the monks, and now the Anabaptists, after they had given up and cast off the Word of God, chose works according to their own judgment, and afterward invented the excuse that they were incited by the Spirit, and that the Spirit must not be hindered by the Law. Hence there followed the dreadful lawlessness of the Anabaptists.

Moreover, we shall say below what it means to be set free from the Law. Now I shall describe it briefly. Those who have been reborn by faith, as it is said, receive the Holy Spirit in order that the new obedience, light, and life eternal may be begun in them, which is a certain beginning of the divine Law in us. Therefore it is said in the Prophet [Jer. 31:33]: "I shall put my Law in their hearts." This beginning must of necessity follow faith, as many statements testify: "If you want to enter into life, keep the commandments" [cf. Deut. 6:2; Ez. 20:11]. Likewise: "Unless your righteousness is better . . . " [Matt. 5:20]. Likewise: "Fornicators and adulterers cannot inherit the kingdom of God" [1 Cor. 6:9]. Moreover the Holy Spirit moves the hearts through the Word of God. Therefore obedience must be governed by a sure Word of God, which we must obey, as Paul says: "We owe it, not to live according to the flesh" [Rom. 8:12]. Neither can faith exist without repentance, because the remission of sins must be accepted by faith. However a person who delights in crime against the conscience does not seek forgiveness. Neither is merely outward discipline demanded, but the beginning of inner obedience, namely, pious impulses of the heart which are in agreement with the Law of God.

When our adversaries talk loudly about good works, they shout about childish discipline, about moderation in dress, in food and drink, and say something about giving alms. Meanwhile there is silence about the works of the first table, about which they are not able to say anything because they do not know the doctrine of faith. However, God demands the works of both tables. He wants us to be shocked as we acknowledge his wrath against our manifold infirmity and our endless errors. He wants us to believe that we are reconciled through his Son, that he will receive us into grace, that he wants to save us, that he wants to help us. In this faith he wants to be invoked, wants us to seek and expect help from him, according to Ps. 49[Ps. 50:15]: "Call on me . . . " He wants us to depend on him by faith, not to seek help contrary to his will. These are hidden acts of worship and are peculiar to Christians. We should understand these as examples of acts of worship as seen in those excellent men whom God has set before us as teachers: Abraham, Isaac, Jacob, Joseph, Samuel, David, Jeremiah, Daniel, and similar men.

Likewise God wants us to burn with zeal to know, propagate, and adorn the Gospel. He teaches that all are chiefly prepared, regenerated, and called for this worship, as Peter says: "Called out of darkness, that you should show forth and celebrate the benefits of God" [1 Pet. 2:9]. And in Ps. 34 [35:18]: "I will confess you in the great congregation." And Ps. 115 [116:14]: "I will pay my vows to the Lord in the presence of all people, in the courts of the house of our God." He wants us to show constancy in the profession of the Gospel, obedience in afflictions, and to seek and expect help from him. He wants us to be careful lest we arouse offenses by our errors or evil examples. He wants us to refute and hate godless dogmas, not go along with the instruments of the devil, which try to destroy the Gospel. (However, it is not my intention here to give an explanation of the Decalog, which pious persons should always study, and consider how many great and arduous duties it embraces.)

Concerning the second question: How can such great works, both within and without, be done in our infirmity? Although human diligence can provide outward discipline to some extent, nevertheless spiritual impulses cannot be brought about without the Holy Spirit. Therefore, when hearts are raised up by faith, the Holy Spirit is given in order that he may kindle a new light in the minds and excite pious impulses which are in agreement with the Law of God, according to the saying of Paul: "In order that we may receive the promise of the Spirit through faith" [Gal. 3:14]. And Zechariah 12[:10]: "I will pour out the Spirit of grace and prayer on the inhabitants of Jerusalem." The prophet most beautifully points out the foremost works of the Holy Spirit in the hearts of the godly, and the chief acts of worship. He calls him the Spirit of grace because, when we are raised up by faith, we are aided by the Holy Spirit to declare that God is propitious to us and that we in turn are accepted by him. Therefore he indicates first of all that faith is excited by the Holy Spirit, in which act he gives us the testimony, as Paul says.

With faith we now acknowledge the mercy and presence of God, call upon him, subject ourselves to him, and begin to render other true acts of worship which are all embraced in the term *prayer*, for this is the highest honor. Therefore it is sufficient that it be understood that faith, about which we are speaking, is also the beginning of the remaining inner obedience, and, as it is called, of good intention. It is not possible to begin keeping the first commandment (which preaches about the wrath of God against sin, not about gratuitous forgiveness) unless first, after the Gospel has been heard, we declare that we receive forgiveness of sins *gratis,* by faith, because of Christ.

Faith looks at the Son of God as he reigns and knows that he is not idle, but wages war assiduously against the devil, who does not cease to go about with the greatest savagery and cunning against the members of Christ. He lures them into sin with his wiles, into sad falls, in order that he may draw them from there into despair. He pours out errors and strengthens Epicurean opinions, which please light minds. He incites tyrants, so that they attempt with the greatest boldness to destroy the name of Christ and exercise the most unjust cruelty. Since it is sufficiently established that human nature is far too weak to be able to defeat so vigilant and rabid an enemy without heavenly aid, faith reminds itself of the rule of Christ and knows that he was always present with the godly after the first promise, when it was said: The Seed of the woman will bruise the head of the serpent [Gen. 3:15], which statement John gives in these words: "Christ appeared that he might destroy the works of the devil" [1 John 3:8].

Christ was present with Jacob, and blessed him, and strengthened him with the Holy Spirit; he was present with Daniel, and indeed conversed with him. Therefore he governs in this way, that he is present with his members, strengthens them with his Spirit, and protects them against the wiles and onslaughts of the devil. The examples of David, Hezekiah, Daniel, and the like show what kind and how glorious such victories are, and Christ will show those triumphs in the resurrection of the dead, although the world now ignores and derides such great things. However, the godly are not totally ignorant of these battles, and individuals need to exercise their faith in their dangers and to acknowledge and invoke Christ, their leader, and with confidence in him do battle with the devil, not forgetting the words of John [1 John 3:8]: "For this Christ appeared, that he might destroy the works of the devil." From this one can know that faith is not an idle investigation, but a light which governs all actions and all dangers.

Therefore we are able to begin obedience, aided by the Son of God, who reigns, who is present with us as leader, and who imparts the Holy Spirit. We must not think that Christ rules idly, as the poets imagine that Jupiter idly holds feasts in heaven. Such is the darkness in the minds of men about God. But these errors must be corrected by the light of the Gospel and by faith. But what can our adversaries say about these exercises of faith and about true invocation, since instead of faith in the Gospel they teach us the philosophy of the Pyrrhonians about doubting.

Concerning the third question: This has been explained less by the ancients than the earlier questions, although it is most necessary. There remains in the regenerate very great weakness. They fear God less than they should; they are not ardent in faith and love. Meanwhile, they seek human aid in ways that are not permitted. They go astray, are negligent in their duties, and become careless in less important matters. They harbor immoderate affections, loves, and hates; they crave forbidden pleasures. In afflictions they rage against God. They are in doubt about the mercy of God. They are oppressed by mistrust; they burn with unjust desire for protection. They do not burn with desire to make known their gratitude to God. They do not give thanks with an ardent heart for so many benefits; they do not value the Gospel highly enough. They aid the propagation of the Gospel coldly. They are not affected by the public calamities of the church and of the state. They do not offer prayers for the church and for rulers. They are inflamed with unjust zeal for acquiring riches, honors, and power. They envy others whom they see are distinguished by virtue or other good things and effort. Meanwhile, they stir up offenses, as ambition brought forth a rebellious spirit in the sister [Miriam] against Moses and Aaron.

These things are not to be considered trivial evils. They are vices that militate against the Law of God, and are worthy of eternal death. They arise from great sicknesses and from original sin, namely, from ignorance of God, and from the fact that the human will is turned away from God. When Paul says about these vices [Rom. 8:7]: "The carnal mind is enmity against God," he is not describing a mild deformity, but a great and dreadful evil. Therefore it is certain that no one satisfies the Law of God except Christ, and that there remain in saints vices which fight against the Law. These sins are worthy of eternal death unless they are forgiven.

Since this is so, this question is constantly raised not only in the schools, but in the minds of the godly, and gives rise to more than ordinary dangers and disputes: whether imperfect and contaminated obedience is acceptable to God, and how it is acceptable. It is necessary that the godly be rightly instructed concerning this question on both sides. Hypocrites, as is the weakness of nature, are pleased with themselves, admire their virtues, make light of the infirmity of nature, and think that they are without sin, that they satisfy the Law of God, that they are worthy of eternal life, and that they deserve eternal life. Such are the thoughts not only of hypocrites, but of all persons who judge according to reason. So Plato and Cicero dispute about the immortality of the soul: Purer souls, which have less contamination from their bodies (that is, who have lived more moderately) fly about in the upper air. But lazier souls, which have more contamination from their bodies (that is, which have defiled themselves with pleasures of the body) wander about on the ground around graves. Don't the monks say the very same thing when they boast about their merits?

Although human reason by its own light judges no differently, the Word of God nevertheless testifies that no one satisfies the Law. It accuses men who trust in their own righteousness, and puts forward the Mediator, the Son of God. It is necessary to rebuke the arrogance and security of the hypocrites. Again, worried consciences need true consolation; they should learn that it is not mistrust but faith which pleases God. Let them also learn in what way life, morals, or works please him, for these also need to please him. Peter in the boat, being terrified, says: "Depart from me Lord, because I am a sinner" [Luke 5:8]. Although in confusion he did not consider what he was saying, nevertheless, as happens in sudden impulses, he sincerely expressed what his mind felt. He fled from God, seeing his own unworthiness. Thus all persons, when they have seen their unworthiness, flee from God, and think they are acting rightly, because unworthy persons are unwilling to approach to God. The voice of the Gospel rebukes this error, which is fixed in human minds. It commands us to approach God although we are unworthy, but are trusting in the Mediator, the Son of God.

Although the new obedience is necessary, as has been said, and also the righteousness of a good conscience, nevertheless, the regenerate do not satisfy the Law, and the original sickness remains in them. This, as has often been said, is by no means to be considered a small evil, and this sickness spawns many evil passions. Since these are vices worthy of eternal death, the regenerate, also after conversion, are not righteous, that is, accepted by God to eternal life on account of their own virtues, but *gratis,* through mercy, by trust in the Mediator, Christ. Likewise they do not merit eternal life by their works or virtues, but must declare that they become heirs of eternal life on account of Christ, *gratis,* by faith; yet as has been said, the new obedience must always follow faith. The following statements testify that the saints do not satisfy the Law, and that sins remain in them:

### Testimonies Where Sins Remain in the Saints

1. Ps. 142[143:2]: "Enter not into judgment with your servant, because no man living will be justified in your sight."

2. 1 John 1[:8]: "If we say that we have no sin, we are deceiving ourselves, and the truth is not in us."

3. Rom. 7[:23]: "I see in my members another law at war with the law of my mind and making me captive to the law of sin." There Paul often

repeats the term sin, signifying that sickness is a vice which really wages war against the Law of God, and is worthy of eternal death unless it seeks forgiveness by faith. He is not talking about a light tickling of only the body, but of the sharpest movements of the mind, of doubting about the the will of God, of shrinking back from the cross, of not being raised up by trust and joy in the Lord, even as we are lifted up by joy, and rejoice when we see physical help. From this mistrust there arise many evil counsels, etc.

Paul used two very clear words: ἀντιστρατευόμενον [warring against]; he says the sickness attacks in a hostile manner, that it wounds the mind through mistrust, terrors, pride, with trust in one's own wisdom and righteousness, carnal security, and that it kindles the flames of a variety of lusts. And it does not appear as a despised foe. Αἰχμαλωτίζοντα [leading captive]: it oppresses weak minds and takes them prisoners, although the prisoners are set free by Christ even as Moses was taken prisoner when he was undecided at the rock and mistrusted. David was taken prisoner when by some human error he commanded that the people be numbered either because he was moved by the desire for glory, since he had enlarged his kingdom by his deeds, or for other reasons. But I omit examples; for the godly have many examples right at home. They experience how diligent the enemy is, and how he oppresses minds more often than we think. For the devil also attacks the godly.

**4.** 1 Cor. 4[:4]: "I am not aware of anything against myself, but I am not thereby acquitted." It is as if he said: Although the righteousness of a good conscience is necessary, nevertheless I am not righteous because of this, that is, accepted before God to eternal life, but by faith in Christ.

**5.** Christ commands the saints to pray for forgiveness of sins: "And forgive us our debts" [Matt. 6:12]. Likewise he says: "Say, 'we are unworthy servants . . . ' " [Luke 17:10].

**6.** Ps. 129[130:3]: "If thou, O Lord, shouldst mark iniquities, Lord, who could stand?" He acknowledges that he has sins, and nevertheless he declares that he is pleasing to God through mercy, and he expects salvation. Therefore he adds [Ps. 130:5]: "My soul sustained itself in his Word," that is, sustained by the divine promise I approach him. I expect salvation and in him I find rest, trusting that he will save me by his goodness.

**7.** Psalm 18[19:12]: "Who can discern his errors? Clear thou me from hidden faults." It is clear that the prophet here, as also elsewhere, is speaking both about himself and about other saints. The very same persons whom he calls servants of God—sanctified through the Holy Spirit, adorned with excellent gifts, who walk in the exercises of faith and govern in great matters, such as Abraham, Joseph, Moses, Samuel, David, Isaiah—exclaim this with one voice: "Who can discern his errors? Clear thou me from hidden faults." Therefore the arrogance of the hypocrites is to be detested, who boast that they merit eternal life with their works, and indeed, as they themselves say, *de condigno* (worthily).

**8.** Psalm 31[32:5]: ''I said. I will confess my transgressions to the Lord; then thou didst forgive the guilt of my sin.'' Therefore let everyone who is godly offer prayer to you [God] at a time of distress. He testifies plainly that the saints ought to pray for forgiveness of present vices and errors.

**9.** Job 9[:20–21]: ''I am ashamed of all my works.''

**10.** Ex. 34[:7]: ''And an innocent man is not innocent before you,'' that is, although he cannot be accused according to human judgment, nevertheless he can be accused by you [God].

**11.** ''To you, Lord, belongs righteousness, to us however confusion of face,'' [Dan. 9:7] that is, I acknowledge that we have sins and that we are justly being punished by you. Thereafter he adds: To us confusion; however, to you mercy and propitiation [cf. Dan. 9:8, 9], that is, I acknowledge that we are sinners, but you, on account of the promised mercy, again hear us and set us free. He repeats the same thought somewhat later, and sets before us an example of faith and prayer [Dan. 9:18]: ''We do not present our supplications before you based on our righteousness, but based on your great mercy.'' These speeches are repeated with great consensus in the sacred books; our infirmity is constantly accused, and we are commanded to take refuge in mercy on account of the promised Mediator, the Son of God.

Thus also Paul does not accuse just some part of men, but simply declares that all persons outside of Christ are guilty before God. Likewise: ''He confined all men under sin, in order that he might take pity on all'' [Rom. 11:32]. Likewise: ''Whoever glories, let him glory in the Lord'' [1 Cor. 1:31]. The godly should set these statements before themselves in order that they may acknowledge that our infirmity is truly sin and they should be terrified with fear of the wrath of God against sin. In this way let repentance grow in us.

In the first sermon about the last judgment it is said in Genesis [cf. Gen. 4:7]: ''Sin lies quiet until it will be revealed.'' Here is revealed the carnal security of the entire human race, which gives no heed to the judgment of God. Sin lies quiet, he says—that is, because God delays punishments, all men will be calm in their minds and will despise threats, but nevertheless finally sin will be brought to view. There it will not be quiet but will strike eternal terrors into the minds and will bring dreadful punishments. Carnal security is therefore fixed in the minds of all. This is the reason why all men make their infirmity small, and are not moved by the greatness of the evil, although the grievous lapses of the saints and the great calamities that befall humans have warned us that we should declare that God is truly angry at this fault, and we should be moved by the voice of the Holy Spirit who rebukes this sin.

In order that the obedience which has been begun may be acceptable, these three things must come together: First it must be established that a person is acceptable to God *gratis,* through faith in Christ. Then we must acknowledge that our infirmity is truly sin, and we must truly grieve that we have these faults. But again we must raise ourselves up and believe that we are forgiven because of Christ after we have been made sons by faith, and that the obedience which has been begun is acceptable, not on account of our own purity or worthiness, but on account of Christ, the Mediator. Since he is our Priest, he now brings our prayers and worship to the Father. Thus Peter teaches [1 Pet. 2:5]: "Offer spiritual sacrifices acceptable to God through Jesus Christ." He adorns good works with an honorable name when he calls them sacrifices, for this term benefits proper worship of God. And indeed, he calls them spiritual sacrifices, that is, impulses excited in the heart by the Holy Spirit. Nevertheless, he says that these acts of worship are acceptable in no other way save through Jesus, the Redeemer and Priest, who diligently makes intercession for us. This is how the godly must be taught and incited to do good. God established the human race to be a society chiefly for this reason, that this might be known among men, and so that some might be able to teach the doctrine of God and of the Son of God to others, as Stigelius says rightly and beautifully:

> In order that some might teach others about religion,
> Piety commanded to have houses near each other.

Therefore he also assigned various duties to men—the governance of the church, of the schools, marriage, the education of children, the government of the state, wars, and contracts. Besides these he subjected the church to very great afflictions. For what purpose was so great a variety of works instituted? For this, that faith might shine forth and grow amid these difficulties and dangers. Faith is to believe that God has not created us for perdition, but that he wants to receive and save us on account of Christ. Let faith invoke God and declare that Christ is present as Leader. He represses the devil and helps us in private and public life.

Let the ruler of the church cry out: "O Lord, open my lips, and my mouth will proclaim your praise" [Ps 51:15]. Let the teacher of the youth consider how dreadfully Christ threatened those who stir up ruinous offenses for children. Let him pray that Christ may rule studies and morals. Let heads of households understand their dangers. Let good rulers consider that they ought to set up the churches rightly; rule the morals of the people; punish Epicureans, unchaste people, thieves, and liars; and pronounce justice, in order that each person may keep what is his. However, the devil is chiefly concerned to disturb churches and governments. He arms tyrants against the church. Therefore let an ardent faith be found in rulers, which believes that Christ will aid them and destroy the works of the devil. Finally, even as invocation [worship], so faith ought to light the way for all actions.

Virtues and the works of the godly do not merit forgiveness of sins or eternal life, nor are they the price of eternal life, since no one satisfies the Law. The merit of Christ ought not to be transferred to our works. The promise would become uncertain if it depended on the condition of our worthiness. Nevertheless, the new obedience must of necessity follow faith, and it is indeed begun when we receive the Holy Spirit by faith. Faith and the Holy Spirit are driven out when the new obedience is lost, when the commandments of God are violated contrary to the conscience. For faith and intentionally acting against the conscience cannot exist at the same time.

Here belong many statements about works: "Man believes with his heart and so is justified, and he confesses with his lips and so is saved" [Rom. 10:10]. All obedience should be a confession, serving to celebrate the glory of Christ and to spread the Gospel. Therefore, although we are righteous because of Christ and heirs of eternal life, nevertheless this obedience must be present, and it pleases, as has been said, and neither could faith be retained without this obedience.

Paul also says elsewhere: "We shall put it on that we may not be found naked" [2 Cor. 5:3]. Eternal life is given on account of Christ, but it is given to the one who believes. In this faith eternal life is begun; this beginning is the new obedience. Our worthiness is excluded, and Christ must be given his honor, both in order that the promise may be certain and that we may have firm consolation against despair.

Therefore there was new obedience also in the thief who was converted on the cross. There was repentance. He bemoans the fact that he has sinned. And a wonderful light of faith arose in this abject person. God showed by this example that he wonderfully preserves and restores the church in extreme difficulties. The scattered apostles were in doubt about the Master. They had seen the greatness of the calamity. Therefore they thought they had been deserted by God, but the thief is not deterred in this way from seeking salvation from him. He had heard him say a little earlier: "Father, forgive them" [Luke 23:34]. He had also heard certain things which had been done by him and a kind of confession. They saw things happening in nature, the sun obscured and the earth quaking, give a testimony concerning him. Therefore he invokes him with great vehemence, saying: "Remember me, Lord, when you enter into your kingdom" [Luke 23:42].

How great was the light of this faith! He acknowledges that this companion in punishment, this dying man, is the Messiah who forgives sins and will give eternal life, who has abolished death and will reign after this life.

Earlier, when things were favorable, the apostles had thought that he would be king after the Romans had been driven out. And this lone person proclaims that the dying man will reign after death. Therefore also Christ, in turn, testifies that he will reign, that he is the giver of eternal life, in order that he may kindle and strengthen his faith: "Today you will be with me in paradise" [Luke 23:43]. Strengthened by these words the thief acknowledges that he has eternal life, not on account of his merits, but on account of this Lord. And together with this faith and consolation, eternal life is begun in him, which is the new obedience before God.

Behold, I ask you, for here the man sent from God [*Apostolus*] hanging [on the cross] preaches from on high, not only to the crowd which was then present, but to the entire coming church. What an outstanding picture is set forth, in order that we may learn from it that we are saved *gratis*, by faith, on account of Christ, and nevertheless, repentance must be present and the other good fruits. In this thief there are seen repentance, faith, invocation, and confession or proclamation. It is certain that these are the foremost good works and the highest acts of worship of God.

He added also another noteworthy work which is necessary chiefly when Christ is being cursed. He sternly castigates the curser and defends the glory of Christ. So also we should, with true ardor of mind, take to task godless teachers, tyrants and their associates, who blampheme Christ. It has often occurred to me that this preacher is significant particularly to the church in the last times. Therefore, let us listen to him diligently, and attentively consider his example and imitate it.

Although eternal life is given *gratis* on account of Christ, afterward, if the new obedience, as I have said, is found pleasing, God also rewards our labors, actions, and troubles. Therefore Christ says: "Your reward is great in heaven" [Luke 6:23]. And although they do not merit eternal life, they do merit their physical and spiritual rewards which come to them in part in this life, in part after this life. For since God wants to preserve the church among men, he bestows many bodily benefits. There is need of food, of peace in the state, and of other comforts of life. There is need also for spiritual benefits: wisdom, learning, fortitude, and successes in one's vocation.

Therefore Christ says: "Seek first the kingdom of God, and the rest of the things will be added to you" [Mt. 6:33]. And Paul: "Godliness has promises of the present and of the future life" [1 Tim. 4:8]. And Mark 10[:30]: "He will receive an hundredfold, but with persecution." And the fourth commandment says: "That you may live long on the earth" [Deut. 5:16]. And Christ: "Give, and it will be given to you" [Luke 6:38]. And Matthew 10[:42]: "Whoever gives a drink of water to one of the least of these, because of the doctrine, will not lose his reward."

Finally there are found here and there in the sermons of the prophets promises about bodily and spiritual benefits, as Is. 33[:16–17] says about the godly: "Bread will be given him , , . and his eyes will see the king in his beauty," that is, they will have food, calm states, etc.

The widow of Zarephath received Elijah the prophet as a guest when the provisions were very short. Here see first the faith of the woman, then the work, and finally wonderful rewards. The prophet commands that what little food was left be given to him, and adds the promise, as a reading of the story shows. The woman obeys his word, although she saw that nothing was left save these remnants. The woman would not have exercised this generosity if she had not been raised up by faith, if she had not thought that God must be obeyed, the prophet helped, and a benefit in turn expected from God. Therefore she receives the reward of her faith and alms. Her family is divinely fed until the scarcity is made easier. Also her dead son is restored to her. The faith of the mother is strengthened even more by this miracle, and the young man is called to piety. Indeed, Epiphanius writes that he was the prophet Jonah, who later preached to the Assyrian King in Nineveh and propagated the Word of God widely and with success.

The saints have at all times received not only spiritual benefits, but also many bodily benefits for the preservation of the church, and some were presented with other gifts, as seemed good to God. He preserved Paul unharmed as long as he wanted him to serve in the ministry, and meanwhile provided him with lodging and the other comforts of life. Thus also Paul writes to the Corinthians about a pestilence, that they were being chastened by this punishment on account of their vices. If they would repent, the punishments would cease. Thus also Zechariah [1:3] says: "Return to me, and I will return to you," that is, I will mitigate the calamities and punishments if you will repent. He is not speaking of one work only, but of true conversion and its fruits. From these sayings one can sufficiently understand both that the obedience which has been begun pleases God, and that it has rewards.

There are many things which should kindle zeal for doing good: the command of God, the fact that faith is extinguished when obedience is lost, and that both the loss of faith and the other faults are punished by present and eternal punishments. Likewise misdeeds are frequently punished by blindness and by more sins. Again, it is not only the promise that invites men to believe and to retain faith, but also the command of God. For it teaches that we should believe the Son. It invites us to exercise our faith, for unless it is exercised faith does not increase, as the parable of the talent shows [cf. Mt. 21:33–46]. And Augustine rightly says: "Love merits an increase of love," for he is not speaking about imputation but about gifts.

Gifts increase through use, and merit increases. The greatness of the mercy of God also invites us. It nevertheless approves of this poor, beggarly, thoroughly contaminated obedience, and judges that honor is shown him through it. Other rewards necessary for life and for the church also invite, which should be prayed for in their place, and which are set forth for the exercise of faith, such as food; peace; good successes in one's calling, in studies, in the governance of church and state; godliness of children; virtue, and happiness.

These are great rewards, but so great is the blindness of the world that it is only lightly affected, not only by the command of God and by mention of eternal punishments and eternal salvation, but it also does not sufficiently understand how great is the need of corporeal benefits, and how important it is that they be used rightly. Therefore let us pray to God for the sake of our Lord Jesus Christ, who intercedes for us, that he may arouse us to true piety, teach us, and govern us by giving us his Holy Spirit, even as he has promised that he will give the Holy Spirit to those who ask him.

About the fourth question, the distinction between sins: When we say that remnants of sin remain in the regenerate, and that at the same time there is faith, it is necessary that sins be distinguished, lest anyone think that adultery and similar gross sins can exist together with faith. In my *Loci Communes* I have spoken at somewhat more length about the distinction between mortal and venial sin. Therefore I shall here remind the reader in a few words.

When we have been justified by faith, the righteousness of a good conscience must follow in the regenerate. The doctrine of Christ makes this distinction openly and frequently, e.g. 1 Tim. 1[:15]: "The sum of the commandment is love out of a pure heart, and a good conscience, and unfeigned faith." And again in the same chapter [1:18, 19]: "Wage the good warfare, holding faith and a good conscience." And 2 Cor. 1[:12]: "Our boast is this, the testimony of our conscience." And 1 John 3[:21]: "If our hearts do not condemn us we have confidence before God." For he teaches that those who harbor the purpose of violating the commandments of God against their conscience cannot invoke God. And 2 Pet. 3: [1 Pet. 3: 15–16]: "With meekness and fear, having a good conscience." Therefore it is said in Gal. 5[:19]: "Now the works of the flesh are obvious: immorality, impurity, licentiousness, idolatry, etc . . . those who do such things shall not inherit the kingdom of God." He calls them obvious because he is condemning deeds which they knowingly do against their conscience.

Paul also distinguishes among sins in Rom. 8[:13]: "If you live according to the flesh, you will die. If by the Spirit you mortify the works of the flesh, you will live." There are in the saints actions of the flesh, that is, vile affections. When they fight against this with the Spirit, that is, not hypocritically, the vile affections will be coerced with true fear of God and true faith, and the saints remain in grace and retain the Holy Spirit and faith. These things are not done without a great struggle in the minds. The lures of the world are of various kinds. There are turbulent attacks in our flesh. And the devil intently seeks occasions through which he can drive minds. Therefore we have need for watchfulness, faith, and prayer. For the victory belongs to Christ when we overcome the devil. But our discipline must nevertheless come to it, and aid must be sought in faith, as Peter says [1 Pet. 5:8]: "Be watchful, for the devil walks about like a roaring lion, seeking whom he may devour." And about discipline: "I pommel my body and subdue it" [1 Cor. 9:27]. The fear of God fights against the evil lusts and wiles: Faith seeks aid and forgiveness for the infirmity, and collects arguments which show the greatness and the punishments of sin, eternal and present.

Thus Joseph, when he was solicited by the lures of his mistress [cf. Gen. 39], did not resist the fury of the woman and the tricks of the devil without a struggle. He sees that the devil is doing this first in order that he may draw him, polluted by crime, away from God, rob him of the gift of prophecy and other divine adornments, and stir up scandal to defame the doctrine which Joseph professed, so that evil might be spoken of God and true religion, which had recently begun to shine forth, might be extinguished. This one voluptuous act would have brought such great ruin in its train. For the devil takes great care and hides from us the webs from which afterward one cannot escape, as David found out, and as many godly persons find out. Gathering all these arguments together, Joseph raised himself up by faith against the lures and dangers, and as he coerced himself with discipline, so he also sought heavenly aid. Thus our leader, the Son of God, overcame and broke the attempt of the devil through Joseph. When pious persons in this way fight against their infirmity, and in faith seek aid and forgiveness, they do not lose grace, the Holy Spirit, and faith. And people everywhere call such an infirmity in the saints a venial sin.

Other lapses are sins against the conscience, which the Greeks call "murderous sins." And Paul says [Gal. 5:19]: "Manifest are the works of the flesh," namely, when someone violates the commandments of God contrary to his conscience, or indulges in a depraved desire and does not fight against it (as Saul hated David) or adds an outward shameful deed (as David seized another man's wife). People who commit such transgressions lose grace, grieve and drive out the Holy Spirit, and cast off faith. Unless they repent and return again to faith, they will be cast into eternal torments when they die. There is no need to bring up here the disputes about predestination. We need to make prouncements about our deeds and about the will and judgment of God according to the express Word of God. If David had not done better, he would have been cast into eternal torments like Saul. Carnal security is deeply fixed in the minds of men, particularly the idle. Therefore we must beware lest we indulge in this evil, which is strengthened by various pretexts. Let us set the Word of God before ourselves, according to the passage: "Your Word is a lamp to my feet" [Ps. 119:105]. The Word testifies that grace is lost and the Holy Spirit driven out through such lapses:

Rom. 8[:13]: "If you live according to the flesh, you will die."

Matt. 12[:45], about the devil returning to those from whom he had been cast out: "He goes and takes seven other spirits more wicked than himself, and entering in, they dwell there, and the latter things become worse than the former."

Matt. 13[:22]: about the seed which is choked by worldly lures.

1 Cor. 6[:9]: "Do not be deceived; neither the immoral, nor idolators, nor adulterers, nor thieves will inherit the kingdom of God." And he testifies that he is speaking to those who had previously received the benefits of Christ. He commands that they should be careful lest they lose them.

Likewise 1 Cor. 10[:8]: "Do not become idolators nor engage in immorality, as some of them did, and in one day 23,000 perished."

Gal. 5[:22]: "Those who do these things will not enter into the kingdom of God." And thereafter [Gal. 6:8]: "He who sows to his own flesh will from the flesh reap corruption; but he who sows to the Spirit will from the Spirit reap eternal life."

1 Tim. 5[:8]: "If anyone does not provide for his relatives, and especially for his own family, he has disowned the faith and is worse than an unbeliever."

Heb. 13[:4]: "God will judge the immoral and adulterous."

2 Pet. 2[:20]: "If, after they have escaped the defilements of the world through the knowledge of our Lord and Savior Jesus Christ, they are again entangled in them and overpowered, the last state has become worse for them than the first."

Matt. 10[:33]: "Whoever denies me before men, I also will deny before my Father who is in heaven."

Matt. 24[:13]: "He who endures to the end will be saved."

Matt. 25[:41]: "Depart from me, you cursed, into the eternal fire, for I was hungry and you gave me no food," etc.

1 Cor. 13[:2]: "If I have all faith . . . . but have not love, I am nothing."

Although we are not righteous on account of our virtues or works, that is, accepted by God, it is nevertheless necessary that there be present in us a beginning obedience, according to the statement [Rom. 8:14]: "Those who are led by the Spirit are sons of God."

1 John 3[:10]: "By this it may be seen who are the children of God, and who are the children of the devil: Whoever does not do right is not of God. . . . He who does not love his brother remains in death . . . Little

children, let no one deceive you. He who does right is righteous . . . He who commits sin is of the devil.'' Human security belittles the magnitude of our lapses, but see how dreadful are these threats. What more dreadful a thing could be said than this: Whoever commits sin is of the devil [cf. John 8:44; 1 John 3:10], that is, he is a captive of the devil, he is moved and driven by him, bereft of the Holy Spirit, cast off from God. The results also testify to this.

How many crimes and calamities one fall of David brought forth. After his desire gained the victory over him, and he had seized the wife of another, he commands her husband to be killed, and together with him many citizens, holy and brave men, perished, and disgrace is brought upon the name of God. Afterward his son stirs up an insurrection, and the wives of the father are seized to be violated by the son—a vicious and more than tragic crime—and many thousands of citizens are killed. Finally, sedition cannot fail to bring forth innumerable scandals and crimes. What evils arose from the idolatry of Solomon! The kingdom of Israel was cut in two, and constant idolatry and wars between brethren followed. What evils the fall of Adam brought forth!

This is what the devil does in order that he may create such a web of troubles when he notices that we regard our sins as small. He cozies up to us to loosen the reign on our lusts; thus faith is extinguished. For faith, which seeks remission of sins, cannot exist in those who knowingly delight in sin and are without repentance, according to this saying: ''Where will God dwell? In a contrite spirit that trembles at my Word'' [Is. 66:2]. For those who knowingly delight in sin are not willing to be set free from it. Therefore the dictum of John should recall to our memory whence sin arises, how great an enemy we have, and what he is after, in order that we may exercise our faith so Christ in us may overcome this enemy.

Until now I have set forth the sum of the doctrine of the Gospel, about justification, as it is called, or about grace, about reconciliation, about faith, and about good works. This concept is plain and clear, since there is in it nothing absurd, dark, or sophistic. It speaks about impulses which are well known to pious minds in the church, and does not argue about idle subtleties. It shows the glory of Christ since it reveals the greatness of human infirmity. Finally, it agrees perfectly with the perpetual consensus of the entire Scripture of the Old and the New Testaments. All the godly of all times in the church experience that this consolation is true and necessary. It is strange in the case of our adversaries that there is such great darkness, and such fury and that they do not cease to fight against it with every evil means.

But the devil pours out errors on human minds in many ways, in order that he may obscure the glory of Christ. Therefore the godly should pray that Christ may preserve his Gospel and not permit it to be destroyed everywhere, and that he may govern us by his light, and show his truth to as many as possible, driving away the fogs which the devil pours out. Also, let our diligence invite Christ. Let the learned labor to set forth this whole matter diligently and clearly so that it is transmitted to those who come after us without sophistry. We also should not shun the responsibilities or labor involved in learning and teaching, or the struggles in confessing the faith. For this matter cannot be explained sufficiently clearly without learning. And there is need for a certain greatness of mind for enduring the hatreds of the mighty and wise, who disapprove of these disputations, some for one reason, others for another. But it is necessary for the godly to share in fighting for the Gospel, as Christ says: "By this my heavenly Father is glorified: if you will be my disciples and bring forth abundant fruit" [John 15:8]. Therefore let us set forth the doctrine in good faith, simply and correctly, and let us pray that God may add his Holy Spirit, that he may, as Paul says, grant a rich increase.

### An Explanation of Arguments from Scripture Which the Adversaries Oppose

I shall however add a few arguments with which the adversaries attempt to shake our understanding.

1. The chief one is the statement in James [2:14]: not by faith only, but by works.

The answer is quite easy: James calls the knowledge of history faith, for he says that the demons believe. But what Paul calls faith is something very different, namely, trust in the mercy promised because of Christ. Therefore he is rebuking the error of those who think they are righteous because of their profession of the history. That is indeed a necessary work like the other good works, but it is not that confidence by which we accept the forgiveness of sins, as is evident.

Thereafter, when he says that he was justified by works, the expression must be observed. He does not want to say that Abraham was reconciled on account of works, but that the works of the reconciled one afterward pleased God. For in the reconciled works do please, as has been said, and some of them are righteousness of the Law, but they do not merit the forgiveness of sins or acceptance to life eternal. Therefore he says that Abraham was also justified by works, that is, also his works were pronounced righteous [cf. James 2:23–24]. This is true of the person who has been justified and believes. And it is indeed necessary, as I have said, that works should follow in which faith lives and is exercised. Let us act openly, without sophistry. James is not treating the same matter as Paul, but is speaking in passing about a faith which is only knowledge of history. Therefore his pronouncements must be set in opposition to Paul, or to the other prophetic Scriptures.

**2.** [Our adversaries also cite,] "If you want to enter into life, keep the commandment [cf. Deut. 6:2; Ez. 20:11]. Therefore eternal life is given on account of works, it is not given [gratis] to the believer." There is a clear, perpetual answer to such sayings. The statements about the Law and about the Gospel must be distinguished. Here the voice of the Law is put forward, which must be interpreted on the basis of the Gospel. For no one would be saved if judgment had to be made according to the Law. Whoever keeps the commandments will enter into life, for no one keeps the Law, and no one is without sin. Therefore add the Gospel to that statement: If you wish to enter into life, keep the commandments, namely, according to the clemency of the Gospel, which promises forgiveness of sins because of Christ.Afterward he begins the new obedience, and he approves it, although it is imperfect, and is not the purchase-price of eternal life.

True, it is necessary that the commandments be kept, and it is necessary that the Law be proclaimed in order that repentance and faith may increase in us. However, what must be taught is not the Law only, but the promise of the Gospel must be added, without which the Law is only a ministry of wrath and of eternal death. And it is certain that Christ is the end of the Law [Rom. 10:4]. Therefore one must not stop with the Law, but when we hear the Law and are terrified, let us think that we are being accused, not in order that we may perish, but that we may seek the Mediator, the Son of God. We should know that he was given to us in order that through him we might be set free from sin, from the tyranny of the devil and from death. Therefore when eternal life is begun in us, we obey the Law, and the commandments are kept as was said: "I shall pour out the Spirit of grace and prayer on the house of David" [Zech 12:10].

**3.** [Our adversaries also cite] 1 Cor. 13[:2]: "If I have all faith . . . but have not love, I am nothing." The answer is the same: I confess that love is necessary, but love for God can neither exist nor can it please unless we have first accepted remission of sins and the imputation of righteousness. It is easy for idle persons to imagine that they love God, but these need to be led back to true sorrow in their minds, and to true impulses in invocation, in dangers. Here some doubt whether God is concerned about human affairs, whether indeed favorable and adverse things happen by chance. Others, feeling the wrath of God, like Saul, succumb in afflictions and rage against the judgment of God. The heavenly voice preaches about these immense storms of the mind, and amid these waves it lifts up the minds by the promise of the Gospel. When the mind sustains itself by faith and acknowledges mercy, there love follows. Therefore it is necessary that faith should come first, which accepts the remission of sins. And this faith cannot rest in our worthiness. Although love follows, it nevertheless declares that we are righteous not on account of our love, but on account of Christ. People in general interpret love as love for God and the neighbor. Therefore I have responded concerning the love to God. However, Paul is here speaking particularly about love for the neighbor; it is even more certain that it does not merit the forgiveness of sins.

**4.** [Our adversaries also cite Luke 6:37:] "Forgive, and it will be forgiven you," [and they say,] "Therefore by our forgiving, we also merit justification for ourselves." The answer is plain. This is preaching of repentance, of which there are many examples in the Prophets, as Is. 1[:16–17]: "Cease to do evil, learn to do good; Then your sins will be wiped away," etc. The first part teaches about our repentance; the other contains a promise. Christ does not say you will be forgiven on account of your forgiving, but only commands that we should forgive; thereafter he reminds about remission which depends on something else, not on the worthiness of our work. How great would be the future consternation of consciences if one had to think that divine forgiveness depended on the purity and worthiness of our forgiving toward those with whom we had a quarrel? For in reconciled minds there also remain scars, as a certain famous person says. Therefore it is necessary to seek another cause of forgiveness. The statement of the Gospel about gratuitous forgiveness must be held fast.

This is what is said in Daniel [4:27]. Part is preaching of repentance: Love justice and do good to the poor who are unjustly oppressed. Defend the church against tyrants, for that is what Daniel wanted. The other part is a promise: And there will be a healing of your transgressions. There must be repentance, and nevertheless forgiveness is gratuitous and to be accepted by faith. For if the promise depended on the condition of our worthiness, it would be void, as is said in Rom. 4.

**5.** [Our adversaries also say that] love is the greatest of virtues, and therefore we are accounted righteous on account of love. I deny the conclusion, and the reason is clear, for this would follow more correctly: Love is the greatest, but since we show hardly any love, there is no way we can be righteous on account of this virtue. If we possessed the virtues which the Law of God demands and were without sin, we would rightly be said to be righteous on account of our love and other virtues. But because human nature is far removed from the perfection of the Law and is not ardent in love, the Gospel sets before us another righteousness. It teaches that we are accounted righteous not on account of our virtues, but on account of something else, outside of us—the Mediator, the Son of God. We declare that we have a gracious God on account of him, by faith. Therefore we are righteous by imputation, not on account of our virtues, although these also must be begun in us.

As for the rest, if someone demands a distinction of virtues: Faith, at the present time, accepts the forgiveness of sins. Hope is an expectation of a future event, or of coming liberation. Faith is assent, by which the will wants and accepts the promise, and finds peace on account of the Mediator, the Son of God. And when the will thus acquiesces, the heart becomes calm and finds consolation and joy, which is the beginning of the new life. Hope and love follow these impulses. Because faith is certain that God is gracious to us, it dares to ask and expect the other benefits. And love springs up because now we know that God is not idle, as reason imagines. Neither is God an enemy, such as the Law shows, but he is a Father who is touched by the greatness of our calamity and desires to set us free. He swears: "As I live, I do not desire the death of the sinner, . . . " [Ez. 33:11]. In this way, when we acknowledge that we are received into grace and are heard by God, we on our part submit ourselves to him, and a certain reverence is kindled, or a certain desire by which we prefer God above other things. Such is love in this life—not burning as it should be, but weak.

**6.** They hold up against us also the [Latin] term *merces* [reward] and say that since eternal life is called a reward, good works must merit eternal life. I shall not seek shrewd interpretations of the term; let the sources of the matter be examined. The Psalm [143:2] says: "Enter not into judgment with your servant, for in your sight no man living shall be justified." Likewise: "Who understands his errors?" [Ps. 19:12]. Therefore we are not able to declare that we merit eternal life with our virtues, or that our virtues are the purchase price of eternal life. Above I have collected many testimonies which show that sin remains in the regenerate which here must be regarded by the mind. And let everyone ask his own conscience whether he prefers that eternal life should be given him because of Christ or indeed that he should be forgiven for the sake of his merits. You may say the zeal for doing right is weak if eternal life is given *gratis*. No—despair debilitates the zeal for doing right even more. For those who imagine that eternal life is given for merits must despair.

The more prudent fathers saw this danger. Augustine and Bernard clearly say eternal life is given to a believer *gratis*, on account of Christ. Also Paul says, "The gift of God is eternal life through our Lord Jesus Christ" [Rom. 6:23]. Neither is the gift uncertain. But God instructs us to believe that we shall certainly receive eternal life on account of Christ, according to what is written John 6[:40]: "This is the will of the Father, that everyone who believes in the Son should have eternal life." However, this faith does not exist without repentance, and faith regards both voices, namely: "As I live, I do not want the death of the sinner, but that he may be converted and live" [Ez. 33:11]. In what way? Through the Son, even as he says: "This is the will of my

Father, that everyone who believes in the Son should have eternal life" [John 6:40]. Although repentance must be present, the condition of our worthiness must not be attached to it. Yes, repentance fights against trust in merit, as the saying reminds us: "Whoever glories, let him glory in the Lord" [1 Cor. 1:31].

Why then is it called a reward? I answer: Although eternal life is given because of Christ, it also rewards our labors and troubles. This is sufficient so far as the nature of the word is concerned, as an inheritance also compensates the labors of the heir, although he receives it for a different reason. But another answer is simpler and truer. The expressions of the Law are: "He will give to everyone according to his works" [Matt. 16:27]. Likewise: "Great will be your reward in heaven" [Luke 6:23]. For the Scripture speaks of righteousness after the manner of the Law, as though about our worthiness, and about faith as though about our virtue, and says that a reward is given to our virtues. Meanwhile it must be known from the Gospel that we are righteous not by our virtue, but by imputation, and that the benefits of Christ are accepted by faith, not on account of the worthiness of this virtue, but because it rests upon the merit of another, namely, Christ. This is a quick and true answer, and it is without sophistry.

## An Explanation of the Scholastics' Esteemed Objections

I shall add also certain scholastic objections which, when they are explained, add much light to this disputation, and meanwhile vex the prattlers.

1. [The Scholastics say] righteousness is obedience to the whole Law, good works are obedience to the whole Law, and therefore we are justified by good works. I answer: First of all the minor premise must be denied. For good works are not perfect obedience to the Law, because human nature fights against the Law of God. Then I answer the major premise. The major premise is true of the righteousness of the Law. For the righteousness of the Law is obedience to the whole Law. But because we do not fulfill this, the Gospel offers gratuitous imputation of righteousness, as also Paul reminds us with respect to the word *imputation*.

This objection is very useful, for it shows the distinction between the righteousness of the Law and that of the Gospel. It shows that the term *righteousness* is used in a different sense in different connections. This deceived the *Sententiarii*[2]: When they had read in Aristotle that righteousness signifies general obedience, they dreamed that it means the same thing everywhere in the Apostles and Prophets. The Psalm [89:16] says: "They shall

---

[2] A *Sententiarius* was an advanced theological student who was trained to lecture on Peter Lombard's *Four Books of Sentences*.

exult in your righteousness." Here it does not signify Aristotelian virtues, but relationally, "in your righteousness," i.e., in the imputation of righteousness by which you account us righteous through mercy, that is, accepted. The righteousness of the law signifies obedience, as when it is said, "I have done justice and righteousness" [Ps. 119:121]. But the righteousness about which the Gospel specifically speaks signifies relationally, the imputation of righteousness, that is, gratuitous acceptance to eternal life, although joined to it is the gift of the Holy Spirit. So when you hear the word *justified,* you should think about the Hebrew phrase which signifies "to be accounted or pronounced righteous," or that the accused person is absolved. And *righteous* signifies "accepted by God to eternal life." 2 Cor. 5[:21]: "He made him to be sin for us who knew no sin, so that in him we might become the righteousness of God," that is, Christ was made guilty for us so that we might become accepted because of him. This is the simple grammatical and true explanation of the words. In different passages the word is used in a different sense. Sometimes it is used for the righteousness of the Law; at other times of imputation. It is necessary to observe this distinction.

**2.** [The Scholastics also say,] "Works against the Law of God are sins, so good works are righteousness. The conclusion is valid from the nature of things that are contrary to each other. It follows also that men are justified by good works, since these constitute justice." I answer: The conclusion would be valid if good works were perfect obedience, but since they fall far short of perfect obedience it can easily be understood that the argument is not valid because it is not a case of true contraries. Things that are faulty are entirely faulty. A great many faults are mixed in with good works, by which they also are contaminated. Pomponius Atticus was a kind-hearted man, righteous in the eyes of the citizens. But he doubts whether God is concerned about human affairs. He is without fear of God. The greatness of those inner defects is not perceived. Therefore the argument deceives those who are not warned. The conclusion must be denied because there is not a true antithesis. I answer the same to the following argument.

**3.** [The Scholastics also say,] "evil works damn. Therefore good works save." I deny the conclusion, and the reason is there is no true antithesis. Evils are bad throughout. Much evil is mixed in with the good works, and although David has good works, he nevertheless has many evil impulses; he had doubts about God. And this darkness draws in its train a great mass of vices, carnal security, and trust in one's own wisdom and righteousness. The heart does not burn with fear or love of God, nor with faith as it should be. I know that there have been some who said that our understanding was powerfully shaken by this argument, but even a moderately attentive reader can easily judge how foolish and futile it is.

**4.** [The Scholastics also say,] "Sin is hatred of God, so love is righteousness." I know that Eck celebrated great triumphs when he tried to use this argument to show that men are not justified by faith alone. However the answer is easy: It is agreed that perfect love is the righteousness which the Law demands, but as was said above, we are not righteous by the Law. For there can be no love unless we are first reconciled by faith. Afterward there follows a certain beginning, and yet there remains a great infirmity which fights against the Law of God, angry and raging against the judgment of God, as the Psalm [4:4] shows: "Be angry, but do not sin . . . " Therefore there is need for another righteousness, namely, by gratuitous imputation.

**5.** [The Scholastics also say,] "righteousness is located in the will, and faith is in the intellect, so faith is not righteousness." I answer: The major premise is true with respect to the righteousness of the Law, which signifies the virtues and qualities in our will. But when Paul speaks about the righteousness of faith, righteousness signifies the imputation of righteousness. For he teaches that men are accounted righteous, that is, accepted, not on account of their own quality, but on account of something outside of ourselves, namely, through mercy on account of the Mediator, the Son of God. It is necessary that this mercy be accepted by faith. Faith is not only knowledge, but assent, for which also the impulse of the will is required, as learned people know. It is to want and to accept the promise, and to find rest in it. This faith is conceived when we assent to the Gospel promise. When a terrified mind sustains itself with this, the Holy Spirit at the same time moves the hearts through the Word to believe.

**6.** [The Scholastics also say,] "we are righteous by faith, and faith is a work, so we are righteous by works." To the major premise the response should be that the argument, rightly understood, could be explained and solved. We are justified by faith, not because it is a work or quality or virtue in us, but insofar as it takes hold of mercy and rests on Christ. In order that the matter may become clearer, the saying must be transformed into its correlative: We are justified by faith, that is, we are righteous through mercy because of Christ, but faith must also declare that this mercy pertains to us. The minor premise is true: Faith is a work, like other virtues—love, patience, and chastity. But as the other virtues are imperfect, so also faith is weak. Therefore we are not righteous on account of the worthiness of the virtue, but because it takes hold of the mercy. For it is necessary, if I may express it this way, that there be some instrument by which mercy is grasped. It is necessary that we look upon Christ, and declare that he forgives us. Therefore the answer to the major premise must be: Faith is a work, but we are not righteous on account of the worthiness of the work, but because it takes hold of the mercy. It cannot follow that we are righteous because of our works.

This also can be learnedly said: there is more in the conclusion than in the premises, for the conclusion wants men to be righteous on account of works. That does not follow from these premises.

7. [The Scholastics also say,] "we are righteous by grace. Grace is love infused in the minds, so we are righteous through love." I respond to the minor premise: Relationally, grace chiefly signifies favor, mercy, or gratuitous acceptance because of Christ. A fitting interpretation of the term must be retained. Moreover, with this acceptance there is connected the gift of the Holy Spirit. But [the Scholastics] explain those terms in this way: We are righteous by grace, that is, we are righteous on account of infused virtues. Here they imagine an explanation that is diametrically opposed to Paul, and which wholly removes from sight the true consolations of pious minds. If, when we pray, we had to look at ourselves and imagine that we would have access to God only when we have been sufficiently adorned with these virtues, then we could hope for eternal life only when we could see this new purity in ourselves. People would lose heart and despair of help and salvation.

The more fear-filled minds are, the more fully they see the uncleanness and infirmity of our nature. For this very reason—because we see that we cannot bring to God merits and worthiness—Paul expounds grace, that is, the gratuitous forgiveness and acceptance because of Christ. Although you do not bring worthiness to God, come before him with trust in Christ, the Mediator, as he says: "Having this high priest, let us approach the throne of grace" [Heb. 4:14, 16].

I have added these refutations so that I might satisfy (as best I could) the learned who argue about the real meaning of the language. We wish to say what is true and right, and avoid improper phrases, in order that we might instruct learners so they may refute scholastic sophistries with greater skill. And I hope that these examples will be useful—first to make clear, and also to sharpen the care with which students learn. For these refutations show that there is need for learning and for a certain amount of practice for those who are attempting to explain such controversies skillfully. Students should not think that those are undertaking a light burden who want to defend an explanation of the Christian doctrine are undertaking a light burden. I pray that God may guide the studies of the godly, and not permit the light of the Gospel and the true knowledge of Christ to be extinguished in the church.

# Chapter 1

## 1a. Paul, a servant of Jesus Christ, a called apostle

An inscription, such as is customary in letters, is placed at the beginning, in a manner most useful for the church, in order that it may be known for certain that the doctrine has been divinely received, preaching not about everyday matters which reason judges, but about the will of God. Thus the fathers, in order that they might know whence the doctrine had been handed down, said expressly: "The God of Abraham, the God of Israel," in order that that Word might be understood and those acts of worship embraced which God taught to Abraham, etc. There the very first authors must be considered through whom the true knowledge of God and the promise of the Gospel has been propagated, lest one rashly think that the profession rose by chance, as so many superstitions in the world either arose by chance or were excited by the devil in order to obscure true religion.

Now this is the sum and substance of the inscription: The Apostle Paul wishes grace and peace for the Romans. But there is inserted a somewhat longer description of the office of Paul and a description of the Gospel. And there is an important reason why he mentions his office—so the church may know that the teaching of Paul must be believed as the voice of God sounding from heaven. Just as Moses prefaced his teaching [cf. Ex. 20:1] "The Lord our God spoke all these words" so the people would know that it was not a human doctrine that was being set forth but one surely and expressly taught by God. Thus Paul says by way of preface that he is an apostle not chosen by human judgment, but by the voice of Christ, and that he is bringing a Gospel that is divinely taught, and that this teaching which he sets forth— about the Law, the promises, sin, grace, and faith—is not a human invention, but was divinely revealed and commended to him so that he would teach it to the church. Therefore it is not in vain that he here and elsewhere continues to mention his office and emphasizes his titles. We must be reminded of these in order that we may read Paul not as we read Ambrose or Augustine (only as a learned interpreter of the prophetic Scripture) but as one who certainly brings the heavenly doctrine to which it is necessary to assent. Here moreover the call of an apostle must be clearly distinguished from the call of the bishop.

An apostle has been immediately called by Christ to teach the Gospel, and he has a sure testimony with respect to his doctrine—that it is divine—

and it is certain that he has the Holy Spirit, that he does not err in doctrine, and that he is able to teach everywhere in all churches.

A bishop, however, has been called by men to teach the Gospel in a certain place, and he can err; neither is it necessary that one be certain that he has the Holy Spirit.

From these descriptions many things can be judged. For as the prophets in the people of Israel were far superior to the priests, and did many heroic things which the Law did not permit to the other priests, so the apostles have a call that is far superior to that of other bishops. They abrogate law. They call Gentiles into the fellowship of the people of God; they explain obscure articles about the Messiah—that he is the Son of God, that his kingdom will not be a political one. They expressly impart remission of sins, which the Levitical priests had by no means done. They explain the article about the righteousness of faith, which few among the people of the law had previously heard. Bishops must accept the sayings of the apostles, not introduce a new or different kind of doctrine. In order that Paul might remind all about the authority of his doctrine, he mentions his call when he says: "A servant of Jesus Christ, a called apostle." Origen here ineptly orates about liberation from ceremonies and about the slavery of Paul, by which he was bound to ceremonies before his conversion. Such declamations don't belong to this passage. Paul here is not speaking of private servitude, but of his office. He calls himself a servant, that is, a minister performing an office pertaining to the kingdom of Christ.

### 1b. Called[1]

This can be understood better from the Epistle to the Galatians [1:1], where he adds that he had not been called by men or through men, but through Jesus Christ and God the Father. He indicates this here when he calls himself not an ordinary preacher, but a called apostle. At this time these statements must be opposed to the Papists, whose impudence is so great that they dare to say openly that one is not to believe Paul any more than the Roman pontiff or the bishops. They imagine Paul to be some beggar or vagabond who wanders about without authority and stubbornly quarrels about religion. However, having heard that he is called an apostle, we should think that he is preaching with prophetic authority and receive what he says as the voice of God sounding from heaven. If we think in this way, his statements will greatly strengthen us.

---

[1] Our 1540 edition has *Vocatus Apostolus,* "Called Apostle."

### 1c. Separated for the gospel of God

He expressly names the kind of business which was commanded to him. He says that he had been chosen for propagating the Gospel. The reader should remember already here that there is a very great difference between these two, between the Law and the Gospel. We have both spoken above in the preface about this distinction, and will have to speak of it below in the third chapter. He also adds a description of the Gospel. The Gospel is a promise, divinely made, handed down in Holy Scripture, about the Son of God, Jesus, born of the seed of David according to the flesh, but declared to be the Son of God, empowered through the sanctifying Spirit, raised from the dead, who is the Messiah or King, through whom liberation is made from sin and eternal death.

This definition will become clearer if an antithesis of Law and Gospel is established. The Law is the doctrine which teaches what manner of persons we ought to be and what we must do, requiring perfect obedience, not promising remission of sins *gratis,* not liberating us from sin and death, but rather giving sin weapons when it accuses us and oppressing us with deadly terrors. But the Gospel is a promise, which promises us remission of sins *gratis,* and liberation from sin and death through the Son of God, born of the descendants of David, according to the promises, and sanctifying us with divine power by means of eternal life. These parts will be explained more fully below.

However Paul in the beginning at once sets forth the definition, in order that we might know what is being taught, and might diligently distinguish the Law from the Gospel, as though he were saying: Paul, divinely called for teaching the Gospel about Christ, not for teaching the law or philosophy.

### 2. Through the prophets in the Holy Scriptures

He inserts this in order that he may meet an unspoken objection. When a new kind of doctrine is being professed, Pharisees will undoubtedly speak against it. Since there has always been from the beginning of the world a church of God, it must have held the doctrine necessary for salvation. Therefore the Pharisees asked whether it held the doctrine of the apostles. If it did not hold it, the Pharisees shout, it is new and an invention.

Paul answers yes—it is one and the same Gospel about the Messiah, the Gospel promised to the fathers, shown to the prophets, and now proclaimed. We are not bringing a doctrine that was unknown to the fathers and prophets (but now buried by you through human opinions about righteousness of the Law), about a political reign of the Messiah. You revile this doctrine as new and invented because you do not understand what kind of liberation the patriarchs and the prophets preached. You imagine that you are righteous through

the Law, that the Messiah will come to occupy a kingdom of this world, that
he will give you provinces to rule, and that you may abound in riches and
pleasures. That is the liberation which you intoxicated people dream about.
But they expected a Messiah who would abolish sin and death with divine
power, who would destroy the reign of the devil. That was the intention of
the promise in which the Seed is promised who will crush the head of the
serpent.

In the same way the Papists now oppose to us the church. They shout
that we are bringing a doctrine that is unknown to the church. We deny that
loudly and testify that our doctrine shone forth in the church of the patriarchs,
the prophets, the apostles, and from then on among the godly. We quote the
testimonies of the church, namely, the prophets, the apostles, and other godly
men. For no kind of doctrine ought to be received which was always unknown
to the true church of Christ. But now for many centuries the understanding
of the true church has been obscured. Popes, priests, and monks scattered
false and Pharisaical opinions in the church about righteousness through
works. They contrived superstitious observances, heaped up heathenish superstitions, invocation of the dead, clear idol-mania, and profaned the Lord's
Supper with horrible impiety.

These things were contrived partly through superstition, partly for the
sake of gain, and partly for the sake of strengthening tyranny. This assembly
of godless popes and monks is not the church of Christ. They unjustly arrogate
this most honorable title to themselves when they oppose to us their invented
authority, not the authority of the true church. Therefore Paul admonishes us
in this passage lest dogmas be received without testimonies of the divine
Scripture. He also admonishes us that we should demand the statements of
the true church, and that we distinguish the true church from the false.

### 3. Concerning His Son

He opposes also this little expression to the common persuasions of the
Jews. The Jews expected a Messiah who would not be by nature the Son of
God but only a man, similar to the other prophets in that he surpasses the
common people in wisdom, justice, and success in managing affairs, so that
he would easily occupy the rule of the world. However, the patriarchs and
the prophets knew that the Messiah is the Son of God who would also govern
and help them. Jacob says: "The Angel who delivered me from all evils bless
these boys" [Gen. 48:16]. There he shows that he is speaking about the
liberator, whom he knew was promised. For the office of this person is to
deliver from all evils. In addition to Jacob, Moses and Daniel saw Him. To
testify that the Messiah is the Son of God and that He was always present
with the fathers, John says [cf. John 1:1 ff.]: "In the beginning was the Word;

all things were made by him . . . '' indicating that all the glorious victories of Noah, Abraham, Joseph, Moses, Samuel, David, Isaiah, and Jeremiah were won by our leader and champion against the devil.

Paul is also preaching here about the two natures in the Messiah. He calls him the Son of God to censure the error of the Jews, even as Christ himself censured it in John 5 and frequently elsewhere. Paul is speaking of the person, and fittingly applies the term *Son of God* to the person. This term is to be applied not only to the divine nature, but to the person of Christ. This, he testifies, is composed of two natures; he says that the Son of God, according to the flesh, is born of the seed of David. Therefore he declares that there is in Christ a human nature. This passage refutes the Manichaeans and many others who took away the human nature from Christ or denied that it had been received from the blood of the virgin mother. Afterward he preaches about the divine nature when he says: "Who had been declared to be the Son of God, powerful through the sanctifying Spirit, by the resurrection from the dead'' [1:4].

**4.** There is particular emphasis in the word ὁρισθέντος (declared), which the Greeks explain by the word ἀποδειχθέντος (pointed out). The meaning is that this person was certainly acknowledged to be the Son of God through these testimonies: that he rose from the dead; that he showed his boundless power by many miracles, as when he resurrected Lazarus; that he now gives to the church the Holy Spirit, who strengthens the minds against the devil and performs many great miracles. Paul, too, revived a dead hearer, and all things were then full of miracles done by the apostles, who asked these gifts from the Son of God. Therefore Paul is speaking of the testimony with respect to us. On account of these testimonies it is declared with certainty and established that this Jesus is the Son of God by nature, since he has divine and immeasurable power. That is what the word ὁρίζεσθαι signifies: to be declared with certainty.

He opposes all these things to Jewish opinions. They expected an outstanding Messiah who still was a man, having only a human nature and being glorious through his heroic victories, who would give wealth, not a new nature and eternal life. But Paul says that this Messiah will be powerful, both to give the sanctifying Spirit, through whom there will be begun in the believers a new light, righteousness, and life eternal, and to overcome the devil. This, he says, is the true liberation which the fathers both understood and experienced in the exercises of faith as they fought against the devil, against death, and in various dangers. It is a far greater liberation than the one expected by you who think the Messiah will partition out provinces, as Alexander distributed kingdoms to comrades in war. Paul censures these errors in this brief description.

When he calls this person the Christ, he lets us look in our mind at all the old promises in the Prophets in order that we may see that they truly agree with this proclamation of the Gospel, so we may kindle in ourselves faith through consideration of the benefits of Christ, and so we may call upon him. Unless faith is exercised in invocation, the kingdom and presence of Christ cannot be understood.

It would take a long time to explain these great things as their greatness demands. Since there must be a certain limit to comments, I shall not dwell longer on this inscription, particularly because the same things recur frequently. The pious reader, informed about the plan of the author and about the sum and substance of the content, will contemplate the greatness of the matters with diligent meditation and will learn how this knowledge of Christ should shine forth in life, in invocation, in dangers, and in every act. By doing so the Son of God may be powerful also for us, a liberator from sin, from death, and from the devil. He will be our high priest, making intercession for us with God. He will be our leader who will help us in our calamities, even as he promises aid to the weak when he says: "Come to me all who labor and are heavy laden, and I will give you rest" [Mt. 11:28].

The simple syntax of the words should be diligently observed. Such observation brings much light to the sentence. The apostle Paul was called as a teacher of the Gospel of Jesus Christ, who was born from the offspring of David's second flesh and was declared to be the Son of God through the resurrection and the gift of the Holy Spirit. Paul desires the salvation of the Romans.

### 5–6. Through whom we have received grace

Although above, when he calls himself an apostle, he says that he had been separated or chosen for the task of teaching the Gospel, he had not said he had been expressly called by Christ. Here he adds this expressly: "Through whom we have received grace," that is, reconciliation with God, and "the office of an apostle for obedience of faith," that is, that the faith might be obeyed, or of preaching the Gospel about faith. "Among all Gentiles"—he adds this in order that he might testify in passing that the Gentiles are to be called to the Gospel. Furthermore, I have said above that the authority of his mandate for his office is defended in order that we may know that this preaching of Paul must be believed. If you read Paul, you should not think that you are reading a human disputation, but that you are hearing God himself speaking with you.

## 7. Grace to you and peace

First he wishes for them grace, that is, reconciliation and the gift of the Holy Spirit. Thereafter peace, that is, the other good things for which there is need. For peace generally signifies, after the Hebrew custom, favorable and joyous things. The church also has need of many gifts: purity of doctrine, increase of virtues, harmony, constancy, food, and hospitality. All these are embraced in the word *peace*. He links together God the Father and the Lord Jesus Christ, first to remind us that grace and the other things are given to us by God on account of His Son, the Mediator. He does this also so that we may know how these things can possibly concern us, namely, if we pray on account of the Son. Thirdly, it signifies that Christ is by nature God, reigning with equal power together with the Father, aiding us with divine power, as is promised in the Psalm: God raises up all who are cast down, and lifts up all who are crushed [cf. Ps. 113:7].

## 8–16. The introduction

The part of a speech must be diligently distinguished, for some things are treated in one place, others in another. Here he prepares the minds of the readers, as is done in introductions. He is not yet concerned with the main issue. But he sets forth certain rhetorical matters. He congratulates them on their knowledge of the Gospel. He shows his good will toward them. He says he wants to aid their zeal. Then he adds causes taken from the function of an apostle.

The learned know that such a reminder of our good will is customary in introductions, and it is not difficult to combine the parts of an introduction with everyday precepts. It consists of four parts: I congratulate you on your knowledge of the Gospel, and I wish that this knowledge may increase in you. Thereafter the proposition of the introduction follows: I desire to instruct you face to face. To this he immediately adds the adversative: But until now the churches in these regions held me back so that I could not come to you. In the third place there follows the reason for his purpose—why he desires to teach them in person: Because, he says, I must aid the study of the Gospel with all, the learned and the unlearned. All these things belong to the matter of gaining good will.

The other cause gains the attention of the reader, being taken from the dignity of the Gospel: "I am not ashamed of the Gospel" [Rom. 1:16]. This word he opposes to the judgment of all the ungodly. For the Epicureans in the world, of whom there is a great multitude, despise the Gospel, and think it is a fraud and a dumb invention. Most governing persons of the state also cruelly hate this kind of teaching, by which they think the calm of the citizens and of the ungodly is disturbed. They desire to extinguish it as a torch kindling seditions and discords among citizens. In addition to them the hypocrites, fascinated by superstitions, and then the Jews, and at this time the monks and persons similar to them hate the Gospel much more intensely, because they think that it brings disgrace on God, since it scolds superstitious acts of worship which those persons admire as the highest piety and ceremonies of the angels.

And the devil, burning with intense hatred for Christ, increases and strengthens these furies in the ungodly, looking for opportunities by which he is able to irritate, impel, and inflame the minds of everyone. He holds them captive and incites them, throwing various opportunities before them, as the power of the devil is seen in idol-mania and other horrendous lapses. Lucian tells of a certain person who violently loved the statue of Venus and was accustomed to embrace it, crying and kissing it. And many things could be told from the histories which are dreadful to hear. Since they are alien from the common custom of nature, it is quite clear that they have really sprung from the devil. When we read these things, let us consider that the devil does not have an idle sovereignty, but dreadfully impels the ungodly to wicked crimes. Therefore we are not surprised that he is able to kindle hatred and savagery in hypocrites and tyrants.

The Pharisees saw that the ceremonies of the Law and their traditions had been abolished. Therefore they raged and complained that disgrace was being done to God, that works that please God were being forbidden, and that permission to sin was being granted. Then they saw that, with the Law abolished, their civil power was changed, the distinction between priest and people confused, the foremost ornament of the state taken away, namely the honored priestly function. Such a change is very painful to the wise. The devil increased these flames; he inflamed the authorities to cruelty, to the killing of the apostles.

So also at this time we are most proudly being ridiculed by the Epicureans because we do not consider the Gospel an invention, because we seriously think that it should be obeyed. Kings and rulers angrily assert that the dissimilarity in doctrine disturbs the tranquility of states. Popes are unwilling for idolatry to be repudiated, lest their authority be shaken. The monks fear for their profits. A few, fascinated by superstition, contend that good works are being forbidden. From so many causes there is immense hatred for the Gospel. But we, on the other hand, declare with great conviction that the profession of the Gospel must not be cast off. We are not ashamed of this doctrine. For it is not a foolish fable nor is it a barbarous superstition. It is the statement of God, divinely revealed, by which he wants to impart to humans eternal salvation.

God is the Founder of all things, and of the human race. He did not want the human race simply to perish, since he had founded it so that the knowledge of God might shine forth in it. Therefore he revealed himself from the beginning to the patriarchs with sure testimonies, and taught them the Gospel. Neither is there any other doctrine which had been received on sure authority, or confirmed with true heavenly testimonies except this doctrine of the Gospel. Therefore we do not reject it, but obey it, and we know that God will truly give what he promises here. Therefore let us firmly fix this statement of Paul in our mind: "I am not ashamed of the Gospel" [Rom. 1:16], in order that it may uphold us against the judgments of the ungodly. Although Paul is not yet arguing in this introduction, nevertheless these ethical teachings contain five useful subjects.

The first is about spiritual worship. He says he serves God in his spirit, through the task of preaching. This, he teaches, is the foremost act of worship: to teach and learn the Gospel. Students and the godly ought to remember this in order that they may offer these acts of worship to God with greater concern.

The second is about mutual strengthening. Paul desires to teach and strengthen them, and in turn to be encouraged by them. Concerning this mutual strengthening, Christ says to Peter: "And you, when you are converted, strengthen your brethren" [Lk 22:32]. It is good for the godly to hear the testimonies of the godly and experienced about the doctrine.

The third is about the apostolic office. I am a debtor, he says, to the wise and to the unwise. Surely, these words seem boastful. The apostle dares to say that he can teach even the wise. To the foremost Romans, what arrogance this was that a wandering Jew should promise that he was a teacher even of the wise! Of all those who are outstanding in intelligence and learning and who have convinced themselves that they are holy, the Romans in particular admire themselves excessively and demand that divine honors be shown them. I have seen some like that. Such look down on Paul with scorn and ridicule these words in which he says that he is a teacher of the wise. But we remember that he is an apostle who brings not a human doctrine, but a heavenly one. As Elijah, Elisha, and Isaiah were teachers and guides of kings and high priests, so let us also hear Paul. Wise men should not be ashamed to hear from God, since we experience so often how shamefully human wisdom hallucinates and goes far astray, as all wise men complain. And God says [1 Cor. 1:19]: "I will destroy the wisdom of the wise," as the histories of all times show, and daily life testifies.

It belongs to the office of an apostle to teach both the wise and the unwise. He must also adjust to a weak understanding, as Paul says in 1 Cor. 3[:1–2]: "I addressed you as men of the flesh, as infants in Christ; I fed you with milk." Teachers and rulers of churches should set forth what is useful and adjust themselves to the capacity of the learners. When inexperienced and unlearned persons do not hear things clearly explained, they conceive false persuasions, as I have often noticed.

Now let popes and monks be compared with the picture Paul paints. Paul says that he must teach; he has been obligated to this task by a command of God. But popes do not even want to teach, but only preserve their rule in a tyrannical manner. In the church they have strengthened idolatry (which has its origin in the devil) namely, profanation of the Lord's Supper, invocation of idols, monkery, and similar things. They have strengthened lusts by the wicked law of celibacy. Now, admonished, they resolutely hold fast to vile errors and shame, and do not even use doctrine as a pretext. They confess that they err, but they say wealth, power, and authority must be fought for. Therefore they defend their crimes with cruel punishments, even as Nebuchadnezzar commanded all who would not worship his statue to be cast into the fiery furnace [cf. Dan. 3:6]. In truth, there is as great a difference between an apostle and a tyrant as between the good angels and the devils. For good teachers are also called angels of God in Malachi [2:7], and a tyrant is truly an instrument of the devil in the world.

Therefore let us diligently weigh these words of Paul, which testify that popes who are adversaries of the Gospel are not to be considered as bishops or successors of the apostles, but to be avoided as tyrants and cast out of the true church. A bishop is a debtor to the conscience of his subject, so he ought not to impose a law on him, such as the law of celibacy, which cannot be obeyed without crimes and offense against God.

Moreover, what about the servants of the tyrants, the writers and monks whom they teach? They propose childish traditions to the wise about dress, about foods, and about the pomp of ceremonies. They adorn these and now are beginning to picture them eloquently, even as now certain ones invent allegories of gestures in the church to excuse the superstition. What good does this teaching do for the wise? They are being called back to a childish discipline and to the poor elements of the world, whereas they ought to hear a doctrine unknown to reason about inner vices, doubting, mistrust, carnal security, admiration of our own wisdom and righteousness, and weakness seeking human aid contrary to the commandments of God, as the kings of Judah sought refuge—now with the Assyrians, now with the Egyptians— when they mistrusted God. They needed to be raised up again by true, spiritual comforts, lest they fall prostrate when human counsels and human errors deceived them. This is the doctrine of the wise, in which the knowledge of God grows.

How do they teach the ignorant? Two kinds of teaching are dominant among our adversaries: Labyrinths of questions in the Lombard, which not even the professors understand, and excerpted summaries from canon law, which gather sins against human traditions. Each of these is endless, full of errors and perplexity. Before these times many good men wished for emendation of the church's doctrine. What matters is that there are as many idolatries as there are futile arguments in one-fourth of the sentences: whether a mouse, gnawing on a part of the sacrament, gnaws the body of the Lord? I shudder to report this. There they ought to have reminded people that the sacraments are actions, not shows foreign to the instituted use of the sacrament. I could cite many examples of idle questions, but there are books available which show sufficiently that there was need for emendation of the doctrine. The little verse of Ovid is well-known:

> "No one can teach what he does not sufficiently know."

The first concern of one who teaches the Gospel must be that he himself rightly holds the sum of the Christian doctrine. Then he will be able to choose what is useful for teaching—both for instructing the unlearned and for admonishing and correcting the wise, as Paul corrected Peter, Isaiah corrected Hezekiah, etc.

The fourth subject is consolation. He confirms this by his own example when he says: "I am not ashamed of the Gospel" [Rom. 1:16], lest we be deterred from the Gospel by the judgments of the world. Although Epicureans ridicule us as insane because we do not think that the Gospel is a foolish fable, and although tyrants and hypocrites attempt to destroy the name of Christ with the great severity of punishments, we nevertheless do not permit ourselves to be drawn away from this kind of doctrine, and we know that this profession is glorious for us in the sight of God, his Son, the good angels, and the entire church. Let us look upon these judgments, and let us know that through this doctrine there are offered to us the promised benefits, namely, reconciliation and eternal life.

The fifth subject is an important and memorable saying about the ministry of the Word, namely, that remission of sins, the Holy Spirit, and the beginning of eternal life are given through the Word of the Gospel when it is heard, read, or pondered. When minds are sustained in the midst of fears by the voice of the Gospel, the Holy Spirit at the same time is at work, as is said below: "Faith comes by hearing" [Rom 10:17]. This word means the same when he says: "The Gospel is the power of God for salvation for everyone who believes" [Rom. 1:16], that is, it is the instrument through which God works and gives the Holy Spirit—not as the Pharisees imagine, *ex opere operato* [from the fact that a work has been performed] without cogitation of the mind—but God commands the Gospel to be accepted by faith. And when the mind accepts it, it fights against fears and mistrust. Therefore it is said to the. Galatians [3:14]: "In order that we may receive the promise of the Spirit through faith." He adds a summary of the Gospel, which is the purpose of the whole disputation which follows: "The righteousness of God is revealed in it from faith to faith" [Rom. 1:17]. This is the sum of all the benefits of Christ. For God is present with the reconciled; he gives them new light and eternal life, and hears and defends them in all calamities. Therefore, when he mentions the righteousness of God, he embraces all the benefits of Christ.

Moreover, let the nature of the speech be observed. The righteousness of God, that is, divine acceptance by which God receives and approves of us, is revealed in the Gospel. Also the antithesis must be noted, as if he said: Formerly you had the Law, in which the righteousness of the Law is revealed, but on account of the Law you did not yet have the righteousness of God; that is, you were not yet accepted by God. But in the Gospel there is revealed the righteousness of God, that is, acceptance by which God is now certainly propitious toward you, forgives your sins, and accounts you righteous. Therefore there follows: He revealed it from faith to faith [Rom. 1:17]. This also is opposed to the righteousness of the Law, as if he said: The Law teaches that righteousness is to satisfy the Law: but now there is revealed the righteousness by faith, that is, righteousness imputed through mercy. For whenever we read the word *faith,* there comes immediately to mind the correlative, namely, by the promised mercy. The speech of Paul smells of the Hebrew way of speaking, for Cicero speaks differently when he says of Caesar: "Your right hand, outstanding in faith (faithfulness)." The way of speaking in Paul must be observed, where faith signifies confidence in the mercy promised because of Christ. When he mentions the righteousness of faith, he understands a righteousness which is imputed through mercy. He opposes this to the righteousness of the Law, which had to be perfect obedience according to the Law. Since no one could furnish this, because this poor nature of man is a slave to sin, there is revealed in the Gospel a new righteousness, namely, a righteousness imputed through mercy. But this must be accepted by faith, that is, by knowledge of and confidence in Christ, as Isaiah [53:11] says: "The knowledge of Christ will justify many." It is as if he said: Since men are not righteous or accepted by God through the Law, but have sins, God wants to forgive them their sins and to be propitious, if they acknowledge that he wants to impart these benefits because of His Son, who is the sacrificial victim and the appeaser. This is the simple and natural explanation.

He says [Rom. 1:17]: "From faith to faith," that is, from an imperfect faith to one more perfect. Mercy is indeed revealed, but it does not come to all because God wants it to be accepted by faith. Since many are unwilling to accept it and spurn this unspeakable goodness, they perish. Faith is not idle knowledge, but needs to grow through constant battle, through calling on God, in all pursuits and dangers. May this always shine in our hearts—that God is propitious to us on account of Christ, the Mediator, and that he will help. And let us call upon him in this faith and ask him to guide us in all undertakings and dangers. In this way, faith and true knowledge of God will increase in the hearts of the godly. He adds a testimony to show that what he set forth is the true meaning, namely, that men are justified by faith, so the hearer may know that the Pauline proclamations truly agree with the prophetic proclamations and that the apostles are restoring the doctrine of the prophets.

### 17. The rightous man lives by faith

There is a clear antithesis in Galatians, where he says [Gal. 3:11–12]: "That no one is justified by the Law is clear, because the righteous shall live by faith. The Law is not of faith, but whoever does these things will live through them." Here he clearly says that the righteousness of the Law is to do the Law, that is, to render perfect obedience to the Law. But no one renders this. Therefore another righteousness is set forth, namely, righteousness imputed through mercy to the believer, who seeks refuge in mercy. When the prophet says [Hab. 2:4]: "The just shall live by faith," he teaches that we shall be just not when we look to the Law, not when we set out virtues and deeds before God, but when we declare that God is propitious to us by faith, that is, by confidence in mercy, that he hears us, wants to save us, and that we expect salvation. These things are on the basis of the prophetic pronouncement.

You will observe, however, that two very great praises are given to faith, namely, that we are both justified and made alive by faith. For God gave his Son for us for this purpose, and he became propitious to us for this purpose, that we may not perish, as he swears: "As I live, I do not want the death of the sinner, but that he may be converted and live" [Ez. 33:11]. When a terrified mind states by faith that sins have been forgiven him, it is set free at the same time from fears and receives true consolation, which is the beginning of eternal life in us, as Christ says: "This is life eternal, that they know you as the true God, and Jesus Christ whom you have sent" [John 17:3]. Therefore we should know that to remission of sins and reconciliation there is joined the gift of the Holy Spirit. We should know that the rule of Christ in the church, that is, for the righteous, is not an idle thing, but that the Son of God is truly present with us, that he truly destroys the works of the devil, that he fights for the believers and helps and preserves them. All these things are embraced in the words of the prophet when he promises life, that is, joy, victory, and eternal salvation to the believer.

But certain deceivers slander the statements quoted by Paul and say they have been badly distorted to the Pauline cause. This, they say, was what Paul was driving at, that people are reconciled to God through faith in Christ, but the prophet is not speaking about Christ in that passage. Likewise, when he elsewhere cites a statement about the faith of Abraham: Abraham believed that he would have descendants propagated from him [cf. Rom. 4:18]. What, they say, has this faith to do with the cause of Paul? I answer: The rule must be held fast, that also when faith has to do with corporeal objects or benefits, faith in the believer always comes before expectation of corporeal benefits. This faith is faith in mercy, and accepts the forgiveness of sins. Jacob expects defense against enemies, David expects victory, but they expect it because they believe they have a propitious God. For the conscience is not able to ask and to expect other benefits from God if it feels that he is angry with us, and that he will not hear us. Therefore it is necessary that confidence in mercy always come beforehand. And the sayings about faith in general always embrace the article about the remission of sins. Thus in our daily prayer, when we pray for daily bread, we should remember that our petition is heard if God is propitious to us, and that he is propitious on account of Christ. There follows at once: "And forgive us our debts" [Mt. 6:12].

If someone asks, "Whence did the fathers know this doctrine about confidence in mercy and about the forgiveness of sins?" I answer: The prophets fought about this article with the teachers of the Law. Therefore all the Psalms, all the pronouncements of the prophets proclaim with a loud voice that men are not just by the law, and inculcate proclamations about mercy. And Isaiah [53:5, 10] says expressly that the Messiah will be the sacrificial victim for sin. Therefore they repeated the promise first given to Adam, afterward to Abraham, about the liberator who would come. They understood that God had promised reconciliation on account of this liberator and bringer of blessing concerning whom it was said [Gen. 3:15]: He will crush the serpent's head. They looked upon this promise and knew that the promise had to be believed; on its account they expected all other benefits.

To this promise about the coming liberator they referred the other promises. The prophets foretold that the people would return from Babylon because they knew that the Messiah must be born of Judah and proclaim the Gospel publicly in Zion. They look to this foremost promise when they promise other benefits, as now also we must believe that God will preserve the ministry of the Gospel, so he will preserve some ministers and provide a defense for them and other commodities necessary for life. Thus we shall include the other commodities in the promise of grace. Since God is propitious on account of Christ, we ask for the other benefits. For the church has need of the life of ministers, food, and civil peace.

This I answer in general to the statements in which mention is made of faith. As for the rest of the statements which Paul cites, they also preach expressly about the promised liberator. Habakkuk [3:18] speaks about the liberator who was expected, who had been promised to the fathers, as the text shows. And Abraham believed not only that he would have freedom, but that he would have seed by whom all nations were to be blessed. I know that many sophistries can be thought out by sly persons for eluding and destroying these testimonies. Human wisdom, which does not know the righteousness of faith, does not rightly accept the sayings of the prophets, but twists them in various ways. But the godly, when they look upon the consensus of the entire Scripture and the true exercises of faith, will easily understand that these sayings are rightly applied by Paul to the present cause about the remission of sins.

### 18a. For the wrath of God is revealed from heaven

Dreadful is the beginning and the lightning with which he begins the disputation, similar to the beginnings in the preaching of the prophets, as in Isaiah 1[:2 ff]: "Hear, O heavens, and give ear, O earth; woe to the sinful generation. . . . " For the form of the prophetic and the apostolic preaching is one and the same. Christ embraced it in these words [cf. Luke 24:47]: "Go, preaching repentance and remission of sins in my name."

When Paul makes a very fitting examination of the Christian doctrine, he sets down the first theme which is the doctrine of repentance or accusing sins. For above he has taken care of the introduction; now he begins to explain the dispute. And he sets forth two propositions, of which the one clarifies the approach to the other.

The first proposition is: The Gospel accuses all men, and declares that all are under sin, that is, guilty of sin and of eternal death, and that they cannot be freed from sin and from eternal wrath by their own righteousness. In this proposition he is detained by two chief points. He wants to call all to repentance. He wants us truly to fear the judgment of God in order that we may seek salvation and acknowledge the liberator, through whom reconciliation and salvation has been promised.

There follows in the third chapter the chief proposition, that people receive remission of sins and are accounted righteous and are freed from eternal death not on account of our own righteousness, but by mercy, on account of Christ, *gratis*. And this comes about by faith, when we believe that the Father has been placated and is propitious on account of the Son of God. That is the chief proposition of this epistle, and the point at issue in this disputation, and the sum of the Gospel.

But before he arrives at this proposition, he first treats the other, for comfort cannot be given unless sins have first been rebuked. And God demands repentance, as both John and Christ begin their sermons [cf. Mt. 3:2; 4:17]: "Repent." And Christ says: "The Holy Spirit will convict the world of sin, of righteousness, and of judgment" [John 16:8]. And Isaiah [66:2]: "Where will the Lord dwell? In the person who is of a contrite spirit, and that trembles at my Word." And Paul uses stern words when he says that the wrath of God is revealed from heaven. He threatens eternal punishments to all who are not terrified and do not flee to the Son of God. Therefore you see that the statements of Paul agree, and that the order in teaching agrees with the preaching of the prophets and of Christ.

The Gospel rebukes not only outward transgressions which even reason can judge, but also the uncleanness of heart in all persons. Therefore he says [Rom. 1:18]: The wrath of God is so revealed from heaven, that is, it is preached in the Gospel, which is divinely taught, against all impiety and righteousness of men. It is a Hebraism when the little word *omnem* (all, every) is transposed, since the meaning is: Over the ungodliness and unrighteousness of all men. For later he will say clearly and expressly that he is accusing all men.

Ungodliness (*impietas*) properly signifies the vices that militate against the first table: ignorance of God; to be without fear, love, and trust in God; to harbor carnal security and contempt of God; anger and raging against God in afflictions; confidence in one's own wisdom, righteousness, or wealth; to seek human aid contrary to the command of God; to place our fortunes, pleasures, reputation, glory, or life ahead of the commandments of God, as those who place these things ahead flee from the dangers of confession; to play with false, invented opinions about God; to delight in Epicurean and philosophical errors, and not truly to assent to the Word of God. Finally, there is a great mass of vices that fight against the first table, which are all embraced in the term *ungodliness.* Unrighteousness (*iniusticia*) is a general term, embracing all sins against God and men, for it signifies universal disobedience as such.

### 18b. They hold back the truth in unrighteousness

They call the knowledge of God, or the natural law, truth. For when sins are rebuked in the preaching of repentance, the Law is being cited, as Paul says [Rom. 3:20]: "By the Law is the knowledge of sin." He is quoting the natural law. He says all men have some knowledge of God. Through this he accuses and condemns all. Because we know the law and nevertheless do not obey it, the Law, which is the judgment of God, condemns all.

Students must first of all be admonished to distinguish Law and Gospel diligently. Some knowledge of the Law is born with us, although in the present ruined state of human nature it is darkened; nevertheless it has not been wholly wiped out. The following are elements of the knowledge of God: there is one God, of immeasurable power, wise, just, good; the founder and preserver of nature; punishing the unjust and criminal; hearing and saving—not *gratis*, not those guilty of sin—but the righteous and pure; that God must be obeyed; that he commands what is honorable, and prohibits shameful deeds; that he implanted in our minds the distinction between what is honorable and what is shameful. These are things known by nature, which we constantly hear speaking to us in our conscience. Natural reason does not know gratuitous forgiveness or reconciliation because of Christ, but has knowledge of the Law which requires the condition of our obedience. It judges that only those who are without sin please God. This is the natural voice of the conscience.

The Gospel promises gratuitous forgiveness and reconciliation because of the Son of God. This knowledge is not born with us, but has been divinely revealed, as John [1:18] says: "The Son, who is in the bosom of the Father, he had told us." And because it disagrees with the natural voice of conscience and with the handwriting written against us in our minds, it is difficult to assent to the promise of gratuitous reconciliation. The reader should remember this at the very start, that the natural knowledge of God is a certain knowledge of the Law, lest he hastily confuse Law and Gospel.

Paul's preaching is wonderful and far superior to the thinking of the philosophers. He says that there is in us knowledge which he calls truth. But the Epicureans and Academicians bury this knowledge. Being liars, they also fight with the nature of man itself. For there inheres in us some knowledge of God, as has been said.

Paul adds that this knowledge is held back in unrighteousness, that is, the will or heart of man does not assent to this knowledge or obey it. It looks into the human mind much more inwardly than do the philosophers. Here it finds very great vices. The mind says there is some kind of God, but because it sees that the wicked prosper and harshly oppress the good and that the good are even cruelly killed by criminals and tyrants, it begins to doubt whether God is concerned about human affairs, whether he punishes criminals or rewards the good. It judges that God either is not concerned about human affairs, or that he is cruel because he has burdened so weak a nature with such great calamities. From this doubt and darkness spring many vices. The heart is devoid of fear, trust, and love of God, and since it is without a rein, it obeys desires which are contrary to natural knowledge. Although Paris knows that it is unjust to snatch the wife of another, he nevertheless follows the custom of his desire, scorning God.

Paul learnedly describes human weakness, grants man a certain amount of knowledge, and nevertheless testifies that man does not assent to that knowledge, and that his will or heart does not obey it because it is turned away from God, without divine impulses. It loves itself, not God. Therefore it is carried along by varied wrong impulses against the commandment of God. Paul indicates all these things when he says that the truth is held back like a prisoner in unrighteousness, that is, by perversion of will or heart, which is, as is said below, enmity against God.

**19–20. For to the extent that God can be known, he is known to them**

The explanation of the above proposition is as follows: Here he appeals to the natural law and tells expressly what that truth is in the minds of men which rebukes and accuses us. It is, he says, knowledge about God, and other items of knowledge, which are called the natural law. The connection of the words must be observed: "The invisible things of him, namely his eternal power and divinity, are clearly seen from the creation of the world, being known from his works" [Rom. 1:20]. His divinity and eternal power means that he is God, eternal, powerful, wise, just, good, punishing the unjust, hearing and aiding the just. These things, I say, the mind acknowledges when it looks upon the creation of the world. For it concludes these things about God from the many traces in the creation. It would not conclude these things if there were not implanted in the mind a certain knowledge or preconception about God. Therefore he says earlier: God had showed it to them [cf. Rom. 1:19]. But the mind, admonished by the sight of the world and the order of the work, thinks that these things cannot have come into existence or have originated by chance, but that they have without doubt been founded and arranged by some eternal mind.

There is no doubt that humans were created chiefly so that the knowledge of God might shine forth in them. God wanted to reveal himself and be known and honored by the human race. There shines in the human mind a wonderful and clear light and noteworthy knowledge about God, implanted in him at his creation. And if there had not come to it a darkness through original sin, the human mind would have been like a mirror, showing (to express it in this way) the image, that is, many clear facts of the knowledge about God. This is why it is written that the mind is a certain image of God.

Neither is there any doubt that the whole world was created so that it might give testimony about God. The order of the works shows clearly that these things could not have originated by chance. And if human nature had remained whole, philosophy would be occupied chiefly with this. It would have pondered the footprints of the Deity in nature, and would have proclaimed the wisdom and goodness of the architect. But since darkness entered the minds on account of original sin, the image does not shine forth. Natural knowledge is exceedingly obscure, and the heart or will, on account of its being turned away from God, does not sufficiently assent to this knowledge, nor fight for it constantly. It easily allows also the true knowledge of God to be driven out of itself, since other persuasions are opposed to it. This is why there has been and remains so great a disagreement about God among men. All the philosophers were in doubt about providence, for although some were moved by nature to declare that there is a God, they doubted whether he was concerned about human affairs when they saw the prosperity of the wicked and the righteous oppressed by criminals. Troubled by this stumbling block, minds fell even more, and the devil, meanwhile, pours out even greater fogs. Many atheists at all times have simply denied that there is a God or any eternal deity, as the Cyclops in Homer and Euripides did. But these are fighting against their own minds, and know that they are lying.

Since there is such a great darkness and levity of the human mind that even true arguments are easily driven out from us, let it be our foremost concern that we may strengthen ourselves by means of the Word of God. For also the divine Law was promulgated for this—that the knowledge of God might be renewed. Because the natural knowledge has not been completely wiped out in our minds, let us stir it up and let us notice the footprints of God in the nature of things.

In the Book of Acts it is written that God is so near to us that it is almost possible to touch him with our hands [cf. Acts 17:27]. And it is not in vain that so many footprints of God are imprinted on nature. God wants to remind us through these marks. He wants them to be considered, and the author acknowledged. Therefore let students seek out these vestiges, but in such a way that they hold fast the rule, namely, the Word of God. Surely it is useful for strengthening good opinions to hold fast to the true reasonings fixed in the mind, which testify that God is the founder and preserver of things. And a learned student of nature will be able aptly to learn many things. The philosophers who treated physical science skillfully thought more honorably about God, as for instance Galen. On the contrary, the Epicureans, even as they confused physical matters, did not want to look upon the footprints of God in nature and therefore wildly professed those Cyclopean ideas about God. Therefore I shall briefly recite nine arguments from nature which testify that God is the founder and preserver of things.

1. The most outstanding testimonies about God are the human mind, and the distinction between what is honorable and what is shameful which is impressed on the mind. From this is taken the argument; Man has a mind; man originated from elsewhere; therefore it is necessary that he have sprung from some eternal mind, because it is impossible that the mind should have originated from unreasoning nature. Of this argument also the Psalm [94:9] reminds us: "He that made the eye, shall he not see. . . . "

2. The distinction between things that are honorable and things that are shameful is naturally known to the human mind. This cannot have come into existence by chance or have flowed forth from unreasoning nature. Therefore it is necessary to confess that God is the originator. This argument no one can shake, even if Cyclopeans, Giants, Epicureans, Academicians, or followers of Mezentius come together and attempt to make war against heaven with combined powers. They must confess that the distinction between honorable and shameful things did not come into existence by chance, but was ordained by some mind.

3. When atrocious crimes are committed, all men naturally are afraid and judge that there is a God, and that he punishes transgressions. Therefore both concepts are implanted in the human mind, both that there is a God, and that he punishes crimes. No matter how much Mezentius rages, he must often be terrified by the consciousness of his crimes. There is a shout in his mind—even if he fights against it—that there is a God who avenges crimes. Otherwise, why does not the mind truly rejoice after an atrocious crime, even as it truly rejoices when it remembers what was rightly done?

4. From the order of things in all nature, we see how sure are the laws that govern the movements of the heavenly bodies, how certain the number of species, and that like propagates like, not some promiscuously from others. We see the ultimate causes of things. All things are born for some use. Also there is a wonderful agreement of superior and inferior bodies. The movements of the heavenly bodies bring about sure alternations between summer and winter for the good of the living. Why are springs and streams ever-flowing? Why the distribution of the individual parts in the human body? Why the recognition of the number and order? Do they not testify clearly that nature did not come into existence by chance, but that they had their origin in some eternal mind? It is impossible that these things always came about as a result of chance. It is impossible that the concepts of number and order originated by chance, or from material things. O, how blind are the minds of men which are not moved by such clear arguments—by such definite footprints of divinity—to think better about God and to revere him!

5. To the consideration of order belongs also a consideration of political order. In this also there shines forth the wisdom and goodness of God, for human nature has been created for society, because it is bound together by many bonds, contracts, pacts, judgments, powers, and punishments. This whole order bears witness that the human race did not come into being by chance.

6. From the punishments of murderers and the preservation and overturning of governments, it is clear that murderers are subject to penalties, not through human diligence but divinely, in order that a society of life may be

preserved. Thus it is manifest that governments were established not by human powers, but by a divine being, and that they are again overturned on account of tyrannies and lusts, because God punishes heinous crimes in the civil society. For example, Tarquin was driven out, and the Lacedemonians were conquered when they had forcibly violated the daughters of a stranger and afterward killed them.

7. From the indications of future things. There are many certain indications in nature, either of the stars or of inferior bodies, and most certain and perpetual experience testifies that a coming together of wet stars in wet signs signifies rains and storms. Likewise, many signs appear without definite regularity but nevertheless signify something. Also there are true prophecies, such as those of Daniel about the sequence of kingdoms. These significations cannot have proceeded save from some eternal mind.

8. Heroic impulses are impulses that transcend human nature, and happen to men because of some great thing, as for instance from the founding of governments, or for illustrating skills useful for life. Therefore they arise from some superior nature and intelligence.

9. From the chain of causes. Causes are ordered in nature, so that it is necessary to go back to one first cause which is not set in motion from elsewhere, but moves the others. If it is the first, it is necessary that it have the power to move itself; therefore it is of infinite power. And it is necessary that there be a first one, for otherwise there would be no succession of causes if they were scattered endlessly. This argument is treated at length in physics and is sufficiently established. But the earlier arguments are superior. They are taken from the nature of the mind, from the distinction between honorable and shameful things, and from order in nature and in society. These indeed testify not only that God is the creator, but also the avenger, and they invite us to fear God. Therefore let young people make up their minds with such considerations. But the more diligently we consider these arguments, the more we agree with them, as Plato says and as we ourselves experience.

Students should know that all these arguments are laws of nature which teach that we should acknowledge God to be the founder of all things, and that we owe him obedience. And that is how Paul makes use of this subject. Although above in the proposition he accuses all men, he now makes a distinction. First he preaches to the Gentiles, and then afterward to the Jews. He says that the Gentiles are under sin because although they knew God, they did not glorify him as God nor give him thanks.

### 21. They did not honor him as God

To honor God as God is to give God, the eternal Creator of things, this honor: that he is God, that is, eternal, of immeasurable power, the creator and preserver of things, wise, just, punishing the unjust, hearing and aiding the just, and to obey him, also truly to fear his judgment, truly to believe him, and to ask and expect good things from him. We all ought to give to God this honor, and that is what he says here: honor him as God.

To give thanks is to believe that God is the creator of things, that he is concerned about us, that we receive life and all good things from him, ask and expect help and defense from him, and therefore acknowledge him as Lord and obey him (lest we be ungrateful and scorn the Lord), and glorify and proclaim his name, power, goodness, and justice.

These are the necessary works of the First and Second Commandments for which we were chiefly created. But the world does not render these things. Therefore the voice of the Gospel at all times accuses the ungodliness of the world. For some men are atheists, others are idolaters. In these two ways men sin against the First Table of the divine Law. Atheists, as the Cyclopeans and the Epicureans, simply deny that there is a God or that he is concerned about human affairs. It is quite clear that these do not honor God, that they do not fear him, do not believe in him, and do not invoke him. They consider his name to be empty; even though they give him some honor, power, goodness, or justice. The crowd of such Cyclopeans is not small, and it is strange that the innate knowledge can thus be destroyed. But the devil, who holds the minds of men captive, pours out greater errors on a nature that is already weak. And now, indeed, some writers, particularly at Rome, consider it wisdom to take pleasure in these Cyclopic opinions.

Idolaters err in yet another way: they transfer the honor which is owed to God to other things. For it is idolatry to ascribe divinity to something which is not God, to invoke something which is not God, to give to someone other than Christ the honor of redemption to put confidence which was owed to God in our works; to tie God to certain acts of worship and to statues, contrary to his commandment; also to fear and love something other than God. This is what idolatry, as the common people call it, really embraces and signifies.

From this one can easily know that the world is full of idol-madness. Concerning this worship, the saying of the poet is true: "Fear first made gods in the world." Cyclopeans are generally carnally secure. Others who seek God in dangers (as reason shows that God is the helper) are worried and do not seek God rightly. For since they hold opinions of the Law and think that God hears the righteous, his worshipers, who think they are well-deserving, indeed call upon him, but without the promise of grace, without knowledge of the mediator. Therefore they either doubt that they will be heard or regarded, or they adorn themselves with a foolish trust in their acts of worship, as a priest says in Homer: "O Phoebe if I have slaughtered victims that are pleasing to you, then hear me.

The first act of impiety is that they are either doubtful that they will be heard by God, or that they put confidence in their own righteousness and do not know the mediator. When this error has gained entrance, many crimes follow. Confidence in their own acts of worship moves people to heap up ceremonies and to think out new acts of worship and new gods. For instance, when rural people thought that good weather was achieved by ceremonies, they instituted an act of worship and they brought certain sacrifices before the statue of Jupiter the thunderer. When soldiers thought that they could get victories from God by means of ceremonies, they instituted an act of worship and brought certain sacrifices before the statue of Mars. Thus human daring devised new acts of worship through confidence in works without a commandment from God, yes, against the commandment of God. Going even farther astray, minds also attributed a certain divinity to statues and thereafter some attributed divinity to other things, wherever the devil impelled them or where some other affection drew them. Divinity was attributed to statues, and to cattle.

Neither should examples be sought only of Gentiles. What is being done now? People invoke the dead, precisely as the Gentiles in ancient times invoked Hercules or Romulus. And different people have different divinities: Soldiers invoke George, sailors Nicolaus, the greedy Anna. People run to statues after the manner of the Gentiles, and divinity is either attributed to the statues themselves, or God is bound to the statues with the opinion that he is more favorable at this statue, although God is not willing to be bound to anything at which he does not command—with an express command—that he should be invoked. There is manifest idolatry in the world, and popes and kings approve and defend it. At Paris they allowed a wooden statue of Mary, perhaps in order to restrain the superstition of the people. It was replaced by another one of silver, with the result that idol-madness was strengthened. Then there is manifold idolatry in various acts of worship. They give to the mass and to vows the honor owed to Christ, saying that they make satisfaction for sins and that they merit forgiveness of sins.

Since ungodliness remains, namely, Epicurean security and superstition of every kind, let us repent. Let us seek the Word of God, and let us learn rightly to worship and invoke God in true faith. Let faith and works be governed by the Word of God, according to the passage [Ps. 119:105]: "Your Word is a lamp to my feet." For when one departs from this lamp, immediately endless errors rush in. Let us embrace the Word of God, and let us pray that God would set us free from all errors and ungodliness through his Son, since he gave us his Son that he might destroy the works of the devil.

Also the greatness of the punishments admonishes us to repentance. Contempt of God and superstition are also rewarded in this life with blindness and insanity. Men forsaken by God rush into every kind of crime, and the devil provides opportunities for minds inflamed with some lust, either love or hate. What shameful things are read in the histories; these I do not want to recite. How foul was Alexander, who saw that he had been gifted with so great a kingdom. He was boastful because he had been adorned with such an outstanding intellect. Nevertheless, while he was drunk, he killed his friends and afterward raged against the most highly deserving rulers. Finally, when he was invited to a banquet by his lover, he meted out punishments when he had fallen into a lethal sickness through his intemperance.

**22–28.** These and similar things, that is, the greater part of the history of the world, Paul embraces when he says: "When they boasted that they were wise, they became foolish and vain." For the madness of Alexander can be seen sufficiently in this great turpitude, although there was hardly any other intellect more excellent than his.

With this in mind, let us also look at the older histories and at the vices of the present times, and let us consider that they are punishments either for Cyclopean contempt of God or for idol-madness. Paul reminds us of this when he repeats a number of times that men are given over to the desires of their hearts because they did not glorify God.

Moreover, here we think of the more unlearned ones regarding the phrase: "He gave them over to their desires," that is, He permitted them to rush ahead. This phrase is customary among the Hebrews: "Lead us not into temptation," that is, do not permit us to be led into it. These things must be understood of permission. For God is by no means the cause of sin, but the devil is, as it is written: "Whoever commits sin is of the devil." [I John 3:8] And he is truly the effective cause and instigator of these acts of madness which are here described.

### 29–31. Filled with all unrighteousness

He adds a great heaping up and mound of sins, in order that he may also rebuke other vices. Ἀδικία (unrighteousness) is a general term, signifying all disobedience against the First and Second Tables of the divine Law, as righteousness of the Law signifies all obedience.

Πονηρία (wickedness) really signifies the desire to do harm. Κακία (depravity) includes sins of omission, as they are called. For the Latins, turpitude is generally the opposite of virtue, so for the Greeks κακία is the opposite of ἀρετή (goodness, excellence). Mark Antony is κακός, a spendthrift, negligent. But Domitian is πονηρός, desiring to do harm and taking pleasure in harming others. Κακοήθεια really is malevolence, which is found in envious people who know how to twist skillfully what has been said simply and straight-forwardly. Κακοήθες μὴ καθαρὸν [malicious and impure] really is the opposite of candor, for Plutarch opposes these to each other. Malevolence is a savage illness and is often destructive to the state, since malevolent natures stir up other moderate persons, or even persons of good merit, with so much sickness of the mind,[2] so that Cato was not favorably inclined toward the praise of Cicero. For this also generally comes to κακοήθεια—the vice is covered over by a simulation of gratuity. There are verses by Menanderin in which certain kinds of men are described. These are verses in which powerful person chiefly delight:

> Life delights most of all in the wicked,
> The flatterer achieves best of all,
> Second the slanderer,
> The malevolent person third,
> Who is a terrible, crafty planner of wicked things.

He gives the first place to the flatterer, for he is the sweetest. The second is the informer or tale-bearer who earns favor by carrying about and inventing tales and constructing slanders. The κακοήθης holds the third place. He knows how to play on the emotions of his master, and can put a different interpretation on things honestly done and knows how to kindle hatreds.

Θεοστυγεῖς is taken either actively or passively. It signifies persons who are openly scornful toward God, as Sennacherib and the Rabskakeh are described in the history of Isaiah, or Mezentius in Vergil, or Antiochus in the history of the Maccabees. And that age has examples of very many tyrants who openly confess that they are enemies of God.[3]

'Ασύνετοι (senseless persons) are mad persons who against the judgment of common sense blindly rush headlong into all crimes and to their end,

---

[2] What follows is different in our 1540 edition from that of the *Corpus Reformatorum.* The Latin is: . . . *ut Scripionis res gestas carpebat Lentulus. Item, ut Aeschines accusarit Demosthenem, nulla lusta causa motus, sed naturae perversitate et malevolentia.* `` . . . as Lentulus slandered the exploits of Scipio. Likewise, as Aeschines accused Demosthenes of rebellion without just cause, but out of a perverse nature and malice.''

[3] Our 1540 edition adds this paragraph:
ἐφευρετὰς κακῶν (inventors of evil): Greek scholia teach that with the compound *epi* those people are indicated who, in addition to old evil schemes and old evil vices, think up new techniques and are the authors of new disgrace, as skillful merchants with depraved characters devise new burdens by changing just prices of coinage. Courtiers invent new pretexts of unjust plunderings, or princes with amazing techniques join or separate property, or contrive reasons for occupying the property of another. Lawyers find new deceptions in judgments, or the erudite find excuses of shame, as many with a false and sophisticated pretext of that which is at hand excuse or confirm usury in order to satisfy usurers. There are inventors of evil from whom disgraceful examples arise, as, for example, those who established contests of naked bodies in the Palestra (wrestling school) in Greece. Likewise, the first Lamech departed from the true institution of marriage, had many wives at the same time, and introduced this disgraceful custom into the world.

as Catiline and Thomas Muenzer, who madly took up arms to destroy all rulers in order to set up a plan where all things were held in common. Likewise, the good-for-nothing Monasteriensis, who called himself king of the temple of God. The prophets often say that this madness is a punishment of ungodliness. Thus Pharaoh, Saul, and others brought about their own end. They lack both a good conscience and moderate counsel.

᾿Ασύνθετοι (faithless) are those not keeping agreements. Συνθῆκαι are agreements in contracts and alliances.

῎Αστοργοι are those who cast off natural feelings toward parents, children, brethren, or people who have merited well. For στοργή signifies good affections divinely implanted in the nature of men, although now, on account of the original sickness, they go astray somewhat. But God nevertheless approves of them and wants them rightly ruled. He commands us to love our spouses, parents, and children. He commands us to be thankful. These are στοργαί (natural affections). Therefore Paul condemns those hard men who cast off natural affections, as did Atreus and Thyestes in the tragedies.

῎Ασπονδοι [found in the textus receptus of v. 31] are implacable persons, as Saul could not be placated by any service to return to grace with David. In the end Paul again appeals to the natural law and calls it the Law of God. Therefore students should remember the rule: whatever violates the natural law is a violation of the divine Law and truly a mortal sin. In the *Loci* I have compared the natural law with the Decalogue which is indeed the way of teaching and sum total of the natural laws, if one understands the Decalogue rightly.

### 32. That those who do these things

Surely, it is a strange statement which says that men know by nature that those who violate the laws of nature are worthy of death. It is easy to understand that crimes which disturb the common peace should be severely punished, like murder and theft. For a civil society could not be preserved if it were permitted with impunity to snatch other people's possessions or to kill innocent persons. Here the common good reminds rulers to establish penalties.

But why does Paul say about all vices in general that both those who do shameful things and those who consent to them are worthy of death? Should an envious person be punished with capital punishment? I answer: Paul is here not speaking of the judgment of magistrates or about punishments which are inflicted on thieves and highway robbers in behalf of peace and common welfare, but he is speaking about the private judgment of the conscience in any and all men. He looks far more deeply into the minds than either the Epicureans or the hypocrites, who, being secure and drunk with pleasures, have not experienced true terrors of conscience. Saul does not judge himself to be worthy of death when, contrary to the command of Samuel, he spares the captive king. But the conscience acknowledges that a sin is worthy of death when true terrors are struck into the mind, when it sees that God has not been obeyed. This sin, as will be said below, becomes especially guilty and damned.

When Adam had tasted the apple contrary to the command, he thought the deed was not a matter of great moment. He had not yet experienced those dreadful terrors of conscience which bring death. Afterward, however, when he had been rebuked by God, he acknowledged that sin is contempt of God. He felt that God was angry. He was terrified and would have died from the magnitude of grief if he had not been recalled from death by the divine promise. The Law, says Paul, is the power of sin [1 Cor. 15:56]. Thus the natural law in the minds of men judges and condemns sin, and shows that God is angry with every and all sin when it is truly recognized, as happens in these terrors.

Paul is here speaking of this true judgment of the conscience, and he condemns not only outward crimes but also the universal internal uncleanness, ignorance and contempt of God, and all evil lusts. Although, different passions break out more in different people—some indulge more in hatreds, others in lusts, others in avarice—nevertheless, the hearts of all wicked persons are without fear of God, without trust. They delight in wicked opinions and errors, in any and all obscene pleasures, although some are more diligent than others in reigning in these inclinations. For example, Pomponius Atticus does not commit murder, but his will is nevertheless turned away from God. He takes pleasure in the opinions of the Epicureans or of the Platonists about God, wants to live softly, and seeks tranquility without recognition of God. Finally, he has many impulses that stray away from God. That is what Paul is after when he condemns not only those who do evil but also those who approve of it, συνευδοκοῦντας. Therefore, he is not speaking only of those who aid the crimes of others, as they interpret consent in court, but about all who take pleasure in such things. That really is the meaning of συνευδοκεῖν. He now elaborates on this statement.

# Chapter 2

## 1. Therefore you are inexcusable

It is necessary that this teaching about the Law should be present in the church, that the Law of God does not only accuse and condemn external crimes, but also inner depravity, doubting with respect to God, and other vices of the heart, and all evil lusts. Christ rebukes the Pharisees in Matthew 5, who interpreted the Law of God only about outward deeds, the way we understand political laws, and he adds a new interpretation about inner depravity. So here Paul, in order to show that all men are guilty of sin as he will say later, accuses also those who, because they live without outward turpitude, think they are righteous on account of these civil morals.

The order of the parts must be observed in order that it can be better understood from where the beginning of the second chapter arises. It is a conclusion, accusing all who judge that they are righteous on account of civil morals. It is a complete syllogism. The major proposition is given at the end of the chapter: "all are worthy of death, both those who commit unjust acts and those who agree with those who do them," [1:32], or who have similar desires.

The minor premise follows in the second chapter [v. 1]: "You who judge another person do the same thing," that is, whoever possesses civil morals and condemns only those who are beholden to manifest turpitude, and does not also condemn himself but thinks he is just because of his morals, does the same thing. In other words he has impiety in his mind and doubts whether God is concerned about human affairs, whether he punishes or hears people. Such a person also has other evil desires, hatreds and loves. That is the meaning of this statement: "You do the same things, namely with the inner impulses of the mind."

Then comes the conclusion [v. 1]: "Therefore, since you do the same things, you are inexcusable, whoever you are that judges," that is, condemns others who are beholden to manifest turpitude. You do not condemn yourself, although you harbor similar inner depravity. This conclusion is a clear and perspicuous accusation of all who think they are just on account of civil morals. Although, they know that those who are beholden to outward turpitude are not righteous, they do not consider that in their mind they are beholden to like sicknesses.

And you should diligently remind yourself of the little word that follows when he says: "You do the same things." For he is talking of inner impulses. Pomponius Atticus does not commit murder with his hand; he does not rob others of their properties, like Sylla. But he does not think rightly about God. He doubts, like the Platonists, whether God cares about human matters. He applauds the customary idolatry. He thinks superstitions are useful so that the common people may be controlled by it as by a prison. Furthermore, he also has many other desires that are evil and directed away from God.

2. Therefore Paul adds: "The judgment of God is according to the truth," that is, he judges not only the outer shadow of actions, but minds that are the source of the actions. If a true opinion about God is not shining in minds, if wills are turned away from God and love themselves more than God, they are certainly not obeying the Law of God which says [Deut. 6:5]: "You shall love the Lord your God with your whole heart." Since such is the infirmity in all men, they should confess that they are not satisfying the law of God. Paul is speaking here concerning this true judgment.

3–5. Then he adds an admonition and calls all to repentance. He teaches why God delays punishments, namely, in order to give us room to come to our senses. He could suddenly have killed our first parent Adam when he sinned. Likewise, Peter in his fall, when he denied that he knew Christ. And fear immediately entered into the minds of both which would bring about their death. But he gives room to the miserable ones in order that they may be able to return to the right way, according to the word [Ez. 33:11]: "As I live, I do not desire the death of the sinner, but that he may be converted and live." Here belongs also the parable of the fig-tree, Luke 13 [:6–9].

### 6–12. Who rewards everyone according to his works

Would that the deceits of sophistries and the cunning perversions of correct statements might be removed from the divine dogmas! It is certain that this is what Paul is driving at in this entire epistle: that men are justified by faith, *gratis,* on account of the Son of God, not on account of our worthiness and merits. Although it is certain that is what Paul is driving at, our adversaries twist this statement, "he will reward according to deeds", to conform to their opinions, against the meaning of Paul. They contend that persons are pronounced just on account of the worthiness of their works. They contend that works are the purchase-price of eternal life. But persons correctly instructed in Christian doctrine will easily be able to harmonize such statements with others which speak about gratuitous imputation and the giving of eternal life because of Christ.

The entire divine Scripture sets forth the Law in some places, in others the Gospel, so some of its statements are statements of the Law, and some of its statements are statements of the Gospel. Nevertheless, the Gospel is the light and interpretation of the Law. This is a phrase of the Law: "He will reward everyone according to his works." The meaning is: "He will give rewards to the righteous, and the unjust he will punish." Neither is there any doubt that the explanation of who the righteous are and what works please God must be added from the Gospel. For the pronouncements of the Law without the Gospel produce despair. Never can a conscience in the midst of true terrors declare that it has works worthy of the forgiveness of sins or eternal life. Thus when Christ says [Mt. 19:17]: "If you wish to enter into life, keep the commandments," it is necessary to mitigate what is said by adding the interpretation from the Gospel. For no one satisfies the Law.

One must answer briefly that the phrase: "He will reward according to works," is Law, that is, he will give rewards to the righteous, and punishments to the unjust. But it is the Gospel which teaches who the righteous are, and in what way works please God. And indeed, the Law speaks about faith as though it were a work, because true faith is the foremost worship of God, and the foremost work is trust in the mercy of God, by which God is truly invoked. Whence this faith arises is taught by the promises or by the Gospel. Afterward also the other works commanded by God, which must of necessity follow faith, are pleasing to Him. Therefore the meaning is: "He will reward according to works," that is, to the righteous he will give eternal life, that is, as the Gospel teaches, to those who are justified by faith. And it is necessary that obedience has begun in these. It pleases not because it satisfies the Law, but because the person has been reconciled by faith and acknowledges its weakness, and nevertheless believes that these acts of worship are pleasing to the Father because of Christ, as has been said above. And below Paul teaches, saying [Rom. 6:14],: "You are not under the Law, but under grace." The explanation is easy for those who understand the nature of faith. For it is necessary that Paul embrace faith when he speaks about the works of the righteous. Whenever mention is made of faith, there is also included this exclusive. Although a beginning of obedience must be present, nevertheless faith rests solely on mercy and declares that we are righteous, that is, accepted through mercy.

### 13. For those who hear the Law are not righteous

The statement about the righteousness of the Law is general. For the Jews arrogated to themselves righteousness on account of the Law. Here Paul opposes the definition of the righteousness of the Law. For the righteousness of the Law is to do the Law, to provide complete obedience to the Law, not merely to hear the Law or to profess the ceremony of the Law. This is what he says: The doers of the law are justified, that is, they are pronounced righteous. Therefore Paul is speaking of the ideal and convicts the Jews that they are not righteous by the Law, because no one satisfies the Law. Therefore this passage cannot be twisted against the righteousness of faith. Neither does Paul here add how the Law is broken and in what way it pleases. For he only refutes those who imagine that they are righteous because of an outward profession of the law.

### 14–16. A Law to themselves

He had said that the wicked would perish, the Jews and also the Gentiles, although the latter did not have the Law. Now he adds the correction: Yes, the Gentiles had the Law, that is, a natural knowledge about morals that distinguishes what is honorable and what is shameful. Here there is again a testimony about the natural Law. And Paul learnedly reasons that the Gentiles have the Law, and declares at the same time what the natural Law is: "They have a conscience that either accuses or excuses," that is, that knows what is honorable and what is shameful. Therefore they have the Law. The conclusion is known from the definition. For the Law is in reality that natural knowledge teaching things honorable and reprehending things shameful.

It must be diligently observed that he says: "They do by nature," that is, by the natural knowledge and light. And with this word, "by nature", Paul testifies that this knowledge is a work of God, founded in the mind as light is in the eyes. For "by nature" really signifies something created by God. Therefore this knowledge is true and is divine Law, as was said above.

Augustine sweats mightily over this passage, although it contains nothing obscure. First he discusses what Paul wants when he says that the Gentiles do the Law, whether he is speaking about a few saints, for instance, about Job and similar persons. Secondly he discusses the little word "by nature." He asks why Paul says that the Gentiles do the Law by nature, although the Law cannot be truly done without the Holy Spirit.

Augustine brings these difficulties to Paul, for the text is not so very obscure. For first, "by nature" signifies chiefly natural knowledge. For Paul is reasoning about knowledge and judgment. Next, it is clear that also unregenerate persons are able to do the outward works of the Law and be outstanding in discipline and civil works. Here it is sufficient for Paul to show that the Gentiles understand the distinction between honorable and shameful things. This shows knowledge, and so he reasons that they have the Law. Therefore he is speaking about doing the outward works and about knowledge, and indeed, he compares Jews and Gentiles. He indicates that the Gentiles accomplished as much from the natural Law as the Jews from the Law of

Moses. For he does not say that the Gentiles were righteous before God by the Law, but indicates that both performed external civil works. Fabius, Scipio, Atticus, and very many others excelled in the most beautiful virtues. Perhaps they surpassed many outstanding Jews in learning and in diligence in every duty. Here Paul is reasoning that the Gentiles have the Law, that is, a natural knowledge about morals. It does not follow from this comparison that any were righteous in the sight of God on account of this learning.

### 17–24. Behold you Jew

As he has in particular accused the Gentiles, so now he particularly accuses the Jews in order that he may arrive at an equalization of Gentiles and Jews, in which it is clearly seen that all men are under sin and that they are not set free from sin by Law. This rebuke is to be taken in this way that we are to understand that both manifest sins and hypocrisy are being rebuked, even as it is necessary that repentance be preached according to the command of Christ [cf. Mt. 28:19]: "Go,[1] preaching repentance and remission of sins." And although a few among the Jews were holy, Paul nevertheless speaks of the Jews insofar as they have nothing except the Law, and are not sanctified by faith and knowledge of the promise of Christ. He wants to make the point that the Law does not suffice for justification. How is this argument valid: "If the law were sufficient for justification, all who have received the Law and are observing the outward acts of worship would be righteous." But these are not righteous, so the Law is not sufficient for justification. It must be diligently considered what Paul's purpose was when he wrote this. He accuses the Jews in order that they may understand that there is need for a different benefit for justification. This is a serious rebuke of the arrogance in hypocrites, who are puffed up with confidence in their own righteousness. Such passages must be noted both in order that we may learn fear and that terrified minds may receive comfort. For such passages do much for both sides because they both curb carnal security and again raise up fear-filled minds according to the saying [2 Cor. 10:17]: "Let him that boasts, boast of the Lord."

### 25–29. For circumcision is indeed profitable if you keep the Law

Here Paul meets the objection about the merits of outward works, since the Jews placed themselves above the Gentiles and objected that they had certain acts of worship instituted by God, and they argued that these acts of worship had not been instituted in vain, but merited forgiveness of sins, etc. Paul answers with a new paradox: "Circumcision is profitable if you keep

---

[1] The text here has "Ita", which does not yield good sense. According to the context it ought to be "Ite", and we have so amended the text.

the Law.'' For it is a general saying about all external acts of worship that they do not profit by the mere fact that the work is performed (*ex opere operato*), as the common people express it, nor merit remission of sins, but are pleasing in those who are righteous. This pronouncement must be applied not only to the Levitical acts of worship but also to outward works and ceremonies in the church.

# Chapter 3

## 1–2. What then does a Jew have in which he is superior?

This is a digression in which, as if he had been interrupted, he meets certain objections. A great and difficult question arises from this equalization of Gentiles and Jews. For if the Jews are not righteous on account of their acts of worship, if they are not freed from sin on account of the works of the Law, then why has the Law been given? Why does God require it? Why does he call them acts of worship and propitiations? Why are the Jews called the people of God if the Law makes no distinction between Jews and Gentiles? What prerogative do the Jews have? Paul responds in a two-fold way. First affirmatively, thereafter negatively. First he says that the Jews are superior to the Gentiles and that they have this advantage: they have the promises. Therefore they are superior not on account of the Law, not because they can merit justification by the law, but because they have the promises. This was a very great prerogative—to know the Word of God and the promise about Christ, and that they indeed have this right, that the promise should belong particularly to this people. Many who heard this Word were saved, and indeed it was certain that at all times some of the Jews were saved, for the promise had been given out in this way, that it should particularly belong to the descendants of Abraham.

Therefore this passage is already teaching about the chief purpose of the Jewish state. The unlearned imagine that these laws were given in order that the people might be justified through them, but Paul takes away the glory of justification from the Law, and shows that the purpose was political. For it was necessary that there should be a certain people in which the promises about Christ should be revealed by sure and clear testimonies of God. Therefore God separated this people from the Gentiles, and bore witness with many evident miracles that they had the Word of God. The cultus and the entire setup of the state were external things ordained chiefly for this political purpose, that they should distinguish this people from the other nations. Meanwhile miracles, laws given out,[1] and other things were testimonies that God had given His Word to this people. The acts of worship themselves had been

---

[1] The text has *editae legis,* which seems to be a misprint for *editae leges.* We have so emended the text.

ordained by God in order to remind men that the Word of God and indeed the promise of Christ, was among this people. And the just had exercises of faith, likewise they admonished others, etc. Therefore this passage of Paul usefully teaches that acts of worship did not merit forgiveness of sins, that they did not justify.

### 3. Does their unbelief

In passing he inserts other questions—whether the Jews have lost the promises and the whole race has been damned because they did not believe but killed Christ. Paul answers, the promise of grace is not rendered invalid, but remains valid for all who believe, although every man spurn it. This passage contains outstanding comfort and reminds us that we should not suspect that the promise of grace made to the church is invalid on account of the very great multitude of the wicked, but know that it is truly given to believers even if they are very few.

### 4a. Every man a liar

He adds an antithesis in order that it may become clearer that God is truthful because he keeps his promises to the unworthy, on account of His truthfulness and goodness. Every man is a liar; he does not judge rightly about God, does not truly fear God; he does not truly believe God; does not think that God is angry at sin or that he takes pity on those who repent. He doubts, neglects, and mistrusts God. Remnants of these sins and of this darkness remain also in the saints. Therefore he says: "Every man is a liar." Therefore the promises do not depend on our worthiness, but on the fact that God is truthful.

### 4b. That you may be justified when you speak and prevail when you are judged

He adds another testimony which takes away from us worthiness or the glory of righteousness and merits, and praises God as being just and keeping his covenants because he is truthful. But let us repeat the entire verse. For it contains the richest teaching and clearly refutes the hypocrites and legal persuasions and also the teaching of the monks, who imagine that people please God on account of their own worthiness or on account of the Law. Again it also offers the sweetest comfort to those who acknowledge their uncleanness, and repent.

These are the words [Ps 51:4]: "To you I am only a sinner, that you may be justified when you speak and prevail when you are judged." The confession of sin is plain and simple. There are many similar ones in other Psalms: "I confess that I am not bringing righteousness to you, worthiness, or merits, but only that I am a sinner" [cf. Ps. 25, 51]. Here the Hebrew way of speaking must be observed. For to the Hebrews, verbs often signify character: "I have sinned against you," that is, I am a sinner. And there is a particular emphasis in the term *sin.* "I am just a sinner," that is, guilty, damned, cursed, refuse. For the term *sin* signifies these two things: sin is either something which fights against the Law of God, which merits the wrath and punishments of God unless it is forgiven, or it is understood simply by its effect, namely, of something which is guilty or condemned, as when sacrificial animals or propitiatory sacrifices are called sins.

Here, when the prophet confesses that he is a sinner and adds the exclusive particle *just* or *only* (*tantum*), he renounces his own worthiness and acknowledges that he has impurity which fights against the Law of God and that he is guilty and deserving of the wrath and punishments of God. What this confession amounts to, the godly experience in true contrition. In the midst of these fears, pride and trust in one's own worthiness or in the righteousness of the Law are driven out.

In order that the hypocrites may be more clearly refuted, there is added the reason for the confession. "I confess that I am a sinner, that you may be justified when You speak" [Ps. 51:4], that is, that I may declare that only you are righteous when you accuse us. Let the glory of being righteous be given to you only. Likewise, "that you may prevail when you judge," that is, that you may prevail, and that the praise that you are righteous may be given to you when the hypocrites accuse you and ascribe to you injustice and cruelty when they are punished and rejected.

After Saul had done such great things for the safety of the people of God, he thought that he had merited that he should not be rejected by God nor cast out of the kingdom. In calamities men are angry with God and find fault with his judgment.

David, on the other hand, in calamity confesses that he is justly being punished. He does not accuse God but offers obedience, as is commanded elsewhere [1 Pet. 5:6]: "Humble yourselves under the mighty hand of God." This is the simple, true, and clear explanation of the Davidic saying, namely, that it is a confession of sin added to the antithesis so that God may be declared to be righteous and that he not be accused of punishing the innocent or of oppressing this weak nature unjustly with such great calamities, as the hypocrites Saul, Cato, and similar persons accuse him.

Perhaps this statement is somewhat obscure for people who are enjoying Epicurean security. Nevertheless it can easily be understood by those who are not entirely ignorant of true repentance or contrition, as it is called.

As for the rest, the grammarians here argue needlessly about the verbs, whether they are to be understood passively: "that you may be justified."

Likewise, "when you are judged." Paul rightly renders them passively, and the passive voice fits the very simple statement which we have recited. I want the passive voice retained, and the Hebrew way of speaking agrees with this, as the learned can easily judge.

However, I will add this: When he says, "that you may be justified when you speak," the statement is to be referred to both—to the Law and to the promise of grace. "I acknowledge that I am a sinner, and am justly accused by you, and I praise you as being the only righteous one, and that we are not righteous."

Up to this point the interpretation is the voice of the law accusing us. He is not yet making mention of the promise. Therefore let us transfer this saying "that you may be justified when you speak" not only to the Law but also to the promise. Although I am guilty and bring nothing to you except the knowledge of sin, nevertheless I flee to the promised mercy. I look for forgiveness, that you may be justified when you speak, that we may proclaim that you are truthful and that you keep your promises, and that you receive through mercy those who call on you, even though they do not bring merits with them.

**5–8.** The hypocrites do not give him this praise. They do not say, "I look for forgiveness, that you may be justified when you speak, that we may proclaim that you receive the unworthy because of the promised mercy." But they deny that the unworthy are received or heard. The former interpretation, which is the voice of the Law, can be understood more easily. The latter is somewhat more obscure, but nevertheless true, and Paul looks back more to this. Therefore he appended the following question: If the mercy of God is enlarged through this—that he receives and justifies the unworthy and those who bring only their sins—then why is God angry at those who sin, if indeed our sins amplify the glory of His mercy? Likewise, if we are not righteous on account of our virtues, what use is it to do good? Likewise, The more sins mercy remits, the more glorious it gets, so let us sin and give free rein to our lusts.

They threw up to Paul these absurdities when he taught that believers are declared righteous *gratis*. If mercy becomes more when we bring our sins, then let us sin freely. He will respond to these absurdities below in the sixth chapter and will dissolve them. For now he merely rejects them by adding a reprimand.

### 9a. What then? Are we superior to them?

Here he returns to his principal purpose—the equalization of Jews and Gentiles, to teach that all men are under sin, that is, guilty of sin and under the wrath of God. You will observe the dissimilar responses to the questions added in the digression. First, he answers affirmatively that the Jews have a great advantage as far as the promise is concerned, but not insofar as merits are concerned. Therefore there is added here the negative response: "The Jews are not superior," namely, so far as merit is concerned. The meaning is: "We are by no means better," that is, we are not righteous on account of our worthiness, nor on account of works of the Law, nor on account of our virtues, etc.

### 9b. For we have shown earlier, giving reasons that both Jews and Gentiles

There is a repetition of the proposition. It must be diligently observed that he is now making it universal and says that all are under sin, that is, that all men are guilty of sin and subject to the wrath of God and eternal death. He is speaking of all men with the exception of Christ, and embraces also the saints, insofar as their nature is considered and they are not understood as having been reconciled through mercy. This equalization ought to admonish us because it terrifies the hypocrites and the carnally secure. And again it raises up those who are cast down because it testifies that God truly wants to forgive us *gratis,* because of Christ.

**10–18.** He confirms this proposition by citing testimonies in which not only civil transgressions are faulted, but the inner sins against the First Table. There is none that knows or seeks God; they are without fear of God and without faith [ Ps. 14:1–3; 53:1–3; Eccl. 7:20]. Therefore they hold Godless opinions and doctrines, and impious plans [cf. Ps. 5:9], and through pride and self-confidence they dare to do many things against the will of God [cf. Ps. 140:3], and persecute those who teach and admonish pious things [cf Is. 59:7–8]. Thus he describes chiefly the secret vices of the hypocrites, which the world takes for outstanding wisdom and righteousness.

### 19–20a. By the works of the Law no flesh shall be justified

In the conclusion he again repeats the universal statement: "That every mouth may be stopped and the whole world be guilty before God." But some, who imagine that men earn forgiveness of sins and are just on account of their good moral works, seek to escape this universal statement, and say that it is a synecdoche, as if Paul were not accusing all, but only most persons, and that from this universal statement there must be excepted a certain few (Scipio, Atticus). Although among the Jews most persons sin, nevertheless they want a certain few to be excepted, as John, Peter, etc.

Minds must be fortified against such sophistries in order that we may retain the true meaning of Paul, and Paul himself prudently cautions us lest this exception could be added. For first he often inculcates what is universal, then he adds the reason which shows what he is accusing. For example, he says that "no flesh will be justified by works of the Law." Here he expressly not only accuses the person, but takes away justification from the very persons whom the former want excepted.

Then the Psalm [143:2] says: "Do not enter into judgment with your servant, for no man living will be justified in your sight." This statement and many similar ones show that exception is false, because they teach clearly that our good works cannot be opposed to the judgment of God. Furthermore, if more works could justify, ceremonies would also have justified the Jews, for with them these also had a command from God. Therefore the statements of the Psalm and of Paul should be understood universally of all men and of all works, nor should a synecdoche be admitted which imagines that some are righteous and merit forgiveness of sins on account of their own worthiness and good works etc.

He adds expressly that they are guilty before God because he is not talking about human judgment but about divine judgment. In the struggle the conscience cannot be pacified by any works, but it must know that God has commanded that we believe that God certainly forgives us on account of Christ, through mercy, etc. And indeed the weight of the words should be observed which exhort all to repentance. For he threatens most gravely those who are secure and who trust in their own righteousness when he says, "That every mouth may be stopped." Likewise, "That the whole world may become guilty."

### 20b. For through the Law comes the knowledge of sin

Paul's concern is that one could object: If we are not righteous by the Law, for what purpose was the Law given? Paul responds (however, more briefly) because this same concern is repeated below. And this response is seen by the world as something wholly new and absurd, that sin is only revealed by the Law, not taken away. For lawgivers make laws for kingdoms not only to show sins, but to take them away. The hearer must be reminded that here Paul is not at all preaching about civil righteousness and external morals. He is treating a different matter: how we may be accounted righteous before God; how we may receive remission of sins; and what the Law contributes there. Therefore the uses of the Law must be distinguished. Moreover we are here talking not only about the law of Moses but about the moral law inscribed in all men.

Now there are two uses. One is the political, namely, to coerce carnal persons from the outside. For God also requires this external justice, although we are not righteous before God on account of it and it does not merit remission of sins. He is not speaking about this use in this statement. Elsewhere he does speak about this use: The law is laid down for the unjust, etc. [cf. Rom. 2:12, 3:19].

The other use is not political, but concerns the judgment of God and the conscience, namely, to accuse and to terrify the conscience, as he says elsewhere [1 Cor. 15:56]: "Sin is the sting of death: the strength of sin is the Law," that is, the Law reveals sin and terrifies hearts. It is of such knowledge that he is speaking here. For he does not have in mind an idle speculation, but such a knowledge in which we acknowledge the wrath of God against sin and are truly terrified. And these terrors truly become eternal death in those who are not raised up by the Gospel. Therefore the meaning is: We are not just in the sight of God through the Law; we do not merit remission of sins. Moreover, when consciences are terrified, they cannot find peace through the Law, which accuses us more and more and drives us to despair, as he says elsewhere [Rom. 7:13]: "That sin might become exceedingly sinful and harmful," that is, killing by these terrors. From this it clearly follows that there is need for another word for comfort and justification.

### 21-22. Now indeed the righteousness of God has been manifested without the Law

Above he made an approach to the principal proposition, for he said that all men are guilty of sin and subject to the wrath of God, neither can they be set free from sin through the Law. Now there follows the principal proposition which is the point at issue in this controversy. This must be diligently kept in mind also because of the greatness of the cause. For this proposition contains the real and chief statement of the Gospel about the benefit of Christ, and because to this issue in this controversy, as to the chief point, the arguments will thereafter have to be addressed.

In propositions, clarity is required most of all. Therefore Paul sets down the proposition accurately, properly, and clearly. But his way of expressing it must be considered, and the weight of the words must be observed: "Justice of God," namely, by means of which he justifies us, that is, acceptance or remission of sins and imputation of righteousness. The meaning is: Now it has been manifested how God justifies; how he wants to pronounce righteous and remit sins and accept us.

He says: "Without Law." This seems absurd to the world. Therefore this little word must be diligently considered. For it shows what the Gospel really is, and what is the distinction between Law and Gospel. For the world has political ideas about Christ. It thinks he is a new lawgiver, bringing a new law somewhat more agreeable than the Mosaic law because it abolishes ceremonies which were not suitable for all people and teaches many things about love. Then they gather the laws which Christ added to the Mosaic laws and imagine that by observing these laws men merit remission of sins and are righteous, and they interpret ''without law'' to mean ''without ceremonies.''

This error must be removed from the minds, for Christ did not come in order to bring a law. Neither is he a Moses or a Solomon, since he has a much greater office. He is the sacrificial victim for sin, and he gives us remission of sins *gratis*, also imputation of righteousness, the Holy Spirit, and eternal life. Therefore when Paul says ''without law'' he is speaking of the whole Law and means that Christ brings remission of sins and imputation of righteousness not on account of any law, nor on account of ceremonies, nor on account of moral works, but *gratis*. And we must know that this statement does not pertain to civil life or to external morals, but to the conscience acting in the sight of God and seeking how it may obtain forgiveness of sins and reconciliation. From this the difference between Law and Gospel becomes much clearer, because it shows that in the Gospel there is announced a gratuitous benefit, not depending on a condition of law or our merit.

This passage must be opposed not only to the Anabaptists (who imagine that the Gospel is a new, worldly state constitution) but is also to be held fast in the struggle of the conscience, so we may truly understand that the benefit of Christ is gratuitous. Therefore the meaning is: ''Righteousness has been manifested without Law,'' that is, we receive remission of sins and are accounted righteous not on account of any law, but *gratis*, on account of Christ, through mercy. For although new obedience is begun in those who have been justified by faith nevertheless this new obedience, or the Law, is not the reason we receive remission of sins and are accounted righteous or accepted. Truly, these are given *gratis*, on account of Christ.

### 23. They come short of the glory of God

They lack the glory which God approves. They lack the righteousness which God judges to be glory. Or, if someone prefers to interpret actively, the meaning will be the same: They lack the glory of God, that is, the wisdom and righteousness which glorifies God, that is, which truly gives the glory to God, knows him, loves him, and presents perfect obedience. They lack the glory of God, that is, the light by which God is acknowledged and glorified. The repetition of the statement is universal. It teaches that all men are guilty of sin and under the wrath of God, that they lack the glory, that is, they are rejected before God, and they are not righteous on account of the Law. This also must be observed: he makes the righteousness of the Law small, including those most holy acts of worship which the Jews thought were certainly the glory of God. He teaches that this outward righteousness is not the glory of God because it is not knowledge and glorification of God.

### 24a. We are justified *gratis*

This means we receive remission of sin and are accounted righteous, that is, accepted, and joined to this accounting is the gift of the Holy Spirit and acceptance to life eternal. We must include these things when we dispute about justification: remission of sins and imputation of righteousness—that is, acceptance—joined to which is the gift of the Holy Spirit and acceptance to life eternal. Paul's description is clear when he says "*gratis, by grace,*" that is, through mercy. Here he shows clearly that he is speaking about a different kind of righteousness than the righteousness of the Law or of our work. For he excludes the condition of the Law or of merit, and testifies that we are justified *gratis,* not on account of any worthiness of our own or because of our works.

### 24b. Through the redemption which is in Christ Jesus

Because God, angered at sin, required a different sacrificial victim, Paul says "through the redemption which is in Christ Jesus." And here our minds shrink back and think first about the wrath of God against sin, then about the greatness of the mercy, because both are here set forth. The world does not see the greatness of the wrath of God against sin, and says that sin is an unimportant thing. But here let us learn that the wrath is so great that no sacrificial victim could placate God, save only the death of his Son. Carnal security is a dreadful sin in those who persevere in sins and despise the wrath of God. Secondly, so great is the mercy that the Father gave his Son for us, and by giving such a pledge wanted us to be sure about the mercy. How great is the blasphemy to transfer the glory of the Son of God to human works and to invent other sacrifices such as satisfactions, Masses, monkery, etc.

### 25a. The Reconciler

He tells[2] in the description of the office of Christ that he is the sacrificial victim, the propitiator, etc. And indeed the term *propitiator* is a title signifying that the benefit which has been promised on account of this propitiator is sure because Christ was not made propitiator in vain. But why does he add "through faith"? This little word must be diligently observed because he is now speaking about the application, that we may know how we receive the benefit of Christ.

---

[2] The text here has *commoratur,* which could perhaps mean "he lingers," but we prefer to read *commemoratur,* and have translated accordingly.

### 25b. By faith

Our adversaries also confess that Christ is the mediator and propitiator. But this very thing they afterward change and corrupt. For they say nothing about the application, neither do they teach one should make use of that Christ the mediator. And first, they say nothing at all about this faith, that is, about trust in the mediator. They do not teach that Christ, the mediator, should be used; rather, they command the conscience to doubt. This doubting clearly militates against the faith which Paul here demands. Secondly, they imagine that Christ is a propitiator only so far as the chance for merit is concerned, as when the head of a family, angry with a servant, is placated by some friend. There the friend procures access to the master for the servant. Thereafter he has no business there, but the servant pleases because of his own service. They give to Christ only this, that He merited this beginning and chance for us to merit.

Thus they themselves say that Christ merited a first grace. Afterward they bury Him and imagine that He is idle, and that people merit remission of sins and are righteous because of their own fulfillment of the Law, etc. On the contrary, we rightly understand that Christ always remains the mediator and must be applied to in faith, that is, it must be stated that we are pleasing to God not on account of our worthiness or fulfillment of the Law, but on account of Christ. We ought not oppose our virtues to the judgment of God, but Christ, the sacrificial victim and propitiator. Paul speaks expressly of the application below when he says [Rom. 5:2] "through whom we have access by faith to this grace," as though he said, "we approach God if we use Christ, the mediator, if by faith we flee to this propitiator and think that we are forgiven because of him."

### 25c. This was to show God's righteousness

The meaning will be clearer if the form of the speech is changed: "For showing his righteousness," that is, that God would declare that he himself is the one who justifies. It is an antithesis. Above he accuses all and says that we are not righteous even when we have the works of the law. But now in Christ, God reveals his righteousness, that is, that he himself is the one who will justify in the way He promised in the promises, that he will give a new righteousness, a new and eternal life, that he will renew the human race by abolishing sin and death. This new righteousness and life he now reveals in the Gospel.

### 25d. On account of the remission

This is a definition of the preceding work, for it explains what he has called "his righteousness." If you change the verbs it will be clearer: "That he may declare that he is the one who will justify, namely, through the forgiveness of sins.'' Thus he sets down a definition, and, if I may express it thus, the formal principle of justification. For in reality justification is the remission of sins on account of Christ, joined to which is the gift of the Holy Spirit, etc. And remission of sins is to be understood not only of actual transgressions but also of the natural impurity. Therefore justification is to be declared righteous not on account of our virtues, but by God remitting sins and accepting the unclean and unworthy through mercy on account of Christ. Thus he elsewhere defines justification to be the remission of sins. "Blessed are those who sins are forgiven" [Rom. 4:7].

### 25e. Of past sins

They say that this little word was added in order that we may know that license to sin is not given us in the Gospel, but that we may know that sins are forgiven to those who repent, in whom sin is being mortified. However, it does not follow from this that those who fall after they are forgiven cannot again find forgiveness if they repent again, because always, as often as forgiveness is given, there is forgiveness of the former sins. Therefore the description of present forgiveness is general; it does not exclude remission of later sins.

**26.** But in my judgment the meaning is simplest if it is understood that these words are set in opposition to the Law, as if he said: "Sin ruled until now." The Law did not abolish sin and death, but through this faith in Christ sin which was present or ruled until now is now abolished. For Paul is speaking not only of actual transgressions, but also about original sin. It is as if he said that sin which was present until now is remitted, as he says below [Rom. 5:13]: "Sin was in the world until the Law came," that is, not even the Law abolished sin. Now sin is doubly abolished, namely, by imputation, because the guilt is taken away, and it begins to be abolished and mortified when there are true terrors in repentance, true comfort, and the beginning of a new creature in the heart.

### 27. Where is boasting?

He adds a call to the proposition. He compares the opposite, namely, what is to be thought about merit. Boasting here really means confidence in merit, or merit itself.

This passage is an outstanding confirmation of our interpretation. It shows clearly that Paul wants the same thing which we interpret, and teaches that the opinions of the monks about merit are false. They imagine that one receives remission of sins because of merits, not *gratis*. They abolish the teaching about faith, as when they teach "If there is sufficient contrition it will merit forgiveness." And because we can never say what is sufficient, they command people to doubt. Finally, they imagine that a person pleases God by fulfilling the Law, etc.

This is the sum total of the imagination of the monks, which Paul openly condemns when he says, "Boasting is excluded by the law of faith," that is, the doctrine about faith teaches that remission is given *gratis,* not on account of merits, and that it is given equally to those who believe, whether they be Jews or Gentiles, that is, to those who do not have the works of the Law. This equalization, as has already often been said, terrifies the carnally secure and comforts the fearful.

It also must be observed that when Paul wholly excludes boasting, he certainly also takes away the condition of merit in reconciliation from moral works. For if forgiveness were given on account of moral works, there would still be boasting. There would be something that would merit forgiveness of sins. Likewise, when he sets faith in opposition to our worthiness, he also takes away boasting. It is sufficiently clear that he understands faith as trust in gratuitous mercy.

The law of works signifies a teaching which requires works and teaches that men are righteous on account of works. The law of faith, on the contrary, signifies a doctrine which speaks of faith, that is, teaches that men are righteous not on account of their own worthiness or fulfillment of the Law or works, but by trust in the mercy promised on account of Christ. For faith does not mean the natural law or the Decalogue, as some falsely interpret, but signifies trust in the mercy promised because of Christ, which Paul opposes to our worthiness. For he is arguing about whether reconciliation is achieved on account of our works or on account of Christ, through mercy, *gratis.* Therefore faith does not signify some law, but relates to the promise, and is trust which lays hold of the promised mercy.

### 28–30. Therefore we judge that a man is justified by faith, without the works of the Law

To his addition he attaches the conclusion in which he briefly repeats the content of the proposition and again inculcates the exclusive, in order that the meaning may be more certain. To be justified signifies to receive forgiveness of sins and be declared righteous, that is, accepted to eternal life. Joined to this acceptance is the gift of the Holy Spirit. Faith signifies confidence in the mercy promised because of Christ. Therefore the meaning is: "We declare that a person receives forgiveness of sins and is accounted righteous before God on account of Christ, through mercy, not on account of the Law." And this mercy must be accepted by faith.

Furthermore, our adversaries mutilate this statement and interpret only that ceremonies are excluded: "Without the works of the Law," that is, without ceremonies. Thereafter they imagine that a person receives remission of sins and is accounted righteous on account of moral works, or, as they say, on account of love, and they understand faith only as knowledge of history. Thus they transfer the benefit of Christ to their own worthiness.

But this interpretation militates against the meaning of Paul, for Paul takes away this glory of merit or of justification from the entire Law, as it clear from what has been said above: "That the whole world may become guilty" and "In your sight no man living shall be justified" [3:19–20]. These statements exclude also moral works from justification. This can be understood easily. In a real struggle, the conscience is not able to say that sins are forgiven us or that we are accepted on account of our virtues and worthiness. Therefore, another reason must be sought for why we should be accepted, namely, Christ, the mediator.

From this it can readily be understood that Paul is speaking about the entire Law, not only about ceremonies, as he shows also below, where he confirms that justification is taken away from the entire Law. And indeed, he himself singles out the moral law [7:7]: "You shall not covet," lest there be an ambiguous discussion. Likewise he says in this passage [3:31]: "We establish the Law." Therefore it is necessary that it be understood of morals. Likewise, when the word *faith* is rightly understood, it is sufficiently clear that justification or reconciliation is taken away from the entire Law, because to be justified by faith is to be accounted righteous by trust in mercy, not on account of our worthiness. Thus this very formula, "we are justified by faith," is opposed to the imagination of those who suppose that people are justified on account of their own worthiness or fulfillment of the moral law. Therefore he excludes also morals from the cause of justification, because no one satisfies the moral law. However, he does not exclude moral works from the effect of justification, for it is necessary that the beginning of a new obedience follow justification.

**31. Do we make the Law void?**

This concern is necessary because when everyone hears this new proclamation—that men are accounted just through mercy, not on account of the Law—ask they immediately whether license to sin is thereby given. They ask whether the Law has been abrogated in order that license to sin may be granted. Paul answers that the Law is not abolished by faith, but rather is very much established, that is, fulfilled.

This passage teaches us how to interpret all statements about works of the Law, such as this: "If you want to enter into life, keep the commandments'' [Lev. 18:5; Prov. 7:2; Mt. 19:17], and similar statements. For here Paul testifies that to the Law there must be added the Gospel about faith. Therefore let these two rules be held fast: Without faith it is impossible to keep the Law. Likewise: By faith the Law is kept and pleases God; by faith obedience is begun and pleases.

The prior rule—it is impossible that the Law be kept without faith—may be understood in two ways. First, of spiritual obedience: When pious hearts feel the wrath of God, then they doubt, flee from God, despair, do not love God, and do not call on him. But when a conscience raised up by faith has come to know the mercy set forth to faith, it begins to love and to call upon God according to the words of Paul [Rom. 5:2]: ''Through faith we have access to God.'' Secondly, it may be understood of acceptance. The things done by a person without faith do not please God without faith. From this it can be clearly understood that the Law cannot be kept without faith. When good works are praised, this must be understood in such a way that we remember that the Gospel of Christ must be included and that we know faith is necessary for keeping the Law, and that the Law without faith does not please God.

The second rule may also be understood in a two-fold way. The Law is kept by faith, first, because faith is the spiritual impulse by which we acknowledge the mercy of God set forth in Christ. Therefore it provides the knowledge of God, love and other good impulses, calling on God, etc. Likewise, the Holy Spirit is received by faith. He arouses good impulses and the new obedience in the hearts. Secondly, the Law pleases God because of faith, that is, although we do not satisfy the Law, nevertheless, because we are in Christ, the new obedience now pleases, and whatever is lacking is forgiven believers because of Christ.

This understanding is necessary in order that consciences may layhold of firm consolation and may acknowledge God's unspeakable mercy which approves of the beginning obedience, in which there is very much both weakness and obedience. Thus Paul says here ''We establish the Law,'' that is, we fulfill it by faith, both because consciences that have found peace by faith acknowledge God, love and call on Him, and because the obedience which has been begun would not please God unless we had been reconciled by faith.

# Chapter 4

**1-17. What shall we say our father Abraham found?**

There follows the proof, in which the arguments must be ordered carefully and referred to Paul's purpose. For these not only confirm the proposition, but also add much light to it. For they clearly teach, fortify, comfort, and lift up our consciences when they are in fear about the forgiveness of sins and about grace. For they show the sources of this question, and learnedly distinguish the promise of the Gospel from the Law, and distinguish between the righteousness of the Law and that of the Gospel.

Moreover, Paul here as nowhere else refutes and rejects the righteousness of the Law in a wonderful manner. One must prudently see where this discussion is headed. He is asking about righteousness before God—whether our righteousness can be set in opposition to the terrors of sin, of the wrath and judgment of God; whether we receive forgiveness of sins on account of our own worthiness; whether our own worthiness can set us free from sin and death; whether in a real struggle our conscience ought to rest on our own worthiness, or indeed on the mercy promised because of Christ. To this debate must be referred these belittlements of the righteousness of the Law, not to carnally secure consciences or to external or civil life. For the Gospel preaches about spiritual and eternal life. It preaches about true repentance and liberates from sin and death. Outward life has need of discipline and Law. But the argument here is not about this external life.

Paul speaks first expressly about Abraham, who possessed many outstanding and heroic virtues, and without doubt excelled all men of that age in gifts of the mind, in wisdom, and every kind of virtue. Paul does not despise these great virtues and gifts of God, but denies that they could offset the wrath and judgment of God. He distinguishes them from that righteousness about which the Gospel speaks, namely, from the forgiveness of sins which is given on account of Christ.

The inexperienced should be reminded of those things in the beginning so they may know where the teaching of Paul belongs, and where this new belittling of the righteousness of the Law is to be applied. For profane people transfer it to the outward life. Afterward certain interpreters, since they dream that Paul is speaking about external life and righteousness, corrupt the statements of Paul and think that he is only urging that the Mosaic ceremonies

106

should be excluded from the external life. They do not apply this teaching to the forgiveness of sins and the struggle of the conscience.

There are five arguments. The first is from an example. Abraham was justified before God by trust in mercy, not on account of his virtues. Therefore we also are justified by faith. The conclusion is plain, because the relationship of virtues is the same. If Abraham, although he had so many outstanding and heroic virtues, was not righteous on their account before God, how much less will inferior virtues in others accomplish this?

The second argument is from the definition. Justification is the gratuitous imputation of righteousness. Therefore, we are not justified on account of our quality or worthiness, etc.

The third argument is from the definition. Justification is the remission of sins. Therefore, it does not come to us on account of our worthiness because we always have need of the remission of sins.

The fourth is from the order of causes and effects. Abraham is pronounced righteous before circumcision. Therefore, he is not righteous on account of this work.

The fifth is from the cause of the promise. A promise that depends on a condition of the Law is not certain. Therefore, the promise of grace does not depend on a condition of the Law, but must be accepted *gratis*, by faith.

## The First Argument

The first argument from the example of Abraham must be diligently inculcated in the minds. For although it strangely offends the Jews, this excessive belittling of the righteousness of the Law brings the richest comfort to pious and fearful consciences. And we should always remember that his preaching does not pertain to the outward life, but to the remission of sins in true repentance.

And here let us diligently magnify the virtues of Abraham. For there is no doubt that this heroic man had outstanding virtues, that he in morals and holy works far outstripped many. Nevertheless Paul dares to take away from him the glory of justification. He has praise, Paul says, but not before God, that is, those virtues cannot be set in opposition to the wrath and judgment of God; they do not set free from sin and death. This example brings great comfort to the godly. Not even Abraham was justified on account of the worthiness of his own virtues. Therefore we declare truly that we are forgiven *gratis*.

Having set down the negative statement, he adds the antithesis from Gen. 15, which is the antecedent of the argument. It was counted for righteousness to Abraham that he believed. Therefore we also are justified by faith, not on account of our works or by the Law.

Some mock this argument in many ways. Some say it is a synecdoche. Believing, they say, is a work signifying obedience as such. Abraham believed, that is, he obeyed God (according to a synecdoche) because obedience must follow faith.therefore, they say, obedience, as such, is signified by faith.

Others say this statement is badly distorted, because Genesis does not mention Christ or this faith which accepts the remission of sins. It is useful to refute these mockeries in order that the meaning of the words in Genesis may be better understood.

This must be noted first: Paul with this statement from Genesis is distinguishing between the righteousness of the law and the righteousness of faith. It is necessary that this statement about faith be properly understood. Likewise, Paul adds the interpretation that the gratuitous imputation is accepted by faith. Here he actually understands faith as assent and confidence by which we accept the promised mercy, that is, by which we declare that God truly wants to forgive us and be propitious through mercy, *gratis,* even if we feel that we are unworthy.

The meaning is "he believed," that is, he was sure he had a gracious God, although he felt that he was unworthy, and in this confidence he expected help and the promised Seed, etc. Thus he was justified by faith, that is, he was pleasing *gratis,* through mercy, not on account of his own worthiness. He was sure of this by this faith, according to the promise, because God had said: "I will be your protector . . . " [Gen. 15:1]. Abraham knew the promise made about the coming Seed, by whom God wanted to do away with sin and death. Therefore we must not invent the synecdoche. Abraham was justified on account of his knowledge of the Word, and on account of his morals that agreed with his teaching and profession. Faith does not rest on the worthiness of one's own virtues, but only looks at mercy. I call attention briefly to these things about the first sophistry in order that the simple and true meaning of the verb "he believed" may be retained.

The second sophistry: The subject of Paul is distorted, because Genesis does not seem in that passage to be speaking about faith in Christ, but about the expectation of a bodily thing, namely, posterity. To this sophistry I answer: Faith is trust in the promised mercy because of Christ, and this trust causes the conscience to be at peace and overcomes the terrors of sin. Therefore the proper object of faith is the promised mercy. Faith always looks first at this object, even though afterward other external things are asked for or expected. In this way, in all statements about faith, it should first be understood that a faith is included which accepts the remission of sins. Thereafter faith also revolves around other, external objects.

The faith of Moses at the Red Sea revolved about the defense of the people. Meanwhile he was certain that he had a gracious God; therefore he expected liberation.

The faith of Jacob, Gen. 28, revolved around the expectation of food and of a return. This he could neither have asked nor expected of God unless he had first been certain that he had a gracious God.

As often as we ask for daily bread, we are sure at the same time that God is gracious because of Christ. This faith which accepts the forgiveness of sins is required in every prayer.

Although external matters differ, the first and chief object, namely, the promised mercy, is the same in all promises and in every exercise of faith. Since faith has this chief object, Paul is quoting this statement correctly.

Furthermore, the patriarchs knew the first promise of Christ, and knew that all promises must be related to this one—that all things are given because of this Seed, on account of which God is gracious. Indeed, Abraham knew that the promise itself properly pertained to the Seed who was to come, that is, Christ.

The third sophistry: To this testimony quoted from Genesis they oppose another passage about Abraham from Gen. 22 [:16–17]: "Because you have done this thing, and have not spared your son, I will bless you." From this they argue: Abraham is praised on account of a work; therefore, he was justified because of a work, not by faith alone.

I answer briefly: The conclusion must be denied. Although a work by a believer has its praise, is necessary obedience, and becomes righteousness, it nevertheless does not possess worth so that a person may have remission of sins on account of the work itself and be righteous, that is, accepted to eternal life before God. It is necessary that a person first have forgiveness of sins and justification. Afterward, the obedience which has been begun is found pleasing, and is worship of God. First, because we have access through Christ [Rom. 5:2]. Likewise, all that is not of faith is sin [Rom. 14:23]. Second, because consciences would become uncertain if forgiveness of sins depended on the worthiness of works. Therefore, it is necessary that a person first have faith.

And these things can easily be judged in a true struggle, because the conscience cannot oppose the wrath or judgment of God according to the saying [Rom. 3:20]: "No man living shall be justified in your sight." Neither did Abraham set his work in opposition to the judgment of God. Rather, in the very work he recognized his weakness and overcame it by faith, and declared that he certainly pleased God through something else, namely, through the promised mercy. Nevertheless, obedience in a believer afterward pleases God, and has great rewards. For this text does not say that Abraham was therefore justified, but bodily rewards were promised to him, although also in these there is repeated to him the promise of Christ.

Therefore both passages in Genesis must be learned. The one teaches simply about the imputation of righteousness, the other about the praise and rewards of obedience which arises from faith and has very great rewards. Therefore one must distinguish where Genesis teaches about justification and judge where it teaches about the obedience which follows.

## The Second Argument

Justification is the gratuitous imputation of mercy, so justification is not our work. The antecedent is that of Paul, for Paul is occupied with the word *impute,* and he interprets it of gratuitous imputation. He opposes it to what is owed.

The way of speaking must be observed. As our adversaries now use the word *merit,* so Paul uses the correlative word *debitus* (something owed). As he takes away debt, so also he takes away merit in justification and clearly declares that an imputation is made not on account of debt or merit, but that it is gratuitous and is accepted by faith.

## The Third Argument

This is a clarification and confirmation of the second argument. Justification is remission of sins, so justification is not made on account of our worthiness or merits.

This argument greatly clarifies Paul's statement about gratuitous imputation, or exclusive [justification exclusively by grace; see on 3:27, 28–30 above]. For Sadoletus and others imagine a synecdoche: We are justified by faith, that is, by faith we acquire virtues; on account of these we please God. But these men are imagining. Paul excludes this merit and says that we are sinners in the sight of God, and so are accounted righteous by the remission of sins.

This is the true meaning of Paul. We are reputed righteous on account of mercy because of Christ, not on account of our worthiness, and this mercy must be accepted by faith. This understanding retains the exclusive and takes away the synecdoche.

As for the rest, this must be known, that connected with imputation and the remission of sins is the gift of the Holy Spirit when we accept the Word by faith. How great is this comfort for godly consciences—to know that justification is the remission of sins! Therefore we are not scared off by the fact that we bring to God sins, not merits. Rather, we know that this is the voice of the Gospel, the eternal will of the Father, and the unchangeable benefit of Christ, that He truly wants to justify us although we are unworthy and bring sins, provided only that we believe. And here note again that the exclusive is repeated: "To whom God imputes righteousness without works" [Rom. 4:6].

But our adversaries mock this passage in this manner: Other passages ascribe blessedness to works: "Blessed is the man who fears the Lord"[Ps. 112:1]; "Blessed are the merciful" [Mt. 5:7]; etc. Therefore, we can argue similarly that we are justified on account of our works, as Paul argues on the basis of a Psalm that we are justified by the remission of sins.

I answer: The conclusion must be denied, because in all passages about works there must be included the passage: "Blessed are those whose sins are forgiven" [Ps. 32:1], because works are not pleasing except in a believer or a righteous person. Therefore Paul cites this passage most correctly, since it speaks about the remission of sins which is gratuitous.

But someone may say: Why do you make a synecdoche in passages about works and not in passages about faith? I answer: Because works are not pleasing except in a believer or a righteous person. Therefore in passages about works we include faith. In passages about faith there is no synecdoche, because it receives remission of sins through mercy and does not rest on the worthiness of works. Instead, it would become uncertain and be driven out if it depended on the worthiness of works or on merit. Therefore it is *gratis* in order that the promise may be firm. Moreover, as often as it is said that works please because of faith, justification is by that very fact taken away from works, because faith does not rest on works, but is trust in mercy alone. And this says that a person must first be reconciled by faith; thereafter works please.

Ps. 31 [32:1]: "Blessed are those whose . . . " is a teaching and a confession in which the Psalm sets before us an example of doctrine. Thereafter in the third place it adds the doctrine of the Law about discipline and about the causes of human calamities. In the beginning it hands down a teaching or proclamation which contains two parts, namely, the teaching that all are under sin, and the promise that God wants to remit sins. It teaches how he remits, how he justifies, namely, *gratis,* not imputing sins, etc.

Therefore the proposition is: "Blessed are those whose iniquities are forgiven" [Ps. 32:1], that is: In this way we are righteous: not on account of our worthiness or merits, but by God not imputing, by God remitting our sins. Therefore all men have sin, and God is able to impute sin to all; all ought to acknowledge that they have sin. Therefore he says: "Neither is there guilt in his spirit" [Ps. 32:2], that is, he who acknowledges and confesses his sin, "He is blest" [Ps. 32:2], etc. Therefore we are accounted righteous in this way: when we acknowledge and confess that we have sins and believe that they are remitted to us through mercy because of Christ.

Then there follows his confession, which is an example of his proposed proclamation. "When I kept silence, my bones waxed old . . . " [Ps. 32:3] He opposes keeping silent to confession. Confession is to acknowledge sin, and to seek and believe in remission. That is what he intends when he says: "I said, I will confess against myself my injustice to the Lord" [Ps. 32:5]. To keep silence, on the other hand, is to feel sin and not to seek and believe in gratuitous remission, but to remain in doubt and fears, or to seek comfort through works, as some do by becoming monks, others through other works. Thus he says: "I remained in fears, and was nearly consumed" [Ps. 32:4]. He adds this about confession, in which he teaches clearly that God remits sins, and indeed remits them to him who confesses, not to him who brings the righteousness of the Law. Therefore he remits them *gratis*.

He transfers this example to others: "For this every saint has prayed to you" [Ps. 32:6] that is, also saints acknowledge that they have sins and ask and believe that they are forgiven. Therefore the remission is gratuitous. By this faith they are saved and are not overwhelmed by the floods. They are not oppressed by terrors. You see that the doctrines of repentance and remission are connected. He does not promise remission to the carnally secure and to persons who do not grieve, but to those who at the same time have repentance and terrors.

He adds a sermon to the people of the Law, whom he exhorts to repentance: "Do not become like a horse and mule" [Ps. 32:9], that is, acknowledge the wrath of God against sin. And he adds concerning the punishment of sin: God burdens the world with calamities and death, and coerces and punishes, also in order that He may humble us, that we may acknowledge our sin [cf. Ps. 32:10]. Thus all disasters in the world are part of the Law, and divine proclamations, which testify that the world is subject to sin, and that God is angry at sin.

He opposes this statement to human judgments. For people think calamities happen by chance and without the counsel of God; or by an unjust judgment of God. But the prophet here proclaims and teaches divinely revealed wisdom, that they happen with the knowledge and by the ordinance of God in order that God may coerce the wicked and declare his wrath against sin, in order that we may acknowledge our sin and seek grace and liberation in Christ. Moreover, it teaches the saints that although they are afflicted at the same time as the wicked, they are nevertheless saved and will finally be set free from death and all evils.

## The Fourth Argument

The fourth argument is taken from the order of causes. Abraham is pronounced righteous before circumcision, therefore that work does not merit remission of sins or justification. This is an important argument because it contains a combination of justification (or reconciliation) and the works that follow. Furthermore, it teaches about the use of the sacraments.

First, however, the sophistry must be refuted. When Paul mentions a ceremony he seems to have taken away justification only from ceremonies. To this we must answer: In the case of Abraham, David, and similar ones, ceremonies had a command from God, just as other good works. Therefore there is here no reason for a difference. If other works commanded by God were meriting remission of sins and justification, then ceremonies together with these did merit this, because they were outstanding works of the First Table. Therefore when Paul takes away merit from ceremonies, he takes it away also from other works.

Second, this topic contains a useful combination of faith and the works that follow. Abraham received remission of sins by faith, and thus, having been justified, his person pleases God. Afterward there follows his obedience. This, in such a person, now has great praise.

Thus David first accepts remission of sins by faith and becomes a son. Afterward the deeds done bravely by him as a soldier, his diligence in ruling, his patience in afflictions, and other virtues are pleasing. And yet he does not oppose these to the judgment of God. He knows that they do not satisfy the Law, that they do not please on account of his perfection, but because he believes that he has a gracious God through mercy, on account of the promised Seed, as he says [Ps. 116:12]: "What can I pay back to the Lord . . . ?" Thus in a believer good works now become sacrifices and offerings of praise, and have great rewards.

In the third place this topic must be most diligently observed with regard to the use of the sacraments, in order that it may fortify us against Pharisaic opinions about the *opus operatum* and against Anabaptist imaginings. For by calling circumcision the seal of the righteousness of faith, Paul testifies that the sacraments are signs requiring faith. Therefore, they do not justify without faith, *ex opere operato,* as the monks were saying.

This passage is teaching the same thing, namely that the sacraments are not just signs of profession before men or symbols of our morals, as the Anabaptists imagine who belittle the sacraments. Truly, the use and the principal purpose of the sacraments is that they are signs of the promise and testimonies concerning the will of God toward ourselves, and they call for faith, just as the promise does.

In Abraham, circumcision was a mark which always reminded him of the promise. It was also a testimony that God would be gracious to him according to the promise. Thus Baptism in our body should remind us of the promise, and ought to testify that God truly wants to impart to us the things which he promised in the Gospel.

The eating of Christ's body and blood is a testimony in ourselves that Christ truly joins us to himself as members, that he truly wants to cleanse us with his blood. Thus the sacraments are to be used in the same way as the Word, and faith is to be aroused and exercised by the sacraments, just as by the Word.

## The Fifth Argument

The fifth argument is taken from the purpose of the promise. No promise that depends on a condition of law is sure. The promise of grace needs to be sure, so the promise of grace does not depend on a condition of the Law, but is to be accepted *gratis*, by faith.

This is the principal syllogism which must above all things be treated in this controversy. It is the thing that contains the chief matter of the disputation, taken from the sources or from the topic of causes. It adds much light to this matter it explains what the promise is and what faith is. Likewise, it shows the difference between the promises of the Law and the promise of grace. Therefore, to understand this controversy, it is necessary to pursue the argument. This will then be most profitable not only for instructing consciences, but also for comforting them. For this topic best explains the little word *gratis,* and shows why the promise is gratuitous.

## Explanation of the Major Premise

If the promise depended on a condition of the Law, it would become uncertain. Paul confirms this proposition with the text [Rom. 4:15]: "Because the Law works wrath," that is, the Law always accuses and condemns us because we never satisfy it, because the Law requires not only outward civil deeds, but perfect inner and outer obedience, perfect love of God. No one furnished this, except Christ. The Law accuses and condemns all other, as Paul says [Eph. 2:3]: "By nature we are all children of wrath." If the promise had a condition of the Law, the promise of grace would become void since the Law always accuses and condemns. Therefore, Paul states the major premise of the syllogism thus: "If those who are of the Law were heirs, faith would be abolished and the promise would be void" [Rom.4:14]. And he adds the confirmation [v. 15]: "The Law works wrath," that is, it condemns and drives to despair. I have stated this confirmation somewhat briefly because he repeats it below where he discusses the use of the Law.

But someone may say: No, the Gospel is certainly conditional, because sins are not remitted unless repentance comes to it, as the text says: "Repent"

[Mt. 3:2]. Likewise: "Cease from doing evil." Likewise Christ says: "If you want to enter into life, keep the commandments" [Mt. 19:17].

I answer briefly: These requirements are not the condition or cause on account of which reconciliation is given, but they are rather effects which necessarily follow. They cannot be the cause for which remission or reconciliation is given, since sin still clings in the flesh, and concupiscence is not idle, but generates endless evil affects. Therefore forgiveness does not depend on the condition of the Law fulfilled, or to be fulfilled, or of our purity. Nevertheless, when forgiveness is apprehended by faith, when the beginning of a new and eternal life has been apprehended by faith, it is necessary that the new obedience should now begin, which, although it is imperfect, nevertheless pleases because of Christ. Likewise, since faith frees us from the terrors of sin, there must necessarily be fears in us, but these terrors are not the purchase price or the cause of the forgiveness of sins. But the conscience should be certain that this benefit is given *gratis* on account of the mediator and high priest, Christ.

But here it could be objected: If conditional promises are invalid, all promises added to works are useless, such as "Give, and it will be given you" [Luke 6:38]; "break your bread to the hungry and the Lord will hear you" [Prov. 25:21], etc.

I answer: The promise of remission of sins and of responsibilities or justification and of eternal life belongs to the Gospel, and is bestowed *gratis* because of Christ, not on account of a condition of Law or of works. This promise must be diligently distinguished from legal promises which have the condition of works, such as: "Give, and it will be given to you" [Luke 6:38]. "If someone only gives a drink of water . . . he will not lose his reward"[Mk. 9:41]. "Honor your father and mother, if you want to live long on the earth" [Ex. 20:12; Deut. 5:16].

These promises have a condition of works and are truly useless and invalid without the promise of the Gospel, because the works in themselves do not please God except in those who are reconciled. But after we have been accepted *gratis* by mercy, the obedience which has been begun thereafter pleases, not on account of our own purity or worthiness, not because it can be opposed to the judgment of God, not because it satisfies the Law, not because a person is righteous because of it, but because the person is righteous, that is, accepted because of Christ through mercy. Therefore, our works are pleasing afterward because we are sons, as Paul says [Rom. 6:14]: "You are no longer under the Law, but under grace." Although such works are not themselves fulfillment of the Law, nevertheless, since they please because of Christ, they are, as it were, a certain fulfillment of the law. Therefore legal promises, that is, promises with such works added to them, now become valid and useful for those who are reconciled.

This is a useful teaching about the distinction of promises and about the use of legal promises. We can know in what way they are valid, and may also learn to exercise our faith in them. Promises are added to works chiefly for this cause, that we may perform our works in such a way that faith at the same time asks and expects spiritual and bodily blessings which are necessary for the state and for ourselves.

### Explanation of the Minor Premise

The minor premise of the syllogism is: The promise of grace must be sure and valid. For first of all, what need would there have been of issuing a promise and of revealing forgiveness if there were no forgiveness? There would be none if it depended on a condition of the Law, because the Law is never satisfied. Rather, reconciliation has been revealed because we were not able to acquire it by the Law. And for this very reason the condition of the Law has been removed. Second, doubting in minds brings forth despair, as was said above: "The Law works wrath" [Rom. 4:5]. Therefore, it is necessary that the promise be known, sure, and valid for us in order that it may be opposed to doubt and be effective comfort.

We must rebuke the popular opinion which teaches that the conscience ought to be in doubt about the remission of sins and in doubt whether God is gracious to us, and that this doubting is not a sin. Doubt indeed inheres naturally in the minds of everyone. For the darkness is so great that carnally secure minds even despise the wrath of God, and are in doubt about his judgment. And then, when the conscience is worried, it unceasingly accuses and condemns. Therefore, let us confess that doubting inheres in the minds, but we also say that that doubting is a sin, and that doubting must be fought. For the promise has been revealed for this reason, that it may correct doubting, that we may have a sure and firm comfort, and that we may say certainly that we are forgiven and we are heirs. The Gospel, even as it sets forth a promise, expressly calls for faith that we should believe the promise itself, as John 3 says. Faith is the opposite of doubting. Likewise, doubting accuses God of lying; it denies that God is truthful, etc. Therefore, we should oppose both the promise and the commandment about faith to doubt, and should learn that doubting is the height of sin.

The scholastics imagined that doubting is not a sin because they saw that it inheres naturally in the minds. Likewise, they did not at all distinguish the Law from the Gospel, neither did they consider the fact that faith is required, or what faith is, because they imagined that faith is knowledge of the Law. By this teaching about doubting—because they command to doubt—they simply abolish the entire Gospel, the promise and command concerning faith. This impious imagination, which commands doubt, must be rejected.

### 18–22. Who in hope believed against hope

There follows an amplification which illustrates the nature and exercise of faith. What was said above must always be held fast, that faith first embraces the confidence which declares that our sins are forgiven, and that God is propitious to us on account of Christ; and that afterward this faith revolves about other (also exterior) objects, as the faith of Abraham in this promise first regarded the promised Seed on account of which God would bless the human race. Then he goes on and expects the promised posterity.

The faith of Moses lays hold of mercy; afterward he expects the liberation of the people, etc. Thus the exterior objects always vary, and yet there is a common chief object of faith, namely, the mercy promised because of Christ. Therefore let everyone also stir up his faith in his danger, in his affliction.

I have spoken here to explain the nature of faith, because its object is described first. The proper object of faith is the Word, which fights with the outward appearance, as Abraham is promised the Seed and posterity whom God wants to bless. Meanwhile, his wife is sterile and he himself was exhausted.

The Gospel promises peace and life. Meanwhile, we are plagued by all kinds of afflictions, and in death life is not visible. Therefore Paul says here: "In hope Abraham believed against hope." Against hope, that is, in the Word, in which he needed to hope. Thus faith looks to the Word and sustains itself by the Word, even if the outward appearance is against it.

Liberation was promised to the Israelites. Meanwhile, the severity of their servitude is increased, and other even greater troubles follow. So we also must exercise our faith during our dangers.

I have spoken about the object; now I shall speak about the formal side of faith. And this subject shows clearly that what Paul calls faith is trust which assents to the promise of the Gospel and fights against doubt. Faith does not mean knowledge of the Law, or merely a knowledge of history. It signifies assent to the promise, not doubt that God will carry out His promise.

This subject must also be observed in order that it may be opposed to those who deny that faith is confidence which fights against doubt. Four descriptions are placed here expressly. Mistrust did not harbor doubt concerning the promise; it was certain. Likewise, it gave glory to God, etc. Thus Paul above puts together faith and the promise, and shows that they are interconnected like correlatives. It is certain that with Paul faith signifies trust which assents to the promise of the Gospel, and which accepts the promised forgiveness of sins and reconciliation. There is no doubt that Paul is speaking about a faith which accomplishes something in the midst of terrors of conscience and comforts consciences, as he says below: "Having been justified by faith, we have peace" [Rom. 5:1]. Furthermore, this comfort is not brought about by knowledge of the Law, or by the knowledge of only history, but by trust in the promise which fights against doubt.

All things are full of darkness and fog in the Christian doctrine where this proper meaning of the word *faith* has been lost. These passages in Paul should be carefully observed in order that one may be able to judge and establish for certain what faith really signifies, and to beat back the twaddle of those who deny that faith is confidence which fights against doubt, but imagine that it is only a knowledge of history.

Let us also transfer to our own use this description here set forth, and learn that this is the true exercise of faith—to fight against the natural doubt and mistrust, and to oppose to it the Word or promise, and to ask and expect that we may be strengthened by God. As the man says in Mark 9[:24]: "I believe, Lord; help my unbelief."

In the third place Paul adorns faith on account of its ultimate purpose. For after he described it according to its essence and its nature, he adds the outstanding commendation that it is an act of worship that gives glory to God, that is, it affirms that God is powerful and true, because not assenting to the promise doubts whether it is true, yes, denies that it is true. Therefore it accuses God of lying, as John says: "Whoever does not believe God makes him a liar" [1 John 5:10]. On the other hand, one who assents to the promise declares that God is true, powerful, etc.

And in order that it may be even better understood that without this faith no glory is given to God, the antithesis must be considered. Reason either has Epicurean opinions about God—that he is idle, neither punishing nor saving (this is the first insult described in the Psalm [14:1]: "The fool has said in his heart, 'There is no God' "). Or reason holds opinions of the Law about God, namely, that God saves the righteous, and because we are not righteous, he will reject us. This is also the second insult, because he who thinks thus about God flees from God and rages against God. Those who judge thus about God do not call upon God. They expect nothing from God. Therefore they do not acknowledge that he is God.

On the other hand, he who believes the promise of grace rejects Epicurean opinions and opinions of the Law, and gives the glory to God that he truly cares for us and loves us, that he does not want us to perish, but wants to hear and save us according to his promise, even though we are unworthy. With this faith a person calls upon God and expects from God help and salvation. Therefore this faith gives glory to God, that he is God, that he is powerful, that is, efficacious, doing something with us, that he is true, that he is merciful, that he hears, and that he saves. This is the glory that belongs to God, and this faith promotes calling on God and true spiritual acts of worship.

Here it is necessary that the hearers be warned about those who are adversaries of the doctrine of faith, and who boast that they are teachers of good works. These men arrogate this praise to themselves falsely because they teach only external and civil works. Meanwhile, they do not teach true and inward acts of worship, namely, the exercises of faith and calling on God. These works are the proper works of Christians. It is about these chiefly that the churches must be taught.

Second, when the doctrine of faith is omitted, then other works do not please God, nor can consciences understand how they may please. Therefore such teachers who omit this doctrine of faith by no means teach about good works, but about certain works of their own which are rejected by God. Since they propose these as worship and transfer to them the honor owed to Christ, they teach idolatrous works. Here belong those speeches in the Prophets, as Is. 41 [:29]: "Behold, they are all a delusion; their works are nothing; their molten images are empty wind."

Therefore in the true doctrine about good works we should consider that first of all faith and the exercises of faith are required. They are the acts of worship which really give glory to God and allow us to practice calling on God in all of life and in all matters. Thus faith itself will grow, and God will give other gifts such as he promises: "How much more will your Father give the Holy Spirit to those who ask" [Luke 11:13]. From that, other good works will come into existence.

### 23–25. It was not written for him alone that it was imputed to him

This is an outstanding passage, and contains two things. The first is that this righteousness about which it speaks was revealed from heaven; it is not known to reason or from the Law. Second, the example of the justification of Abraham pertains to all. Both subjects contain important teaching.

The first, about revelation, shows the distinction between the righteousness of the Law and that which is by imputation, and leads us to the Word and promise. It clearly teaches the same thing which John teaches when he says [John 1:8]: "The Son, who is in the bosom of the Father, he has told it to us," because neither reason nor the Law teaches or makes us certain that God forgives sins—and that to the unworthy—and that he pronounces people righteous, although they do not satisfy the Law. This promise (which is Gospel) about remission of sins and imputation of righteousness has been divinely revealed, and has a different meaning from the teaching of the Law and reason. one must carefully note here what he says: "It has been written that it is imputed,'' as though he said: ''This will about imputation is not known to reason like the Law, but is a different pronouncement and a new revelation.''

This also must be considered—that it leads us to the Word. It does not want us to seek other enlightenments, but wants us to begin with the Word and comfort consciences with the Word, and declare that this is the sure and valid will of God which is set forth in the Word. Anabaptist and Manichaean imaginings, which seek enlightenments without the Word of God and outside the Word of God, must be rejected.

Second, this contains outstanding comfort. He here transfers the example of Abraham to all, and teaches first that Abraham is a model of the people of God, so we may know that the others are accounted righteous, even as he was justified.

It is most lovely to see that he makes all people the equals of Abraham as far as the forgiveness of sins and the imputation of righteousness is concerned. For there is a difference of gifts. All should know that they are loved and accounted righteous as God testifies that he loves and justifies Abraham. Testimonies of true and great love are revealed concerning him in order that we may know that we are similarly loved and heard. This passage in Paul must be applied so as to transfer the example of Abraham to us.

That which we have often said should be inculcated in consciences should be referred to this passage—that the promises are universal. Since this is so, God commands and teaches that all should believe that they are equally loved and accounted righteous.

Finally, it is not enough just to speak about faith or trust in the promise. It is necessary to embrace the mediator. Paul says that it is imputed to those who believe in him who raised from the dead Jesus, who was delivered for our offenses and raised again for our justification. Here again you have an argument that faith does not signify knowledge of the Law or only of history, but signifies trust which lays hold of the imputation made on account of Christ, the mediator, who suffered and now reigns.

Paul distinguishes death and resurrection, and when mention is made of resurrection, the reign of Christ and his priesthood should be understood. We belong to Christ because Christ, our high priest, makes intercession for us with the Father and accounts us righteous [cf. Rom. 8:34, Heb. 7:25]. Likewise, because Christ lives and reigns, he gives the Holy Spirit and makes alive, frees from wrath and eternal death, and raises the dead. And faith apprehends both and applies them to us, namely the death of Christ and the resurrected mediator, high priest, and giver of life. It apprehends the death of Christ in order that it may hold fast to the sacrificial victim, it declares to be the sure ransom of our sins, because God wanted some victim for sin.

And indeed he is so angry at sin that no sacrifice placated him except the death of his Son. This testifies both that the wrath of God against sin is unspeakable, and that his mercy toward us is infinite he made his Son the sacrificial victim for us.

Not only the death of Christ must be apprehended, but also that our high priest with the Father has been raised again, that he truly hears us, is truly efficacious, truly gives life, gives the Holy Spirit, helps us, frees us from eternal death, will raise the dead, and will give new and everlasting life, wisdom, and righteousness. Paul has included all these things when he says, "He rose again for our justification."

# Chapter 5

### 1–2a. Therefore, being justified by faith, we have peace

The closing words are for confirmation. They repeat the proposition and add an outstanding amplification about the first effect of faith, or about the real advantage which faith has. Afterward he adds on comfort full of the strongest emotions, which must always be kept in sight and applied to bodily and spiritual afflictions.

But I return to the beginning of the closing words: "Having been justified by faith we have peace with God through Jesus, our Lord." The meaning is that we are reconciled by faith, and being reconciled, we from then on by the same faith please God and have pacified consciences, not on account of fulfillment of the Law, but on account of Christ.

This statement must first of all be opposed to the imagination of the scholastics, who suppose that the regenerate are thereafter righteous on account of the fulfillment of the Law, and, as they themselves say, the virtues and works of the regenerate merit eternal life because they are worthy *de condigno*. Thus they destroy faith and imagine that the regenerate thereafter have no need of Christ, the mediator. This is to bury Christ once more.

Second, this statement should be used to teach and comfort pious consciences which acknowledge their weakness in order that they may be recalled to Christ, the mediator, and may learn that they are accounted righteous by faith on account of Christ—not on account of their own beginning and imperfect obedience, but by faith on account of Christ.

Third, the testimony about justification should again be noted. For here he says expressly that we are justified by faith.

Fourth, Origen twists this passage to refer to peace before men and the duties of love, spoiling the reading. We have peace, that is, we have peaceful morals toward others. This meaning is simply unsuitable here. For Paul says clearly, "We have peace with God." He therefore talks about peace, that is, consolation of the conscience with God or liberation from fears. Therefore the meaning is: God is no longer angry with us. And we in turn have quiet consciences, freed from the terrors of sin and death.

Here it should be noted that the first and most characteristic effect of faith is to give a person a pacified or tranquil conscience, set free from the terrors of sin and death. This comfort is a return to life, of which the Scripture speaks when it teaches that we are brought to life: That a righteous person will live by his faith [Rom. 1:16]. Now if we are set free from terrors by faith, there must necessarily be fears and repentance in the godly.

Fifth, this passage teaches that the opinion which commands to be in doubt about the remission of sins is false, because this text says "We have peace." A conscience that doubts by no means has peace. Therefore, it is necessary that minds be raised up against doubting.

Sixth, this passage teaches that the imagination is false which separates the remission of guilt from the remission of eternal punishment. For since we are brought to life by the remission of guilt and find peace, that is, we are freed from the terrors of sin and eternal death, at the same time that the guilt is remitted there must also be remission of eternal punishment, and that eternal punishment is not remitted because of payment in purgatory.

Moreover, the remission of guilt and the remission of temporal punishments in this life should be distinguished. There is peace and comfort for the conscience in the godly, even if they are oppressed externally by bodily afflictions, as David retains faith and peace of conscience even when he was driven into exile [2 Samuel 15–19].

Seventh, from here on the argument about justification should be taken from its effect. We receive remission and are justified only by that thing which makes our consciences at peace before God. They are rendered at peace by faith alone; therefore, we receive forgiveness and justification by faith alone.

The major premise is clear because justification is bringing to life. The minor premise in this passage is Paul's own: "By faith we have peace," and it can be explained from what has gone before. If faith rested in part on mercy and in part on worthiness, it would become uncertain; it would be cast out. For the exclusive word excludes worthiness. It does not teach that there need not exist in us newness, repentance, or contrition.

Eighth, it is a noteworthy passage because it says: "Through whom we have access by faith." It teaches about the mediator, and teaches how the mediator should be accepted, and what faith is, namely, that sins are remitted on account of Christ, the mediator. The Law does not do this, neither can one be pleasing except on account of Christ.

He also refutes the opinion of the monks who, although they say that Christ is the mediator, nevertheless say nothing about faith by which the mediator must be apprehended for the remission of sins. They only say that sins are remitted on account of contrition, or of other works. They do not teach that it is necessary to have faith, that is, confidence which states that sins are remitted to us *gratis,* on account of Christ, the mediator. As he has said about above [3:25], "Whom he made the propitiator through faith," in order that we may know that the benefit of the mediator is applied to us by faith.

This passage must be noted in order that it may be opposed to the hypocritical opinions which, although they appear to speak about the mediator, nevertheless in fact take away the mediator because they do not teach about this faith. Faith is trust which applies the benefit of the mediator to ourselves or which rests on the mediator, and which declares that sins are remitted to us *gratis* for his sake, etc.

Ninth, again there is a testimony here that faith signifies trust in the mediator, or trust which apprehends grace, that is, mercy, because the passage says: "By faith we have access into this grace." These things cannot be understood about knowledge of history, but about trust that lays hold of grace, that is, gratuitous mercy—the remission of sins and imputation of righteousness. For that is what "by grace" here really means.

### 2b. We glory in the hope of the glory of God

In the closing words he has repeated the chief proposition about justification, and reminds us that even as we have been justified by faith, the saints should thereafter declare that they are righteous by faith, not on account of their own worthiness.

Now the question could be asked: Of what kind is that righteousness and liberation from sin, since sin still clings to us and we are subject to death, yes, and are oppressed by all calamities? What have believers acquired that all other people do not have? Many ridiculed the Christians when they proclaimed liberation from sin and death, although no kind of person was more beset by calamities. Yes, also the consciences of saints grieve when they acknowledge their infirmity and fight with doubt, questioning whether they please God since they are so weak. This is not a trivial temptation. Although faith ought to depend on the Word and declare that God is certainly propitious on account of Christ, our infirmity attempts to grasp this with the eyes and senses. This is why the Anabaptists revile the doctrine of faith and say that other heavenly enlightenments are to be sought. And there are others who dream that they already possess glory, that is, perfect obedience, and that they please God because they satisfy the Law and are without sin.

Therefore Paul does both: he comforts the saints who acknowledge their infirmity, and he exhorts them to glory—but in hope—and to declare that they have glory, that is, newness and eternal life, which, although it has not yet been revealed, is certain for us. Therefore, consciences ought to be calm and not doubt or despair, although they still feel their infirmity. He commands that they should glory in hope, that is, they should not think that they already have perfect newness, nor ought they to seek other enlightenment, but should remain with the Word. They should declare that they are pleasing by faith on account of Christ, and that this newness is not yet perfect since sin still clings in us.

The meaning is this: although the world and our reason judge that we do not have glory, that is, liberation from sin and from death, we still glory, that is, we conclude that we have that glory with which God will glorify us, but as something hoped for. Now we hold this by faith, but this hope is nevertheless certain; it does not deceive. In the same manner he says to the Galatians [5:5]: "For through the Spirit, by faith, we wait for the hope of righteousness," that is, although we are still unclean, we are pleasing by faith and await perfect newness. Thus he teaches here that the saints do not yet have perfect newness but still are pleasing by faith, and glory in hope, that is, by faith they have a new nature, eternal life, new wisdom, and new righteousness.

### 3a. Not only this, but we glory also

He adds a correction. Yes, we have glory in reality, not only glory hoped for, but present. What is it? Afflictions!

He opposes this needed comfort to the judgments of the world and of reason. The world sees that we are afflicted, as though forsaken and rejected by God, and by this offense it is scared off from the Gospel. Also, reason itself judges according to the law that afflictions are curses, that is, evils and signs of the wrath of God. Paul on the contrary teaches us that afflictions are not signs of the wrath of God, but signs of the goodwill of God.

Therefore, the meaning is: We glory in afflictions, that is, we conclude that afflictions are good things, not disgraceful things, not curses, not signs of wrath and rejection. We conclude that bearing up under them is a good work, and an act of worship pleasing to God not on account of one's own worthiness or perfection, but because the person has already been accepted by faith, as we have said elsewhere about the obedience which has begun.

The meaning is: We have a twofold glory. The first is the chief one, but until now it is one hoped for: the new nature and eternal life. This glory we possess for now in hope. The second glory we have at present: afflictions. For although the world judges afflictions to be signs of God's wrath nevertheless we know them to be signs of the goodwill of God, and obedience in afflictions is a new act of worship of God.

### 3b. Knowing that affliction produces patience

Earlier he had said that afflictions are our present glory, because until we die this life is a constant battle, and the flesh has been subjected to afflictions in order that the remnants of sin may be mortified. The law judges these mortifications to be curses and signs of wrath. But the Gospel, on the contrary, teaches that they are transformed into another shape, namely, that they are signs of the goodwill of God. Therefore he now speaks of the comfort in this statement, and preaches about the purpose and use of afflictions.

Paul connects a series of steps. Afflictions produce patience, patience approval, approval hope, etc. To sum it up, these words want to say that afflictions are exercises of faith or hope, and that God requires obedience and faith or hope in afflictions. Therefore they are not signs of wrath. That is the sum and substance of this statement, but before we treat the individual words, the teaching about afflictions must first be considered. There are four precepts which one must know about afflictions.

1. First, that it must be declared that we are not afflicted by chance, but according to the sure counsel and permission of God.

2. Second, it must not only be declared that afflictions happen according to the plan of God, but one must also add that God punishes not in order to destroy, but that he may recall us to repentance, or that he may exercise our faith. Afflictions are not signs of wrath, but of the goodwill of God, according to the statement: "I do not want the death of the sinner" [Ezek. 33:11]. And it is profitable in these precepts to have before our eyes as many testimonies as possible.

3. The third precept is that God requires obedience in afflictions, and ill will and impatience are sin. God chiefly subjects the church to afflictions, and this obedience is to be rendered for God's sake.

4. Fourth, it is not sufficient that there be obedience. More is required: faith and invocation, by which we seek and expect help, according to the command [Ps. 50:15]: "Call upon me in the days of trouble."

These four precepts must be held fast in all afflictions. Pondering these leads to true Christian patience, which differs from philosophical patience. For philosophical patience is obedience in the sight of reason in enduring adverse matters from some honorable cause. But Christian patience is obedience which is rendered for the sake of God, and which is accompanied by faith or hope and expectation of help. I have stated these things (though briefly) because from them the meaning of Paul can be understood more easily. Now I return to the text.

"Affliction produces patience." These words should not be understood only after the manner of the Law, that obedience is required in afflictions, but also as comfort. For when God demands patience and hope, it is clear that the afflictions are not signs of wrath, but exercises. God wants to exercise our obedience and faith. For according to the judgment of the Law or of reason, affliction does not produce patience, but indignation, as our weak nature murmurs against God and is angry that this weak nature is burdened with such great calamities. It flees from them as much as it can. But according to the judgment of the Gospel, affliction produces patience, since the mind recognizes that they are signs of the goodwill of God, and that faith and invocation are to be excited in these exercises.

### 4a. Patience [produces] approval

This means that the exercise or test arouses faith in order that it may not be idle, not feigned, but true, that it may not languish, etc. For Peter says [1 Pet. 1:7]: "After your faith has been tested, if it is found to praise," that is, after it has been exercised in order that it may be true and not feigned.

The purpose of afflictions is described here, as if he said. Afflictions are not a sign of wrath because they are tests, that is, exercises in which faith is aroused and strengthened. We experience true comfort and a real struggle. As Isaiah says: "Their cry in difficulty is for them your discipline." Because in idleness and pleasure there is no struggle of faith, it languishes and is extinguished; likewise, there is no earnest invocation, etc.

### 4b. Approval [produces] hope

This means that in this exercise, faith and hope are aroused and strengthened. For although faith and hope are related impulses and are not separated from each other, there is some difference. Faith is confidence by which we at present accept forgiveness of sins and declare that we have a gracious God. We are comforted at present by this mercy; its object also is God, apprehended in the Word by which the remission is bestowed. But hope is the expectation of future deliverance. It speaks not only about present mercy, but also about a future event.

These impulses, he says, increase in that exercise, and patience does not consider itself as merit on which hope depends, but considers itself an occasion for its exercise. For faith and hope are there when in affliction they fight against doubt and despair. Neither does patience come before hope, but Paul wants there to be hope in that struggle. That struggle is patience, obeying God and expecting liberation. And faith and hope depend on the gratuitous promise, otherwise they would become uncertain.

### 5a. Moreover, hope does not make ashamed

The expression is Hebraic. Hope does not confound, that is, it does not deceive the one who hopes. That is the true interpretation of the verb *con fundere,* "to deceive," as elsewhere [Is. 28:16; 49:23]: "No one hoped and was confounded," that is, deceived. There is a statement similar to this one which will be examined in the ninth chapter [v. 33]: "Everyone who believes in God will not be confounded."

But someone may say: "Why is faith not deceived? What if we are unworthy?" The godly must be reminded that this objection is an intensification of the struggle about faith and hope, namely, whether God wants to save the unworthy. Here the exclusive word must be held fast—that God wants to save us *gratis* on account of Christ, although we are unworthy. And finally the topics of faith and hope help consciences when these exclusives are understood in them.

It should also be considered that with respect to the remission of sins and to eternal life, there is the express commandment of God that we should believe the remission and hope for life eternal. We should ask and hope for this without any condition. But liberation from bodily afflictions should be asked with the condition "if it pleases God."

### 5b. Because the love of God has been poured out

The reason for the conclusion seems obscure. Hope does not confound, because the love of God has been poured out. The conclusion would seem less obscure if he said: "Hope does not confound, because the promise is sure and valid." This reason is taken from the nearby efficient cause, namely, from the nearest object, and in fact it says this, but adds something. For the meaning is: "Hope does not confound, because God certainly loves us. And we lay hold of this love, even when faith, by which the Holy Spirit is efficacious, is dying. The reason for hope is that God loves us. But this love is not apprehended except through the Word.

The love of God in this passage signifies the love with which God loves us. This is the simplest and least intricate interpretation, and it is useful for consciences. Hope does not confound, because the promise is sure and valid in which we apprehend the love of God toward us.

This is the plain meaning, and it contains a very weighty teaching about the impulses of faith and hope: what the struggles are in which the conscience is raised up and declares that we are loved by God. This is the highest and most difficult article. The mind cannot retain it without a great struggle, because that is the very message of the Gospel—that God loves us because of Christ, although we are unworthy and unclean. The Son, who is in the bosom of the Father, revealed this message. But human hearts are so pressed down by mistrust that they not only do not see this will of the Father, but also shrink back greatly from this voice.

Let us learn here what kind of impulses faith and hope are. They lift up minds with this comfort they can declare that we are loved by God. The statement below teaches the same thing: "You have received the Spirit by which we cry 'Abba, Father' " [Rom. 8:15].

Second, it also should be noted that these impulses—faith and hope—

arise from the Holy Spirit. The monks turn this statement upside down and patch on the reason for the conclusion of hope as the cause in this way: "Hope does not disappoint because we have love, that is, because we love God." Thus they argue from merit; when merit has been paid as the price, the result follows.

This interpretation is foreign to the meaning intended by Paul, and the conscience would be upset if it judged that one would have to build his hope on merit. The promise would become conditional and uncertain. The cause for hope is not some quality in us. One must know that the cause for hope is the gratuitous promise which shows the benefit of Christ, and the love of God toward us because of Christ; therefore, the interpretation of the monks must be repudiated.

As for the rest, if one adds on thus: "Hope does not deceive, because we have the Holy Spirit as the guarantee," that connection does not displease me, and the subject is from the order of the effects of the promise, and from the auxiliary cause, as if he said: "We already have the beginning and first fruits of eternal life, namely, the Holy Spirit, who also comforts us and helps us, and is the pledge of future glorification."

But here one must know that we are not to look at some quality in ourselves, but comfort is to be sought in the Word. For the Holy Spirit finally works through the Word; he does not come before the Word. He is with us and helps us in this way—that we may lay hold of the love of God and sustain ourselves by means of the Word. This interpretation agrees with the first. For the meaning is: "Hope does not deceive, because when we lay hold of the Word, the Holy Spirit at the same time works and helps us to apprehend in the Word the love of God toward us. One can more clearly add on this: "hope does not deceive because God loves us, and you have already laid hold of this through the Holy Spirit; you have declared certainly that he loves you, which is the basis for the hope that he will do you good." The argument proceeds from the causes, because knowing that he loves is the cause for hoping.

This statement again reminds us that faith signifies trust in mercy, because Paul says in effect: "Through the Holy Spirit you have laid hold of the love of God, that is, that God loves you." Therefore faith is confidence that God loves us; faith is to apprehend this. Thus the passage reminds us that those who command us to be in doubt about the forgiveness of sins are not teaching correctly.

### 6. For Christ, when we were still weak

An amplification follows which gathers the signs and testimonies that God loves us, namely, this highest and unspeakable benefit he gave his Son for us, and indeed wanted Him to be a certain guarantee of his true and unchangeable love.

### 7a. Scarcely for a righteous man will anyone die

He amplifies this love by putting together two things. "Scarcely for a righteous person will anyone die," that is, even when we must die we meet death unwillingly. A thief dies unwillingly, although by law he ought to die. Understand Paul's phrase "for a righteous person" as meaning when the cause is righteous or owed.

### 7b. For a good person someone may dare to die

The other connection is: "For a good person someone may dare to die." We risk dangers for something good and pleasant, incited by desire or by the thought that something is useful, for instance, for the defense of a spouse or children, for honor, or when a brave man meets death, etc.

He argues from these two propositions and amplifies the love of God and Christ from the combination of causes. If anyone bestows a benefit, especially if life depends on it, although he neither owes it nor is moved by some personal desire, this must necessarily be the result of a great and powerful love. Even those who owe the legal penalties die unwillingly, and others who go to meet death are motivated by some opinion that this is useful. Christ died for us although he did not owe it to us and was not motivated by any usefulness to himself. Therefore there must be an immense and unspeakable power of love toward us.

### 8–10. But God commends his love to us

Afterward he amplifies it on the basis of the minor premise: If he died for the unrighteous how much more will he save the righteous. This comfort is necessary for those who, although they are sanctified, but still see that they still have the remnants of sin and are subject to terrors and fears. Likewise, they are overwhelmed by the roughest and most dreadful calamities, and are struggling against mistrust, desperation, etc. These have need of this teaching and comfort. Although they are unworthy and impure, they are pleasing by faith *gratis,* because of Christ, as I have said above [on 5:1]: "Being justified by faith we have peace." Likewise: "By faith we have access to this grace in which we stand" [5:2]. Likewise: "Then the death and resurrection of Christ are the pledge that God wants to set us free" [cf. 5:10].

### 11. Glorying in God through Jesus, our Lord

This bit has been added for a particular purpose and emphasis: "Glorying in God through our Lord Jesus Christ." For he is again inculcating the teaching which is most necessary for everyone, namely, how the conscience may be rendered certain. For especially in true afflictions, our unworthiness cries out against us. We question whether we are really being heard, whether God certainly wants to bestow the things which are promised in the Gospel, etc.

To these doubts Paul opposes this little statement: "Glorying in God . . . " For to glory is to think that we have glory, that is, righteousness, wisdom, etc., a conscience which declares truly and with certainty that we are pleasing to God.

But he adds: "Glorying in God through our Lord Jesus Christ." Here he teaches about the cause of this glory and certainty, as though he said: "We do not glory—we do not please—on account of our own worthiness, but we glory in God, that is, we believe that we have glory and are righteous through the mercy of God because of Christ." In sum, he teaches that the regenerate declare that they are certainly pleasing on account of Christ, *gratis,* not on account of their own worthiness or fulfillment of the Law, as he also says to the Corinthians [1 Cor. 1:29]: "In order that no flesh may glory before him." Likewise [1 Cor. 1:31]: "Let him who glories glory in the Lord," that is, let him declare that he pleases God on account of God's promise, not on account of our worthiness.

This statement must always be kept in view so that Christ may be given his honor, since he is always the mediator, and so that we may know our own unworthiness[1] and nevertheless so that the conscience may have firm comfort. It is a commandment of God that we should believe that we have remission of sins and are pleasing and are heard on account of Christ.

What he says above, "we glory in afflictions," is said elsewhere about the obedience which has been begun. It is not glory, that is, righteousness which can be opposed to the judgment of God. Nothing defective is permitted before God, but on account of him we are righteous and have the forgiveness of sins. Therefore, this judgment remains firm: "Let him who glories, glory in the Lord" [1 Cor. 1:31; 2 Cor. 10:17]. After we are reconciled by faith, we resolve to be pleasing through mercy on account of Christ. Then the beginning and imperfect obedience follows which results in worship and praise. This is not opposed by God's judgment, but God approves of it because we have been made sons.

## The Solution Follows

### 12a. Therefore, as through one man

The earlier part of the Epistle is a comparison of opposites. For a proposition had been set down and strengthened with arguments. Now there fol-

---

[1] The text has *dignitatem,* but the context appears to call for *indignitatem,* unworthiness.

lows, as it were, a new book. For here no argumentation is undertaken, but a certain solution of the individual parts of which mention was made above. For the earlier disputation contains these propositions: "All men are under sin" [3:9]. Likewise: "Men are not justified by the Law, because no one satisfies the Law [3:20]. Likewise: "We are accounted righteous by faith, on account of Christ, through grace" [3:22]. In these propositions there are individual members: sin, law, and grace.

Now this analysis is both customary and useful in teaching, as when a physician discusses whether veins, arteries, and nerves are born from the heart. Surely there is need that the unlearned be taught how veins, nerves, and arteries differ. Such a description of parts is called analysis.

1. Veins carry nutritious blood and have thin garments. The arteries carry the purest blood and the vital spirit. The nerves are the finest threads, which carry the animal spirit; they are the instruments of the senses. The veins have their origin in the liver, because the liver is the source of the blood. The arteries originate in the heart. Sleep was given because there is need for repose.

2. During repose the whole body is watered and moistened.

3. Because warmth must be recalled to the inside in order to generate breath in the heart, the outside becomes colder during sleep[2] and the inside warmer. After sleep, bodies become more lively and fit for doing all kinds of things. The nerves originate in the brain.

Thus also Paul, after that argument, returns to the proposition and picks out the individual members, explains them, and compares them with one another. This comparison brings much light to the earlier propositions because definitions and causes are the source of all kinds of transactions. First he speaks here of sin; then about the Law; and third, about grace. These are the chief topics of the Christian doctrine which need to be found in the church, which all need to know.

Paul does not distinguish between the terms *original sin* and *actual sin,* because he embraces the root and its fruits, although he is actually speaking about the propagation of original sin. Meanwhile, he also makes a distinction, as when he names sin and the fruit of sin. However, there was need in the church of a new term for avoiding ambiguities.

### Concerning Original Sin

What is original sin? Original sin is guilt or imputation. On account of the fall of Adam, all who are propagated according to nature are guilty because of it. It is also the corruption of human nature which followed the fall of

---

[2] The text of *CR* has *summo.* The context clearly calls for *somno,* "during sleep," which is the reading of our 1540 edition.

Adam. Because of it human nature is not able truly to obey the law of God, but has defects and lust against the Law of God.

The popular definition of Anselm says precisely the same thing as ours, as he also explains it at length, although popularly only a few words taken from it are recited, namely, ''Original sin is the lack of original righteousness which ought to be in man.'' For original righteousness was to be not only acceptance, but also wholeness of man's powers, or rectitude, which would have rendered perfect obedience to the Law of God. Neither would there have been doubt in the minds of men about the will of God, and lack of fear, trust, and love of God. But there would have been born in the minds or created together with them a light, and a firm knowledge about God, and inclinations in agreement with the Law of God. Now, on the contrary, the nature of man is guilty and corrupt. From this antithesis the definition can easily be understood.

Why are there disagreements about original sin? Because people do not see the uncleanness of the heart, namely these sins: doubt about God; lack of the fear God, trust, and love; and harboring dreadful impulses agains the Law of God. They do not see these vices, much less the fact that they are sins. Therefore the ungodly imagine that original sin is nothing.

Then they patch on philosophical statements, saying that nature is good or that nothing is sin unless it is done voluntarily. In their place these things are rightly said, but they are not to be twisted to apply to original sin. Therefore darkness and blindness in human minds is the reason many either minimize original sin or deny it entirely, and then smartly corrupt the Scripture and escape it, as Pelagius and many others did. Minds must be fortified against such sophistries with true and firm testimonies.

### The Original Cause of Sin

The original cause of sin is the devil, and the will of our first parents which, although it was free, turned away from the Word of God and did not retain obedience toward God. Therefore Adam became guilty and made his descendants guilty, deprived of the integrity of the gifts of nature which God had added to nature. Then he procreated such persons as he himself was. The guilty and corrupt nature is propagated.

### The Effects

The Scholastics said concupiscence is not sin but only a punishment, and they called it ''the tinder.'' We say that concupiscence is both a punishment in guilty nature and a sin.

The second punishment is death, and all the calamities of humankind.

The third punishment is that this infirm nature has been subjected to the tyranny of the devil, who is eager to destroy with bodily ills and terrors and drive men to sins of all kinds—to blasphemies, heresies, unbridled lusts, and other sins.

The philosophers wondered from where in the outstanding nature of humankind so great a number not only of calamities, but also of crimes might come, although it is indeed according to nature to do right. However, only the Christian doctrine shows the cause, namely, original sin.

Since such dreadful effects and punishments followed, original sin dare not be minimized. But so great is the darkness of minds that we not only do not see sin and the wrath of God, but do not even understand the greatness of the disasters. Therefore, some teachers also either publicly were indifferent to or minimized original sin. However, the Scripture reveals this sin to us in order that having been humbled, we may seek grace and may acknowledge the benefits of Christ, as John says: "For this the Son of God appeared, that he might destroy the works of the devil" [1 John 3:8].

### 12b. Sin came into the world

That Paul is speaking of original sin is clear, because he speaks about the sin of Adam, on account of which all men are guilty, as he says a little later: "Because all have sinned," that is, are guilty; Likewise: "Through the transgression of one, condemnation came upon all" [5:18]. Likewise: "On account of the disobedience[3] of one the others are sinners" [5:19]. Now if there were only actual transgressions, then everyone would be guilty only of his own transgression. But Paul here testifies that all are guilty on account of one, Adam. Therefore there is another sin beside actual sin, etc.

### 13a. For until the Law, sin was in the world

He wants to say not only that there was sin in the world before the Law was promulgated, but he also adds this: Sin has not been destroyed by the Law. Therefore this statement should be understood as including: "Until the Law, sin was in the world," that is, also since the law of Moses was given, sin nevertheless remained. Thus he reminds us briefly that sin and death are not taken away by the Law because the outward righteousness of the Law does not liberate from sin, neither is it the beginning of eternal life, but only a certain outward bodily discipline. And when the conscience is troubled and seeks justification in the Law, then the Law has its chief effect. It accuses and casts consciences into terrors and despair. This is what Paul wants to say when he adds:

---

[3] The text has *propter obedientiam*. However the context clearly calls for *propter inobedientiam*, "on account of the disobedience," which is the reading of our 1540 edition.

### 13b. But sin is not reckoned where there is no Law

That is, where there is no Law, sin is not acknowledged, is not rebuked. Paul is speaking of the judgment of our conscience. Therefore the Law was given in order that the conscience may acknowledge sin, be rebuked, and be terrified, as he says above: "By the Law is the knowledge of sin" [3:20]. Afterward, however, he will speak more fully about the uses of the Law; for at this time he only touches on it briefly, in passing, as it were. However this follows:

### 14a. Death reigned from Adam until Moses

By this statement the above words are explained. As he said before that sin was there until the Law came, and that it had not even been abolished by the Law, so he says here that sin reigned from Adam until Moses, and that it has not even been abolished by the Law. However he adds:

### 14b. Death reigned also in those who have not sinned after the likeness of the transgression of Adam

That is, that also infants are subjected to death, although they do not have actual sins. For Paul calls actual sin transgression. He says this in order to confirm the first proposition, that all are guilty. For if also infants are subjected to death, therefore they have some sin, because death came into the world through sin. There is therefore another kind of sin besides actual sin.

### 14c. Who is a type of the coming One

Until now he has been speaking of original sin, that this human nature is guilty and corrupt. Therefore, it is not just by the Law or by works, but there remain in human nature corruption, blindness, concupiscence, and horrible attacks against the Law of God. Therefore there is need of some other righteousness, namely, the grace of Christ. He now begins to discourse about this: "Who is (he says) a type of the One who is to come."

### 15a. Concerning grace

As above he spoke about sin, about the cause of sin, about its propagation and effect, so he now teaches about grace, about the cause, the propagation, and the effect of grace, in order that he may teach that sin is taken away through grace.

He links together grace and the gift through grace. The word *grace* signifies gratuitous mercy. Here it most truly signifies forgiveness of sins and gratuitous acceptance, which comes about through Christ. The gift through grace signifies the giving of the Holy Spirit, who begins the new and eternal life in the minds, and excites new impulses.

First he compares Adam and Christ. This comparison powerfully illustrates both parts. It explains the manner of the merit, what each merited for others. Adam merited guilt for others; Christ merited reconciliation for others. This comparison clearly refutes our adversaries who imagine that people are righteous by their own worthiness. For here he says clearly: As others are guilty because of Adam, so others are righteous because of Christ. This statement is repeated frequently. He is speaking of this kind of merit when he says Adam is a type of Christ, namely, so far as this is concerned, that each merited for others. For in a comparison it is not necessary that all things should be similar.

Paul himself adds a correction in order to remind that there are many dissimilar things in this comparison, for he says: "But the gift is not like the transgression," that is, there are many dissimilar things in this comparison of transgression and gift.

To begin with, the matters are very different: guilt or sin, and forgiveness or grace, eternal death and eternal life. By Adam there is propagated guilty nature, sinful and subject to death, and it is propagated by fleshly generation. Contrarily, by Christ there is given reconciliation. This is not propagated by fleshly generation, but is accepted by faith. As is written in John 1 [:12]: "He gave them power to become sons of God, to those who believed . . . " Likewise John 4 [3:3]: "Unless a person is born again . . . "

This dissimilarity of propagation must be diligently observed on account of the Anabaptists who here mingle together a prodigious amount of idle talk. Some simply take away original sin altogether; others imagine that after the resurrection of Christ no one is born with original sin. The passages cited from John fortify us against these fanatical opinions. But see how great is the madness of the Anabaptists! If there were no original sin, all men would live without sin and without death. Since this is clearly false, it is necessary that the cause remain, namely, original sin.

The third dissimilarity which Paul also treats and enlarges upon here in the text must be diligently considered: Grace overcomes sin. This dissimilarity should be diligently inculcated; for if sin and grace had equal power, how would grace save, particularly since sin is felt more? Thus the benefit of the Gospel would be nothing; there would be no firm comfort.

Therefore this dissimilarity must be clearly shown, as Paul says later, that grace overcomes sin. However, it overcomes it doubly, by imputation and by its effect. It overcomes by imputation, because God accounts those who lay hold of grace to be righteous, although in fact they still have the remnants of sin. Thereafter, it also overcomes it in effect, because in them, although they are weak, there are new impulses which resist sin. Likewise these persons, although in this life they were weak, are nevertheless resurrected to eternal life. It is necessary that these things be known in order that the benefit of Christ may be understood and so firm comfort may be retained. And Paul himself thereafter discusses and magnifies this dissimilarity.

**15b. For if by the transgression of one**

He repeats the comparison in clear words: As on account of the transgression of one others became guilty, along the same line, others were reconciled to God and became accepted by God on account of One, Christ. This comparison shows clearly that we are reconciled to God and are accepted not by our own merit, but by that of another.

Here Paul joins together two things: grace and a gift through grace. Grace signifies gratuitous acceptance because of Christ, that is, gratuitous remission of sins, and gratuitous imputation of righteousness because of Christ. The gift through grace signifies the giving of the Holy Spirit and eternal life. In the remission of sins the Gospel at the same time offers the Holy Spirit, which we accept by faith when hearts are raised up and find comfort through the Word. This is the benefit of the new testament or of the Gospel, given because of Christ: the forgiveness of sins, the imputation of righteousness, the gift of the Holy Spirit, and eternal life.

[Some say,] "We are righteous by grace; grace is our love, etc., therefore we are righteous by our love." I answer to the minor premise: Even if for the time being the word *grace* is understood in this way, it is done improperly, since grace signifies forgiveness of sins.

[Some say,] "We are righteous by righteousness; righteousness is a quality of ours; therefore we are justified by a quality of our own." I answer to the minor premise: Righteousness in these discussions signifies acceptance, and to be righteous is to be accepted.

[Some say,] "Righteousness is located in the will; faith is in the intellect, therefore we cannot be righteous by faith." I answer: The righteousness which is our quality is located in the will. But righteousness, that is, acceptance, is a restoration, not something inherent in anyone. Finally faith, insofar as it is a will that accepts, is not only in the intellect, but also in the will.

The Scholastic teachers generally understand grace as a quality in us, and they call it charity. Thereafter, when it is said that we are righteous through grace, they imagine that men are righteous on account of a quality of their own, namely, on account of charity, that is, the new obedience. Thus they do not teach that one should apprehend Christ, the mediator, and they leave consciences in doubt. Finally, to teach in such a way that one must think that we are righteous because of a quality in ourselves is a doctrine of the Law, and is fraught with much that is harmful.

Therefore "by grace" should be understood relationally, as gratuitous acceptance, so that "we are righteous through grace" is the same as "we are accepted by God, God accepting us *gratis* on account of Christ" according to the promise, in which this grace, that is, acceptance, is set before us. And the conscience declares that we are righteous, that is, accepted, because of Christ. It does not look to our own worthiness, but to the Word or promise, and according to that it speaks about the will of God toward us, and thus apprehends Christ, the mediator. When this happens, the Holy Spirit is given and new impulses come into being in us.

Therefore, let both be held, both that new impulses must come into being in us, and that the conscience should look outside of ourselves on Christ the mediator and declare that we are righteous for his sake, that is, accepted. This is what it means to say that men are righteous through grace, namely, that they are righteous, that is, accepted *gratis* for Christ's sake, God accepting them. So also this should be understood: "We are righteous by faith," that is, correlatively we are righteous because of Christ, who must be apprehended by faith. In this way the conscience learns to look at the Word and has firm comfort because that grace, that is, that will of God which accepts because of Christ, is set before us in the Word. It must also be known that the Holy Spirit works when we lay hold of this Word. So much about the word *grace*.

Paul adds: "The gift through grace, which is Christ's." For he teaches that the gift, that is, the Holy Spirit and eternal life, is given because of Christ, as is written elsewhere [John 1:16]: "Grace for grace," that is, we are pleasing not for our own sake, but because the Son pleases. Likewise to the Ephesians [1:6]: "He accepts us in his beloved Son."

### 16. And not as through one sin

The language in the text can be satisfactorily explained in this way: And the case of the gift is not like the case of sin, which destroyed men through the one who sinned. Paul adds this statement most prudently and necessarily to show the dissimilarity of the reign of sin and the reign of grace. He teaches that the dissimilarity is that grace is more fruitful and more powerful than sin. This dissimilarity needs to be set forth. For if sin and grace had equal power, how would we be saved if sin damned equally? The conscience must know that grace is more powerful, first, because it does away with sin through the forgiveness of sins and the imputation of righteousness, by which imputation we are accepted, although sin and infirmity clings in us. Also, the effect is more powerful because it resists sin and the devil, and brings new and eternal life.

The godly should diligently consider this superiority of grace in order that they may oppose it to the magnitude of their sin and to their present weakness. No sin, no matter how great, ought to be considered greater than grace. Likewise, although the saints are still weak, they should know that grace is more fruitful.

Paul exaggerates this dissimilarity and adds: "Judgment from one [resulted] in condemnation," that is, the one sin of Adam brought universal condemnation to posterity. Moreover, grace abolished many sins, that is, both original and actual, both the roots and the fruits, etc. For this reason they are pleasing because of Christ.

### 17–21. As death reigned through the transgression of one, through One

As before he compared sin and grace, so now he compares their effects: death and life. However, the emphasis is in the word *reigned*. Death remains in those who are sanctified, but it does not reign in them. Those who are sanctified overcome the terrors of sin and death by faith. Likewise, they are set free from eternal death. Likewise they have comfort in human calamities. For by the term *death* also the other calamities of the human race should be understood. Therefore, he says expressly here "Death reigned," that is, the ungodly succumb to the terrors of sin and death. They are not set free from eternal death. They do not have comfort in great afflictions, as Saul and Cato inflict death on themselves.

Also this emphasis should be considered: "How much more will those who receive the excellence of the grace . . . " He is pressing the dissimilarity of which it was said above, "grace is more powerful than sin"; I have reminded above how important it is that this be inculcated.

Then follows a repetition of the comparison, in which the above statements are inculcated in nearly the same words. This article about original sin must be noted first. For because he says clearly that by the transgression of one all have been condemned, then others must be guilty and condemned not only on account of their own crime, but of that of another, namely, Adam. Therefore there is some original sin.

He says that righteousness came upon all men on account of the righteousness of one. This should be understood about the promise or about the Word which offers grace universally to all, even though not all accept it.

[Some say,] "Not all are saved, so grace did not come to all." I answer: The promises are universal. As far as the will of God is concerned, he wants all men to be saved. We ought not to inquire about other things. Each proclamation, that of repentance and of grace, is universal.

## What Is Grace?

Grace is remission of sins and imputation of righteousness, or acceptance which is made *gratis* by God for Christ's sake. And joined to this acceptance is the gift of the Holy Spirit and eternal life.

## The Causes

The efficient cause is the will of God, which wanted Christ to become the sacrificial victim for us, and in this way to take pity on us for his sake, not on account of any worthiness of ours.

## In What Way Does Grace Touch Us?

The Word of God is the instrument, and this must be accepted by faith. For when hearts receive comfort from the promise which has been revealed in the Gospel, they declare that they truly receive the things which the Gospel promises, namely, remission of sins, the imputation of righteousness, and the Holy Spirit, because God is truthful and wants this glory of truthfulness to be given to him. He wants us to worship him with this faith by assenting to his Word. Yes, this is the greatest immutable precept that we should believe that the things which the Gospel promises are given us for Christ's sake. And in order that we may fight against doubt we must know that the promise is gratuitous and universal, because these two things trouble consciences: our unworthiness and the idea that grace is only for a part of humankind.

## The Effects of Grace

Of the changes which come about through the Spirit when we accept the Gospel, the chief one is faith, by which we are raised up and declare that God is propitious to us on account of Christ. This change is called vivification, because by this confidence the terrors of sin and death are overcome. Other changes follow: beginning obedience toward God, calling on God, fear, love, patience, chastity, and other changes which conform to the Law of God, as has been said: "I will put my law into their hearts" [Jer. 31:33]. Effects of grace are also liberation from the power of the devil, and help against the devil and the infirmity of the flesh. So are comfort and help in present calamities, as Christ says: "I will not leave you orphans" [John 14:18]. An effect is also liberation from the Law so that it does not condemn believers. The final effect is the completion of our entire nature, also newness and eternal life.

## The Effects of the Law

To begin with, the reader must be reminded that Paul is not speaking about the political use of the Law, or about the pedagogical, but about the use of the Law in a conscience which is dealing with God and seeking justification. The first is the pedagogical or political use, namely, to coerce the flesh and to furnish outward works commanded by the Law. This use in those who have not been sanctified is called discipline. Though it does not justify in the sight of God, it is necessary that we know that this discipline has been commanded by God also for those who are not sanctified, and that it can to some extent be performed by human powers. With respect to this political or pedagogical use one must also know that the Law is needed because it is the highest gift for bodily life, which God also gives and preserves.

Four purposes must be considered which should urge us to undergo this training with the greatest care and diligence. The first is because God demands this obedience also in those who are not sanctified. The second is the God also adds rewards and punishments. The third purpose is for the sake of the peace of the common society. The fourth purpose is because it is training toward Christ.

Three things pertain to this training. It is necessary that there be order and peace in order that people can be taught. Second, it is necessary for people not to fight against the Word of God, and not to continue in manifest crimes. For the Word of God is not efficacious in a person who remains in them. In the third place, this training is not only a guardian of peace—it does not only coerce—it also teaches. This is what training really is. The Law has ceremonies, rites, and exercises, like any pious head of a family. In order that this custom may teach the unlearned and weak, we sing, we read, and we meditate on some passages of Scripture at certain times for the purpose of training, that is, that the Word may be inculcated, that, having become accustomed to it, we may understand the Word of God. The Holy Spirit works through the Word.

These uses are not to be despised, because these two things certainly are necessary: not to remain in manifest sins and to learn and to meditate on the Word of God. Meanwhile, people must be taught that these outward exercises are not righteousness in the sight of God, but that righteousness before God is something different. As for the rest, when faith in Christ comes in those who are godly, these exercises by which the flesh is coerced are good works and pleasing to God, if they are done for a purpose that is owed.

Let this be sufficient for a reminder about the first and political use of the Law. It is also profitable often to inculcate in young people what the difference is between this training, between the righteousness of faith and the fruits of faith. It is also useful to admonish them to undergo this training, that they may learn that the barbaric, or Cyclopean, or Neronian life, which is spent in manifest shame, is displeasing to God. They also may learn that exercises and studies in the Word of God are profitable. So the meaning is this: The Law is a schoolmaster, that is, an exercise by which people become accustomed to and are taught in order that they may understand the Word.

In this sense Paul said [1 Tim. 1:9]: "The Law has been given to the unjust," that is, God wants to coerce the unjust, and there should be in the church the teaching about the distinction between this discipline and the righteousness of faith. Also, it should be taught that it is a command of God that the unlearned should be coerced. Also the godly, who are still weak and unlearned, have need for such exercises in order that they may be coerced and may learn as Paul says [Eph. 6:4]: "Educate children in the discipline and admonition of the Lord." So much about the political use of the Law, about which Paul does not speak here to the Romans.

The second and chief use of the Law is to accuse and terrify consciences when it judges and condemns sin. This is a hidden use which the Law has in the conscience. It is not understood by hypocrites, but only when minds are truly terrified as they recognize their sin. These terrors are frequently described in the Psalms [38:3]: "There is no peace for my bones in the face of my sins."

Paul speaks of this use in the entire Epistle to the Romans and to the Corinthians when he says [1 Cor. 15:56]: "The sting of death is sin; the power of sin is the Law," that is, on account of sin men are destined to die. And sin indeed brings terrors, despair, and death. But sin would not be recognized if the Law did not judge and accuse us. That is also what he wants above, when he says [4:15]: "The Law works wrath," that is, it accuses and terrifies consciences. Also this [5:20]: "The Law increases sin," not in a civil sense, but it increases it in the conscience, that is, it makes it more powerful so that it terrifies and brings on despair and death.

Thus sin is increased within, in the conscience, when it is recognized to be sin, that is, when we recognize that God is truly angry and feel the wrath of God, terrors, and death. Thus David felt true and dreadful terrors when he heard the rebuke of Nathan. Hezekiah also describes his terrors: "Like a lion he has broken all my bones" [Is. 38:13].

Paul teaches that this is the foremost task of the Law—that it accuses, terrifies, and condemns. It does not justify; it does not announce forgiveness of sins; it does not liberate from sin and from death. Thus Paul distinguishes the Law from the Gospel. The Law, or external discipline, coerces the body as best as it can. When it does its proper and highest work, it accuses, terrifies, and condemns.

This twofold use of the law is signified by a type, namely, by the face of Moses. The face of Moses being so shiny that the people were unable to look at it signifies that the Law terrifies when it is truly understood of perfect obedience, not carnally of outward discipline. Afterward Moses spoke to the people with his face veiled; thus the people heard him. This figure signifies that men do not truly understand the Law with the judgment of reason, but understand it only of outward discipline. Then veiled reason imagines false opinions, that fulfillment of the Law consists of outward discipline, and that it is righteousness before God. But God uses the word of the Law to judge and condemn sin, and for accusing and terrifying consciences. As later in Rom. 7, this entire topic is repeated [7:13]: "Did that which is good become death to me? By no means! But sin, that it might become exceedingly sinful, worked death."

# Chapter 6

**1–2.** Before he completes the comparison of the Law and the Gospel which he started, he inserts objections which people make and does away with certain absurd things. For a great mass of questions arise here. If we are not righteous by the Law and by our works but through mercy for the sake of Christ, then what is the need of doing good? If the Law does not justify nor bestow eternal life, what need is there of the Law? The reader will more easily understand these objections of Paul if he will consider the controversies of our time. For just as our adversaries now shout: "If we are not just on account of our works, then what good does it do to do well?" The Pharisees threw up the same absurdities to Paul. From this it is sufficiently evident that we are dealing with the very same matter about which Paul is arguing, and that we are giving the genuine and true meaning of Paul.

The godly should weigh also this here that it is not only the adversaries who raise these objections which I have stated, but there is in all men so great an infirmity of nature that when we hear the teaching about gratuitous imputation, we become less fruitful for doing good and carnal security is strengthened. But this knowledge of mercy ought to have excited our zeal for doing good. For doubting deters the minds. Therefore now, when we have learned in what way works are certainly pleasing and with what honor God adorns them—that he approves and calls them sacrifices, and promises rewards—this certainty ought to have kindled the minds even more for doing good.

Now to the question: If we are not just because of works, then what need is there for doing well? We answer as usual: The benefit of justification has been transferred to Christ in order that it may be certain, that is, a person is righteous, that is, accepted, for the sake of Christ. And in order that this may be certain, it does not depend on our worthiness, but it is imputed to the believer because of Christ, that is, to him that accepts it by faith. Thereafter the new obedience is necessary as an effect which necessarily follows the imputation, because with the imputation there comes about renewal, which is the beginning of new and eternal life. The beginning of the new and eternal life is truly new and spiritual obedience. Therefore new and spiritual obedience is necessary. This is the sum and substance of Paul's answer.

But he divides renewal into two parts, namely, mortification and vivification, and he argues from the efficient causes. Dead nature is not effica-

144

cious; it is necessary that the old and corrupt nature in us should be mortified. The old and corrupt nature ought not to be efficacious, nor ought it to be obeyed when it fights against the will of God.

The other syllogism is this: Living nature ought to be working. We receive the new nature and light when faith raises us up and comforts the conscience. This new life ought to have works that are in harmony with it, that is, obedience toward God, whom we begin to acknowledge already in this new life.

Paul recites these two syllogisms here in which we see the renewal of man described, and he here uses the terms *mortification, vivification,* and certain related terms. It must be diligently considered what these terms properly signify. The conversion of man or his potential is being described, as it is customarily called. Let us always look upon this as the chief topic of the Gospel and see what meanings may be given it; also that the Gospel preaches repentance and remission of sins. Thus each is set before us in the death of Christ: the wrath of God against sin, for it is necessary that the wrath be great and unspeakable, since no other sacrifice could make satisfaction to God. Since he wanted his Son to die and be crucified, the wrath is very great and inexpressible. And this very death is the pledge which makes us certain about the forgiveness of sins.

Thus it is necessary in our conversion or repentance that there be true terrors and pain in which our hearts truly feel that God is angry at sin. Again, it is necessary that hearts receive true comfort by faith when they declare that on account of Christ they certainly have forgiveness of sins. Neither should one imagine that these things happen only once. In this life faith ought to fight assiduously against these terrors, and in this struggle faith and spiritual newness increase. Therefore both words are diligently set before us, the word which rebukes sins and the promise about Christ which proclaims forgiveness, etc. The Gospel rebukes unbelief, and the ministry of the Law shows the other sins: adultery, hatred, etc. Yes, God applies punishments and calamities which are also the voice of God rebuking sin. Mortification without faith causes dread, such as is in the wicked, in Saul and Judas, and brings on despair and eternal death. But terrors together with faith and knowledge of Christ become both an act of worship of God and a good work, as the Psalm calls them a sacrifice [cf. Ps. 51:17].

This explanation of the sayings and their application to repentance is necessary lest foolish people imagine that mortifications are monastic works and observances supplied by us, or leisurely speculations, as Monetarius and also the Platonists foolishly imitated these terms. But we must know that mortification is genuine terror and pain, and vivification is the faith which comforts us.

### 3. As many of us as have been baptized into Christ Jesus

In the first syllogism he wants to say that it is necessary that there be mortification or repentance in those who believe, or that faith is not in those who are secure and despise judgment, because he says: "You have been baptized and buried together into the death of Christ," that is, on account of the death of Christ you have forgiveness. But that death shows also the wrath of God against sin, in order that sin may be put to death also in us, that is, that as we acknowledge the wrath of God, we may also comfort ourselves with the benefit of Christ. Likewise, remission of sins is made in such a way that sin may at the same time be destroyed. However, having been destroyed, it should no longer be active.

### 4–11. Therefore we have been buried together with him

The comparison of our conversion with the death, burial, and resurrection of Christ is most meaningful. For that is how he makes his response: You have forgiveness on account of the death of Christ. Because of the death of Christ, sin is destroyed, and our vitiated nature begins to be mortified. The Holy Spirit is given at the same time in order that he might put to death our old nature and begin the new. We are buried with Christ, because after our nature has begun to be mortified, sin has been buried in a twofold way: first, by imputation, for although the remnants of sin remain, they are forgiven, and second, as far as the effect is concerned, because our sinful nature ceases to be active, or begins to be mortified. The rest of life, after mortification has been begun, is burial. The sin has indeed been wiped away by imputation, but we have not yet been glorified. Although we are righteous, we lie buried, awaiting glorification. As Paul says: "Our life is hidden with Christ" [cf. Col. 3:3], that is, although we have glory, righteousness, and life, this glory still remains hidden with Christ until we are raised from the dead.

Second, so far as the effect is concerned, we lie in a tomb, that is, under a cross, in afflictions of all kinds. The devil troubles and persecutes the godly in horrible ways. All these calamities, and finally also death itself, are (as it were) a sepulcher in which our old nature lies dead, so that it can no longer be active. This comparison with burial is a clear picture of dead sin, so far as imputation and effect are concerned, and reminds us what the Christian life should be.

Then he adds a third part. Not only is there mortification, but vivification is also begun. Furthermore, the new nature is active, so it is necessary that there be new obedience. He repeats this comparison: "If we have been united with him in the likeness of his death, we shall also be united with him in the likeness of his resurrection," that is, as our old man has been crucified together with him, so also, having been renewed, we shall live together with him. Since there is new life, or a new nature, a new light and knowledge of God, there is also a new obedience.

[Some say,] "Whoever has died has been justified from sin. Nero has died, therefore he has been justified." I answer that the major premise is said of actual sin. "He has been justified," that is, "he has made satisfaction for his sin." This is a figure taken from everyday speech, as we say when a thief is hanged: "Now he is through sinning."

[Others say,] "There is in man a certain amount of good knowledge, that God is to be obeyed, etc. Therefore, the old man is not wholly to be condemned." I answer that there is this knowledge in man, but his emotions do not obey it. Therefore the distinction between desires and knowledge must be diligently noted. Natural affections are good by nature, but they become evil because they are found in a nature that has been vitiated, and are not directed at the glory of God.

The old man does not signify only a part of man, namely, the senses and the desires of the senses, but also man's reason and will. It is not only the desires that fight with the Law of God, but also man's reason, where there is ignorance of God, doubt whether we are heard, and blasphemies. There are also desires, carnal security, contempt of God, mistrust, love of and trust in present things contrary to the commandment of God, despair, etc. These vices do not belong to man's feelings, but to his higher part. Therefore Paul, describing man without the Holy Spirit in 1 Cor. 2 [:14], says: "The natural man does not perceive the things which are of the Spirit of God."

By contrast the new man is described insofar as he has new light and new impulses excited by the Holy Spirit, namely, knowledge of Christ, trust in God, fear of God, calling on God, love, and similar emotions. Of this newness Paul says in 2 Cor. 3 [:18]: "With unveiled face, beholding the glory of the Lord, we are being changed into his likeness from one degree of glory to another; this is from the Lord who is the Spirit." That is, when mercy is shown us in the Gospel, we are raised up by knowledge and trust in God. We feel that God cares for us, and we call on him. In this knowledge and in these impulses God is acknowledged and shines forth, and we are renewed by a certain image, that is, by the knowledge of God. Newness does not signify the thoughts and movements of reason without the Holy Spirit.

### 12–13. Do not let sin reign

This is the conclusion of the objection which has been raised, which follows from the above argument: because sin has been destroyed on account of the death of Christ, it must not reign or be efficacious.

Dead nature ought not to be efficacious. On account of the death of Christ, sin has been forgiven, so it should at the same time begin to be abolished because of the death of Christ. Since it is abolished, it ought not to be working in us.

However, he says expressly "it should not reign," in order to indicate that the evil nature has not been totally extinguished. There is a remnant of sin in our nature, but it is beginning to be mortified, so it should not reign. Paul himself explains these words: It should not reign in such a way that you obey it, that is, do not obey the evil affections, but fight against them. He also says below [8:13]: "If by the Spirit you put to death the actions of the flesh, you will live."

These and similar passages show the difference between mortal and venial sin. There remain in the saints concupiscence and evil desires; but since they resist these, and in faith seek and declare that these sins are forgiven them, the sins become venial, because when such sins are present, the Holy Spirit and faith can exist at the same time in the godly.

But they become mortal sins in those who have been sanctified when they obey the evil desires contrary to their conscience. As is said below [8:13]: "If you live according to the flesh, you will die." And here: "Do not yield your members as instruments of wickedness." He teaches that when the Holy Spirit is working through the Word of God, urging the godly on, urging us to obey, then we ought not to resist the Spirit, as Paul says elsewhere [2 Cor. 6:1]: "See that you do not receive the grace in vain." He commands us to exercise the gift, and in this exercise the godly go forward according to the admonition [1 Tim. 4:15]: "Practice these things, in order that your progress may be apparent."

Significantly, he says here: "Yield your members, that they may be instruments of righteousness." For he wants to excite and sharpen their fervor. As he says elsewhere [12:11]: "Fervent in spirit," that their members should not be languid, that they may not be idle inasfar as they have impulses of their old nature, but that they may be lively and have sharp impulses. Thus the members of our renewed nature ought not to be languid, but have sharp and true motions for doing good.

And he uses the word *instruments* in order to indicate that in this Christian warfare there must be a very sharp struggle against the devil, the flesh, and every kind of trickery and temptation.

### 14. Sin will not have dominion over you

He is responding to an unspoken objection. For when we hear preaching about obedience, a godly mind at once asks: Since we are not able to satisfy the Law, how will our obedience be found pleasing? Thus here, when Paul said: "Yield your members as instruments of righteousness," the godly are troubled and argue: How can that obedience be pleasing, especially since there is an infinite difference of gifts, since there is great weakness, since our obedience is deformed by many great offences? Here Paul answers: "Sin will not have dominion over you. For you are not under the law, but under grace."

[Some say,] "No obedience pleases except that of the saints. Our obedience is not like the obedience of the saints, so it does not please." I answer: I deny the minor premise. Although our obedience is in fact not as great, by imputation it is similar to it because we believe in Christ. God counts every kind of obedience as perfection of the Law, although there is a difference in gifts. God wants this difference to be there, etc.

This teaching and comfort is necessary for the godly in order that they may know to what extent and in what way the beginning obedience pleases, although it is imperfect, and there is a great difference of gifts, and we are troubled by innumerable offences and terrors. Therefore this statement should be understood as comfort and promise. Sin will not have dominion over you, that is, it does not condemn you, it is not imputed to those who believe in Christ, but the beginning obedience pleases because of grace, that is, because we believe in Christ, although it is imperfect.

In the same sense he says below [8:1]: "There is now no condemnation for those who walk in Christ Jesus." The reason or explanation is added [6:14]: "You are not under the Law, but under grace," that is, under mercy which accepts you on account of Christ according to the promise. Believers are pleasing on account of Christ, although they do not yet in fact satisfy the Law. The Law has no authority to judge and condemn believers. So also he says to the Galatians [3:13]: "Christ has redeemed us from the curse of the Law . . . " That is the simple and genuine meaning of this statement.

Here the meaning of the word *grace* should be prudently observed. For the entire meaning is corrupted and ruined by those who explain: "You are under grace, that is, under the moral law," since the moral law condemns very sternly. But grace is to be understood of imputation, by which believers are righteous, that is, accepted because of Christ. This imputation is proclaimed in the Gospel. Although effects and renewal accompany imputation, the conscience must nevertheless look to the promised imputation and to Christ, the mediator, and not to its own qualities or condition. This statement sets before us a very rich teaching and comfort: "You are not under the Law, but under grace," that is, the Law has no right to condemn believers. Therefore, although obedience is imperfect in believers, it is nevertheless pleasing because the persons are accounted righteous or accepted on account of Christ, the High Priest.

Here mercy must be greatly exalted in order that it may arouse us to doing good. The goodness of God is very great and inexpressible, that God approves of this obedience in believers, even though it has strange weakness and dissimilarity and is contaminated with much filth and offences. Doubt should not weaken or scare off minds. The very greatness of the mercy which approves of all kinds of weak persons, provided only that they believe in Christ, etc., invites us to do good. It is necessary that this teaching and comfort should be found in the church, in order that we may know to what extent and where good works are to be rejected, and to what extent required, and how they may please God.

### 15a. What then? Shall we sin?

Paul inserts a necessary concern. For what he had said before [6:14]: "You are not under the law," seems most absurd, for good natures love nothing more greatly than the Law. Therefore, it is bound to happen that they will be greatly offended by these seemingly imperious words, by which they think the Law is abrogated in such a way that license is given to sin. It has, however, frequently been said elsewhere that this discussion of Paul has absolutely nothing to do with life in the state, that it does not take away discipline or civil morals, but that an entirely different thing is being treated here. Others easily get around this because they refer this liberty only to the abrogation of ceremonies and of the Mosaic state, not to the entire Law.

It has already been said often that Paul is here speaking chiefly about the moral law, and in sum, he wants us to be freed from the whole Law insofar as justification is concerned. A different thing is set forth here, on account of which we have remission of sins and are accounted righteous in the sight of God—the merit of Christ. For we are set free from the Law if we declare that we have remission of sins and are accounted righteous in the sight of God because of Him, not on account of the Law. And joined to this imputation is the renewal of our nature, repentance, or beginning obedience.

The Gospel does not grant license to sin, since it preaches not only about imputation, but also about repentance, and it brings in the new obedience, and shows in which way it is pleasing. Meanwhile the Law remains, as far as discipline and external life are concerned. Likewise, as far as rebuking and mortifying the old nature is concerned, but in such a way that when faith is victorious the Law has no power to condemn. Therefore, I answer simply: The law has been abrogated as far as justification is concerned, but not as far as obedience is concerned. Obedience must be rendered, and indeed is begun. Nevertheless we must know that we are righteous because of Christ, in order that the benefit may remain sure. In my judgment, this response contains nothing perplexing or intricate; however, I leave the judgment about this to the prudent.

## 15b–23. By no means! Do you not know?

Paul dissolves the objection by means of two arguments, both of which are taken from the ultimate purpose or from the effect. Christ appeared in order to abolish sin and death and to restore nature, in order that having been restored, it may have eternal life, which is the new and eternal obedience and wisdom. Since this newness or restoration of nature is the purpose, it is necessary that the new obedience be begun and furnished, because this very spiritual newness is that obedience. And in sum, when the Gospel gives reconciliation on account of Christ, at the same time it subjects us to obedience toward God and begins the obedience. Therefore it is necessary to obey. There is no one who does not see that this is a fitting argument taken from the ultimate purpose. Paul states the same meaning in a syllogism.

Everyone obeys him to whom he has become subject: You are not subjected to sin, but have been freed from sin, and have been transferred into the kingdom of God, and made subject to God. Therefore you ought not to obey sin, but God.

This can be applied also to the formal cause, as if you were to say: "A healthy body has healthy actions," or "A warm body makes warm," so in this proposition: Righteous people have righteous actions; you are righteous, so you also ought to have righteous actions. The minor premise I explain thus: For although we are righteous, that is, accepted by imputation on account of Christ, it is necessary that virtue also be begun in us—righteousness, that is, obedience. Righteousness brings forth virtues, righteous actions. Nevertheless, we must know that we are righteous on account of Christ, our High Priest, that is, accepted by God not on account of the worthiness of our obedience or qualities.

# Chapter 7

## 1–3. Or do you not know, brethren?

The other picture is also taken from the ultimate purpose. We have been reconciled for this: that we may now obey God. There are two parts to the comparison. The first teaches what kind of nature is subjected to the Law. The second part of the comparison speaks about the ultimate purpose, namely, about the new obedience.

The earlier part is this: The Law pertains to the living fleshly nature. However, you are dead, that is, if you are truly in Christ. Therefore the Law does not accuse, does not condemn you. He proves the major premise with a picture: A woman is subjected to her husband as long as her husband lives; so the Law dominates the living.

The later comparison is as follows: As a woman, married to another after her husband has died, ought to cling to him, so we, having been set free from an earlier slavery, now belong to the one who set us free; we owe it to cling to him and to obey him. This is a simple, uncomplicated application.

The first part signifies that the liberation is not just an imaginary thing, but that our nature has died to the old, which formerly was under the Law. Now, since there is a different nature, the power of the Law does not pertain to it as it did to the old, but insofar as we believe, the Law neither accuses nor condemns us. The other part is clearer, namely, the part which speaks about the ultimate purpose: We have become the property of the one who set us free; therefore let us adhere to him and obey him.

## 4. You are dead to the Law through the body of Christ

This is the conclusion, in which Paul applies the above picture in the same sense as he applied it. You are dead to the Law through the body of Christ, that is, you have been set free from the Law, that is, lest the Law condemn and accuse you. And indeed, you have been set free through the body of Christ, that is, through Christ the sacrificial victim, who has satisfied the Law for us, in particular the condemnation and eternal death. Moreover, on account of the death of Christ, our nature is being restored, as I said above [6:4]: "We have been buried through Baptism into death . . . "

## 5. For when we were in the flesh

He attaches an antithesis to the conclusion in order to describe in passing that prior servitude under the Law, and on the other hand, to describe that newness which exists when we have been set free from the Law. The servitude, he says, was such that the Law even increased sin. For when it accuses and terrifies, doubt is kindled, and there follows indignation against God and despair. He is really speaking of sins of this kind here when he says: "The sinful emotions aroused by the Law were working in our members," that is, doubt and anger against God turn the heart away from God, and forbid us to call on him, etc.

In the first place, that very great doubting which clings in the minds of all men certainly works in their members. On account of this doubting, men rush against the will of God with the result that, because they do not trust God, they do many things in fear and distrust against the will of God, seeking wealth, aid, etc. The Law increases this doubt or mistrust because it always accuses. It turns the hearts away from God so that they flee God, do not call on him, do not trust him, and do not seek help from God. These things happen much more and are seen more in the midst of terrors and struggles of the conscience, as in Saul the terrors aroused by the Law were indeed working in his members, and led to anger and raging against God, despair, and death, and prevented him from calling on God.

This topic must be diligently noted in order that we may learn that this doubting is sin, that we may resist it and raise ourselves up by the Gospel, and that we may know that to fight against doubt and distrust in the midst of these terrors is worship of God. But the greater part of mankind lives in this perpetual doubt and distrust. It neither calls upon God, nor does it seek or expect anything from God. Men do not discern these hidden sins. But Christians should understand them in order that they may learn to resist mistrust and to comfort themselves with the Word of the Gospel, so they may comprehend true faith.

Paul uses very meaningful words when he mentions the emotions and says expressly that they are aroused by the Law. He adds that they are active in the members. These are very clear descriptions. We see in Saul how violent is the anger, how burning are the impulses. In individual persons, doubting turns the hearts away from God and holds them captive. These things are not said in an ordinary judgment by Paul, but Paul looks with spiritual eyes on the captivity of human hearts and at the secret mistrust and doubt which afterward brings forth endless sins.

**6b.** What he says afterward belongs to the same subject: "Being dead to the Law by which we were held captive.'' For he points to that captivity by which human hearts, oppressed by doubt, mistrust, and fears, are turned away from God, flee from God, and are not able truly to call on him, neither are they certain that they have been forgiven. But when they have heard the voice of the Gospel, have raised themselves up, and comphrehend true faith, then they begin to acknowledge God and call on him, and they declare that they are forgiven, that they are heard, and they expect good things from God. In this way he speaks about freedom in 2 Cor. 3 [:17]. And here he says that liberation from that captivity comes about in this way: once hearts are set free from mistrust, they truly acknowledge God. Therefore he says: ''That we may serve in newness of spirit.''

### 6a. Now we have been set free from the Law

He has described the servitude under the Law in a few words in the latest conclusion, namely, that the Law holds hearts captive and increases mistrust and doubting, which lead to despair and blasphemy, and turn the hearts away from God, and rush them into various sins.

Then he adds a description of freedom and says first that we are dead to the Law, that is, freed from that captivity, because the Gospel brings forgiveness of sins. One cannot call on God or obey God unless one has first received remission of sins. As long as we are prisoners of the Law and have not yet heard about the remission of sins, and the goodness of God is not yet known to us and hearts do not feel that we are heard, we flee from the wrath of God and are turned away from God. But after the remission of sins has been received through the Gospel and the knowledge of Christ, then obedience begins because now we know the will of God—that he wants to hear us, wants to take pity on us; then we call on him. This is why he says here that obedience is begun when we are set free from the Law through faith, that is, when in Christ we now acknowledge the will and the goodness of God. This statement teaches clearly that without faith and outside of faith in Christ, no works please God, nor are they righteousness or obedience in the sight of God, or worship of God, as he says above [5:2]: ''Through whom we have access to God.''

He distinguishes the new obedience from the fleshly. He calls the new spiritual, the other he calls the oldness of the letter. It was said above that the letter signifies all thoughts, attempts, good intentions, and works which reason does without true fear of God, without true trust in Christ, and without the Holy Spirit. Thus Saul has good intentions—good purposes—because he wants to serve God. Likewise, he sacrifices, and meanwhile he has neither fear nor true faith. Contrition, when there is no true grief but artificial sadness, is the letter. It is called the letter because it is not a true and living movement of the mind, but is an idle imitation either within or without. Neither can there be true invocation if the heart does not lay hold of the remission of sins.

The Spirit, on the other hand, signifies true spiritual impulses, namely, true fear of God and true trust, which are conceived in true comfort when hearts raise themselves up in the midst of terrors by the promise of the Gospel and lay hold of the mercy promised because of Christ. When they acknowledge the mercy, they begin truly to call on God, and truly to expect help from him, truly to love, etc. These impulses are true acts of worship, and are the new obedience of which he speaks here. These are aroused by the Holy Spirit, who is received in that consolation when we are raised up by faith. As Paul says in Gal. 3 [:14]: "That we may receive the promise of the Spirit through faith." Spirit and letter are distinguished. The Spirit signifies the impulses excited by the Holy Spirit, while the letter signifies the thoughts, intentions, purposes, and imitations without true movement of the heart; nevertheless, the letter pertains to discipline.

He uses the phrase "Let us serve" not because the new obedience is a servitude like the righteousness of the Law, but in order to teach that the new creature is subjected to God and ordered to obedience, although that obedience is voluntary. As he says to the Ephesians [2:10]: "We are his workmanship, created in Christ Jesus for good works which God ordained, that we should walk in them." And Is. 61 [:3]: "They shall be called righteous trees and little plants for glorifying," that is, that they may glorify God, not that they should bring shame on God through offenses.

### 7–13. What shall we say therefore?

Having completed his digression, he returns to the comparison which he began above between the Law and grace. And most of all he speaks here about the use of the Law, in order that he may correct two opinions which persist not only in Jews, but universally in the minds of all. For all imagine that the righteousness of the Law which man is able to offer satisfies the Law and is righteousness in the sight of God. People do not see sin and the corruption of nature, nor do they see that the discipline which they offer as best they can through the Law, does not satisfy the Law, nor is it righteousness in the sight of God. Although it was the Jews who most of all defended these opinions about the Law, they are nevertheless common to all. But they are refuted by the Gospel, which teaches that the Law is not only an external discipline, and that people are not righteous by means of the Law. Therefore it is necessary that the apostles speak about this matter. Neither is Paul here quarreling only about ceremonies, but he is speaking about the whole Law, and chiefly about the Decalogue, since he cites an example from the Decalogue and argues that no one satisfies the Law, and that all are accused by the Law, and that for this reason the Law is a ministry of wrath and of death

It is necessary that this be taught in the church in order that the benefit of Christ may become clear, and that the need of the Gospel, and the need of grace and righteousness other than the righteousness of the Law, may be understood. Because we are not justified by the Law, God gave his Son for us. God reveals the Gospel—that he wants to forgive us *gratis* on account of his Son, pronounce us righteous, and renew us.

I have said these things by way of preface to this topic in order that students may consider more diligently why these things are being discussed by Paul, to what they pertain, and how necessary they are. For they explain what kind of sin inheres in our nature, and what corruption of nature. Likewise, they explain that the Law requires not only outward civil duties, but perfect obedience, they explain how much the Law accomplishes, and that there is need of another Word and the benefit of Christ. Likewise, they are useful so that the distinction of Law and Gospel may be correctly and truly understood. It is essential that the knowledge of these topics be found in the church.

This part of the Pauline epistle must be pondered in a particularly careful manner, because the ancients also sweated greatly in explaining these things, and few of them treated them skillfully and correctly. They did not see that Paul was speaking about a struggle of the conscience, but thought that he was speaking about the civil use of the Law, so they invented many foolish interpretations which did not pertain to the matter. It is of great importance to the church that the true meaning of this passage be retained. If this is overthrown, it cannot be satisfactorily understood what and how great original sin is, what the difference between Law and Gospel is, what grace is, and what the righteousness of faith is.

Now I come to the text. This, in sum, is the meaning: We are not righteous by the Law, because the corruption of our nature is such that no one can satisfy the Law. Therefore, the Law always accuses. And when hearts feel this judgment and wrath of God, they become terrified and are driven to despair and eternal death. Thus the Law is a ministry of wrath and death, and it increases it not outwardly but inwardly, that is, it arms sin so that it terrifies and kills us. As he says to the Corinthians [1 Cor. 15:56]: "The sting of death is sin; however, the power of sin is the Law." And Paul, as a diligent teacher, adds an example from his own experience.

To begin with, he sets forth a correction: The Law is not a ministry of death because of a defect in the Law, but because of our sin, since our corrupt nature is not able to satisfy the Law. Therefore, the Law accuses us. He gives an example from the commandment [Ex. 20:17; Deut. 5:21]: "You shall not covet," in order to remind us that the Law does not rebuke only external civil transgressions, but also the corruption of our nature. He uses these words: "Sin, taking occasion," that is, sin recognized through the Law, "riled up lust," that is, it made me afraid, and in the midst of these terrors it arouses doubting, mistrust, and anger against God, so that the heart flees from God and is angry at the judgment of God.

"Without Law, sin is dead," that is, if the Law did not accuse us, there would not be those terrors and the confusion of the conscience. "At one time I lived without Law," that is, when I was a carnally secure Pharisee, I thought that I was satisfying the Law, that I was righteous. He calls this living without Law, not hearing the Law which shows sin and rebukes it, not being influenced by that rebuke, not feeling grief.

Therefore, people fall in three categories. One is the carnal who live secure, either as the Epicureans or as the Pharisees, and who do not have true fears of conscience. This is to live without Law, namely, the Law judging and accusing, etc. The Law does not have its chief effect in them: to show and rebuke sin. For the Law is truly Law when it judges and accuses, not when it is written on the walls.

The second category is those who are oppressed by fears and torments of conscience, such as Judas or Saul. Because these do not hear the voice of the Gospel, they succumb to these terrors and think they are damned. Therefore, he says here: "When the Law came, sin revived," that is, it began to work and to frighten, "and I died." If Paul had not heard the voice of the Gospel, he also would have perished in such terrors.

The third category consists of those who are raised up in the midst of their terrors by the voice of the Gospel, as he says above [5:1]: "Having been justified by faith we have peace, . . . ."

When these three categories have been considered, Paul's text can be understood more easily. What he says: "Without Law sin is dead. At one time I lived without Law," belongs in the first category because in carnally secure and idle Epicureans or Pharisees there are no terrors; there is no knowledge of sin. In such persons sin is dead, that is, it does not terrify, it does not oppress them with terrors and with the sense that they are damned, because they do not feel that they are being accused by the Law.

Those who are in true terrors belong in the second category, such as those frequently described in the Psalms, as in Ps. 38 [:3]: "There is no health in my flesh in the face of my sins." And Isaiah [38:13] says: "Like a lion he has broken all my bones." In this sense he says [Rom. 7.9]. "When the Law came, sin revived," that is, it was working and inflicting terrors and a feeling of damnation.

Those who are raised up in the midst of their terrors belong in the third category. This struggle remains in the godly: faith fights against fears. Paul sets forth his own example so he may teach the entire church about this struggle.

Some imagine that Paul is not speaking about himself but about some ungodly person. This imagination can be openly refuted through examples in the Psalms. For if we grant that David speaks in the same way about himself, why may we not grant the same about Paul? And the example of both has been set forth in order to testify that things happen and are done in this way in other pious persons. In the end Paul repeats the correction when he says the Law itself is not bad, but our sin, which the Law attacks and accuses, is the cause of the terrors and of damnation [cf. v. 12].

This short phrase must be diligently noted [v. 13]: "In order that sin may become exceedingly sinful." This is the meaning: The greatness of sin is not discerned by the idle and the carnally secure, so that while David's mind was idle he did not see what a dreadful thing sin is. Because a secure mind does not think that God is truly angry at sin, and since it does not feel the wrath of God, it does not see the most important thing about sin, namely, guilt, that is, that God is truly angry at sin. But when hearts are terrified, they truly declare that God is angry, and they see the real and chief thing about sin, namely, guilt and the wrath of God. Then it is truly seen to be sin, and it becomes exceedingly harmful, vicious, or guilty, and brings on damnation.

### 14. The Law is spiritual

He does away with an unspoken objection. It could have been objected: "What about those who are obeying the Law, such as hypocrites, whose life is full of guilt, and also saints, like Isaiah, John the Baptizer, etc?" The question is whether they are righteous by the Law. Does not the Law give them the benefit of life, that is, the remission of sins and vivification? Here Paul responds: "Rather" he says, "the Law is spiritual, but I am carnal," as if he said: "Neither I nor anyone else satisfies the Law, because the Law is spiritual and requires spiritual and perfect obedience which carnal nature cannot render."

What he calls spiritual must be diligently noted. He opposes it to civil or external discipline, which is called carnal discipline and righteousness, as if he said "the Law is not a mere civil doctrine, that is, one which outward discipline could satisfy. It demands spiritual obedience, that is, spiritual impulses, clear knowledge of God, fear, trust, love of God, and other ardent pious impulses without concupiscence. However, because the heart of man is not like that, the Law is a ministry that condemns sin and truly terrifies hearts."

The interpretation of Origen is foreign to the statement of Paul, as is the interpretation of similar people who think that spiritual means the same thing as allegorical. They understand the whole Law to be only a doctrine about external morals, and think that it is possible to satisfy the Law. But let us hold to the opposite, that spiritual is the opposite of outward discipline, which is carnal righteousness—not spiritual—because spiritual denotes impulses that deal with God. Therefore, this antithesis adds much light when we interpret "The Law is spiritual," that is, the Law is not only civil, but demanding spiritual and perfect obedience. And its ministry is not just external, but one by which God judges and condemns sins and terrifies hearts. Furthermore, although human reason understands the Law only of civil morals, the Gospel, by preaching repentance, takes away the veil of Moses from human hearts, that is, the false opinion about the Law, and argues that the righteousness of the Law, that is, outward righteousness, does not satisfy the Law. And it testifies that the Law demands perfect obedience, etc.

Thereafter Paul explains what he has set forth: "The Law is spiritual, but I am carnal," since he recalls that he does not satisfy the Law, but has in his flesh impulses that fight against the Law of God. He also adds a clarification about what he means by the words "I am carnal"—because he adds these words: "Sold under sin." By these words he indicates that nature does not have spiritual obedience, but is evil and a slave or captive of sin, that is, it is corrupted. This entire topic explains what this corruption of nature is like, and that original sin is not merely imputation, but in reality a corruption in nature. It is necessary that this be taught in the church in order that we may acknowledge our sin, and that the greatness of the benefit of Christ may be known. These words, "I am sold under sin," must be diligently weighed in order that the greatness of the sin and the slavery may be understood, namely, that our nature has truly been corrupted and made evil.

Some mock these things and imagine that Paul is here speaking not about his own person, not about the converted and holy, but about the ungodly. This sophistry must be rejected. David is speaking about himself and about all saints when he says [Ps. 143:2]: "In your sight no man living shall be justified," and when he says [Ps. 51:5]: "Behold, I was conceived in iniquity." Thus Paul is speaking about himself, and he includes all saints by his example. Since this interpretation of Paul has firm and clear testimonies in the Psalms, it is certain that foreign interpretations should not be invented.

Carnal nature signifies the nature of man which does not itself understand or seek spiritual things. It has doubts about God, is devoid of the fear of God, is carnally secure, and either despises or is angry at the judgment of God. It seeks the things of the flesh, pleasures, wealth, and glory, not trusting in the help of God which it does not know but in present things, such as the powers of wisdom or righteousness. Such is human nature without the Holy Spirit.

But when a person is renewed by faith through the Holy Spirit, spiritual newness begins to fight against the fleshly corruption which still remains while we live in this mortal body.

### 15a. I do not approve of what I do

Paul then describes this strife: "What I do, I do not know," that is, I do not approve of it. It is as if he said: "I feel that my nature is fighting against the Law of God, that I do not have ardent emotions of fear, faith, and love of God. Likewise, in afflictions my nature fights against the will of God, desires to cast off afflictions, and seeks physical aids." Doubts about God often rush into the mind. Paul refers to such inner motions when he says: "I do not approve what I do," that is, the spiritual newness in me fights against these evil impulses and disapproves of that kind of life.

### 15b–23. I do not do the good which I want

He then describes this battle with many words: "I do not do the good which I want," that is, "although I have a beginning of fear, it is hindered by natural security so that it is not as great as it ought to be. Although I have a beginning of faith, it is hindered by natural doubting so that it is not sufficiently firm. Although I have a beginning of love, it is hindered by concupiscence so that it does not burn sufficiently brightly."

He is not speaking about small affections and temptations but about very severe impulses. He uses powerful words—war service and captivity—to indicate that the impulses are vehement, like those we experience in calamities or in death. How difficult it is to obey! Our whole nature rages, is angry, and resists. Likewise, natural doubting and the sight of sin terrify in such a way that even the godly are oppressed and about to despair as David frequently complains. This captivity is clearly seen in impatience and fears. But the carnally secure and ungodly do not discern these inner sins, so they minimize original sin and concupiscence.

Let us hold fast to this topic and oppose it to false opinions about the Law and sin. From this we learn that fulfillment of the Law is not mere outward discipline. Original sin is in fact a certain corruption in the nature of man which is condemned by the Law of God. Also concupiscence in the saints is sin by its very nature but it is forgiven to the godly. Likewise, not even the saints satisfy the Law of God. The saints always need the forgiveness of sins. Our fulfillment of the Law, our love, and our works are not good enough for us to be righteous because of them, that is, accepted; neither are they worthy of eternal life. But we receive remission of sins by faith because of Christ, the mediator, and life eternal by imputation of righteousness.

This chapter contains rich teaching about sin, the Law, and the remnants of sin in the saints. Let us remind ourselves diligently how this chapter should be used, because it refutes many false and carnal opinions about sin and the Law.

Furthermore, we must refute the false imagination of those who say that Paul is assuming the artificial guise of an ungodly person here. They deny that the struggle which is described here fits the person who is converted and sanctified, as though in the sanctified there were no remnants of sin, or that nature had been wholly renewed and there are no evil impulses.

This imagination can easily be refuted by the consensus of the Scriptures. For also in Galatians this struggle in the saints is described in a similar manner when he says [Gal. 5:17]: "The spirit lusts against the flesh, the flesh against the spirit." Frequently in the Psalms, David, who was converted and sanctified, complains about his present sin, as in the Psalm [130:1]: "Out of the depths . . ." and Ps. 19[:12]: "Who understands his transgressions? Cleanse me from my secret ones." Also Ps. 143[:2]: "Enter not into judgment with your servant, for in your sight no man living will be justified." And Ps. 33[32:6]: "For this will every saint pray to you, . . . " These testimonies of the Psalms agree completely with this passage of Paul, and teach the same thing which Paul discusses here: no one satisfies the Law, remnants of sin remain in the saints, but the saints are righteous, that is, accepted through mercy, believing that their sins are remitted for Christ's sake. In the Psalms, by the example of David, all the converted and saints in the church are described. So also here Paul is speaking of himself as a converted, sanctified person, and by means of his example he describes all the saints in the church.

The very words show this when he says [7:22]: "I delight in the Law of God." Likewise: "With my mind I serve the Law of God" [8:25]. Likewise: "To will is present with me" [7:18]. For although there is some knowledge of the Law in the ungodly, that is not the same as to will or to delight in the Law of God, of which he is speaking here. For these words must not be coldly understood: "I delight in the Law of God; to will is present with me," etc. Paul testifies here that he has a beginning obedience, to acknowledge God, to trust God, not to remain in doubt, but to be raised up by faith. Likewise, to obey God willingly in afflictions. This is what the words "I delight in the Law of God" signify; these things are certainly not found in the ungodly.

The reader should also be reminded of the distinction between the inner and the outer man, about the mind and about the flesh. The inner man signifies a person insofar as he has been renewed by the Holy Spirit, that is, insofar as he has true fear and true trust. Here the mind does not signify only the part which knows, but both parts: knowing and laying hold of, as far as it has been renewed by the Holy Spirit, as he says: ''With my mind I serve the Law of God'' [7.23].

By contrast, the outer man or the flesh signifies the entire man insofar as he has not been renewed by the Holy Spirit. They signify not only the appetites of the senses or the external members, but also the higher powers, reason and will, insofar as they have not been renewed, as will have to be said again below.

When he says [7:24]: ''Miserable man that I am, who will deliver me from the body of this death?'' these are not the words of a godless or carnally secure person, but of one who is converted, who is engaged in this struggle which goes with repentance. Therefore, let us place this passage among the examples of repentance, and let us learn that such is the never-ending repentance of the godly, namely, to acknowledge our wretched state with immense grief, that is, to be shocked, as we see in some measure the sickness of our nature, because pious impulses are not ardent in us. Fear, faith, and love are cold. Meanwhile, fleshly cares and affections show up strongly, and a great part of life is directed to fleshly plans. The glory of God is not being sought with a total attack. The godly ought to see these faults. They should repent in order that we may exclaim with Paul: ''Who will deliver us from the body of this death?''

### 24–25. Who[1] will deliver me?

The form of the speech should be noted. He does not say: ''Who will deliver me from this death,'' but ''from the body.'' For he is not speaking only of the punishment, but of the sin. And he testifies that the body itself, that is, this carnal nature, is immersed in sin and death. For when he calls it a body of death, he understands nature immersed in sin and subjected to death because of sin, that is, subjected to the wrath of God, to punishments, to terrors, to eternal death, etc. As is said in Ps. 28[:3]: ''On account of his iniquity you have carried a man away.''

---

[1] The text of *CR* has *Quia liberabit me.* The entire context suggests that *quia* is a misprint for *Quis.* Our 1540 edition has *Quia liberavit me.*

# Chapter 8

Until now he has spoken about sin and the Law. Now he returns to the description of grace. One might ask: If there is still sin in the regenerate, how can they be righteous? How are they saved? Here he answers and explains the richness of grace. It was said above that grace signifies gratuitous acceptance, which he here describes negatively.

### 1. There is now no condemnation for those who walk in Christ Jesus

The justified please God on account of Christ, although sin still clings to them, namely, concupiscence and evil affections. He does not say that there is no sin in the pious, but no condemnation. That is the chief proposition in this topic about grace, and this teaching is genuinely needed in the church, namely, that the regenerate are righteous, not on account of their fulfillment of the Law or their own worthiness, but by faith, on account of Christ, that is, accepted, although sin still clings them, that is, concupiscence.

In the proposition he adds: "who walk according to the Spirit." This has been added for two reasons: The first is to show that faith is not a human cogitation, but a work of the Holy Spirit. The other reason is that we may know that this faith is not found in those who walk according to the flesh, that is, who are without repentance and who rush into sins against the conscience. For in these, because they delight in sin, there is neither contrition nor remission of sins.

Paul teaches in what way the justified may be pleasing, namely, not because they satisfy the Law, but because they believe in Christ. He also teaches that this faith is a work of the Holy Spirit and is not found in those who walk according to the flesh, that is, who are without repentance and indulge in carnal affections against the conscience.

**2.** Then he adds the reason or explanation of the proposition: "For the law of the Spirit of life . . . " That is: I am justified because by faith, by which I have laid hold of Christ, I have been set free from the terrors of sin and death. And this liberation is vivification, that is, the beginning of a new and eternal life.

"The law of the Spirit of life . . . " Therefore the law justifies. The law signifies the teaching [Deut. 6:5]: "You shall love the Lord your God

. . . '' He adds the response: "The law of the Spirit," so he understands the Spirit which governs, that is, that governance, a spiritual impulse, which gives life through apprehending Christ; that impulse is the Spirit.

Here the words must be diligently considered. For in these words "the law of the Spirit of life," the term *law* does not mean the doctrine of the Law. For he says: "The law of the Spirit," that is, the Spirit which governs, or motivates, or makes alive. This is a figure of speech: "The law of the Spirit," that is, the governance or motivation of the Spirit.

So that the faith which apprehends Christ may be clearly understood, and not be understood as some work of the Law, Paul himself adds: "The law of the Spirit of life in Christ Jesus." Therefore he wants us to be vivified by faith and knowledge of Christ and be set free from sin and death, as though he said: "Not because of fulfillment of the Law, but because you have apprehended Christ."

Therefore he makes a contrast. He sets faith and knowledge of Christ over against that which is properly called Law, as if he said: "Faith and the knowledge of Christ takes away the Law which accuses and condemns." Thus he says later [8:2]: "He has set me free from the Law of sin and death." Therefore, the sum and substance of his statement is that for the justified there is no condemnation, not because they have fulfilled the Law, but because they have been made alive by faith in Christ and set free from the curse of the Law and from damnation.

### 3a. Because it was impossible for the Law

There follows the reason, in which the contrast between the Law and the benefit of Christ is again set forth. First, however, consider the grammatical connection and construct a sentence in the following manner: since it was impossible for the Law to take away sin, and because the Law could not be kept by the flesh, God sent his Son in the likeness of sinful flesh, and through sin condemned sin in the flesh, in order that the requirement of the Law might be fulfilled. This entire statement is instructive, and contains the foremost testimonies about the Law, works, and justification or the merit of Christ. First of all, it says clearly that the Law is not done or fulfilled by this corrupt nature. It teaches also that our works do not take away sin or set us free from sin and death. Therefore, the imagination of our adversaries is false. They suppose that people earn forgiveness of sins by their own works, or that people are righteous by their own fulfillment of the Law.

These things are taught in the first part of the sentence: "Since it was not possible for the Law to take away sin." Likewise, when he says later: "Because it was made weak through sin," that is, it could not be done by this corrupt nature.

### 3b. God sent his Son in the likeness of sinful flesh

There is great emphasis on these words: "He sent His Son in the likeness of sinful flesh." Likewise: "On account of sin He condemned sin." For he understands that Christ was sent in this way in order that he might be subjected to the punishments of sin, to pains, anguish, and death, as he says in Phil. 2[:7]: "Being made in the likeness of men, and found in fashion like a man." And afterward he calls Christ "sin" when he says: "Through sin," namely, Christ, he condemned, that is, he took away or made sin and damnation in men void. After Christ himself was made the sacrificial victim that made satisfaction for us, we are freed from sin and punishment, etc.

First the phrase must be noted. He says that Christ was made sin, or the sacrifice for sin. For here in "on account of sin," the word *sin* after the Hebraic manner signifies the sacrificial victim for sin, that is, the penalty or satisfaction for sin, or as the Latins say, the propitiatory sacrifice, and the Greeks κάθαρμα (that which is thrown away in cleansing). It means the same thing in the words *curse* and *anathema*, which signify things destined for making satisfaction, for placating the wrath of God. Thus Isaiah [53:10] says of Christ: "Because he will make his soul sin," that is, a sacrifice for sin. For this reason Paul so often inculcates, as in 2 Cor. 5[:21]: "Him who did not know sin he made sin for us," that is, he was made the sacrificial victim, who should bear the punishment of sin and make satisfaction for our sins. And to the Galatians [3:13] he says likewise that Christ was made a curse, that is, a propitiatory sacrifice, bearing the curse and wrath of God against sin.

Second, one ought also consider how great the humiliation of Christ is. For since he suffered for the sins of all, he bore the wrath of God and the true terrors against sins in our stead as the lowest and most abject of all sinners, as Isaiah [53:6] says: "The Lord laid on him the iniquities of us all."

We ought to think of these things in order that fear and faith may be aroused, and that we may not think that these things were done in vain, but should consider the greatness of the wrath of God against sin. And again let us raise up our faith when we consider what kind of sacrificial victim this was, how he was humiliated, how dreadfully angry God is at sin, since he wanted his Son to become such a sacrificial victim. And again, how great a pledge of mercy we have because that victim took the wrath on himself, etc.

These things are set before us also in the words: "Behold the Lamb of God, which takes away the sins of the world" [John 1:29]. He is called the Lamb because he is the sacrificial victim. And the sacrifices from the very beginning of the world signified that such a sacrificial victim would come who would die for the sins of the human race. In the text we read περὶ ἁμαρτίας which can be rendered "because of sin", that is, on account of the sacrificial victim, or for this sacrificial victim. The picture has been taken from the book of Leviticus, where the Greeks rendered sacrifice for sin with this formula, περὶ ἁμαρτίας. Therefore you could interpret: He condemned sin in the flesh, that is, the sins of men: On account of sin, that is, on account of the sacrificial victim which was delivered, or for sin, that is, for the sacrificial victim who was delivered.

Also the histories and the ancient rites help somewhat for understanding the force of the words. The word καθάρματα was used for those those who were polluted with the most atrocious misdeeds, whom both God and men cursed, and on account of whom the nature of things appeared to be polluted, and that God would punish others, such as Atreus, who gave his brother his children to eat; Nero; and similar monsters. Such are blasphemers, idolaters, heretics, tyrants, incestuous persons, and parricides. As a certain man in a tragedy says: "Go away from me, lest your shadow harm the good people."

### 3c. He condemned sin in the flesh

The language is Hebraic: "He condemned sin," instead of "he punished," that is, he abolished and destroyed it so it should now be void, or that it simply should not be left. It is a different way of speaking if you say that sin had formerly been condemned by the Law, for then *condemn* does not mean "to take away sin," but "to declare guilty the sin which remains," with both the guilt and the wrath remaining. But in this passage, Paul says that sin was condemned on account of Christ, who is the sacrifice. To condemn signifies to take away or to extinguish sin, and to take away the guilt and the wrath.

This dissimilarity in language should be noted. This is the meaning: On account of Christ sin has been abolished in the flesh, that is, in the nature of men. And this should be understood in a twofold way: First, by imputation, because sin has been remitted and is not imputed to us who believe. The sin that still clings to our nature has therefore been abolished, that is, made powerless so that it cannot accuse and condemn those who believe. Second, it has been abolished so that it now really begins to be extinguished. Spiritual newness is begun which will be consummated when in the resurrection we are clothed with the new nature and with righteousness without sin.

**4.** Here belongs also what is said afterward: "That the requirement of the Law might be fulfilled in us," that is, that we may have perfectly what the Law requires, that is, that we may be accounted righteous. It should first be understood about imputation that the Law is fulfilled in us by faith on account of Christ, namely by imputation. We are accounted righteous by faith on account of Christ, just as if we were satisfying the Law, in spite of the fact that sin still clings to us and we are a long way from fulfilling the Law. In the second place, it should be understood of the effect, namely, that newness is begun because the Holy Spirit has been given to us. This newness will be perfected, righteousness and obedience will be made complete, and the Law will be fulfilled when this infirmity of the flesh will have been completely destroyed and we are clothed with entire spiritual newness, which is complete righteousness and obedience without sin.

The reader should know that this reasoning must be applied to the proposition which the apostle set up [Rom. 8:1]: "There is now no condemnation for those who are in Christ. . . . " To confirm the proposition he adds the following, the sum and substance of which is this: Believers are righteous, that is, accepted because of Christ, although they do not satisfy the Law. The reason is because Christ was made the sacrificial victim for us, so the Law now no longer accuses believers. We are righteous through faith because of Christ, just as if we were satisfying the Law. As he says in Galatians[3:13]: "Christ has set us free from the curse of the Law, having been made a curse for us." This is the sum and substance of the application.

The use must also be considered, for it contains a twofold teaching, as I mentioned above. It comforts the godly so that they know how they may please God. Again, it also humbles the proud so we may be reminded that we have sin and are not satisfying the law. Therefore the opinions of our adversaries about earned merit, about perfection, etc., must be repudiated. It is necessary to remind people of these things about the application and its use. For unless it is used, the greatness of this benefit cannot be understood.

Moreover, there is added in the text [Some Greek manuscripts of Rom. 8:1 add]: "To those who do not walk according to the flesh, but according to the Spirit." This, as I have said above, testifies that the Holy Spirit is given. Likewise, that those persons who are without repentance and do not fight against fleshly lusts do not retain the righteousness which was given them.

### 5. For those who live according to the flesh set their minds on the things of the flesh

An antithesis is set up in order that human righteousness may be distinguished from that which is spiritual and eternal, about which the Gospel speaks. The chief argument here is about the meaning of the term *flesh*. For some have imagined that the flesh means only the desires of the senses. Thereafter they imagine that reason and will are able to obey the Law of God and to bring about love of God, faith, and similar impulses, even without the Holy Spirit. And by *spirit* they understand the thoughts and undertakings of reason and will without the Holy Spirit. Thus they transform the Gospel into philosophy.

This perversion of the Pauline statement must be widely repudiated. On the contrary, it must be stated that *flesh*[1] truly and properly signifies the total nature of man, the desires of the senses and both reason and will without the Holy Spirit. And, by way of contrast, *spirit* signifies the Holy Spirit, or the impulses that arise from the Holy Spirit within us.

Therefore, to be according to the flesh signifies to be without the Holy Spirit. And to set the mind on the things of the flesh signifies that one's thinking or rational judgment and the affections of sense and will are such as are without the Holy Spirit: to think about and seek pleasures, riches, tranquility, and glory. And this is the highest step, to understand civil righteousness, both to regard it very highly and to seek it, while at the same time the heart is without fear of God, full of doubt about and ignorance of God. To set the mind on the things of the Spirit, on the contrary, is to judge spiritually, that is, to have spiritual impulses, that is, light by which God is acknowledged, and genuine fears, and true confidence which fights against doubt.

### 6a. The sense of the flesh is death

Here *sensus* [translated here as "sense"] signifies thinking and the desires of the senses and of the will. For Paul includes speech and the passions, and speaks about thinking and desire as seen by God. Therefore the meaning is that human righteousness, philosophy, the laws of states, yes, even the Law of God, as reason, without faith and without the Holy Spirit, considers it and tries to do it, are death, that is, things which do not make alive in the sight of God. Rather, when the impulses of reason deal with God without faith, they also are sins. Therefore they truly are death, that is, things which are condemned.

From this it does not follow that philosophy or laws are bad. However, philosophy and laws serve bodily life, and they are good things when we use them in their proper place. Nevertheless, they do not make alive in the judgment of God, neither do they vivify with life eternal. Rather, even the Law of God does not vivify with eternal life, and it is not even sufficiently understood without the Holy Spirit.

---

[1] Our 1540 edition inserts the following paragraph in the middle of the hyphenated word *flesh*. The paragraph appears to relate to Melanchthon's explanation of Rom. 8:6a below.

λόγον: when he divides reason and desire, they understand the will as repeatedly submitting to reason and intellect, affecting desires in so far as they are not ruled by reason. The organ of the body where desire resides is the heart. The heart is an organ totally at the service of the appetite of the senses. A lively appetite does not pertain to this."

### 6b. The sense of the Spirit is life and peace

True comfort, which comes into being through the Holy Spirit, is an impulse by which God is truly acknowledged, apprehended, and invoked, and new light, knowledge, life and joy of conscience are received. As he says below [8:15]: "You have received the spirit of the adoption of sons by which we cry, 'Abba Father,' " that is, by which we truly acknowledge God. And these impulses are liberation from eternal death, and the beginning of eternal life, as Christ says in John 17[:3]: "This is life eternal, that they know you as true God, and Jesus Christ, whom you have sent." Such impulses are not found in persons who are without faith and without the Holy Spirit. Paul instituted this comparison in order to show the difference between spiritual and carnal righteousness. Then follows the reason, which explains what kind of impulses are in the nature of a person who is without faith and without the Holy Spirit.

### 7. To be carnally minded is enmity against God

This passage completely refutes the Pelagians and all who imagine that people without the Holy Spirit obey the Law of God, in fact, even satisfy the Law. But this error arises from the fact that they think that only outward discipline is required by the Law of God. This imagination leads them away from the right path.

One must know that the Law of God requires inner obedience, and indeed perfect and complete obedience. Paul is speaking here of inner faults, of the original sickness, of ignorance of God, of constant doubting, of concupiscence. A carnally secure mind that is without the Holy Spirit does not see the wrath and judgment of God. This doubting and carnal security is contempt for God. Again, a mind that is terrified—as in Saul and Judas, where there are terrors without faith and without the comfort of the Holy Spirit—flees from the wrath and judgment of God, and conceives a dreadful rage and anger against God.

Paul is here accusing not only inordinate desires of the flesh—such as lusts and other well-known vices, hatreds, greed and similar things—but even much more the sources of these evils, namely, ignorance of God, doubting, contempt, and anger against God. Finally, he embraces all impulses which fight against the Law of God when he says: "To be carnally minded is enmity against God." Paul uses a harsh word in order that the reader may consider the infirmity of human nature to be much greater than human reason can sufficiently see and judge it to be.

### 8–9. For those who are in the flesh are not able to please God

This antithesis should be diligently noted because it shows clearly what it is that Paul calls *flesh* and *spirit*. Because he says "the Spirit of God" and "the Spirit of Christ," it is quite certain that he is speaking of God the Holy Spirit. On the other hand, *flesh* should be understood of whatever is in man without the Holy Spirit, namely, not only the desires of the senses, but also reason and will without the Holy Spirit. This passage should be noted in order that we may have a testimony about the meaning of these terms.

This clearly refutes the Pelagians and similar errorists who imagine that persons without the Holy Spirit are righteous. Likewise, the scholastics said that remission of sins is merited without the Holy Spirit. Here consciences may be instructed in order that they may learn that the impulses of the Holy Spirit are brought about through the Word, and that the Holy Spirit accompanies the Word. Spiritual impulses come about when in the midst of true terrors we again comfort ourselves with the word of the Gospel, as the text says [Rom. 10:17]: "Faith comes by hearing." Likewise he says to the Galatians [3:14]: "In order that the promise of the Spirit may be given through faith."

### 10a. If Christ is in you

What he says: "If Christ is in you," must be understood through the Holy Spirit, as he says later [8:11]: "His Spirit, which raised Jesus . . . dwells in you."

### 10b–11. The body indeed is dead because of sin

This statement explains why there are in the saints remaining afflictions and death. For it could be objected that if believers are righteous children of God, and heirs of eternal life, why are they still burdened with death and other ills? In fact, no other kind of people suffers more calamities than the godly because the devil and the world practice dreadful savagery against them. For what reason? Paul answers: Because there is still sin left over in the flesh.

Although calamities and death are simply punishments of sin in the ungodly, in the saints they are exercises in which the spiritual newness ought to grow. Through death, when sin has been wholly cast out, we are clothed with the new nature. This distinction should be diligently noted: in the ungodly afflictions are simply punishments, but in the saints they are exercises and the way in which corrupt and unclean flesh is destroyed. So let this passage be understood in this way: The body is dead, that is, it has been mortified on account of sin, namely, present sin, which still clings to the flesh of the saints and must be destroyed by this death in order that we may be clothed with the renewed flesh.

Here disputes about satisfactions are added—whether after the guilt is remitted God imposes other penalties which are to be compensation for eternal death, as the office of the keys does. I answer briefly: The power of the keys does not have a command to impose penalties.

Second, although God does at times impose penalties, as on David after his adultery, this is not made into a universal rule. We certainly should not believe that no sin is forgiven without a penalty, because the promises so often teach that also the penalties are forgiven us. This also applies to the assertion that when God imposes bodily punishments on some persons, such as sicknesses, wars, and other calamities, they can not be forgiven by the power of the keys.

Moreover, special afflictions are imposed on saints, as Isaiah was sawn in two, Jeremiah stoned, John the Baptizer beheaded, etc. These afflictions are not punishments for particular sins, but extraordinary works in which God wants to show his glory. As also the prophet says: Also the innocent will drink the cup, etc. [cf. Is. 51:17; Mt. 20:23]. Here belongs also the argument of Job, who denies that he is being afflicted because of sins. For he teaches the godly both that they are not rejected because they are afflicted, and that afflictions are imposed also by another counsel of God—they are not always punishments for particular sins.

From this it is clear that no rule must be made that afflictions are satisfactions or punishments for particular sins. As afflictions are not always punishments, so sins are frequently forgiven without special penalties, as God promises in the Scripture that he will lessen the calamities for those who repent. Also Paul says: "If we would judge ourselves, we would not be judged by the Lord" [1 Cor. 11:31].

Finally, we must know also this: although punishments or exercises are imposed, they are not compensations for eternal death because only the death of Christ is satisfaction and compensation for eternal death. As it is written: "Because he will lay down his life for sin" [Is. 53:12]. Likewise: "O Death, I will be your death . . . " [cf. Is. 25:8; 1 Cor. 15:55]. Therefore the opinion of our adversaries about satisfactions must be rejected.

As for the rest, it is useful that both should be inculcated in the churches—both that God punishes sins, also with bodily punishments, and that he lessens penalties or alters them on account of repentance. The godly should also be taught to know that afflictions are not signs of wrath. Even if they could be punishments, they are not always punishments, but exercises or individual works in which God wants us to acknowledge our infirmity and again be raised up by faith and prayer in order that the spiritual newness may increase.

Thus the church has been subjected to afflictions, as will be said again below [8:29]: "We need to become like the image of the Son of God." And here he says that the church has been subjected to death on account of the present sin, in order that the evil flesh may be destroyed. However, he adds that believers are freed from death, because they live in the Spirit, and God will raise up their bodies again.

## A Final Word

He teaches in this comparison that human nature is not able to satisfy the Law of God, and that fleshly righteousness is not righteousness in the sight of God, neither does it make alive. A remnant of the flesh remains in the saints. Nevertheless, they please God on account of Christ and have been set free from death so they may live by the Spirit. Christ is working in them and has begun to vivify them through the Holy Spirit. However, the flesh has been destined to death on account of sin, so that when the old has been done away with, we may again be clothed with flesh in which there is nothing evil.

This topic contains rich teaching. First, human nature is not able to satisfy the Law of God. Second, fleshly righteousness neither justifies nor vivifies in the sight of God. Third, the saints are pleasing and are set free from death, although sin still clings to them. Fourth, the church has been subjected to afflictions and death for a purpose. Fifth, what the words *flesh* and *Spirit* really mean.

## 12. Brothers, we are debtors

Up to this point he has completed the teaching about justification. Now it is necessary that the teaching about the new obedience be added. For also this part needs to be found in the church, in order that people may understand what the obedience in the saints is like, and what is the nature of the sin on account of which they fall from grace and lose faith and the Holy Spirit.

Paul sets up the proposition: "We are debtors, not to obey the flesh." For when we are born again by faith, spiritual newness is begun, which is beginning obedience toward God or the beginning of the Law in their hearts, as it is written: "I will put my law into their hearts" [Jer. 31:33]. That newness has its effects; it acknowledges God, obeys him, and fights against the impulses of the flesh which carry a person along against the will of God.

He says distinctly: "We are debtors." He opposes this declaration to those who misunderstand evangelical liberty, which sets us free so that we may not be accused by the Law; it does not set us free that we may not obey. For it remains an eternal and immutable ordinance that we should obey God, and the Gospel not only initiates this obedience but also subjects us to obedience to God.

### 13. For if you will live according to the flesh

He adds two reasons to his proposition. The first is taken from punishments. This topic must be considered in order that we may hold fast to the distinction between mortal and venial sins, that is, of such sins as are found in the saints. For when he says: "If you mortify the actions of the flesh by the Spirit," he testifies that there are in saints some sinful actions, namely, concupiscence; various evil desires; doubt about God; not being ardent in the fear of God, in faith, or in love; sluggishness in prayer (which they called ἀκηδία [indifference]); impatience; the flames of lusts; not obeying superiors; being inflamed with desire for revenge; hatred; avarice; etc. Such sicknesses in the saints, although they are by their nature mortal sins, that is, worthy of eternal death, are nevertheless condoned in those who believe in Christ, who both fight against these sicknesses and apprehend Christ, the mediator, by faith. They become venial, that is, tolerated.

On the contrary, they become truly mortal sins when those who had been sanctified indulge in and obey such desires, do not fight against them, and are without repentance. Such persons lose faith and the Holy Spirit and are condemned to eternal death unless they return to repentance. Thus when David had become an adulterer, he was without faith and the Holy Spirit, and would have been lost if he had not afterward been restored through repentance.

Here belongs what is said in this passage: "If you will live according to the flesh," that is, if you will obey the evil desires, "you will die." The same thought is frequently repeated in Scripture. Mt. 5[:20]: "Unless your righteousness exceeds that of the scribes and the Pharisees . . . " 1 John 3[:10]: "Everyone who does not do right is not of God." 1 Cor. 6[:9]: "Do not be deceived; neither the immoral, nor idolaters, . . . will inherit the kingdom of God." Gal. 5[:21]: "Those who do such things shall not inherit the kingdom of God." Col. 3[:6]: "On account of which the wrath of God is coming on the disobedient . . ."

But here the question is asked about the degree of sin. When do these lapses become mortal sins? First, this step is without doubt mortal sin when men rush against the commandments of God against their conscience. In describing the nature of the life of saints, Paul makes this the first step: they should not act against their conscience. 1 Tim. 1[:15]: "The sum of the commandment is love from a pure heart, a good conscience, and unfeigned faith." When acts are committed against the commandments of God, against the conscience, or when evil desires are not resisted, they become mortal sins. This step is clear.

But outside this step there happen also more obscure lapses, many of which become mortal sins, which reason cannot sufficiently judge. Such was David's error when he commanded the people to be numbered [cf. 2 Sam. 24]. Truly, also these lapses are forgiven to those who return to faith, but as long as the purpose remains to act against the conscience, there can be no faith, for it is impossible for faith to exist with an evil conscience. For faith is confidence which declares that we please God because of Christ. A bad conscience fights against this confidence when it conceives a plan of acting against the commandments of God.

These are the things which Paul teaches here about the distinction between sins. Therefore we should diligently remind ourselves of this passage, in order that we beware, lest we lose the benefit of Christ and rush into destruction, as also Peter says [2 Pet. 1:10]: "Strive to make your calling and election firm," that is, continue in this newness which you have received, lest your calling and election, by which you have been separated from the world—from the ungodly—again become void.

### 14. Those who are led by the Spirit

The second argument is taken from the efficient cause. The Holy Spirit works in those to whom he has been given: You have received the Holy Spirit; therefore let him work in you. Paul here quotes the major premise: As many as are led by the Spirit of God, these are the sons of God. He uses the term "to be led" in order that we may understand that the Holy Spirit moves us.

### 15a. For you have not received the spirit of servitude

After explaining of what kind the impulses of the Holy Spirit are, he also distinguishes this new Word—the Gospel—from the Law. For persons terrified by the Law rush into despair if comfort does not come to them; they flee from God and do not call on him. These terrors—doubting and flight—he calls the spirit of servitude in fear. Conversely, when minds are raised up by the Gospel and by faith, they receive the Holy Spirit who makes them alive, and acknowledge that God has already been placated and wants to hear them. This true comfort in true fears is an impulse and testimony of the Holy Spirit. Therefore Paul perceives that another Word has already been revealed, by which we are made sons, when remission of sins has been imparted and the Holy Spirit has been given us.

The fact that he calls them adopted sons distinguishes the other saints from Christ, and this distinction must be held fast in order that we may know that Christ is the Son of God by nature, both equal with the Father and of the same essence, as it is written: "We beheld his glory, like the glory of the only-begotten of the Father. . . . " [John 1:14] But the saints are sons by adoption, because they have been received because of Christ, and have been given the gifts of Christ, namely the Spirit, and new life, wisdom and righteousness, etc.

### 15b–16. In whom we cry "Abba, Father"

As long as the conscience is without faith and about to despair in fears, it flees from God, doubts whether he hears, whether he has regard for them, etc. It does not call on God. Therefore Paul links together comfort and calling on God, and ascribes this only to those who have already been raised up by faith through the Gospel. For when he says: "We cry 'Abba, Father,' " this signifies: Now we acknowledge that God is a Father, that he truly hears us, and by means of this faith we receive comfort and call on God.

This faith and acknowledgment of the mercy of God really makes a distinction between the Christian and the ungodly, because doubt and anger against God remain in the wicked. But in believers faith is a new recognition of the mercy of God. It fights against doubting and declares that we are truly heard on account of Christ. This same faith is the comfort and vivification, and the testimony of the Holy Spirit in hearts about which he says here: "The Spirit bears witness to our spirit." The Holy Spirit works comfort in the midst of true terrors through the word of the Gospel.

[Some say,] David's sins had been forgiven, so he did not have mortal sin. Likewise, David had been ordained, predestinated from eternity. Therefore all sins were for him venial, and he had no mortal sin. I answer: One must not judge according to election or predestination, but according to the present word. This teaches David that adultery is a mortal sin, and that it will not be forgiven to him unless he repents. One must judge about sin and about righteousness according to the present word, not according to election and a will that has not been revealed. These cogitations about predestination must be removed; they do not agree with the statement of Paul, who declares that one must judge according to that doctrine, etc.

### 17. But if sons, then also heirs

After he delivered the teaching that there must be new obedience, he attaches a graduation about glorification which follows justification. And into this topic he mixes a proposition about afflictions—that this new obedience is practiced amid afflictions, because it fights against the flesh, the devil, and the world, that is, the entire rule of sin.

Since he says that we are coheirs of Christ if indeed we are similarly afflicted, this proposition describes a necessity, as if he said: It is necessary to suffer since Christ also suffered. With that word he embraces the entire new obedience which is practiced in the midst of afflictions. It does not follow that if we suffer, we will be glorified, therefore our afflictions are the purchase price or merit of eternal life. For then the promise would be rendered uncertain, for no one is sufficiently patient; no one satisfies the law. Likewise, Paul says clearly [Eph. 2:8]: "You are saved *gratis*." And Christ [Luke 17:10]: "Say, we are unprofitable servants." And here [Rom. 8:18]: "The afflictions are not worthy of future glory." Also Augustine says: "Eternal life is given for no human merits, but is given by the grace of God who gives bountifully." Therefore this statement must be held fast, that our obedience or afflictions are not the merit or price of eternal life *gratis* on account of Christ; in this way certainty remains.

What then does the condition, "if we suffer with him," say? I answer: Not purchase price or merit, but a necessity, because obedience is the newness itself by which eternal life is begun in believers according to 2 Cor. 5[:4]: "If we shall not be found naked." It is necessary as a necessary effect following justification.

### 18–21. However, I judge that the sufferings of this time are not worthy

He establishes a very ample and beautiful comfort which you can separate into six arguments.

The first is taken from the outcome of the affliction, and is similar to the topic about rewards. Very great glory will be given us for these afflictions. Therefore let us patiently await the outcome and our liberation.

### 22. We know that the whole creation groans

The second example is taken from the example of creation. Everything in nature is subjected to corruption and to the abuse of the ungodly in the meantime until it is liberated. Therefore, we are awaiting liberation.

This is a sublime impulse in Paul, by which he looks on the horrible confusion of human life and the corruption of all things, murders, wars, devastations, and other ills of the world. He sees how great the power of sin is, how great the tyranny of the devil, and how unworthy it is for the nature of things to be subjected to the devil and death on account of the sin of man.

Here one should first consider the feeling of the godly in every affliction. Delay tortures their minds, as does the fact that we do not foresee the mode of liberation. Likewise, troubles grow assiduously. Thus also the minds of the godly are tormented by public worry when they see great dangers threatening the church, and see that liberation from them is being deferred and evils are increasing.

Whether our afflictions are private or whether we grieve for a public cause, he sets before us comfort from the example of heaven and earth and of all nature, which has been subjected to the abuse of the ungodly. Tyrants rule, wicked persons enjoy the riches of the world, but the church, for whose sake all these things were created, is being hacked to pieces; it is not granted the use of life, light, and other creatures. Yet things have been created that they may serve the godly, and the glory of God. Since they are being dreadfully abused and have been subjected to corruption on account of the sin of Adam, the creatures themselves also look for liberation.

This is the comfort: Heaven and earth are bearing an immense burden, namely, the abuse of the ungodly, and still they look for liberation. Therefore let us together with them endure these common troubles and bear the delay, for although liberation is delayed, it still will reach us at some time.

Paul uses very meaningful words and personifies: "All creation groans and is in travail." With these words he signifies that the creatures are suffering injury, but the pain from that injury reaches the church, against which the wicked rage at the same time as they rage against the creatures, as when tyrants and wicked persons ravish the creatures and persecute the church.

### 23. But also we who have the firstfruits of the Spirit

The third is from the example of the apostles. Do we who have more excellent gifts suffer afflictions? We struggle with the consciousness of our sins and offenses, with terrors of the devil, with our infirmity, with dangers and persecutions on the outside, and await liberation. Therefore you also should await it.

### 24. For we are saved in hope

The fourth argument is taken from the definition of hope. Hope has to do with things which are not yet present: "We are saved in hope," that is, by hope we have been set free from death and all evils. Therefore the liberation from death and other evils is not yet a present reality.

But here we must ask whether we have not in the present been set free from sin. I answer: By imputation we are at present righteous and freed from sin. But there still remains in our nature the sickness from which we have been set free in hope, that is, we hope for complete newness. Therefore, we in fact still labor with infirmity and are plagued by the terrors of sin and by other afflictions. But in the midst of these troubles we ought to raise ourselves up and declare that at present we have remission of sins, are righteous by imputation, and please God for Christ's sake. As he says above [5:1]: "Having been justified by faith, we have peace."

Here we see an important difference between faith and hope. Faith in the present accepts the remission of sins and the imputation of righteousness. Hope has a different object; it awaits complete liberation.

With respect to hope these two things must chiefly be held: First, it has been commanded that we hope for eternal life. For whoever does not look for the things which have been promised denies that God is truthful. Therefore, in order that the glory of truthfulness may be given to God, it is necessary to hope for the things he has promised. We must know that hope is not doubting, but that it fights against doubt and conquers it.

I know the command; but the condition of merit or of our worthiness is demanded. Should also the unworthy hope for salvation? It is this question which particularly troubles minds and drives out hope. This is the voice of the Law and of the handwriting in our minds which condemns us and forbids us to hope because we are unworthy.

Therefore this second teaching is very necessary, namely, that the reason for hope is not our merits nor our worthiness, but the gratuitous promise of Christ. It has been commanded that we should hope for salvation, and it has been commanded that we should hope—not on account of our worthiness, but *gratis,* on account of Christ, because eternal life is given to the believer on account of Christ, not on account of our own worthiness. Therefore, although we are unworthy, gratuitous hope should still be held fast and our unworthiness acknowledged. The statements about hope are to be taken in this way. God commands us to hope because our unworthiness scares us off. Hope is not to be cast off on account of our unworthiness; rather, it is to be opposed to our unworthiness because of the promise.

Thus Ps. 42[:5] acknowledges and confesses unworthiness. Then it sets hope in opposition to it: "Why are you cast down, O my soul, and why are you disquieted within me? Hope in God, for I shall yet confess him."

Thus in the beginning of Ps. 130[:3] he confesses his sin: "If you, O Lord, should mark iniquities, who will stand?" Then he sustains himself by hope [v. 5]: "My soul has sustained itself with his Word; my soul has hoped in the Lord, for with the Lord there is mercy. . . . "

In such sayings it should always be understood that hope depends on the gratuitous promise, not on a condition of our merits and worthiness or on a condition of the Law. Thus those statements become sweet and bring forth true and efficacious comfort. And this hope is to be exercised in calling on God, as is said in Ps. 28[:7]: "In him my heart hoped, and I was helped." And Ps. 34[:8]: "Blessed is the man who hopes in him . . . " And Ps. 25[:3]: "All who wait for you shall not be confounded." Ps. 4[:5]: "Offer right sacrifices, and put your trust in the Lord."

Up to this point he has spoken about the fourth argument, namely, that we have been liberated in the present, so far as imputation is concerned. Next, we have been liberated in hope, so far as complete newness is concerned. This also has been said with respect to hope: we have been commanded to hope for the things which have been promised, and that there must not be patched on to it the condition of our worthiness or merits. Men are in great need of being reminded of this. For that is how hope must be defined; hope is the sure expectation of the salvation promised to believers because of Christ, not because of our worthiness.

## 25. We wait patiently

He says distinctly: "We wait patiently," in order to indicate that liberation is not only deferred, but deferred in such a way that meanwhile great and extraordinary struggles must be endured. The saints are troubled by terrors of sin, snares of the devil, offenses, persecution, and various experiences by which faith is shaken, and in some persons extinguished. In order that we may foresee and understand these dangers and so our minds may be prepared for these struggles, he commands that patience be added to hope.

Here we need to consider what patience really signifies; this can be understood better from a comparison. I shall say first what patience means to the philosophers. Patience, according to the judgment of reason, is a certain obedience to reason which moderates grief and forbids us, when overcome by some grief, anger, or cupidity, to act against justice. Saul, driven by grief when he had suffered disaster, inflicted death on himself. Catiline, angered because he had been rejected, stirred up civil war. In such examples one can see what impatience is. From their standpoint, philosophers call patience something that moderates grief and keeps us from rushing ahead against justice.

But there are far more factors in Christian patience. First of all, the causes are different. There are three different causes. The first is the commandment of God. For all should know that it is a commandment of God that we should be obedient in afflictions, and that anger or impatience in afflictions is a sin. Therefore Christ commands [Luke 21:19]: "Possess your souls in patience." And the Psalm [4:4] says: "Be angry and sin not," that is, when you are angry, when in afflictions nature rages, do not succumb, but overcome the anger. Also Paul says [Col. 3:15]: "Let the peace of God rule your hearts."

The second cause is the Gospel, which explains that afflictions are not signs of the wrath of God. This cause is unknown to reason and to the Law; it is revealed only in the Gospel. Obedience can be rendered when the mind looks not only at the command of God, but sees also the other thing, namely, that afflictions are not signs of wrath but of the good will of God. What was said above about afflictions, that they are not to result in a fall, that they are not signs of the wrath of God, etc., should be considered here.

The third cause is the promise of help, which lessens and lightens the appearance of evil in afflictions. David is obedient because he sees that they are not signs of wrath, and he awaits liberation. But philosophical patience is without hope of help when human supports have been lost.

Christian patience is a certain obedience in afflictions, but on account of the commandments of God and with the addition of faith, which according to the Gospel feels that afflictions are not signs of wrath, but expects and seeks help, according to the passage [Ps. 50:15]: "Call on me in the day of trouble, and I will deliver you, and you will glorify me . . ." Paul is describing such patience here. For he demands not only that we should be obedient in afflictions, but also that we should declare that we have not been cast off, that we should call on God, and that we should expect help.

He immediately adds on the fifth argument about the aid of the Holy Spirit and about calling on God, as though he said: I demand the kind of obedience in which you at the same time call on God and hope for help, which indeed has been promised to you. Thus Christ says [John 14:18]: "I will not leave you orphans. . . ."

### 26–27. The Spirit also helps our infirmity

Because he has above spoken about patience and hope, he adds a fifth argument, taken from help. It is necessary for hope to be shown in order that patience may be retained, and so calling on God and hope may not be driven out in so great a magnitude of afflictions, in such great infirmity of the human heart which is filled with doubting. Therefore he argues thus: God is truly present and helps us in afflictions. So let us not succumb; let us not cast off faith and confession, overcome by despair.

Here it is profitable to have at hand and to keep in sight similar promises, such as: "Ask, and you shall receive" [Lk 11:9]; "How much more will your Father give the Holy Spirit to those who ask him" [Lk 11:13]; "Come to me, all who labor" [Mt. 11:28]; "I will not leave you orphans" [John 14:18]; "I shall ask my Father and he will give you another comforter, that he may remain with you always" [John 14:16].

But how is the Holy Spirit given, and how does he work? I answer: When we sustain ourselves by the Word in these struggles, and call upon God. Paul here links these two together, as it is said very often in the Psalms: "My soul sustained itself in his Word" [Ps. 119:50]. Likewise about invocation, in Ps. 4[:1]: "When I called upon him, the God of my righteousness heard me." And Christ says about invocation: "He will give the Holy Spirit to those who ask him" [Lk 11:13].

Paul is here describing in brief words an immense struggle which our weakness undergoes. For in dangers, persecution, death, and all kinds of afflictions, and in bodily or spiritual troubles, nature finds it difficult to obey and at once seeks to cast them out. Therefore Paul says [8:26]: "We do not know what we should pray for," namely, in our natural ignorance we ask to be set free at once, and we bear the cross impatiently. Meanwhile the Holy Spirit brings it about that we in some part obey and call on God. This obedience and invocation Paul calls "sighs too deep for words." Through the Spirit we subject ourselves to God and ask for liberation according to the will of God, not according to fleshly desire.

Paul is speaking about a true and very great struggle, not about cold and idle thoughts. These things cannot be understood by the carnally secure, but everyone in his way in his temptations ought to experience the power of this comfort in some part as he calls on God. Nothing greater can be promised than the presence and working of God; this is what is promised when the Holy Spirit is promised.

Moreover this topic also supplies us with a testimony against the Pelagians, who imagine that people are made righteous and are saved without the Holy Spirit. Against this Paul openly testifies here that the Holy Spirit is given, and that these impulses—faith and calling on God—are aroused by the Holy Spirit as he works and moves people.

### 28–29. We know that for those who love God

The sixth argument is taken from the outcome. God is glorified in no other way except through afflictions. Therefore endure them, since they are the road to glorification. He proves the antecedent by setting forth the picture of Christ. We need to become similar to the image of the Son of God; he was glorified through suffering. Therefore it is necessary that we also be afflicted. This is the chief comfort of the godly, to gaze upon this picture of the Son of God. No philosophy and no human wisdom can see why this infirm human nature should be burdened with such extraordinary calamities. Reason wonders whether they happen by chance. The Law of God proclaims that they are punishments of sin and signs of the wrath of God which testify that we have been rejected.

But the Gospel chides both errors and sets before us the Son of God. It testifies that we are subjected to afflictions not by chance, but according to the sure counsel of God, not in order that we may be lost, but that we may be exercised. When God comforts us, faith and the knowledge of God increase in us. This wisdom about the cause and purpose of human calamities is wholly above and beyond the grasp of reason. It is revealed only in the Gospel, and is seen chiefly in this picture of the Son of God.

### 30. Those he elected, he also called

Why does he begin from election? "Those whom he elected, he also calls, thereafter he justifies and glorifies them." I answer: He wanted to embrace the whole order, according to which the church was founded by God. And first he reminds us that the election is the cause for the calling, not human merit or the righteousness of the Law. This is useful to know in order that we may hold fast to the comfort against the opinion about merit, and against those people who falsely arrogate to themselves the title of *church* on account of the righteousness of the Law, etc. We must declare that the church has been elected not on account of worthiness and human merit, not on account of righteousness of the Law, not on account of human authority, and not on account of the prerogative of succession. Likewise, we must know that the church which has the title is persecuting the true church. Therefore, he reminds us at the start that there is another church which has been elected, in order that we may look to and acknowledge the true church.

Immediately he weaves in something about the calling in order to lead us to the Word, and this reminds us that the calling is not invalid. God is truly present in his calling, and he justifies and glorifies those who have been called. He wants us to regard our calling highly and to remember that it has been brought about by God, in order that we may persevere in it, because God will stand by this his calling and Word.

### 31–34. What then shall we say?

The seventh argument meets the foremost question, for it is taken from the object and cause of the fear. The cause of fear and despair is that in the midst of our afflictions, the sight of our sins terrifies us, and we judge that God is angry at us.

Paul here comes to the aid of this question and shows that another object must be apprehended. He argues thus: God testifies by the giving of his Son that he is propitious to us, and indeed the Son is busy interceding for us. Therefore, we should not cast off faith and hope of liberation. "What shall we say to these things?" means "what is more ample or greater that can be set forth for our comfort than that we have a God who is favorable toward us?" He amplifies this with the added pledge of grace, namely, that he gave us his Son. And lest our sins scare us off, he adds plainly: "Who will accuse?" as if he said: "Although we feel that we are unworthy, and that we still have sins and very great weakness and uncleanness, nevertheless, no one will accuse us after we have become righteous on account of our high priest, Christ, that is, accepted. He says: "It is God who justifies," that is, pronounces righteous. He justifies us on account of Christ, who intercedes for us.

He amplifies this statement by mentioning Christ, the mediator, and he mentions first death, then the resurrection, third, the kingdom, and fourth, the priesthood. He mentions these things briefly, but they are not to be looked at only in passing.

First, he speaks about death and about the sacrifice in order to remind us that it is the height of disgrace make any sin greater than this sacrifice.

Second, by his resurrection Christ overcame all the power of the devil. We should know that this victory is efficacious and that it will profit us also.

In the third place, his reign is not idle: He sits at the right hand of the Father and saves the believers with divine power, sustains and vivifies them, if only we do not fall away from him.

Fourth, he adds the priesthood and intercession of Christ. Neither is there any sweeter comfort than knowing that Christ is the priest and intercessor for us. However, it would be a disgrace against the priesthood of Christ if we were to think that his intercession was ineffective, or if we were not to join our calling on God to his intercession.

### 35–39. What then will separate us?

The conclusion of the last argument is as follows: Since God loves us so much he certainly will not cast us away, even though we are weak and are troubled by every kind of affliction. He calls the love of God that love with which God loves us, as Paul himself later interprets: "Because of Him who loved us" [8:37]. At the end of the consolation Paul repeats this proper and chief voice of the Gospel—that God loves us—because that is the most effective comfort in all afflictions, yes, in every act of calling on God. It far surpasses the understanding of the human heart, which is filled with doubting and fear and does not dare to declare that we are loved by God. Paul makes this comfort great with many words, as though he said: "Do not let the greatness of the afflictions break you, but in all terrors look upon this comfort, that God certainly loves you." These words do not need a lengthy interpretation. But let us learn in life and in calling on God that God demands that we should declare that we are loved, and raise ourselves up, and in this faith truly call upon him.

The readers must be reminded about the inappropriate questions which are raised here. The scholastics disputed whether a righteous person could lose his virtues, since Paul says: "Who shall separate us from the love?" as if he wanted to say: "In what way could we lose our love?" They thought that love should be interpreted of our virtues, that is, the love with which we love God. But this unsound interpretation must be rejected. It is certain that saints can fall and lose the Holy Spirit, faith, and love, as the prophet Nathan condemns David on account of adultery.

Why then does he say that the love of God is everlasting? I answer: As the evangelical promise is perpetual and valid, but in such a way that it requires faith, so Paul is here speaking to believers, as if he said: "As long as you believe, as long as you do not fall from faith, it is most certain that the love of God toward you is in force." The meaning is this. Without doubt the love with which God loves us is always valid, firm, and certain for the believer. This is the proper message of the Gospel, as was said above. Therefore Paul enlarges it here, at the end of the comfort.

Others have twisted this to refer to predestination, but there is no need to turn to that in this passage, for he is speaking of our victory. And we shall conquer through the mercy and love revealed in the Word when we set this comfort in opposition to the terrors of sin and death. The meaning will be simple and plain if it is understood of believers. These ought to declare truly and with certainty that they are loved by God on account of Christ.

# Chapter 9

An entirely new discussion is begun. Although he at times repeats and interweaves the doctrine of justification, he chiefly treats two other matters: Who truly are the people of God (or which is the true church), and the calling of the Gentiles.

The Jews were objecting that the promises had not yet been fulfilled; they contended that the Christ had not yet appeared. For they were arguing thus: The people must receive the promises when Christ comes, but the people have received nothing, so the promises have not yet been fulfilled, neither has the Christ appeared. They proved the minor premise by saying that "the people" signifies not just a certain few, as though they were inciting a rebellion, but it signifies the princes, the priests, the learned, the good, and the most flourishing part in the respective state. And in the Jewish state the princes, the priests, and the chief part of the people did not feel that they had things better. Rather, the entire state was falling down more and more. Therefore, they judged that they certainly had not been helped by Christ. The weak were greatly moved by this argument. The apostles contended that the promises had been fulfilled and the people had been saved, but the others on the contrary objected that the apostles were a small number of seditious men who were not the people. To overcome this argument, Paul has to dispute about this offense of fewness and distinguish the people of God from those who just have the title. This teaching is also useful.

There are at all times two bodies of the church, the one of the true church, the other of the one that has the title but which persecutes the true church. The church which bears the title has great authority, great power. Therefore, lest the weak be deceived, it is necessary that the godly be fortified against this external appearance in order that they may understand which is the true church, who are the true people of God.

It is also now being argued: The church cannot err; the assembly of the bishops and priests and of their adherents is the church. Therefore, this assembly cannot err. They prove the minor premise by the fact that for many centuries these alone were in the ministry of the Word; they have the examples of the fathers, etc., so they are the church.

Here it is necessary to show that although they hold the position of the ministry, they do not have the ministry of the Gospel if they teach wicked things, and neither are they the church. It is not a small offense that this highest honor the title of church—is taken away from popes, princes, and all the most beautifully ordered clerical estate, and to confer this august title on a few who are poor and calamity-ridden, and who indeed seem to be rebelliously shouting against the ordinary form of the church. By this offense many are being scared away from the Gospel and from the true church. Therefore people must be taught about the election, that the true church is not any and every crowd, but those who are elected and called to the Gospel, who retain the true Word of God and fight for it against the wisdom and power of the world.

That is the occasion for Paul's discussion here. For the Jews were pressing these two arguments, that they were the people of God, and unless things were better for the entire Jewish state, the promises had not yet been fulfilled. Similarly, because they are the seed of Abraham, the promise does not pertain to the Gentiles.

Here Paul opposes a contrary statement, that the people of God is a certain multitude chosen through mercy, called through the Gospel, and sanctified through the Holy Spirit. The people of God are not made by fleshly propagation and the worship of the Law. This is the sum and substance of the statement, and the principal proposition. Therefore, he is speaking of the effect of the election, that the true church has been elected through mercy, and he takes away two causes, fleshly propagation and the Law.

He is here disputing about predestination, about the freedom of the human will, and about certain other matters—the general and the special activity of God, and contingency. It is useful to consider the things which are said about such great matters, but those things are to be chosen piously and in the fear of God, since they are taught in the Scriptures, have the testimony of received and approved writers, and are profitable for consciences. Therefore we shall compare a certain few briefly.

First: The writers do not disagree about the reprobation of the wicked, but all confess that the cause of reprobation in those who are damned is their wicked will and their sins. However, in the matter of the cause of the predestination or election of those who are to be saved, they do not speak in the same way.

The more recent scholastics, following only human judgment, said that merits or the good works of human free will are the cause of election. This imagination had its origin in ignorance of the Gospel. Because they thought that a person is justified on account of his own worthiness, merits, or fulfillment of the Law, and likewise they thought that the Law was being fulfilled, they patched on this imagination that those who were to be saved were elected on account of their fulfillment of the Law. But the Gospel declares that no one satisfies the Law; therefore it takes away merit, so far as justification and salvation are concerned. And it teaches that men are accounted righteous through mercy, because of Christ, not because of their own worthiness. Therefore one's own worthiness, merits, or fulfillment of the Law are not causes of the election.

The other understanding is that the mercy of God is the cause of election, as Paul clearly teaches here and elsewhere: If it is of works, it is no longer of grace [cf. Rom. 11:6]. For the church is not dependent on human counsel, or on human powers, but God in Christ loved and chose those who are to be saved.

Here two questions about election torment the mind. The first is about worthiness or merit. The mind argues: If I were worthy, sufficiently pure, or had merited well, I would declare that I also would receive mercy and the other benefits which have been promised. This trial arises from the judgment of the Law, which requires worthiness and merits. Here it is very useful to hold fast to the teaching of the Gospel about gratuitous mercy. The Gospel of gratuitous mercy is proclaimed not to drive minds to despair, but in order that it might be a remedy for our mistrust and despair. And mercy is shown not in order that we might do nothing, or so that we might not accept the Word, but in order that our worthiness might be taken away and that the benefit of God might be certain.

The other cause of unrest comes from particularity. Because we hear that mercy is the cause of election, and that few are elected, we experience even greater anguish and wonder whether God shows partiality. Why does he not have mercy on all? To this attack also there should be opposed the universal promises of the Gospel, which teach that God offers salvation to all on account of Christ, and *gratis,* according to the passage: "The righteousness of God through faith in Jesus Christ on all and over all" [Rom. 3:22]. And elsewhere: "The same Lord of all is rich toward all" [Rom. 10:12]. Likewise: "Everyone who will call on the name of the Lord. . . . " [Rom. 10:13]. These universal statements must be opposed to the temptation stemming from particularity. Thereafter we must declare that one must not judge about the will of God from reason without the Word of God. Likewise, just as about justification, so also about election, one must not judge from reason or from the Law, but from the Gospel.

When we wonder: If merits make no difference, then why is not mercy shown to all? I answer: As far as the Word and the promise are concerned, we must hold fast to universality. But not all attain the benefits because very many resist the Word. And it is evident that resistance is an act of the human will, because God is not a cause of sin.

If we speak for the benefit of the conscience according to our judgment, let us say as we say about justification: That those who believe are righteous, so the elect do not resist the calling, but believe the Gospel, and do not in the end reject it. Nevertheless, it must be held in the meantime that to believe and not to resist are results which come about when the Holy Spirit impels. I am speaking about our judgment, which does not search out the hidden majesty without the Word, but looks at the God who calls through the promise and apprehends his will in the Word, which is universal. Thus Paul says [Rom: 9:16]: "It is not of him who wills and runs, but of God who has mercy," that is, mercy is indeed the cause of election, not our willing and running. Nevertheless, these things are done in the will and in running, not in resisting.

### 1–5. I tell the truth in Christ Jesus

Now I come to the text, in which we establish this as the aim: it teaches that one must distinguish the true and elected church from the one which has the title and the fleshly prerogatives. This is a necessary teaching against the magnificent show which the false church puts forth, namely, its antiquity, the examples of the fathers, and the consensus of the crowd. When these things meet our eyes, let us distinguish the churches, as Paul here distinguishes the people of God. The true people has been elected through mercy; it is the people which has the Gospel.

But the Jews contended that they were the people of God because they were descendants of Abraham, had the law, the fathers, examples, and miracles. From this they reasoned as follows: Christ has not yet come, because when Christ comes he will save the people; the people has not been saved, but a certain few seditious persons boast they have been saved. Therefore Christ has not yet come.

Here Paul responds to the minor premise and teaches that the people had been elected through mercy, not on account of fleshly prerogatives or because of the Law. If the discussion of Paul is to be referred to this understanding, it will be easier, and it can be transferred to our use in order that we may learn which is the true church.

Paul begins with a very serious complaint, in which he testifies that he is grieved by the destruction of his race. All holy persons suffer intense grief when they consider that so great a multitude of persons is being damned, and wonder at this secret counsel that the church is such a tiny crowd, weak and downcast. Chiefly it was a matter of grief to persons born in this people that this race should be rejected, since the fathers and the prophets came from it. Here let us ponder Paul's argument in order that we may learn to fear God. If God did not spare those who were descendants of the fathers and of the prophets, about whom the promises openly spoke, how much less will he spare the Gentiles.

### 6a. Not however that the Word of God has failed

Correction: Although I deplore the destruction of the race, I do not command anyone to despair. Rather, I exhort all to believe. For my thinking is not that none of the Jews could be saved. Rather, the promise still pertains to us, nor is it void. Would that you would believe the promise, for as many as do, will be saved.

### 6b. For not all who are of Israel

This is the chief proposition in which he answers the objection concerning which is the true people of God.

The Jews contended that they were the people of God, that they were the church, and that the promises pertained to them alone. Paul responds that the elect are the people of God, and he distinguishes the true people from those who have the title. The true church must be distinguished from that kingdom which has the title but which makes war against the true church.

Paul states the proposition clearly: The sons of God are not made by fleshly propagation, not by natural gifts or merits, but by the election of God. In order to clarify this statement, he leads us to the Scripture so that we may see how God at all times separated some by his election. God did this to prepare a church and to show that the church does not come into being by human counsel. If sons were made by nature or merits, there would have been no need for God to separate the son of his promise from the rest.

The Chaldaeans and the Egyptians were not inferior to Isaac in natural gifts or merits. Alexander, the Macedonian, Fabius, and Scipio were better endowed with natural gifts than we, and yet they did not have the Gospel. Therefore, the church is by election, not by natural gifts or merits.

### 7–11. But in Isaac your seed shall be called

He applies this passage about Isaac to this understanding. The first proof of the proposition is this: He is the son whom God chose for himself by his promise, and he separated him from the sons of Abraham, sons of God are made by election. These things do not impress us sufficiently because of the brevity of the words, although they contain a most important teaching, namely, that the church does not come into being by human counsel, by natural gifts or merits, but by divine election and promise.

### 12–13. Not as a result of works, but as a result of him who calls

The second proof. Jacob becomes a son not on account of works, but on account of the one who calls. Therefore, sons of God are made by election, not by gifts or natural merits, or by the Law.

### 14–16. Is there injustice with God?

But Paul sees that these things are far too high for human reason to perceive. Therefore he interrupts himself, and puts forth and refutes a common argument which must come into the mind of all sane people. If Esau and Jacob are equals, then God should have chosen or rejected both, because a just judge renders equal things to equals. Paul refutes this in this way: Equal things are to be rendered to equals when a debt is paid. In the case of a gift or when something is done through mercy, there is no need to render equal things to equals.

Thus also Christ, in the parable about those brought into the vineyard, shows that through mercy equal things are given to persons who are not equals. In accord with this understanding this saying is cited [Rom. 9:15; cf. Ex. 33:19]: "I will take pity on whom I will take pity," that is, on whom it seems good to me to take pity, as if he said: "Salvation comes by mercy, not through a debt." And he attaches the conclusion [v. 16]: "It does not depend on anyone's willing or running, but on God who takes pity." This statement testifies that men are chosen and called through mercy in order that they may will and run.

Earlier he cited statements about mercy and showed that mercy is the cause of election, and that the people of God are truly that church of the elect. Now, on the other hand, he adds testimonies and a discussion about the reprobate, that there is a certain crowd of reprobate persons whom God permits to exist in order that in time of persecution the glory of the Gospel may be more clearly visible. He says this in order that we may be fortified against the offense of the crowd, and should not think that one must follow the example[1] of the crowd.

Gamaliel sees that the greater and more prominent part of the people are still enemies of the Gospel. Therefore, he thinks that he also must remain in this assembly. So also now, innumerable persons judge about the church which arrogates the title of church to itself. Paul draws us away from these judgments and reminds us that few are chosen to be the church, and that there is a very great multitude of the reprobate who make war against the Gospel.

---

[1] The text here has *exemptum*. The context clearly calls for *exemplum*. Our 1540 edition has *exemplum*.

## 17. I raised you up for this very thing

He quotes the history of Pharaoh, which contains two things, namely, that he was a reprobate, and that he was tolerated in order that the glory of God might become more conspicuous under persecution.

## 18–24. Therefore he has mercy on whom he wills

Paul adds the conclusion: "Therefore he has mercy on whom he wills; whom he wills, he hardens." This conclusion is not understood equally so far as the causes are concerned, but of the effect of the election, that some are elected, while others, who are adversaries of the Gospel, are hardened.

First you should learn about the phraseology. For the Hebrews, transitive verbs most commonly have the meaning of permitting. For instance: "Lead us not into temptation," that is, do not permit us to be led into it. Likewise: "You have made us to go astray," that is, you allowed us to fall into error. Thus "to harden" signifies not to liberate others, but to permit them to fight against God in order that they may perish. The meaning is: "Whom he wills he hardens," that is, he does not set them free, does not convert them because they continue to fight against God who is calling them.

Second, Paul is not saying here that the cause of hardening or reprobation is not in the ungodly. Prudence must be exercised here, and one must think that the cause of hardening or reprobation is in the ungodly themselves because they do not cease to resist God who is calling them. These things that Paul says are certain, that there is a great number that is hardened or rejected, which fights against the Word of God. If someone obeys the Word of God, he is not in that number.

Let us learn here what the judgment is about those who fight against the Word of God. Because they fight against it, they are hardened and show that they are of the number of the reprobate.

When he says: "Whom he wills, he hardens," he immediately adds the objection: If hardening occurs by the will of God, that multitude cannot be converted; if it cannot be converted, then why is it accused? He answers, conceding that it cannot be converted, namely, from necessity of the consequence, as if he said: "It is true that the multitude is rejected and that it cannot be converted, because it has been rejected; but it has been rejected on account of its own ungodliness. If someone obeys God who is calling, he is not of that number." Thus he answers by way of a concession, and adds the ultimate cause why God ordained things in this way—in order that both the wrath and the mercy might be more clearly seen.

I apply Paul's answers: "Why do you quarrel with God?" means that when you see this wonderful counsel of God according to which he chooses few and rejects many, you should obey God and fear his judgment, lest you be offended by the example of the multitude. Know that God is showing mercy in saving us, and is showing his wrath in punishing those who do not obey.

This is the least intricate explanation. It should not be thought that there is no cause of hardening or reprobation in the ungodly themselves, nor does Paul say this. Also the picture of the clay and the potter does not imply that the wicked do nothing, but it fits insofar as from the one mass of the human race God saves some according to his decision, and damns others. The causes cannot be fitted in completely in a picture. For the idea must be retained that God is not the cause of sin. This also must be held fast: the promise is universal. Thus Paul himself later adds the reason: Israel is perishing because it is unwilling to accept the Gospel. While pursuing righteousness it does not achieve it, because it is not of faith, etc. Here he expressly sets down the cause of reprobation, namely, because they fight against the Gospel.

### 25–26. I shall call a people that is not mine "my people"

After he has set down the thesis that the people of God is the church of the elect, he now comes to the hypothesis that the elect are from among Jews and Gentiles. He proves this with testimonies of Scripture in order to show that the Gospel pertains to the Gentiles. First he quotes the passage from Hosea [cf. Hos. 2:23; 1:10]. The testimony is sufficiently clear.

The reader must be reminded of this in passing. As often as the calling of the Gentiles is spoken of, one must know that grace is being commended, that we are pleasing not on account of the Law, but *gratis,* on account of Christ, etc.

### 27. If the number of the children of Israel were

The second testimony is from Isaiah [10:22, 23], and it prophesies about the falling away of the people. First he says: "Even if there should be an immense multitude of people, only a few shall be saved." That is what the phrase intends when he says "Remnant," for *remnant* signifies a few who are left after the others have been carried away. Then a repetition of the same statement follows.

### 28–29. The consummation will be shortened

The shortened consummation will overflow righteousness [the variant Greek reading of v. 28, quoting Is. 10:22, has "righteousness"]. For the Lord will make a consummation, a shortened one. The consummation signifies the end or the downfall of the people, as if he said: "A great downfall or destruction of the people will come, but righteousness will then overflow," that is, then the promised righteousness and blessing will be revealed and given. About the time of the end, a great multitude of the people will perish, and some will be saved, who believe the Gospel and accept the promised righteousness. An abbreviated consummation is one that is certainly predetermined or constituted. Paul quotes the Greek version, which is less clear, but which contains the same meaning if you understand the word for the thing it signifies, as the Hebrews are accustomed to speak. The Lord will make a shortened word, that is, a shortened thing, or end. And in that consummation, righteousness will overflow.

Others have thought up varying interpretations. They interpret the shortened word as being the Gospel because the Law is a long doctrine, yet it does not justify. This interpretation is unsuitable.

A certain other person interpreted: The completed sentence overflows righteousness, that is, the wise judge will bring a just sentence. This runs totally off the road.

Let us hold fast the one, simple meaning which fits the general narration in the text. The people will perish, but a short time before Christ will come, and some of the people will have received those very rich promises made to the fathers but rejected by the remaining multitude. Also the emphasis of the word ''overflow'' should be noted, which signifies a rich measure of grace.

### 30–32. What shall we say?

Here he expressly sets down the cause of reprobation, namely, because they are not willing to believe the Gospel. I said above that the picture of the clay is not to be taken in such a way as if the cause of reprobation were not in the human will. For here Paul expressly sets down the cause, and adds the reason which prevents the ungodly from believing: because the Gospel accuses human righteousness and worship, and sets forth another righteousness. ''Wise'' men here judge that it is most absurd to take away the praise from righteousness—from outward obedience—and from worship. They see that when worship has been changed, states are changed and destroyed. Therefore, they begin to hate and persecute this kind of doctrine as though it were blasphemous, as if it injures the glory of God, abolishes worship, loosens the rein on the license of the people, is seditious, and destroys the state. This has always been the chief cause of persecution, and it fired up the Jews very greatly, because they had a law that was divinely given and worship that was divinely ordained.

So now our adversaries persecute us furiously and cruelly because we say that men cannot satisfy the Law nor be justified in the sight of God on account of good works, but only through faith for the sake of Christ. They also rage all the more when acts of worship are reprehended, such as Masses, monkery, and similar things. For when these ordinances are changed, the state seems to be made to totter, to be cast down, and to be destroyed, and the glory of God seems to be harmed. From this, hatreds are kindled and immense struggles arise. These "offenses" greatly move human reason, which thinks the glory of God is injured and the common society is destroyed. And it is difficult for the saints to strengthen themselves so that these "offenses" do not drive out their faith.

Therefore Paul says afterward [10:12]: "I confess that the Jews have a zeal." And to the Corinthians he says that the reason why the Jews do not believe the Gospel is because they look at the Law covered with a veil [cf. 2 Cor. 3:15], that is, because they think the righteousness of the Law is righteousness in the sight of God. Because this is disapproved by the Gospel they are incited to persecute. Thus Christ becomes a rock of offense because reason thinks it is a blasphemous and seditious doctrine to disapprove of outward righteousness and worship.

### 33. Everyone who believes in him will not be confounded

"He will not be confounded" means he will not be deceived, but will receive what he hopes for. For it is customary for the Hebrews to say "be confounded" instead of "be deceived," as if I were to say; "The messenger that was sent to ask for money is confounded," that is, deceived. Thus it was said above: "Hope does not confound," that is, it is not in vain, it is not disappointed.

In these statements about faith, the little word *gratis* should always be understood. Let us not think, "If I shall be sufficiently worthy, then I will believe," for this is not putting confidence in Christ, but trusting in one's own worthiness. Therefore he says: "He who believes in him," that is, he who trusts in him—that God is favorable toward us on account of Christ, not on account of our own worthiness—he will be saved.

# Chapter 10

### 1–2. They have a zeal for God

He undertakes nothing new, but repeats the earlier statement about the cause of the defection of the Jews and the cause of the persecution of the Gospel. He says they wage war against the Gospel because they are not willing to have the righteousness of the Law belittled, neither do they understand that there is need of another righteousness in the sight of God. Therefore they stubbornly hold fast to the righteousness and worship of the Law.

**3.** He adds a complaint about the destruction of the race, as above, and ascribes to it a zeal, that is, eagerness for piety, but connected with an error. The error is the chief one in the articles of faith, namely with respect to the nature of Christ's office and kingdom, whence forgiveness of sins comes, what is true righteousness, and what sin is. A great threat is added against those who defend wicked opinions about the righteousness of the Law, when he says: "They have not submitted themselves to the righteousness of God." He clearly condemns all who oppose the true doctrine about the righteousness of faith.

### 4. For Christ is the end of the Law

Here he begins a comparison of the righteousness of the Law and of the righteousness of the Gospel, and defines each, and puts forth a statement opposed to the Jewish imaginations about the Law. It is as if he said: "The Jews seek righteousness from the Law; they do not understand that Christ is the end of the Law," that is, that it has been promised that he would take away sin and death, which the Law only reveals.

The meaning is: "Christ is the end of the Law," that is, its fulfillment or consummation. He gives that which the Law requires. Whoever believes in Christ has that which the Law demands—righteousness by imputation—and is set free from sin and death. But this liberation is only begun in this life, although the believer is truly righteous by imputation.

### 5. For Moses writes

Some have imagined that the point at issue in this antithesis is in the words: "He shall live in them," that is: In the matter of rewards two kinds of works are being compared; the works of reason have temporal rewards, but the good works which have their origin from the Holy Spirit have eternal rewards. This interpretation is foreign to the discussion of Paul, for it is not a comparison of rewards, neither is it about ultimate causes. Rather, the dispute is about the formal cause: what in fact is the righteousness of the Law, and conversely, what is the righteousness of the Gospel.

The point at issue in the comparison lies in the two phrases "to do" and "to believe." The righteousness of the Law is to do the Law, that is, to render perfect obedience according to the Law. So, he says, righteousness is described by Moses when he says "doing them," as though he said: "The righteousness of the Law is this very obedience by which the things which the Law prescribes are truly and wholly done: to glorify God, to burn with love of God with all one's heart, to love the neighbor, to be without concupiscence, to be without any vicious affect, to be without sin." That is the righteousness which the Law requires, which human nature is so far from fulfilling that it does not even know what that love of God is.

On the other hand, the righteousness of faith is not to be righteous on account of fulfilling the Law on account or of our virtues, but it is to believe that we are righteous, that is, accepted by God, on account of Christ.

From this the distinction between faith and love can be seen, and why one must say "We are just by faith" and how this is to be understood. One must not imagine "We are just by faith" means that on account of our renewal or our new virtues we are righteous, but instead that we are rightous because of Christ, who can be apprehended in no other way than through faith. To say that we are righteous by love is the same as to say that we are righteous through our virtues, or through our fulfillment of the Law. However, it is certain that we do not satisfy the Law. Therefore, it is necessary that this saying be retained in purity: "We are accounted righteous by faith," in order that it may be understood that we are righteous—accepted—not on account of our virtues, but on account of Christ, the mediator, through mercy, *gratis*. That is what Paul intends in this definition, which he amplified wonderfully by quoting certain words from Deuteronomy [Cf. Deut. 30:12–14].

### 6. Do not say in your heart

Paul changes the description of faith from the statement of Moses, but does not twist it to a meaning that does not fit. For there Moses also describes and requires faith. But the statement about the Word and about faith is general. Paul applies it to this word about Christ and to faith in Christ.

Let us first examine the statement of Moses, who pictures the wickedness of the human heart with clear figures. Although the heart knows there is a God, it doubts whether God is concerned about us, denies that the will of

God toward us can be known, and denies that he hears or saves us. It is apparent enough that these doubts cling to human minds. Therefore, the Law of God rebukes them and requires faith. "Do not say in your heart: 'Who will ascend into heaven?' " that is, do not be an Epicurean, or think that God is nothing, or doubt whether there is a God, or whether he is concerned about human affairs. Do not think that God is so hidden that his will is not expressed in some word. Do not think that his will is unknown just because he is not discerned with bodily eyes. Do not think that he does not hear, that he does not take pity, or does not require this worship which he taught in his Word, etc.

How then can God be found and apprehended? "The Word," he says, "is near" [v. 8]. Hence I lead you to the Word. Hear it, if you believe that God is apprehended and his will is seen when you hear the Word. Believe that this is the will of God, that he wants to be worshiped in this way, that He wants to hear, as he has promised. It is quite clear that this is the meaning in Moses. It is also not doubtful that Moses is here speaking about faith, and that he requires faith. Faith believes not only that there is a God, but also that God wants to be known through his Word, and to be invoked that he wants to hear, that he wants to take pity according to his promise, and that he demands these acts of worship.

These things which are spoken in general, although they contain the doctrine about faith, are nevertheless somewhat obscure, and are voices of the Law. Therefore Paul puts forward another Word and mentions the mediator in order that he may set forth gratuitous mercy promised because of Christ. When we acknowledge this, faith becomes certain that we are heard, saved, etc., *gratis* on account of Christ, not on account of the Law.

He applies this in this way: "Do not say in your heart, 'Who will ascend into heaven?' for that is to lead Christ down from heaven." This means first: Do not be an Epicurean; then, do not doubt that it is the will of God that Christ should be the mediator, that God wants to save us because of Christ. If you do not believe that Christ is the mediator, that he saves us, you pull him down from heaven, you deny that he rules and accuse God of lying, as if his promise were void.

### 7. Do not say, "Who shall descend into the abyss?"

This means, do not think after the manner of the Epicureans that there is not another life after death; neither think that men cannot be set free from sin and death. If you doubt, you deny that Christ rose from the dead. You imagine that Christ still lies dead, is yet to be resurrected, that he is not the victor over death and sin. The sum and substance of the statement is: Do not doubt that for his sake God truly takes pity on us, remits our sins, hears and

saves us. Thus Paul adds to the statement of Moses the Gospel about the
mediator, and includes the exclusive word in order that faith may be certain.

Let us oppose this very weighty speech of Paul to our infirmity and
doubting, and in it contemplate how great is the wickedness to doubt whether
God wants to remit sins, whether he wants to hear, help, save, and finally
grant us the things which he promised through Christ. Every time we pray,
let us think about these words: "Do not say, 'Who shall ascend into
heaven?' " For that would be to bring down Christ. Instead, declare that
Christ is truly sitting at the right hand of the Father, that he is our intercessor,
that we are heard. When we do this, we learn the power and meaning of this
saying. For those who do not pray deny that Christ is sitting at the right hand
of the Father, and that he is our intercessor, etc.

### 8. The Word is near, in your mouth

Earlier he reprehended doubting. Now he adds the affirmative description
of faith: "The Word is near, in your mouth." He defines the righteousness
of faith: it is not doubting, but believing this word about Christ and declaring
that Jesus is Lord, the one through whom the blessing has been promised
which liberates from death and sin.

There is a clear antithesis: The righteousness of the Law is to do the
Law. It is our obedience according to the Law, either perfect, or civil. But
the righteousness of faith is to believe that we are accepted because of Christ,
not because of our own worthiness, qualities, or virtues. Therefore, he opposes
this to the earlier definition, in which he says "to do." In the other definition,
he says "the Word is near, in your mouth and heart," because we accept
Christ through the Word, and we are righteous and accepted for his sake, not
because of our own worthiness.

This is worth observing also about the need for the ministry and for the
spoken word, and about the manner in which God deals with us. For one
must not imagine that God sends the Holy Spirit without his word. Paul leads
us to the ministry and to the spoken word. God is found nowhere outside of
his Word, or without his Word; he wants to be known through it. By means
of this instrument he wants to work. Therefore let us seek God through the
Word in every temptation, and let us resist with the Word. And let us declare
that this certainty is the will of God which is set forth in his Word. He is
saying this about a very great thing, namely, about salvation: "The Word is
near, in your mouth," and "The word of faith which we preach." And later
he will repeat this mode: "Faith comes from hearing, hearing through the
word of God" [10:17].

## 9. If you confess

"If you confess the Lord Jesus" is to be explained in this way: If you confess that Jesus is Lord, that is, not an idle lord, but that Lord about whom the promises were made, who liberates the human race from sin and death, who has been made the sacrificial victim for us, who sits at the right hand of the Father in order to save. For here one must learn from all the promises what the honor of the Lord is, and what benefits it embraces, as it says in the Psalm [110:1]: "The Lord said to my Lord," and in others.

### 10a. For with the heart one believes to righteousness

It is a clear testimony that we are justified by grace, but clearly to our adversaries these words are idle and signify nothing. Afterward they imagine many sophistic interpretations for them. Truly, we do not corrupt the saying of Paul, and truly we ascribe to faith what Paul ascribed to it. Neither is what he calls faith obscure, namely, that which the Word expresses.To believe in Christ, as he himself here explains faith, is faith which believes that Jesus is Lord. As above [10:9], it is that which accepts the promise. And here: "Everyone who believes in him," certainly means "who has confidence in him," that is, who is confident that God is favorable to us on account of him.

### 10b. With the mouth confession is made to salvation

Many people imagine this: Even if good works do not merit remission of sins, nevertheless afterward they merit eternal life. Many have said: Although people do not merit the first grace, nevertheless afterward they merit eternal life. For this they quote many statements: "With the mouth confession is made to salvation." Likewise: "I was hungry, and you gave me food" [Mt 25:35]. Likewise: "If I have all faith, but do not have love, I am nothing" [1 Cor. 13:2].

I answer all these statements in one and the same manner. I grant that a beginning of obedience is necessary, but it does not merit eternal life. Neither is it the purchase price of eternal life, nor is it pleasing except because we believe in Christ. Since obedience is pleasing because of faith, it is a contradiction to imagine that works either justify or that they merit eternal life. By faith we declare that remission of sins and eternal life are given us *gratis*, because of Christ. Nevertheless, the effect necessarily follows, namely, beginning newness when hearts are made alive by faith.

There is nothing troublesome about this interpretation. It grants that obedience is necessary. It takes away the opinion about merit. It teaches how one pleases in order that Christ may be accorded his honor, and that faith may remain certain. For it would become uncertain if one had to think that we pleased God when we had sufficient merits. This is profitable to know in general about all statements of this kind.

Now let us return to the text. It is certain that Paul does not approve of confession unless faith is present; he does not grant to confession that it is the purchase price or merit of eternal life. As has been said, that would be a contradiction. Yet he demands confession because, as has been said, obedience is necessary, and Paul wanted to show that he was speaking not of a hypocritical faith, that is, of idle thinking, but about a true impulse of the heart which lays hold of the mercy promised because of Christ. Therefore, patience and every kind of good work shines forth in confession.

Moreover, he distinguishes righteousness and salvation for the sake of perseverance. For although someone is righteous and is an heir of eternal life, it can happen that a righteous person again loses his righteousness. Therefore, he says: "If you confess," namely, because you have faith, as though he said: If your faith is firm and persevering." For he does not approve confession except because of faith.

**11–13. For all who call upon him**

First we must observe that he stresses the universal particle, and remind ourselves that the promises are universal. Second, we must consider what the purpose of this new statement is, and whether the statement "Every one who will call" agrees with the Gospel.

I answer: This is a new prophecy, distinguishing the Gospel from the Law, because the Law also teaches us to call on God, with the condition of perfect obedience. But this prophecy promises salvation to those who call on God, to those whom the Law formerly could not help, and who are still such that they cannot render the obedience which the Law demands. To those he now promises salvation if they call on the name of God, that is, if they call on him as the Lord who reveals himself in his Word which he gave to the fathers, which he handed down in the coming of his Son.

Here it is necessary that calling on God be understood together with the little word *gratis*. For it demands that we believe that we are heard and saved *gratis*, because of the promised Lord. This promise must be opposed to the Law, as if he said: "Because the Law could not help you, because you are under sin and death, salvation by another way is promised. God will give a teacher, he will pour out his Spirit, and by calling on the Lord, you will be saved from these very evils, from sin and death, from which the Law did not set you free."

That is the simple and true meaning of this promise. Therefore it squares perfectly with the Gospel, and adds a measure of light to the definition of the righteousness of faith which he handed down above: The righteousness of the Law is to do the law [10:5]. But the righteousness of faith is to call on the Lord, and to declare that on account of the Son of God we are set free from sin and death and from wrath, from which the Law could not set us free.

The promise will become sweet when the little word *gratis* is understood in it. Calling on God is to be practiced in this way, lest our own unworthiness scare us off, so we may know that it is a command of God that we should call on him. Likewise, that it is commanded that we believe that we are heard because of Christ, not because of our own worthiness. Therefore let us obey God and render him this act of worship.When we call on him, let us remember that we are bringing unworthiness and sins, and let us pray that we may be set free and heard because of Christ. When we do this we are at the same time repenting. Now it is easy to reconcile the dissimilar statements: God does not hear sinners, namely, those who call on him without repentance and without faith.

### 14a. How shall they call on him in whom they have not believed?

Paul adds the manner in which the benefits of Christ come to us, namely, through the ministry of the Word of God. This foremost passage about the necessity and the dignity of the ministry must be most diligently noted in order that we may know in what way God works in us, and may not seek other illuminations outside of the Word, nor grant entrance to imaginations and opinions about God without a sure word of God. This precept about the Word of God is wide open, for it is difficult for a man to stand fast by the Word of God and to say for certain that what he sets forth in the Word is the will of God, and so he easily slips into other imaginations. Thus Eve, thinking lightly of the Word, adds the imagination: "Perhaps God does not think so harshly."

So it happens in many articles. The Word says clearly: "We are righteous by faith because of Christ." Bad teachers, holding this word but weakly and following their own imagination, thought it would be more fittingly said that men are righteous on account of their own virtues and merits. Then they added that one ought to doubt, and completely destroyed the teaching about faith. So also now the Anabaptists despise the doctrine about faith. They loudly proclaim that people are righteous through the greatness of their afflictions and by certain illuminations of theirs, and so they cast off the Word and teaching about faith. Once upon a time such things were entirely the babblings of the Manichaeans and Enthusiasts. It is not an error of one time only, for people easily slip into such imaginations when they think lightly of the Word of God.

These Enthusiasts are to be avoided and cursed. And we must know that

God does not want His will about sin and about grace to be known and apprehended in any other way except in the Word, and that the Holy Spirit works through the Word. Let us hold this rule fast, and for this great reason show all honor to and defend the public ministry of the Word. And let us always keep these statements before our eyes: "Faith comes from hearing, hearing through the Word of God" [Rom. 10:17]. Likewise: "How shall they hear without a preacher?" [Rom. 10:14]. Likewise: "How beautiful are the feet of those who preach the Gospel of peace" [Rom. 10:15].

In the second place, this passage teaches that in calling on God faith is required, that is, this very faith, by which we believe that our sins are remitted to us and that we are heard on account of Christ, as Christ says [Mt. 6:23]: "Whatever you shall ask the Father in my name," that is, not bringing your own worthiness, but believing that you are accepted and heard because of Christ. So also this [10:14] teaches: "How shall they call on him in whom they have not believed?" If they do not believe that God is favorable toward them and that he hears their prayers, they cannot call on him. Therefore it is certain that faith is required in invocation. And this makes the difference between the invocation of the godly and that of the heathen or hypocrites. The Gentiles also pray, but with this doubt: they do not believe that God is reconciled to them and that he regards or hears their prayers. All who do not know the doctrine of the Gospel about justification and about faith pray in the same way. Such prayer is useless and condemned.

From this it can be understood how great is the darkness of those who boast that they are teachers of good works and yet reject the teaching about faith. For they destroy the chief and proper works of the godly, namely, calling on God. For this reason, not only the ceremonies and public prayers of the enemies of the Gospel, but also their private prayers are condemned, just like the prayers of the heathen such as are found here and there in poems. This must be diligently considered in order that we may learn what invocation or prayer should be like, and what is the difference between the prayer of a godly and an ungodly person. Likewise, what kind of faith the godly should have when they call on God. Wherever the teaching of this faith about which we are speaking here is ignored, it is impossible to have true prayer. Doubting and disbelief is strengthened that God does not hear, is not concerned, yes, that he will reject the one who is calling on him.

Let us Christians learn that such unbelief is sin. Let us fight against this sin and raise ourselves up by the true doctrine about faith. Let us know that faith must be brought to our calling on God, namely, that we believe that God is truly favorable toward us and receives our prayers because of our high priest, Christ.

**14b. How shall they believe if they do not hear?**

In the third place, this passage teaches that worship instituted without the Word of God is not pleasing to God because there can be no faith without the Word of God. That is why it is said here: "How shall they believe if they do not hear?" This passage contains rich teaching about how the benefits of Christ come to men through the ministry of the Word; how great is the need and the dignity of the ministry; and what is true calling on God, what acts of worship please God.

**15. How beautiful are the feet of those who proclaim peace!**

He adds a very sweet statement from Isaiah [52:7] which describes the kingdom of Christ. It reminds us that the kingdom must be administered through the Word, and indeed through the preaching of a new Word, namely, the Gospel, in which there will be proclaimed peace, that is, health and salvation which is divinely given. The contrast is opposed to the Law and sin and the miseries of mankind, as though he said: "Then will sin be taken away and the other ills which the Law could not take away, and there will be true comfort and the gift of righteousness and eternal life."

"The feet are lovely" is a figure of speech about the messengers of the Word, as if he said: "The ministry of the Word which will be preached in that new kingdom will be wonderfully lovely beyond measure because it brings the best things, knowledge of the mercy of God, righteousness, and eternal life. The prophet opposes this praise to the judgment of the world. For there is the greatest bitterness of hatred against the Gospel and the ministers of the Gospel, as Paul indicates that the apostles are considered refuse [1 Cor. 4:13]. Therefore, the world by no means judges these feet, that is, the messengers, to be salutary and lovely. The prophet comforts us against such judgments of the world and teaches us that we should love this ministry, although it is spurned and hated by the world, and we should know that it is efficacious and brings salvation to the believers. Thus Paul also says: "I am not ashamed of the Gospel" [Rom. 1:16]. Let us strengthen ourselves against the wicked judgments of the world, and let us consider how great a crime it is to practice cruelty against the godly ministers of the Gospel.

# Chapter 11

**1–7.** He tones down the above complaint about the falling away of the people, and testifies that the promise still belongs to the people, and that many will follow it, namely, those who believe. First he argues from his own example: I am an Israelite, and I have received the promise, so Israelites are able to obtain it. The other reason is taken from the example of the time of Elijah [cf. 1 Kings 19:10–18]. Thus he reminds us that the church is always small, and that the number and power of the wicked is much greater.

He adds the teaching that the church has not been elected on account of the Law, on account of the form of government, but that the people of God which accepts the Gospel by faith has been elected. He adds that the cause of election is mercy, not the Law, not the form of government, as was said above about the distinction between the two peoples. The synagogue has the title "people of God," and wages war against the true people and the true church. We need to be prepared against this offense, and forearmed in order that we may know that the church is not that crowd which persecutes the Gospel, even if they have the worship and the form of government.

### 8. He gave them a spirit of remorse

A spirit of remorse is an angry spirit, embittered with hatred of God and the Gospel. For there is a certain dreadful bitterness of hate in enemies of the Gospel, such as is described in Cain, Pharaoh, and similar persons. First, it is because the devil inflames those attacks. Second, because human reason itself is vehemently offended by the dissolution of acts of worship and of the state. It imagines the doctrine to be blasphemous and seditious, for they think the glory of God is injured by a change in acts of worship. So it was when the apostles abrogated the Levitical ceremonies, and it is also now, when human acts of worship like the abuses of the Mass are reprehended. Changes of acts of worship change also the form of government, and now it certainly tears the church apart. Each brings forth immense hatred because it is thought to harm the glory of God, and others are grieved that the authority of the church is shaken, that the order of the church is being destroyed, etc.

### 9. Also David says: "Let their table become. . . . "

He heaps up many statements which describe the punishments of wickedness. Blindness and hardening accompany contempt for the Gospel, which so occupy the mind that they are unable to return to reason. Then that very blindness heaps up errors and increases madness, offenses, and dreadful evils, both bodily and eternal. Thus he says about the blindness: "They have been blinded . . . " [v. 10; cf. Ps. 69:22, 23]

About other punishments: "May their table become a snare, an offense . . . " [v. 9]. "Table" signifies that in which men chiefly find repose, which seems to bring comfort, help, restoration, and quiet. Thus the table of Pompey was the king of Egypt, the one with whom he sought refuge, by whose aid he hoped he would be safe, but it turned out to be his destruction. As for the Jews, their table was the Law and their form of government at the time, and the most glorious title "people of God." They knew that these things had been divinely handed down and had been so long defended, and they thought that they could not be changed. Therefore, they condemned the doctrine which seemed to be against them, and hoped they would be victors, as their fathers before them had been triumphant. These things were a snare, that is, they held fast the minds that were caught in a net of evil persuasion, and afterward destroyed them, etc. And now the title "church" is the table of the adversaries of the church. It ensnares minds with a false persuasion, and it will be their destruction.

### 10. Bend their back forever

This means, burden them more and more with errors, offenses, sins, and calamities. Finally, oppress them with eternal servitude, lest they begin again to bloom, lest they recover their authority and rule.

The Anabaptists furnish a clear example. They brought forth new errors. Then they added the foulest offenses, seditions, lusts, and blasphemies so that now their madness might become manifest until they were finally utterly destroyed. Similar things happened to the Jews after they persecuted the Gospel. Let the threat of such dreadful punishment warn us not to despise the Gospel, lest we bring down such punishments on ourselves.

### 11–12. Did they stumble so that they might fall?

The proposition set forth above is repeated. The Jews were not caused to stumble in order that the race might perish. The reason is sharply delineated and has an obvious meaning. For the argument is taken from the ultimate cause of the reception of the Gentiles, in this way: the Gentiles have been received in order that the Jews might be challenged to believe when they see that the Gospel is efficacious in the Gentiles. Therefore, it is necessary that there be some remnants among the Jews who will believe. For what need would there have been to challenge the Jews if none were going to believe?

Paul appends the consequence in this way: if their downfall served to challenge them, then there is some remnant that is unharmed, that is, there must be some part that can be healed. This idea can also be enlarged from the minor premise: If their downfall served the acceptance of the Gentiles, how much greater will the safety be of those who obeyed when they were challenged, because God challenged them for this purpose, that he might heal them and render them whole and unharmed.

### 13–15. For I say to you Gentiles

He adds his own example to the reason taken from the ultimate cause. I, he says, am eager to propagate the Gospel among the Gentiles with all the greater diligence, in order that the Jews may be challenged to believe when they see that the Gospel is effective among the Gentiles. What he is saying is this: I glorify my ministry, that is, I teach with great confidence and diligence the Gospel by which the glory of God is adorned and shown, in order that I may challenge the flesh, that is, the Jews. And he adds an amplification from the minor premise: If their rejection was profitable, how much more glorious will their restitution be since it will be, as it were, a resurrection from the dead. This is the simple and least involved interpretation.

### 16–17. If the firstfruits are holy

The third argument, that the people of the Jews here not been rejected, is taken from the promise, which is immutable and pertains equally to the ancestor and to his descendants. The root is holy on account of the promise, since the fathers believed. Therefore also the branches are holy, because the promise pertains also to them, but it is necessary that the promise be accepted by faith.

### 18–24. Do not boast against the branches

Now he turns to the Gentiles. He exhorts them not to despise the Jews out of carnal security, nor run securely up against God, trusting in this title, that they are the people of God or the church. Thus now the popes promise themselves in carnal security that they are the church, and as a result of this opinion they establish and do many things against the Word of God. God will without doubt punish this wickedness according to the Second Commandment. As Ezekiel [36:23] says: "On account of us the name of God is in bad repute among the heathen."

What Paul here prophesies about the downfall of the church of the Gentiles shows the outcome. The church in Asia and Africa, having scarcely been founded, was destroyed by the rage of Mohammed. In Europe it is being dreadfully oppressed by idolatry and ungodliness, by the profanation of the

Masses, the invocation of the saints, by the superstitious opinions of human acts of worship, by ignorance of the doctrine of faith.

But we should comfort ourselves in the midst of these offenses with the fact that the promises of the Gospel are always valid for believers, and that there is always some true church, namely, those who repent and truly believe. Christ promises that the church will always remain and that the promises are immutable.

### 25–31. I do not want you to be ignorant

He adds a prophecy about the conversion of the Jews which should perhaps be understood in this way: It will come to pass that later, before the end of the world, some from among the Jews will be converted. But I do not know whether he wants to say that there will be a conversion of a great multitude about the time of the end of the world. Since this is a mystery, let us commit it to God. The prophecy of Isaiah [59:20, 21] preaches about the liberation of the people, namely about that liberation which the Gospel actually describes, that is, about the remission of sins. It is a sweet statement because it teaches clearly that in the New Testament forgiveness of sins is to be preached. This liberation of the people is to be understood as extending from the beginning of the preaching of the Gospel until the end.

### 32. God has confined all things

This is the closing word, in which there is an equalizing of Gentiles and Jews. Confidence in merits is taken away from both. He exhorts all to repent. Thereafter he sets forth comfort equally to all. There is most profound teaching in each part, for to be confined under sin is not to be understood without fear, but embraces guilt, fears, and judgment on and punishments of sin, as if he said: "All are guilty, all will be subjected to the judgment of God, to death and afflictions."

So David was confined under sin when he was driven into exile, when he was troubled by dreadful pains. In these afflictions, this comfort which is taught here must be held fast above all things. For it teaches about the cause of afflictions and judgment, and about its outcome. He says that we are subjected to these evils because of sin, but not in order that we may perish.

He adds the manner of the liberation. It is promised by gratuitous mercy, in order that the comfort may be sure. He commands us to believe that we are justified and saved through mercy, not because of our worthiness or merits. Yes, he commands us who are confined under sin, who are truly guilty, to flee to mercy, not to spurn the offered mercy, but to declare that we receive remission of sins *gratis*, because of Christ.

This statement will become clear and sweet when we put it to use, when in true fears and afflictions we feel that it pertains to us, and we will support ourselves by this promise of mercy. It is a useful statement and it should be used in all afflictions because it reminds us of the ultimate cause of afflictions, and also of gratuitous mercy.

The universal word should also be observed in order that we may know that the promise is universal, and in order that we, each and every one, may truly include ourselves in this universality.

### 33–36. O, the depth of the riches

An exclamation is added in order that he may rein in human arrogance and human thoughts about the counsel of God, by which he wonderfully established and governs his church. For many things offend human reason, for example, that only a few—and those being downtrodden people—make up the people of God, and that so great a multitude—which is outstanding in terms of number, virtue, and glorious deeds—is damned. The Jews were strangely offended when they heard that the synagogue had been rejected, since it had the most honorable title "people of God." Also now the minds of very many people are offended, and they murmur when they hear that those who hold the title "church" are not the church.

To these offenses Paul opposes this exclamation, in which he teaches that we should subject ourselves to the wisdom and the Word of God, and that we should not fall away from the Word, even if we do not understand why God governs the church according to such a wonderful plan.

We should do both, acknowledge the greatness of God's wrath in the rejection of so many peoples, for so many centuries, and so many persons. Let this wrath admonish us to fear, lest we despise the Word of God. Again, let us also acknowledge the mercy, that God has afterward renewed his Word and finally disseminated it in the whole world. Let us be strengthened by this testimony of the mercy, and declare that God truly wants to receive us, truly wants to make us his people, and truly wants to save those who call on him.

This is the sum and substance of the Pauline exclamation by which he meets the offenses and forbids human judgments about this secret counsel of God. Likewise, he forbids arrogance, lest we trust that we become the people of God on account of fleshly prerogatives or merits, as the bishops contend that they are the church on account of the succession.

# Chapter 12

He begins a new part consisting of precepts about good works. Above he taught the particular subject of the Gospel—the doctrine about justification and about faith. That is not the doctrine of the Law, and is far removed from the Law, as was said in the proper place. For first the remission of sins, justification, and the gift of the Holy Spirit must be accepted by faith, on account of Christ, *gratis*. Afterward it is necessary that the new obedience follow, which is a certain beginning of fulfilling the Law. Therefore the commandments are taught after the doctrine concerning faith.

But why must the commandments be taught, since it is the Spirit who obeys God? I answer: First, there is need for the Word, in order that the carnal part be coerced. Thereafter, it is necessary that the doctrine of repentance be constantly taught, and the remnants of sin in us mortified, so that repentance may increase. In the third place, there is need of the Word for the righteous, through which they are taught what works please God, and through which spiritual impulses are aroused. Therefore, after the doctrine of the Gospel and faith has been set forth, also the commandments or the Law are taught.

## The Doctrine concerning Good Works

Here now the doctrine of good works must be known—what kind of works are demanded, and how they can please.

First, what kind. For demanded are the good works which have been divinely taught, within and without, namely, fear of God, faith, love, repentance, patience, and calling on God. These inner impulses are not found in the ungodly, even if external civil discipline is present. Therefore, one must diligently consider what kind of works should be found in believers.

But in what way do they please? This teaching is necessary for the church, and is treated above in chapter 8. Both must be held fast: The first, that we are not righteous because of our virtues or works, and that sin still clings to us, which also defiles good works. Therefore, knowledge of our infirmity and repentance ought to increase in us. Next, although we are not righteous because of our virtues, after we have been reconciled by faith and are righteous, even beginning obedience is pleasing. This is not because it satisfies the Law or is without defect, but because of our high priest, Christ, who Inteicedes for us, etc.

This teaching is a great comfort for the godly, and the greatness of the mercy exhorts us to perform good works. For when a godly mind hears that even a small and contaminated measure of obedience is an act of worship of God and a sacrifice, it will without doubt be incited to furnish it with greater zeal. This entire topic has been treated above in the eighth chapter, where it has also been said what kind of sins are found in the saints, and also the distinction of venial and mortal sin. These topics, which belong to the doctrine of works, must be considered here in the beginning.

Now I return to the text. The twelfth chapter is about ethics; it deals with private virtues. The thirteenth is political, about the government and obedience. The fourteenth is ceremonial, about the use of ceremonies.

### 1. I implore you, brethren

To begin with, he puts forward a general command that we should practice some kind of worship of God, and indeed, a rational one, that is, such a one in which we acknowledge and apprehend God, or in which there are divine impulses, namely, fear of and trust in God. Then he gives a name to this worship. We should offer our bodies as sacrifices. Our bodies should be mortified and thus become sacrificial victims by mortifying our carnal affections and enduring afflictions.

It is a general command. It is noteworthy that he wants this obedience to be a rational worship, and that we should become sacrifices. Here, first of all, the entire doctrine about the priesthood and the difference in sacrifices must be reviewed.

Second, it must be diligently observed that he demands faith in that obedience and in all good works.

Third, note what kind of emphasis there is when he calls us sacrifices. Priests properly have three duties: to hold fast and to confess the Gospel, which has been divinely revealed; to have a command and promise about invocation; and sacrifice.

These belong first to Christ, through whom the Gospel has been revealed, who alone has the right of interceding for us, and of offering his sacrifices for others. Thereafter, Christ imparts the honor of the priesthood to the believers, because he gives them his Word, adds the promise that God will hear those who call on him, and gives them the fruit of his sacrifice. Then he demands sacrifices from them themselves, namely, confession and obedience in good works and afflictions.

Since believers are priests, Paul also preaches here about sacrifices, as Peter says: ''You are a holy priesthood, to offer spiritual sacrifices, acceptable to God through Jesus Christ'' [1 Pet. 2:5]. Here he says expressly that our acts of worship are accepted not on account of our worthiness, but on account of Christ, the high priest.

Here also the customary distinction between sacrifices must be maintained. One is the propitiary sacrifice for others, that is, which merits remission of sins for others, namely, the death of Christ. First of all, believers have that sacrifice by another which has been given to us so that we may declare by faith that the fruit or merit of this sacrifice has truly been given to us. Next, the believers also render their own sacrifices, but these do not merit remission of sins either for him who brings them or for others. They are pleasing in the reconciled on account of Christ, the high priest, as Peter [1 Pet. 2:5] says: ''That you may offer. . . . '' These sacrifices are called sacrifices of thanksgiving. For it belongs to the nature of this sacrifice to perform a work commanded by God to this end: that we may give thanks to God and glorify him, that is, that we may bear witness by this obedience that he is truly the God on whom we are calling, and that the things which we preach about him are true, and thus invite others by our example. This is the chief purpose of the sacrifice: that the glory of God may shine more brightly, and that God may become known.

Sacrifices are either ceremonial or spiritual. In the Old Testament slaughters of cattle and other ceremonies were performed which at that time had a command of God and foreshadowed the benefits of the Gospel. These shadows ceased after the Gospel was revealed. Since the New Testament brings righteousness and life in the hearts, worship and sacrifices should now be true and constant impulses of the heart, a constant glorification of God, as Christ says [Jn 4:24]: ''The true worshipers will worship God in spirit and in truth,'' that is, with true and spiritual impulses of the heart.

That is what Paul wants here when he calls for a rational worship, that is, worship of the mind, in which God is acknowledged and apprehended, in which there are true impulses toward God—fear, faith, calling on God, and confession. Paul rules out not only animal sacrifices, but also the works of men, and not only the traditions of the monks, but also moral works whenever they are done without fear of God and without faith. The saying of Paul fights everywhere with the opinion of the *opus operatum*; for the error of our adversaries must be detested, since they imagine that a Mass is valid *ex opere operato* [by virtue of the fact that the act has been performed] without a good impulse in the one who uses it.

When Paul here demands a rational worship, he demands a good motive in the user, namely, true impulses of fear and faith toward God.

This is what Paul says: ''I implore you that you present to God true, spiritual acts of worship, or impulses of the heart, so that your bodies may obey and become sacrifices, or that you may obey and become sacrifices."

But what is the emphasis in the word "sacrifices"? First, an offering is a certain confession or testimony that we acknowledge God. Sacrificing signifies that it is destined to death for sin, that this sinful nature must be destroyed, and that obedience must be rendered to God by that death. Therefore, he includes these three things when he mentions sacrifice: recognition or glorification of God; mortification of ourselves, or that obedience must be shown in such mortification; and faith, by which we believe that these sacrifices are pleasing to God on account of Christ, the sacrificial victim, to whom all sacrifices at all times pointed, and on account of whom they were accepted. Therefore the meaning is this: Become sacrifices, that is, acknowledge, proclaim, or glorify God, and undergo mortification, and believe that these acts of your worship are pleasing to God on account of Christ, on account of whom you also are sacrifices. This is the very simple meaning.

If now we consider that we are sacrifices, we shall understand that we have been called, not to the pleasures, riches, and power of this world, but to a violent death, dreadful hatred, and afflictions of every kind as we are attacked by the devil and by wicked men. And even as the sacrificial animal stands by the altar, constantly waiting until it is struck down, so let us stand at the altar, that is, in confession and glorification of God. Let us render obedience to God in persecutions and calamities as we are besieged. In the midst of them let us call on God and believe that these acts of worship are pleasing because of Christ, for whose sake we shall also be set free at some time.

He adds "life" because the New Testament brings perpetual righteousness and life. Therefore now perpetual sacrifices, perpetual praises, and giving of thanks are required. No longer are cattle to be slain, but such sacrifices which, although they are mortified, nevertheless at the same time receive new life in order that they may glorify God forever.

"Holy" means destined for divine uses, for calling on God, for proclamation, glorification, and other good works, but in such a way that they are directed to the end that the glory of God may be served.

"Pleasing to God": In order that a work may please God, two things are required: that there be a command from God, and that it be done in faith or trust in Christ, as it is written: "The just shall live by faith" [Rom. 1:17]. This faith is required in all good works so that we believe that these works are pleasing, not because of our worthiness, but on account of Christ, the high priest. As Peter also says [1 Pet. 2:5]: "Offering spiritual sacrifices acceptable to God through Jesus Christ." And in the last chapter to the Hebrews [13:15]: "Through him we offer the sacrifices of praise."

The sum and substance of this proposition is this: He commands that we obey God, and that this obedience be rendered in true fear of God, true faith, and to this end—that it may make known the glory of God and may invite others to godliness. Because he has transferred the doctrine about good works to the subject of sacrifices, he has embraced very many things, including that it is necessary to offer worship to God, and that it is necessary that we be subjected to afflictions. Also, it is necessary that all good works be done in faith, and be an example for inciting others, in order that God may become known. In addition, since they are sacrifices, they please God on account of Christ, the high priest, when accompanied by faith.

## 2. Do not imitate the attitude of this world

In this saying the earlier statement is repeated by way of contrast: Let us not have desires similar to those of the world, but new desires that obey God. When he forbids us to imitate the world, he is not criticizing the things which God has ordained for our use. He is not forbidding the use of foods, marriage, courts, contracts, and other ordinances of God, but is prohibiting wicked desires. Therefore, he says: "attitude," that is, the impulses of our minds are not to be similar to those of the world so that, contrary to the will of God, they desire pleasures that are sinful, seek wealth and power by unjust methods, and fall from the cross. He condemns such desires; these are the concerns of the greater part of the world. We see everywhere the minds of men inflamed with various kinds of desires—avarice, ambition, lusts—and because of these they trouble the whole world with tumults, murders, and wars, as daily life shows, as well as the histories of all times.

Against these, he commands us to be renewed in the mind. He commands us to think differently, to conceive different ideas about God and have other desires, namely, true fear of God and true faith, so that we place the will of God ahead of our desires.

He adds: "That you may know what is the good will of God." I understand this simply as the will of God set forth in his commandments and promises. He commands us to be renewed in such a way that we conceive a new concept of God and put on new feelings, namely, true fear of God and true faith. These feelings will exercise[1] themselves in all kinds of good works and afflictions so that we understand that obedience in afflictions is pleasing to God, and therefore bear adversities and do not flee from the cross.

---

[1] The text of CR and our 1540 edition both have *exerant*; we take this as a misprint for *exerceant*.

### 3–5. I say to you by the grace which has been given me

Among the virtues which pertain to the ministry, or to government or to administration, there are chiefly two: obedience in one's calling, and not to depart from the prescribed rule or mandate in judging or instituting something. To begin with, he speaks about these two virtues and says: "Let no one think arrogantly of himself," that is, let no one storm outside of his calling and arrogantly undertake something other than what the nature of his duty demands. Likewise: Let no one dare arrogantly to judge about dogmas contrary to the rule which has been handed down, or spread new opinions, or institute new acts of worship, inflated by the persuasion that he possesses great wisdom and holiness, above the measure of his gift.

Both commandments are necessary, most of all in the church. As in civil states meddling does much harm, when private persons push their way into what is being done and hinder ordinary activities, as Marius, Brutus, and others disturbed the state, so there is great danger in the church when some, either from foolish zeal or incited by other desires, break forth outside of their calling and try to reform many things in doctrine or in rites. This is also true when teachers, outside of their office, assume power in civil affairs and have one foot in the court, the other in the church. As Aristophanes said about Cleon, he had one foot in the camp, the other in the assembly.

Let us first remember here the command not to get confused about our calling. Everyone should diligently attend to the duties of his calling. The other commandment forbids us to judge contrary to the prescribed rule, that is, against the Word of God and saner judgments. Thus some, being puffed up with the foolish persuasion that they possess special wisdom, spread new opinions, institute new acts of worship, and pour out darkness on true and necessary articles. Let us remember that this audacity is particularly forbidden here when he commands that everyone should recognize the measure of his gift, that is, that he should obey his calling, and not take to himself judgment above the measure of his gift, nor affirm uncertain things.

Paul calls the measure of faith the measure of the gift. It should be exercised in faith, and it is given through faith. In the army one is the leader, another a tribune, another a quaestor. So in the church some teachers have greater gifts than others. Therefore Paul afterward adds an enumeration in order that each one may be mindful of his calling and his measure.

### 6–21. Whether prophecy

In the enumeration he prescribes rules for certain persons, for instance, prophets. Prophecy signifies revelation, predictions about future events, or interpretation of Scripture, for which there is also need of some revelation.

No one knows what true faith is, what true comfort for the conscience is, or true knowledge of sin, without a divine impulse. And some have clearer impulses than others.

Now he teaches that the interpretation of the Word of God should be analogous, that is, in agreement with the faith. It should not depart from the articles of faith, nor extinguish the true knowledge of Christ or faith in Christ. In earlier times, Ebion [the Ebionites], Paul of Samosata, and others who contended that there was only a human nature in Christ, departed from the faith. Thereafter the Arians, who denied that the Son of God was God by nature; the Manichaeans, who imagined two gods and condemned marriage, courts, and eating meat. Thus they imagined that people are righteous not by faith, but by such observances.

The Pelagians departed from the analogy of faith because they denied that there is such a thing as original sin and imagined that the Law of God is satisfied through such rational works as people can perform as well as possible. They felt that a man merited remission of sins by these works, and that he is righteous on account of rational works; they taught nothing at all of justifying faith. They added that people are righteous and saved without the Holy Spirit.

These pharisaical opinions destroy the Gospel of Christ completely. For Christ was given us because we do not satisfy the Law and because we are not righteous because of the Law. A different righteousness is set forth, namely, that we are accounted just by faith on account of Christ. Because Pelagian opinions take away the benefits of Christ, they certainly are not according to the analogy of faith.

Such are also the opinions of our adversaries, who imagine that people can satisfy the Law of God, and merit remission of sins by means of works, and be righteous because of works. They have said nothing about justifying faith; therefore their teaching is not analogous to the faith.

Also the opinion about the Mass, that it is a work which is to be applied to others, militates against the faith because the Mass benefits only the person who calls to memory the death of Christ, as the text itself testifies. Therefore one must not believe apparitions of spirits which beg for Masses.

Likewise, the opinions of the monks—that the works taught by traditions are worship of God, that they are perfection—disagree with the faith.

Neither is the invocation of the saints analogous to the faith. One must not believe apparitions or miracles which confirmed those acts of worship, because one certainly must not believe miracles or apparitions contrary to the clear Word of God, as Deut. 13 clearly teaches. Paul is here alluding to this passage when he opposes the rule about the analogy of faith to the authority of those who appear to be prophets.

# Chapter 13

Above he set forth precepts about private morals and taught ethics. Now he adds precepts about the life in the state. It does not belong to the Gospel, but to the judgment of reason and the counsel of the magistracy. Passing laws about contracts, successions, court actions, punishments, war, and similar civil or forensic things belongs to reason, like matters of architecture, or the art of physicians. Nevertheless, it is necessary that there be a word of God about the use of these arts for two reasons: that the works of God may be acknowledged, and that we may know their use is permitted to the godly, because our works need to have a testimony from the Word of God.

Let the readers here note first to what extent the Gospel speaks about political matters in general. They should remember that the Gospel does not set up any kind of worldly government, but approves the forms of government of all peoples and the laws about civil matters which are in agreement with reason. Thus it approves of medicine and the art of building. Meanwhile, the Gospel teaches the godly properly about spiritual and eternal life in order that eternal life may be begun in their hearts. In public it wants our bodies to be engaged in this civil society and to make sure of the common bonds of this society with decisions about properties, contracts, laws, judgments, magistrates, and other things. These external matters do not hinder the knowledge of God from being present in hearts or fear, faith, calling on God, and other virtues. In fact, God put forth these external matters as opportunities in which faith, calling on God, fear of God, patience, and love might be exercised.

There is a certain wisdom worthy for a Christian to know. God cast the church into the midst of these occupations because he wants to become known among men in a common society. He wanted all offices of society to be exercises in confession, and at the same time exercises of our faith and love.

Minds must become accustomed to think reverently about all areas of civil society because minds are greatly hurt by fanatical opinions that governments, laws, courts, and contracts are things thought out by human ingenuity and are only instruments of human greed; that governments are instruments for exercising unjust power against those who are weaker; and that courts serve the desire for revenge or avarice. So the monks regard these things, and so they disapprove of them or certainly obscure their dignity.

On the contrary, we should think honorably of them. They are gifts and ordinances of God, handed down for this purpose first, that this society may be preserved for the purpose of teaching. Second, that these offices of society themselves may be exercises of confession. Third, that in these works we may exercise fear of God, faith, prayer, love, etc. Therefore let us realize that it is wicked to despise or harm these divine things.

### 1–4. Let every soul be subject to the higher power

To begin with, he teaches simply and clearly that everyone should obey his own government. The words "which are over you" were not added without cause, but exclude foreign governments. It is not necessary for a citizen of Cologne to obey the government of Paris. But this is what Paul teaches: we should obey that government which is over us, or that everyone should obey his own government.

Then he adds the reason for this precept: "for there is no power, except from God." He teaches what government is and whence it comes. He shows that it must be obeyed in a different way from the way someone endures unjust violence from a robber or thief, in such a way that we remember that also the form of government or the government itself is a good thing, divinely ordained, and declare that this obedience is required by God, to be rendered as by God's own ordinance. There was need in the church of this reminder in order that the godly might know what is to be thought about political matters, lest they condemn governments, courts, and other political offices, chiefly because many misuse these words. When a person who is not rightly instructed looks on these evils, he does not distinguish between governments and robberies.

Thus the Manichaeans totally condemned forms of government. Also the monks darkened the true doctrine about government when they imagined that abstaining from civil offices would constitute perfection. On the contrary, they should have taught whether there is such a thing as perfection. These works have been put forward by God in order that God might become known in society, and in order that we may have exercises of confession, patience, faith, and love. Therefore, to flee from these exercises would be weakness rather than perfection, as it is customarily said: "Government shows the man." Finally, improper ideas have at all times been scattered in the church about civil matters. Therefore it is very profitable to maintain the true teaching about this business.

This proposition of Paul is first that government, that is, the order of rules or the form of the state, is a good thing, which God by his own work both instituted and preserves. Also the order of the movements of the heavenly bodies has both been instituted by God and is preserved by him. When Paul says that governments are from God, we should understand that they are not only permitted by God, as sins are said to be permitted, but that they are rather works of God, instituted and preserved by him, and confirmed through his Word. Paul clearly calls government an ordinance of God, that is, a thing which is instituted by the counsel of God in order that it may be in harmony with his will, or that it may be approved by him. Sins are not ordained by God; rather, they are the violation of his ordinance.

These things are said briefly by Paul, but they are very important. First it is necessary that this teaching be found in the church, lest a work of God be ascribed to the devil, and so that the works of God and the works of the devil may be distinguished from each other. Second, we may know that these offices have been set before us to be exercises of confession, calling on God, and other virtues, to become acts of true worship of God. Third, obedience may be strengthened, lest we violate a divine ordinance, and may remember that God is the protector and preserver of his ordinance. Fourth, the government and all of us in civil life may have the comfort that God governs these dangers of civil life and preserves kingdoms, civil righteousness, and peace in the world, and punishes tyrannies and robberies.

This is a very great comfort to all godly persons in light of the great dangers to governments. The godly should consider the magnitude of these things, namely, that states are overthrown not only by human audacity, but much more by the fury of the devil, who is the enemy of discipline and of things honorable. Therefore Christ calls him a murderer [cf. John 8:44]. And in Daniel [10:13, 20–21] it is written that a good angel defended the Persian kingdom against an evil angel. The devil incites his members to destroy public harmony. Neither should only the authors of danger be considered. Remembering this comfort of the Scripture—that God wants to preserve governments—we should add prayer, as the Scripture teaches in many places.

I have briefly related these things in order that we may consider the benefits of this doctrine and carry this over into life for application. In public office, we exercise confession and prayer, which are the chief purpose of civil society.

Then let a comparison be made. No philosophy is able to speak so honorably about governments. For although reason is moved by certain signs to think that governments are from God, it is in doubt because of various scandals when it is not strengthened by the Word of God. It certainly does not see that God wants to govern our dangers in civil administration, that he wants to be invoked, and that the administration of these matters becomes an act of worship of God. Therefore, let students gather testimonies from other passages of Scripture which confirm the meaning which Paul here teaches. Let them also observe how to refute things which are put forward as objections, about the prohibition of revenge and other things.

Now that this proposition has been set up, that governments are good things which God both establishes and approves, Paul's conclusion follows: One must obey the authorities because God does not want his ordinance to be violated. Then is added an argument from punishment, which should be understood not only of those punishments which the authorities impose, but in general about all punishments into which seditious and contumacious people fall because they are divinely dragged toward punishments, even though no danger threatens them from the authorities. As Solomon says, an ungodly person cannot escape war [Prov. 19:5].

Up to this point he has taught two rules, that authorities or government are good things and approved by God, and also that it must be obeyed, where he includes the teaching about punishment, which he repeats later. Meanwhile he inserts a description of the government—what it is—in this way: The government is a minister of God to us for good, a protector for defending right actions and for punishing transgressions with the sword, that is, with corporal punishments.

This definition is complete and better than the Aristotelian definition, which is as follows: The government is the guardian of the laws. For Paul adds the efficient cause—that it has been instituted by God. And with respect to the ultimate cause he adds the clear words: "To you for good," where he distinguishes the tyrant from the true ruler. For a magistrate should think that he had been divinely placed in this office so that he should plan what is useful for others, as Aristotle reminds Alexander that he should think that the kingdom had come to him in order that he might do good to the entire human race, not that he might be unscrupulous and scornful toward others. Daniel also says to the king: "Free yourself from sin through justice, and do good to the poor" [Dan. 4:7]. Also the saying of Xenophon is praised: "A good ruler is not different from a good father." Thus a magistrate should think that authority and wealth have come to him not so that he can misuse them to fulfill his desires, but so that he may be able to counsel for the common good, and that right actions may be protected, such as the true worship of God, discipline, the courts, and peace.

But in connection with this definition people ask how we know what are right actions. I answer: Paul here avoids a longer discussion and speaks generally in order to approve the laws of all peoples about civil matters, if only they are in agreement with the law of nature. For from it he wants right actions in civil matters to be judged. Therefore, he is here teaching the third rule: A Christian is not bound to the Mosaic form of government, but is permitted to use the laws of all nations which are in harmony with reason. A Christian owes obedience to his present government, as was said above [13:1] in the words: "To the authority which is over him." He owes obedience to the present laws which are in agreement with reason. Therefore it is permissible to hang thieves; it is permissible to divide inheritances according to our laws, because the Gospel does not establish a new, worldly form of government, but preaches about eternal and spiritual life. Meanwhile, it permits us to use various forms of governments, even at various times of days. Because obedience toward present laws is taught, it is taught also that we may make use of present laws. In Luke 3 [:14] service in the Roman Army is approved. And in Acts 15 [:19–21] the apostles forbid that the Gentiles should be burdened with the Mosaic form of government. Paul also says: "In Christ there is neither Jew nor Greek" [Gal. 3:28].

### 5. Therefore you must obey, not only on account of wrath

To the precept about obedience he adds a necessary explanation, in order that the church may know why it is necessary to obey and what a sin it is not to obey. The question is often argued whether or not obeying the government is a mortal sin. And the opinion is urged that since the government is not able to understand eternal punishment, the laws of the government do not seem to obligate under eternal punishment.

But in reasoning thus, those who follow this do not see that they deceive themselves. Eternal punishment is inflicted because of a violation of the divine commandment, which prescribes obedience. For God made us subject to the government and added the commandment that we should obey its laws. With respect to the punishment, he adds that he will punish those who do not obey. Therefore, one must set down as a rule that not to obey the government or the one who bears the sword—about whom he is speaking here—is a mortal sin, because Paul says clearly: "It is necessary to obey," and adds: "For the sake of conscience." Therefore he means that consciences are rendered guilty in those who despise the government. The things which make the conscience guilty are mortal sins, and drive out faith. He explains the necessity so that it may be understood of an obligation to the conscience and about eternal punishments. Who does not see what a rein is here cast on all persons for observing obedience to the powers that be?

Elsewhere it is said that believers are free from the Law. Here, however, they are subjected to the laws of the government, and subjected in such a way that Paul says they are condemned if they do not obey. One must know that spiritual freedom does not exclude this obligation, which remains on account of our bodily life. We are free from the Law as far as it concerns justification in the spirit, that is, we must think that we are forgiven and that we are accounted righteous not on account of the Law, but on account of Christ. Nevertheless, obedience is necessary in our bodily life. For our bodily life has been made subject to ordinances which pertain to the body, such as laws of health and marriage, and also the civil laws.

Then this obligation must be widened. If the conscience becomes guilty, the curse and wrath of God follows, which brings present and eternal punishments. For example, sometimes evildoers escape but are divinely brought to punishment. Likewise, scornful persons, even if they cannot be coerced at present, nevertheless later fall into other snares in order that they may pay the penalties, as happened to Clodius, Catiline, Mark Antony, and others, who had from time to time stirred up new tumults. God curses the counsels and undertakings of such persons, so that they rush into civil and eternal punishments. Paul includes all these things when he says: "For conscience sake."

These things do not pertain only to subjects, but also to magistrates. When these become tyrants, they destroy the ordinance of God no less than do seditious persons. Their consciences become guilty because they do not obey the ordinance of God, that is, the laws which they ought to obey. The threats set down here pertain also to them. As the Scripture says elsewhere: "You are not exercising man's judgment, but the Lord's. Whatever you judge shall overwhelm you" [cf. 1 Pet. 2:13–17]. For this statement must always be kept in mind—that government is an ordinance of God. Therefore whoever violates it sins, whether he be a subject or a superior, and God will impose punishments, for instance, if in church he despises the sacraments.

The severity of this commandment should move all not to think that violation of the political estate is a small matter. On the contrary, let us learn that in those who believe in Christ, the works of political and economical life are good works and acts of worship of God, not merely secular works, because society must be preserved in order that God may become known in it. This purpose is not a worldly matter, since all activities of the political life are aimed at this purpose: God wanted them to be exercises of confession, and on account of this purpose he imposed them on us. Therefore the prophets demand these works, and even more so than ceremonies, as in Isaiah 1 [:17]: "Judge the fatherless. . . . "

But here the question is asked: If violation of civil laws is a mortal sin, what should be thought about the violation of ecclesiastical laws which are laid down by the bishops? I answer: First of all, one must not obey traditions which militate against a commandment of God, whether they originated with magistrates that bear the sword or with bishops, because one must obey God rather than men. Such are the traditions about celibacy, about the misuse of Masses, and about prayer to the saints. And although the eating of meats and certain other similar things are of themselves adiaphora, they are taught with an ungodly opinion and for strengthening ungodly acts of worship, so those who do not obey them are acting rightly, even as the brothers in the history of the Maccabees acted rightly when they refused to eat pork. When doctrine is at stake, actions must be examples of confession, as also Paul did not permit Titus to be circumcised.

Second, if there are traditions about indifferent things made for a political purpose, such as the observation of a certain day or the reading of a certain history for the sake of learning, a violation of these traditions, except in the case of offense, is not a mortal sin, because Paul says [Col. 2:16]: ''Let no one judge you with respect to a festival day.''

But here there is set before us an example of why civil laws obligate more than ecclesiastical laws. I answer simply that the Scripture teaches this difference. It says clearly that consciences are defiled if one does not obey the magistrate who bears the sword [Rom. 13:5]. And again it says clearly that consciences are not defiled through violation of traditions which bishops lay down, as statements to the Galatians and the Colossians testify [cf. Gal. 4:9; Col. 2:8]. Let this reason be sufficient for the godly.

Someone may object: Is greater reverence owed to the civil power? No, the greatest reverence is owed to the ministers of the Gospel, and without doubt all who do not obey the Word which has been entrusted to the ecclesiastical power sin mortally. Second, also those who in a matter of offense violate the teachings of the pastors sin mortally, for instance, if someone, by his example in a church which is rightly set up, invites others to show contempt for the teaching and the ministers. But one who violates them without scornfulness and without an evil example does not sin mortally. Christ wants this freedom to be found and understood in the church.

Reasons may also be gathered from the difference of authorities. God committed to magistrates that they should lay down just laws; therefore, he wants us to be subject to those laws. But to pastors he gave his sure Word; he does not want us to be over and above lawgivers, or to add other laws. Therefore, he requires that we should be subject to the Word that has been handed down, not to new laws which will be added over and above this. The difference of powers adds some light to this question. Nevertheless, it is safer to depend on the other reason, namely, that the apostolic teaching demands that we consider the violation of civil laws to be a mortal sin. On the other hand, a violation of church tradition, with the exception of the case of offense and scornfulness, is not a mortal sin.

Earlier he spoke in general about obedience; now he mentions certain duties in particular, and first tributes, under which term he includes all things which are owed to the authorities for the defense of discipline and peace, namely works, military service, wages. He again repeats the praise of the authorities, because he calls them servants of God. Therefore he testifies that the function of the government is a good work, because the devil is an enemy of God, not a servant, and sins are not a function by which service is rendered to God, but they offend God, and destroy the functions by which God is served. This argument becomes clearer when the circumstance set down above is added, namely that it is a service that is divinely ordained. For it is clear that sin is not something divinely ordained, but rather the destruction of the ordinance of God.

**6.** There is added here also an important word about the diligence which is required in magistrates. For Paul says [v. 6]: "They attend diligently to this," that is, to the service of God, that is, to the propagation of true worship, and to the defense of discipline and peace, which are divine benefits. And diligent attendance is a great effort of the mind, which does not relax its care, vigilance, and labor, even as it is most true that government is a burden to which no human wisdom can be equal. Nevertheless diligence, which he here calls *assiduitas*, is required of magistrates, which, God helping, is successful.

**7.** Thereafter he adds a general precept about all civil offices: "Render to all what you owe them." In this saying he embraces all duties that are necessary in society. He commands that we render the obedience we owe to superiors. He commands that we pay the money we owe to anyone in contracts. He commands that we render the duties we owe to the family, citizens, parents, spouse, children, and servants. The Decalog shows what the duties are which are owed to each individual which he repeats here [v. 9] in order that we may have a sure teaching about which works are necessary. For it is necessary that the conscience have a sure word also about works, according to which they are regulated, lest acts of worship be imagined without a word of God. About such works Christ says: "In vain they worship me with the commandments of men" [Mark 7:7].

**8–10.** Many twist this statement against the doctrine of faith because Paul here says that the Law is fulfilled by love. From this they argue: Fulfillment of the Law justifies, and love is the fulfilling of the Law; therefore love justifies. I answer very briefly to the minor premise: The minor premise is true with respect to perfect love, but not with respect to the kind of love which any human beings demonstrate. Paul says rightly and properly about the ideal, or about the essence, that love fulfills the Law, that is, that which the Law demands. But it does not follow from this that the Law is fulfilled by our love, because our love is unclean and far removed from perfection.

Since nobody could furnish perfect love or fulfillment, we have need of another righteousness, one which by faith apprehends the mercy promised on account of Christ. This faith is fulfillment of the Law by way of imputation. The believers are accounted righteous just as if they had fulfilled the Law. Thereafter there is added also that faith begins the fulfillment of the Law in us, and this beginning pleases because we are in Christ.

### 11a. The hour is at hand for us to wake from sleep

He adds an exhortation taken from the circumstance of the time, namely, that now salvation is being bestowed; the Gospel has been revealed. Therefore let us not spurn so great a gift, but let us eagerly embrace it and obey. Thus it is also elsewhere frequently argued from the time in 2 Cor. 11[1] and Hebr. 3 [:7, 13, 15]. Such a time is whenever God gives the true light of the Gospel, which was widely dispersed among the Gentiles after Christ appeared, although before they had not known the promises and the Gospel.

By sleep he understands ignorance of the true doctrine. Watchfulness must mean the new knowledge of the Gospel and new actions. And that he commands us to wake up signifies that we are being called to great struggles, dangers, and watchfulness. But the world, by contrast, becomes all the sleepier when the Gospel is heard, and falls asleep anew. For carnal security brings forth negligence, through which various evils slip in little by little. He censures this negligence when he commands us to wake up. Therefore he commands afterward to put on the armor of light, for he indicates that there is need of a great struggle, lest we be lost [v. 12]. For the armor of light is knowledge of the Word of God, knowledge of God, and the other virtues with which those who use the Word of God fight against the devil. Conversely, the works of darkness are ignorance of God and the evils which this ignorance gives rise to, for there the devil rules.

### 11b–13. For salvation is now closer

Salvation should be understood of Christ himself, and of the ministry of the Gospel, not about the effect. Christ has now been revealed, and remission of sins has been openly promulgated and given, and the ministry of the Gospel has been instituted. The patriarchs expected and believed that Christ would come. Therefore salvation is closer to us, because Christ has been revealed, and the remission of sins promulgated, and the ministry of the Gospel instituted. For the patriarchs knew that Christ would come, and they knew that forgiveness of sins was wrapped up in the promises, but they did not have the ministry instituted with the express command to remit sins. As for the effect, we must know that the patriarchs were saved by faith in the promised Christ, even as the church is saved after Christ has been revealed. Neither is

---

[1] Our 1540 edition has 2 Cor. 6 [:2] which fits the context much better.

there any other salvation of the patriarchs, or of the church after Christ has been revealed, but there is only this difference: they believed in a Christ who would come, we in one who has come.

### 14. But put on the Lord Jesus

To put on Christ signifies not merely imitation, as if he said to put on the ornament of Christ and imitate his virtues. It means more, namely, to apprehend Christ by faith and to believe that because of him the Father is favorable toward us. Likewise, that he works in those who call on him. For Christ is not merely our example like the other saints. He is the cause and author of our salvation, the sacrificial victim and Savior. Therefore let putting on Christ be understood in both ways, that we apprehend him by faith as our Savior and acknowledge that he is the umbrella by which we are protected against the wrath of God. Then follows the imitation of his example.

# Chapter 14

Earlier it was said that there are three kinds of works: private, political, and ceremonial. Since the most useful precepts about the others were taught above, now the teaching about ceremonies is added. Because this life cannot be without ceremonies, that is, some regulations of times and certain exercises, it was necessary that the church be reminded of their use. For error about ceremonies brings forth many very great troubles.

First, the doctrine of the Gospel about faith and the benefit of Christ is obscured when the opinion creeps in that such observances merit forgiveness of sins, and that we are righteous on their account, as the Jews imagined about their rites. This opinion naturally occupies minds unless they are rightly instructed from the Gospel.

Second, the teaching about the difference of works is extinguished when ceremonies are preferred to political life, yes, preferred also to inner spiritual exercises, to patience and prayer. Thus the monks called their observances perfections.

Third, the opinion that they are necessary creeps in, which is a dangerous torture of consciences.

Fourth, the opinion that they are necessary brings forth discords that cannot be healed, as were the disagreements about Easter long ago.

Fifth, when the true use of ceremonies is not known there is falsely ascribed to the bishops the authority of instituting new acts of worship. Thus the teaching of the New Testament is ignored, ungodliness is strengthened, and the tyranny of the bishops is increased.

Since error about ceremonies brings forth such great and numerous difficulties, it is necessary that their use be rightly taught. Paul here teaches in sum that neither the Mosaic ceremonies nor similar ones instituted by men are to be observed as being necessary, because the righteousness about which the Gospel speaks is not observance of Mosaic or similar rites, but knowledge of Christ, new and spiritual life in the heart. In the outer life, while it is lawful to use various intervals of days, it is also permitted to use different rites. He does not want the opinion of righteousness and necessity to be imagined for ceremonies.Neither does he want discord to be sown about rites, either Mosaic or human. This is the sum and substance of this chapter, which does not talk about sacraments, which have a command, because they are signs added to the promises. Likewise, they are testimonies of confession, but here also it is profitable that human traditions be distinguished.

There are three kinds of ceremonies. The first kind is traditions which teach something that cannot be done without sin. Such is the tradition about celibacy, since it is imposed on those who are not fit for it. Likewise, the profanation of Masses and the worship of the saints. About this kind, the rule must be held fast: "We must obey God rather than men" [Acts 5:29]. Therefore such traditions are condemned by divine authority.

The second kind is traditions which make rules about things that are adiaphora according to their nature such as feast days, dress, and food. With respect to these, the purposes must be considered. If the purpose is political, they are lawful traditions, as when festival days are observed not as though this were an act of worship, but for the sake of order, that people may know at what time they should come together to hear the Gospel and for the Lord's Supper. Since man naturally understands order and needs to arrange his activities in an orderly manner, church activities also ought to have their order. Neither can life be without such rites and ordinances that make for good order. Therefore also Paul commands: "That in the church all things should be done decently and in good order" [1 Cor. 14:40].

The third kind is traditions regarding adiaphora that are thought to be acts of worship, meritorious, or necessary. Such traditions obscure the doctrine of the Gospel, and the opinion which comes to them makes godless traditions of adiaphora. Therefore they are rightly violated and abolished in order that the false opinion may be corrected, for it is necessary that errors about worship, merits, and necessity be rejected.

[False] worship can be such a work. The immediate aim of [true] worship is not something useful for the body, but that God may be honored by this work. But the people think about the distinction of foods that this work is done because it is an honor which God requires and approves. About them Christ says: "In vain they worship me with commandments of men" [Mark 7:7].

Frequently they add to it the opinion of merit, which is even more openly ungodly—that such a work merits forgiveness of sins or eternal life, that it is righteousness, that it is perfection, or that it is satisfaction. These errors must necessarily be condemned.

The opinion of necessity prevails when people think that the violation of something is a mortal sin. The Gospel condemns this opinion according to the passage: "Let no one judge you in matters of food, of drink . . . " [Col. 2:16]. Therefore one should hold that the Gospel has ordained this freedom in matters which are permitted by the Word of God, and that it does not want to have such things made matters of right or wrong. It is profitable to keep these kinds of tradition in mind in order that one may know which traditions are to be rejected and which ones may be retained.

## Regarding Christian Liberty

Here it is necessary also that we speak about Christian liberty. For the purpose of teaching, I distinguish four degrees of Christian liberty.

The first is that remission of sins, imputation of righteousness, and eternal life are not given on account of the Law or our virtues, but *gratis*, on account of Christ, only that we should believe that these things come to us on account of Christ. About this degree Christ says: "If the Son makes you free then you are truly free" [John 8:36].

The second degree is that in the remission of sins the Holy Spirit is given, who helps us to begin to obey the Law of God, rules us, and defends us against the snares of the devil. Although this degree is linked to the one above, I distinguish it in the enumeration so that the benefits of Christ may be more clearly seen. Here belongs the saying of Paul: "Where the Spirit of the Lord is, there is liberty" [2 Cor. 3:17]. For that lifts up hearts so that they are not oppressed by the terrors of sin, other terrors, or death. The Spirit moves them so that they begin to obey God, as is said elsewhere: "The Holy Spirit helps our infirmity" [Rom. 8:26]. This liberty will be complete after the resurrection. Meanwhile, however, it must be begun in this life in the exercises of faith and prayer. In these exercises it is understood and grows when we sustain ourselves with the Word of God, in order that we may overcome terrors and griefs. These two degrees chiefly constitute Christian liberty and pertain to spiritual and eternal life (which must be begun in this life) and their knowledge affords great comfort to the godly.

The third degree is that the Gospel frees us from the ceremonies and the civil or judicial laws of Moses. This degree pertains in some measure to the outer life, but has its cause in the earlier degrees. For the reason why the Gospel does not require the Levitical ceremonies is that it teaches that we are pronounced righteous not on account of those acts of worship or other works of ours, but by faith through mercy on account of Christ. And since the Gospel teaches about spiritual and perpetual righteousness of the heart, it does not require the form of government or the civil laws of Moses, but permits us in this bodily life to use the laws of all governments under which we live, as long as they are in agreement with reason, even as it permits us to use the architecture and medicine of all nations.

Here someone may ask: If the Gospel abrogates the law of Moses, then why does it not also abrogate the Decalogue, particularly because that part of the law is the most difficult? I answer, first most bluntly: The Decalogue is not retained because it is written in the law of Moses, but carnal persons must be coerced by the moral law because it is the common law of all men. The regenerate indeed begin to obey that law not because it is the Mosaic form of government, but because the Gospel preaches repentance and brings the Holy Spirit, because it begins spiritual worship in us. Therefore the Decalogue—that law which is common to all men—is retained because it condemns sins and teaches spiritual worship.

That is the bluntest kind of answer, and although it is true, not enough has yet been said about this matter. Therefore it is necessary that the chief reason be added, also the teaching about the abrogation of the Law or freedom from the Law. First, as far as justification is concerned, the Gospel truly frees us from the whole Law.It declares that we are pronounced righteous because of something else—on account of Christ, not on account of the Law. Therefore, those who believe in Christ have the forgiveness of sins, although infirmity still clings to them, which keeps them from fulfilling the Law. The chief reason why the abrogation of the Law must be taught is that it is necessary to teach consciences correctly about justification. Therefore it is necessary that this response be added to the earlier one.

Second, although we have been set free as far as justification is concerned, the Law has not been taken away as far as obedience is concerned, because the Gospel preaches repentance, subjects us to God, and begins spiritual obedience in us. Therefore, it is necessary that those acts of worship be begun which are contained in the moral law. Nevertheless, because we do not satisfy the Law, it meanwhile teaches that we are righteous by something else—because of Christ, by faith. Thus it frees consciences from that dreadful burden, from the terrors and the condemnation which the Law would bring, since we do not satisfy it, if we were not set free and righteous because of something else. This is what Paul is teaching when he says that we have been freed from the curse of the Law [Gal. 3:13]. For he says clearly "from the curse" in order to signify that freedom from the Law is freedom from the terrors and from the condemnation which the Law brings unless we lay hold of the mercy promised because of Christ by faith. It can be known from these facts that we have been set free from the whole Law as far as justification is concerned. Nevertheless, it is necessary that obedience be begun.

The fourth degree of Christian liberty is that while the Gospel permits some ordinances about times and practices in the church to be made by men in the interest of good order, it wants us to think that these observances are not acts of worship, that they do not merit remission of sins, and that they are not righteousness or perfection. Also, except in case of offense, they can be omitted without sin. Concerning this degree Paul teaches in Col. 2 [:16]: "Let no one judge you in food, in drink." He is not speaking only about Mosaic rites, but in general about Mosaic and all other ceremonies which are instituted in the church by human authority. Therefore he expressly names human traditions later when he says [in Col. 2:22]: "according to the precepts and doctrines of men."

Knowledge of this degree is very necessary for the churches to avoid many errors. Men are naturally inclined to false acts of worship, and in dangers they take refuge in their own righteousness or merits, so they erroneously think up and heap up acts of worship. Therefore, it is necessary that the churches be forewarned so that they may truly understand the teaching about faith, true prayer, and the worship of faith, and may know that acts of worship instituted without a divine command are displeasing to God.

David says about Levitical sacrifices [Ps. 51:16]: "For if you desired a sacrifice, I would give it; but surely you will take no pleasure in whole burnt offerings." In this verse he indicates that human minds seek sacrifices when they are afraid, but he calls them back from works to faith and acknowledgment of mercy. Since this is said about Levitical sacrifices, how much more is the opinion of worship or merit to be taken away from human traditions. If someone were now to restore circumcision or the Levitical burnt offerings, all would rightly be disgusted with him. So also we should detest monasticism and the ceremonies of the ungodly which are performed with the idea that they are acts of worship or merit. This picture must be set before the godly so that they may declare more firmly that such acts of worship are to be disapproved and avoided.

I have listed many reasons above why knowledge of this fourth degree of liberty is necessary for the church. Also, the opinion that a thing is necessary becomes a dangerous torture of consciences. Therefore, it is profitable that this should be the rule: except in case of offense, traditions in the church made by human authority can be omitted without sin, even if they do not bring on any godless work. Nevertheless, the godly should still be taught in churches which are rightly constituted that they may observe useful rites with a free mind for the sake of the example and good order, because this human life is not able to continue steadfastly without certain ordinances.

## Regarding Scandal

Scandal signifies an offense which deters minds or invites imitation. It is twofold. The one kind is called pharisaical scandal. That is an offense which hypocrites conceive on account of the true doctrine or an act which God requires or approves. By this offense, hypocrites are incited to hate the true doctrine and the godly. This scandal cannot be avoided, and the godly do not sin on account of such rage of the ungodly. Rather, it is necessary to obey the commandment of God despite the judgments and hatreds of the ungodly, because Paul says: "If anyone preaches another Gospel, let him be anathema''[1 Cor. 16:22; Gal. 1:8]. And the godly must be diligently taught and fortified, lest the hypocrites deter them from confession when they place dangers, insurrections, and destructions in their way after persecution. Minds should be thoroughly fortified against these terrors, lest they grow weary and discard the truth.

The other kind of scandal is wicked doctrine, or an evil deed, or an indifferent one, wilfully undertaken among the weak, which scares them away from the Gospel or wounds their minds in some way. These scandals are to be avoided. The most harmful of all is godless teaching, because it harms the glory of God and ruins innumerable minds of hearers.

Furthermore, every evil deed is a manifest offense. Bad examples invite others to imitation and lessen reverence for God. They often cause the church itself and its teaching to be in ill repute, and reasonable persons are scared away from the true doctrine. Thus the doctrine would have been in ill repute if Joseph had committed adultery. In contrast, his continence glorified the godly doctrine in many ways and brought great advantages to the entire kingdom. Since this is an outstanding example, it shows how much good it does to shun scandals of this kind. Let us remember that all our actions concern not only ourselves but also the glory of God. It is written: ''The name of God is blasphemed among the Gentiles because of you'' [Rom. 2:24; cf. Is. 52:5; Ez. 36:22].

Finally, one must beware of thoughtlessness in the use of indifferent things lest indifferent customs be changed among those who either have not yet heard the teaching about liberty or are still too weak. The danger is that they may be deterred from the Gospel by the changing of such customs. They do not persecute the godly teaching, but are teachable. However, after the doctrine has been taught and the hypocrites are opposing it, it is right that examples of liberty be shown them, and these examples are a part of confession according to Galatians 1. Thus the apostle violates the pharisaic traditions.

### 1–2. Welcome the person who is weak in faith

As he is about to speak about the use of ceremonies and liberty, he sets down, first of all, an admonition about tolerating the weak. He teaches a precept which is not to be practiced toward wicked persecutors—enemies of the Gospel—but toward our members, that is, toward such as permit themselves to be taught and who hear the Gospel. He forbids these to be deterred by unusual examples so that they do not embrace the Gospel.

He calls him weak in the faith, not yet sufficiently learned in the doctrine of liberty. Furthermore, when he says that such a one is to be raised up lest he fall into a state of doubt, he reminds us of two things: that he should not be compelled to do something against his conscience which his conscience disapproves; and that he should be moved forward little by little and be snatched out and set free from the state of doubt. For doubting in any article, if it is not corrected and increases, is a terrible sickness. It casts out faith and causes despair, hatred of the entire Gospel, and manifest ungodliness. Thus it happened to Julian [the Apostate] and to many similar persons.

### 3. For God has welcomed him

First you will note the precept to beware of doubting. Then you will note than an outstanding comfort is set forth here. For Paul testifies that the weak have been welcomed by God. But he understands not enemies or persecutors, but those who hear the Gospel, who are teachable, and have the beginnings of the fear of God and faith in Christ. Thus the apostles were righteous before Christ's resurrection, although they had their weaknesses, as is apparent in the gospel history.

Let us transfer this example to ourselves, and remember that we also have many weaknesses. Nevertheless, we do not abandon our faith because of them, since the Scripture here testifies that the weak are welcomed, but also admonishes at the same time that the weak are to be carried forward little by little.

In the third place the precept against doubting is taught. We should not do anything of which our conscience disapproves. Let everyone be certain in his own mind. This statement forbids one to act against his conscience. For whoever acts against his conscience openly despises the commandment of God. It is easy to understand that this contempt is a sin. Therefore every act against the conscience truly is a sin.

### 4–12. Who are you to judge another?

He hands down a rule which is necessary in the church: we should not do anything against our conscience. Afterward he forbids us to condemn one another in the use of indifferent things such as rites about foods, days, and other things of this kind. And he adds the argument about judgment. Judgment belongs to Christ; therefore we ought not to arrogate judgment to ourselves, namely, about the conscience of another (not about an outward deed that is clearly unlawful). This rule is wide open, as also that one: "Judge not" [Mt. 7:1; Luke 6:37]. But ministries are not forbidden, namely, teaching, brotherly admonition, or the duties of the magistrate. For these have commandments of God and are divinely instituted courts. What is prohibited are private judgments, that is, condemnations outside of these three courts which I have enumerated, judgments that have originated from a sick mind, ill will, or vanity. A judgment which is made by a man must be made about an external unlawful act. However, it is very common in the world that what others say and do lawfully is deceitfully misinterpreted. Paul disapproves of such judgments in the use of indifferent things, and forbids that condemnations be made on account of dissimilar rites in indifferent matters, as at one time there were fights about the date of Easter, about fermented drinks, and other things of this kind.

### 13–14a. But rather judge this

He adds a precept about avoiding offenses. He spoke above about various kinds of offenses. Now he is speaking only about this one kind: when libertine persons misuse freedom, or the more hard-nosed ones (who are not enemies of the Gospel) criticize the use of liberty. Both are to be admonished. Although the misuse of liberty is to be scolded, there is more wrong on the other side, which also does more harm on account of the appearance of authority.[1] The more rigid wound the consciences of the godly who make use of their liberty. They scare away many simple people from the Gospel, and in many cases grieve the Holy Spirit. Since there is much danger on both sides, Christians have need of great diligence lest they sin, either with harsh criticisms or with the misuse of their liberty. Christians should adhere to the fundamental principle, the doctrine, because here the use is an indifferent thing, as Paul says in 1 Cor. 8[:8]: "Food does not commend us to God."

To the precept about avoiding offenses, he adds four reasons full of Christian instruction. The first is taken from the kind of works, because the use of things divinely ordained and given is not of itself unclean or prohibited. "I know," he says, "that nothing is unclean in itself." He uses the term *unclean*, that is, profane, unlawful, prohibited, not holy, after the Jewish manner. Since the Jews are called the people of God and holy, that is, separated from the Gentiles for the worship of God, they called all things which were granted to them to use sacred. And indeed they were sacred, because they had been ordained by the Word of God. On the contrary, they call things profane and prohibited common, that is, not holy, not separated for the use of the holy people, but which the Gentiles used. These things I said about this term only. Now let also the rule be considered which is briefly taught here (elsewhere it is more fully explained) that the Gospel does not demand certain observances about foods, days, or clothing. Similar cases have been treated above because the Gospel teaches that sins are remitted *gratis*, because of Christ, not on account of our works or observances. Likewise, the Gospel brings righteousness and spiritual and eternal life. External observances of foods and similar things profit nothing for this.

---

[1] The text has *gratuitatis*, which is not recognized by the Latin dictionaries. It apparently is a misprint for *gravitatis*, which is the reading of our 1540 edition.

### 14b. Except for the person who thinks

He adds an appendix to the rule. Clean things, that is, permitted things, become unlawful for those whose conscience judges that they are unlawful. This subject must be diligently considered so we may learn that it truly is a sin to act against one's conscience. The meaning of this saying is this: The kind of food is indeed in itself lawful, but he who eats it while his conscience disapproves, sins. To do something when he is in doubt or when his conscience disapproves is to act in contempt of God and without faith.

### 15. But if because of food your brother

The second reason has been taken from the duty of brotherly love, and it is emphasized greatly. To harm others is against brotherly love; beware lest your examples hurt others. The argument can be applied both to those who wilfully misuse their freedom, and to the hard-nosed who judge harshly about those who use their liberty. Frequently this harshness in judging deters the weak from the Gospel and wounds the minds of those who are only moderately confirmed. Yes, it grieves the Holy Spirit, in this way: some who are about to despair fall away from the Gospel and lose the Holy Spirit. These offenses are to be avoided with great care, according to the saying: "Woe to that person through whom offense comes" [Mt. 18:7].

### 16. Your good may be blamed

The third reason is taken from the dignity of the Gospel. We must beware lest the Gospel sound bad to people, for the glory of God is harmed when his Word is reviled and the good of men is hindered. People do not accept a doctrine which they despise. Controversies do not necessarily alienate the minds of the inexperienced and simple from the Gospel so that they begin to hate a kind of doctrine as a seedbed of hatreds, but there are also those offenses which do alienate minds. Those who misuse liberty increase the licentiousness of the common people. On the other hand, hard-nosed persons deter the weak with the virulence of their judgments, etc. He commands us to shun diligently these offenses of minds on account of the glory of the Gospel, in order that more may love and embrace the doctrine.

### 17. For the kingdom of God is not

The fourth reason is taken from a comparison of necessary and unnecessary things, and it is a useful statement about the distinction between true and false acts of worship. Necessary things are not to be ruined by unnecessary things. Indifferent rites are not necessary, so do not let necessary things be harmed by them, namely, faith, the peace of the church, and the edification of the neighbor.

Moreover, the Scripture teaches frequently elsewhere that true acts of worship of God are repentance, faith, love, chastity, and similar spiritual impulses, as Paul elsewhere embraces this same meaning: "In Christ Jesus neither circumcision nor uncircumcision avails, but faith which works through love" [Gal. 5:6]. Likewise: "They will worship the Father in Spirit" [John 4:23]. On the other hand, he says about human traditions: "In vain they worship me with commandments of men" [Mark 7:7].

This teaching is greatly needed in the churches so we may know that works thought up without a command of God do not constitute worship of God. Minds should be recalled to works commanded by God. It is a great comfort to the godly to know these true acts of worship, to know that God truly requires prayer and faith, that he wants to hear us, and that these common duties in home and state are pleasing to him if they are done in faith.On account of the common afflictions they are indeed exercises of faith. Therefore, this teaching is so often repeated: "Call on me in the day of trouble and I will deliver you" [Ps. 50:15]. Also Isaiah 1 and 58, Micah 6, and Zechariah 7.

With respect to this Paul also says here that the kingdom of God is righteousness, peace, and joy in the Holy Spirit. Righteousness means to be righteous, that is, accepted by God, at the same time submitting one's self to God with beginning obedience. Peace and joy in the Holy Spirit signify the same thing, namely, peace of conscience before God when we truly know that our sins are forgiven. This knowledge of mercy is followed by prayer, patience, diligence in keeping harmony, and avoiding offenses with the help of the church. Thus Paul embraces all acts of spiritual worship, as he frequently does elsewhere.

### 18–22. Whoever serves Christ in these

There is a small but important addition: "Whoever serves Christ in these pleases God and is approved by men." This passage contains a clear testimony that good works please God. But Paul says expressly "Whoever serves Christ" in order to testify that he is speaking about the good works of those persons who are righteous by faith in Christ, who know that this worship pleases on account of Christ, the mediator and high priest.

Then there is added the useful teaching that when we serve Christ we will also be respected in the judgments of men, and most of all of the godly or of the church. However, he is speaking of those who serve Christ in order that we may know that the judgments of men are not to be put above the teaching and commandment of God. But when we hold fast to the commandment and teaching of God, we must be careful that our morals adorn the Gospel and invite others to believe and to glorify God, according to the saying: "Let your light shine before men" [Mt. 5:16].

## 23. Moreover, whatever is not from faith

In this chapter he has often inculcated the rule that we should do nothing contrary to our conscience. Now at the close he adds also that this work should be done from faith. This addition should be considered diligently, for this addition is not sufficiently clear to those who do not know the true teaching of the Gospel. For the common people, the statement of Paul is explained as follows: "Whatever is not from faith is sin," that is, whatever is done contrary to the conscience is sin. But they do not explain this sufficiently, for they apply it only to the Law, that stealing is done contrary to the Law, and therefore is a sin, and against the conscience in the person who steals knowingly. This interpretation is true and necessary. For in our actions it is necessary first of all to consult the Law in order that we may know what works God forbids or commands, and there is no doubt that works against the Law of God are sins.

But when Paul mentions faith he demands not only the Law or knowledge of history, but true faith. He teaches that works commanded or permitted by God must be done in faith, that is, with the confidence that God is propitious to us on account of Christ, the mediator, and our works are pleasing on account of that high priest. Therefore it is necessary to apply the statement of Paul not to the Law only, but also to the Gospel.

But someone may ask: How can we declare that we or our works are pleasing to God, since they are rendered unclean by the contagion of concupiscence? I answer: The carnally secure, who are without repentance, do not understand this teaching about faith. But in genuine afflictions, their mind begins to see the light when they consider that they are not being heard by God. They begin to see that we may declare that God truly forgives us because of Christ, that he truly hears us and cares for us.

Where there is such comfort, it is possible to understand what faith is, and then faith fights against natural doubting and overcomes mistrust. By this faith a person first pleases God on account of Christ. Thereafter God declares that also our good works are pleasing on account of Christ, the high priest, although they are imperfect and unclean. It is necessary also that people be taught that God demands that we serve in faith, not in a perpetual state of doubting. Let them not think: "Although I serve God and call on him, I should doubt whether these things please him." This doubt contains many sins; it denies the Gospel, it denies that God forgives sins, it expects nothing from God, it is silently angry, and it murmurs against God. These are the things which properly result from through the Law, as Paul calls them.

Such doubting must be reprehended in the church, and the doctrine about faith must be opposed to it. Also to be reprehended is the very common error which has been disseminated in the church that a Christian should doubt whether there is grace for him, and that such doubting is not a sin. For this they quote a statement from Ecclesiasticus: "A man does not know whether he is worthy of love or wrath." Then they seek conjectures from works—whether we are in grace—and our adversaries say that one should doubt, and that doubting is not a sin. This entire idea militates against the doctrine of faith.

Moreover, we do not deny that doubt inheres naturally in minds, as does mistrust, which we all experience. But it must be known that this very doubt and mistrust is a sin, and that it arises from our natural blindess, which rejects the promise of the Gospel. And although this doubting inheres in the minds, these two things should be opposed to it: the promise of the Gospel and the commandment which teaches that we should believe that promise. Therefore doubting must be resisted and mistrust overcome, and we must declare that God truly forgives believers and that he truly accepts, cares for them, and hears them. And we should know that this faith is worked and nourished by the Word.

It is not only the promise which demands that we believe. The commandment which is added to it is unchangeable. It commands us most sternly to believe that the things which have been promised will certainly be imparted to us on account of the Son of God. Thus we read 1 John 3[:23]: "This is his commandment, that we should believe in the name of his Son." Likewise: "Whoever does not believe God makes him a liar, because he does not believe the testimony which God has testified about his Son" [1 John 5:10]. And Hebr. 4[:16]: "Let us approach the throne of grace with confidence." The teaching which commands us to doubt militates against these commandments and promises.

One must struggle against doubting, and faith must be raised up in every prayer. James [1:6] also teaches this: "Let him ask in faith, without doubting." Neither do acts of worship please God in those who do not fight against doubt and who silently retain their mistrust that they are not being regarded, that they have been rejected. We ought to recognize these sins, resist them, and arouse true exercises of faith.

Paul's statement should be understood: "Whatever is not of faith is sin." Let us remember that we should perform works commanded by God, and that they are to be done in faith that God is propitious to us on account of Christ, the mediator, and that for Christ's sake he hears us and cares for us, pardons our Infirmities and approves our good works.

Now let the hypocritical acts of worship be compared with this statement. When they do works not commanded by God, they cannot believe that such worship is pleasing to him because they have no word about the will of God. Second, because they disapprove of the doctrine about faith and command us to doubt, another piece of ungodliness is added. They pray like the heathen, silently thinking that they are not regarded, not cared for, not heard by God, and that perhaps they have also been rejected. This perpetual doubting is ungodliness, even if the world does not judge it to be a sin.

How is the saying of Solomon [cf. Ecclesiasticus] to be understood: "A man does not know whether he is worthy of love or of hate?" I answer very simply: Solomon is not speaking of the judgment of the conscience before God, about grace or rejection, but about events in this life. These, he says, are uncertain, and good things and evil things alike happen in this life. This uncertainty offends Epicureans, and moves them to deny providence. Abel is pious, and yet he is slain by his brother. John the Baptist is killed; meanwhile the tyrant is enjoying all pleasures, and many wicked persons did not meet a tragic end. Solomon collected these arguments in order to warn us that we should not fall away from God on account of this offense, neither judge from the events about the will of God, except from the Word. Likewise, that the godly should not become carnally secure and forsake the fear of God, nor from trust in their own righteousness undertake anything without a call, etc.[2]

---

[2] Our 1540 edition ends the discussion of Romans 14 here.

# Excursus on the Authority
## of Scripture and the Fallibility
of the Church Fathers

## Regarding the Church and the Authority
### of the Word of God

People often argue how much authority should be given to the pronouncements of the church, the decrees of synods, and the sayings of writers.
Although we hold fast the rule that we embrace the Word of God, nevertheless,
because ambiguous passages seem to occur in the apostolic writings, some
argue that we should follow the pronouncements of the church rather than
the writings of the apostles.

These people imagine that the authority of the church is to be placed
above the Word of God, and that the church is able to change what is taught
in the Word of God. In favor of these opinions they cite a saying of Augustine:
"I would not believe the Gospel if the authority of the catholic church did
not move me to do it." Under the false pretext of the name of the church,
popes decree and command many things contrary to the Word of God, just
as they please. They strengthen and establish ungodly teaching and ungodly
acts of worship, and the mere name of the church now also deters very many
from the true doctrine of the Gospel, which we profess. Therefore it is necessary that people be correctly advised about the authority of the church.

Certain ingenious but particularly impudent persons imagine new opinions from badly distorted statements of Scripture. They completely reject the
consensus of the true church and all synods without distinction. For example,
Servetus fights with the church of all times and distorts the statement about
the Word in John 1, seeking a more elegant interpretation, as he thinks. In
order that such impudence may be held in check, the church needs a certain
fence, so to speak, as the ancient synods and writers quote the earliest testimonies received from the apostles and from trustworthy writers.

Tertullian says against Praxeas that this rule must be maintained against
all heresies: "Whatever was first is right; whatever is later is adulterated."
Then he calls what the apostles clearly taught "the first," and in this way
he explains what he means.

Irenaeus, writing against Florinus, quotes the authority of those who

239

were before him. He quotes Polycarp by name, who listened to the apostle John. He says that he would have cursed the dogmas of Florinus if he had heard them, and would shun the place where they had been spoken as polluted.

Basil quotes his wet-nurse, whose piety had then been very highly praised. He said that she had received the teaching from Gregory of Neo-caesarea [Pontus], who at that time was famous for learning and miracles, and who refuted Paul of Samosata and left behind a brief confession of faith, which contains a clear witness about the Trinity. It is found in book 7 of [Eusebius'] Church History.

Origen quotes the apostles about the baptism of infants. He says on Romans 6 that the churches received from the apostles the teaching that infants should be baptized. These quote the authority of the church correctly. Therefore I shall tell in orderly fashion what the church is, that it should be heard, that approved testimonies should be used, and that nevertheless the doctrine should be judged from the Word of God in order that the highest authority should remain the authority of the Word, according to the saying: "If anyone teaches another Gospel let him be anathema" [Gal. 1:8].

First, when I say *church,* I do not understand popes, bishops, and others who approve of their opinions. For these are enemies of the true church, being in part Epicureans, in part manifest idolaters. I call the church the assembly of those who truly believe, who have the Gospel and the sacraments, and are sanctified by the Holy Spirit, as the church is described in Ephesians 5 and John 10[:27]: "My sheep hear my voice."

It is necessary that this true church always remain, because the kingdom of Christ is everlasting and it is written [Mt. 28:20]: "I shall remain with you until the end of the world." Nevertheless, we must know that this true church is not always flourishing equally, but often is only small, and is to be divinely restored later when true teachers are sent, as in Noah's time the church was oppressed and an assembly of only a few persons.

After the deluge Melchizedek, who was Shem, the son of Noah, retained the true doctrine. When idolatry increased among the Chaldaeans and the true doctrine had been extinguished almost everywhere, God renewed the church through the calling of Abraham. Then the family of Abraham and a few of his hearers, were the church. Meanwhile, the Chaldaeans and the Egyptians were boasting that they were the descendants of the fathers, that they retained the examples and the worship of the fathers. They proclaimed that they were the people of God, although they had not retained the Word of God (even if they had retained the ceremonies, to which they had attached perverse opinions and added idolatry).

At the time of Ahaz when the church was nearly extinct in Israel, it was again increased through Elijah and Elisha. Afterward it again collapsed.

When Christ was about to be born there was in Judah only a small church: Mary, Joseph, the family of Zachariah, Simon, Anna, the shepherds, and a few others. Meanwhile, the church government was with the Pharisees and Sadducees who were openly ungodly. The Sadducees were also Epicureans. Nevertheless, they, most of all arrogated to themselves the title *people of God*.

At the time of the prophets the true church was small. Isaiah 1[:9]: "If the Lord had not left to us a seed, we would have become like Sodom and Gomorrah." These words admonish us most earnestly that we should not think of the church as a secular state, nor measure it by the succession of bishops, nor by the degree or position of popes, but declare that the church is with those who retain the true doctrine of the Gospel. It is necessary that there be in that assembly some who truly believe. For to this assembly belong the promises. Isaiah takes away this venerable title from his princes and high priests, and says a small seed is left in the people who were called the people of God.

In the time of Jeremiah, when both kings and priests were against him, the church was not the assembly of priests, but those who believed the preaching of Jeremiah. Amos 3[12]: "Israel will be liberated in this way, as when a shepherd rescues two legs out of the jaws of a lion." Finally, the church was small compared with the multitude of the wicked when all peoples, with the exception of the people of Judah, had totally lost the knowledge of God.

The Scripture also foretells that after the apostles there will be disaster for the church. Matthew 24[:11]: "Many false prophets will arise and will deceive many." Likewise: "When you shall see the abomination of desolation standing in the holy place" [Mt. 24:15]. This signifies that in the church which bears the name there will arise idolatry, by which the true doctrine and true acts of worship will be destroyed, and the church will become a waste, that is, it will be forsaken or extinct; and so it happened. After the abuses of the Masses and the worship of traditions arose, there followed darkness about true acts of worship, about faith, about calling on God in faith, and about the duties of one's calling. This happened because a conscience that looks to its own merits is not able to understand the remission of sins, true prayer, the expectation of divine help, etc.

Finally, they will perform signs and wonders so that, if it were possible, even the elect would be misled [Matt. 24:24]. 2 Thess. 2[:3]: "A falling away will come." Luke 18[:8]: "Do you think that the Son of Man will find faith when he comes?" Ps. 88[89:47]: "Have you created all the sons of men in vain?" This is a complaint about the coming ruin of the church. These sayings testify that although the church must be preserved, it will, especially in the last time, be only small and an assembly of few persons who are spurned and rejected in this life, as Paul says: "Not many wise, not many powerful" [1 Cor. 1:26].

I have cited these testimonies for this reason, so that first it might be considered what the church is, and so that the mind may be led away from the carnal opinions which imagine that the church is the papal state tied to the orderly succession of bishops, as kingdoms are upheld by an orderly succession of rulers. But with the church it is a different matter, for it is an assembly not bound to an orderly succession, but to the Word of God. The church is reborn where God restores the doctrine, and gives his Holy Spirit. Paul testifies in Eph. 4[:11] that the church is ruled and preserved in this manner, not by orderly succession: "He gave gifts to men, apostles, prophets. . . . "He teaches that the true church is where Christ is at work and where he bestows true teachers.

Therefore, when the name and the authority of the church is opposed to us, let us first consider whether they are speaking of the true church or about the papal assembly and its succession and form of government. Let us not permit ourselves to be scared away from the Word of God by the false protection of the name *church*.

Second, after it has been said what the true church is, one must add that the true church is small and consists only of saints. It retains the true doctrine of the Gospel, the articles of faith, or, as Paul calls it, the source of the truth. Yet this same true church sometimes preserves the doctrine purely and clearly, but at other times less so. It also has many weak members, as the apostles were the church although they did not understand before the resurrection of Christ what the future kingdom of Christ would be like. Even after the Holy Spirit was given, Peter imagined that the works of the Law were necessary. Warned from heaven, he learned that the kingdom of Christ is not a Jewish state, but spiritual and eternal acts of worship (Acts 9).

Afterward, when the preaching of the apostles had been begun, the doctrine shone forth pure and clean in them. Nevertheless, there were many who were weak. Although they were true members of the church and held fast the articles of faith, they added something erroneous, as did those who observed the acts of worship of the Law and did not sufficiently understand the abrogation of the Law and the true acts of worship. This was not an insignificant error, and it poured out a certain amount of darkness on the articles of faith. Thus Christ predicts about the church of the last times that there will be great darkness which will hinder even the elect, that they will not have the pure doctrine [cf. Mt. 24].

There remains some true church, which holds fast the articles of faith, but at times less pure, obscured by some incorrect opinions and holding some erroneous views. I am still speaking about true members of the church and saints, not about the others who, when the light of the Word has been lost, lose the Holy Spirit and follow the judgment of reason. Although they think that they are teaching only godly things, they are really teaching foreign and wicked things. Thus also now there are many outstanding teachers—persons of good morals with a show of piety—who think they are speaking very holy things, although they are far removed from the true light, that is, from the true understanding of the Word of God. I am not yet speaking about such persons; now I am speaking only of true members of the church, who in large part are weak.

For Paul says: "No man can lay another foundation except that which has been laid. But one builds on it gold, another wood, stubble . . . " [1 Cor. 3:11] He understands the foundation as the article of faith, that is, the sum and substance of the Christian doctrine, the doctrine about the benefit of Christ. But to this, he says, some add useful teaching, explanation, and true spiritual acts of worship; this he calls gold. Others add stubble, that is, opinions which are not fitting and contain something erroneous, even as in the beginning immediately ceremonies were laid down which brought errors in their train.

Thus I consider Ambrose a true member of the church. Nevertheless, he says about the forty-day fast: "The other fasts are voluntary; this one is necessary." This opinion is stubble added to the doctrine of faith.

Basil added monasticism, although it is stubble, and praises this kind of life with excessive and false praise, although he was rebuked by his bishop. Scripture frequently reminds us that it is not a light error to institute new acts of worship. This is shown us by this one statement: "In vain they worship me with commandments of men" [Mark 7:7]. It is a serious sin against the First Commandment to institute or to approve of acts of worship not commanded by God. It is against the First Commandment, because this commandment forbids strange acts of worship.

Cyprian urges canonical penalties which were in use at the time, and promotes the view that they are necessary, and that sins are remitted because of them. At the same time, he says that absolution without these punishments is useless. Perhaps he thought better than he spoke. Nevertheless, these are not small errors, but very thick stubble, obscuring the pure doctrine about the benefits of Christ and about faith.

Furthermore, writers often felt more correctly than they spoke, because most were quite negligent and improper in speaking, and they borrowed many statements and formulas from the common people which contain something erroneous. Thus Augustine takes the term *satisfactions* from the common people, although he openly rebukes the errors about satisfactions. He tortures himself in explaining the statement "Every sin is voluntary" when he discusses original sin, although the saying is a civil saying that speaks about outward transgressions.

Thus they call the Lord's Supper an offering, after the manner of the people, although it was not instituted as an offering, since Christ himself was the sacrificer, offering the sacrifice. And there was not even in ancient times an offering of the body and blood in the ceremony of the Supper. Before the consecration, bread and other things were offered, and the priest said that he was offering prayers, thanksgivings, and the entire worship which was customarily done there. Therefore, although *Offering* was not understood in one and the same way, it was later twisted to offering the body; very great abuses followed from this.

In the book in which the ceremonies of the church are contained, Dionysius, when he diligently describes the order of the rites, makes no mention whatever of the offering of the Lord's body. Neither does the canon of Basel contain this offering. But I shall say more about the Lord's Supper later. I have added these things in order to show that the ancients at times borrowed unsuitable ways of speaking from the people, as is accustomed to happen in all ages.

Meanwhile, men are defeated by the judgments and examples of the crowd—which is not godly—so that they are drawn into superstitions by some human imagination, as at the Synod of Nicaea. If the one man Paphnutius had not objected, the opinion of those who wanted a decree made that priests should abstain from their wives would have been approved. Custom defeated Cyprian and many others, so that they approved prohibition of marriage.

Likewise, the entire Nicene Synod, overcome by the consensus of the crowd or of the time, approved the canons of penitence which afterward brought forth intolerable errors. Great examples frequently deceive even the godly, as the example of Antony darkened the understanding of many. Until now I have been speaking of the godly. Although they are holy, very many are weak. Now I shall add something about the fallen.

At times the godly waver completely and lose the Holy Spirit, as I judge that Origen has completely fallen, especially if he affirmed those monstrous errors of the world which were innumerable, namely, that the devils would finally be saved. Tertullian also wickedly condemns second marriages. However, perhaps they returned to their senses. For many who truly lapse in life and doctrine nevertheless return to their senses. And it happens very often that saints truly waver and do not judge according to the Word and spiritual light, but are deceived by the imagination of reason, yet nevertheless afterward return to their senses. Thus Gideon fell completely when he instituted a form of worship guided by human counsel.

From all this the conclusion follows: Although the true church, which is small, retains the articles of faith, that true church can hold errors which obscure the articles of faith. Moreover, many fall in such a way that they completely approve of wicked errors against the articles of faith, although some do perhaps return to their senses.

First of all when the authority of the church is appealed to, one must ask whether it was the consensus of the true church, agreeing with the Word of God.

Then one must say that extant writers often were persons who had lapsed, and perhaps some are not even members of the church.

In the third place this distinction must be added: In the assembly which is called the church there is a great multitude of ungodly persons, many of whom enjoy higher authority than others, through a show of religion or a reputation as teachers. Such were the high priests at the time of Jeremiah among the people of Judah, and the ungodly priests who appealed against Jeremiah [18:18] to the authority of their position and the law and to the promises: "The law shall not depart from the priests." They denied that their assembly could err, while at the same time they were completely in error and disagreed with Jeremiah. Likewise, at the time of Christ there were very few godly people, for instance Zachariah and Simeon.

Moreover, when an ungodly crowd has control in the church, it establishes many false and ungodly things in the name of the church. Such a crowd embraced the application of Masses for the living and the dead, the worship of vows and of the saints; afterward this example harmed the godly. Such a crowd also decreed at a synod that the marriages of priests should be torn apart. However, it often happens in the church that wicked persons with ingenius minds make an attempt to establish a religion by human wisdom. Since they are not influenced by the Word of God but are led by the imagination of reason and seek eloquent suppositions, they bring forth wicked dogmas. Such were Paul of Samosata, Arius, and Pelagius. Others seek merits, a showy administration, or discipline of the people, and they are moved by these causes to institute and to heap up acts of worship, as did the monk Gregory. At the present time popes, princes, and many learned men who desire to set up the church are moved by human wisdom, and having ignored the Word of God, they want to set up the church according to their own imaginings. They do not see that it is a dreadful act of impiety to depart from the Word of God, to seek God without the Word, to institute acts of worship by human judgment, to alter true dogmas without a command from God, and to oppress the purity of the Word of God.

The authority of the church is held up against us, as for instance about the application of Masses: "The church does not err; the church has applied Masses for so many centuries, the custom must be preserved." One must answer to the major premise: The entire church, which is the multitude of those who dominate in the church, can err, as high priests and priests erred at the time of Jeremiah and of Christ. Although beside that multitude there are some pious persons who hold fast to the articles of faith, these also, moved by the examples, can assent to certain errors. It comes about that they retain the articles of faith less purely. For example, Bernard appears to have thought more correctly than others, although he assented to many errors, such as the abuse of the Masses, the power of the papacy, vows, and the worship of the saints.

Therefore, the authority of the crowd must not be appealed to against the Word of God, but it is necessary that one return to the rule: "If anyone shall preach another Gospel, let him be anathema" [1 Cor. 16:22; Gal. 1:8]. Let the highest authority be that of the Word which was divinely taught. Thereafter that church which agrees with that Word is to be considered authoritative as Christ says [John 10:27]: "My sheep hear my voice." As Augustine said: "The question is: 'Where is the church?' " What, therefore, shall we do? Shall we seek it in our words, or in the words of the church's Head, our Lord Jesus Christ? I think that we should seek it in the words of the One who is the truth, and best knows his own body.

But here the objection is raised: "If the authority of the church is repudiated, then too great a license is granted to the wantonness of human minds. When the statements of the church have been rejected, many will think up new and impious interpretations of Scripture." Although this danger is not to be despised and it is profitable to curb that licentiousness, one must see, on the other hand, to what extent the authority of the church is to be consulted. For when Servetus renews[1] the impious error of Paul of Samosata by denying that "the Word" signifies a person in the statement: "In the beginning was the Word" [John 1:1], he magnificently proclaims the authority of the Scripture, and commands that this be preferred to the decrees of the church. Then he slyly argues that the speech is to be understood simply. For since in common human speech *word* does not signify a person, he denies that it is to be understood of a person in John, so that if Demosthenes were to read this saying: "In the beginning was the Word," he would certainly not think that a person is to be understood.

I ask, therefore, whether it is not profitable to oppose the authority of the church to such men. Here I answer: As the Gospel teaches that the church should be heard, so I always say that assembly which has the Word of God and which is called the church should be heard, even as we also command

---

[1] The text here has *revovat,* which is not recognized by the Latin dictionaries. It appears to be a misprint for *revocat.*

that our pastors be heard. Therefore let us hear the church when it teaches and admonishes, but one must not believe because of the authority of the church. For the church does not lay down articles of faith; it only teaches and admonishes. We must believe on account of the Word of God when, admonished by the church, we understand that this meaning is truly and without sophistry taught in the Word of God.

Perhaps Demosthenes would not think of a person if he were to read: "In the beginning was the Word." But a hearer, admonished by the church that *Word* signifies a person—the Son of God—is now aided by the church as it teaches and admonishes, and believes the article, not because of the authority of the church, but because he sees that this meaning has firm testimonies in the Scripture itself. He sees that it is spoken of a certain person, who, having assumed human nature, dwelt in the world with men. He sees that this person is called λόγος. He gathers fitting and firm testimonies about the two natures in Christ, for he knows that with respect to the nature of God the heavenly voice must be believed, and that it is the height of ungodliness to invent opinions about the nature of God without God's own testimony, according to 2 Pet. 1[:17], and Matt. 16 [17:5; cf. Mark 9:7; Luke 9:35]: "Hear him!"

Also the first church has authority as witness of the apostles. I am speaking of dogmas, not about human traditions. For dogmas are intended to be firm and perpetual. Human rites are not intended to be perpetual or immutable. Neither did the apostles err in doctrine. Therefore it is profitable to hold fast where the most ancient writers appeal to the authority of the apostles.

Thus about the Trinity they cite these: Origen, Tertullian, Irenaeus, Gregory of Neocaesaraea [Pontus], Alexander the bishop of Alexandria, and many others who, since they testify that the doctrine of the Trinity was received from the apostles, powerfully strengthen the godly. Therefore such testimonies are not to be despised.

I said that the writers are to be heard, as now we say also that preachers are to be heard, because some remain in the church who hold fast the truth, some more purely, others less purely. But one must add that the hearers should judge according to the Word of God which always remains the rule for doctrine.

## Examples

Augustine contends more sharply about original sin than do the rest. For he teaches and reminds, and when we see that he truly and without sophistry sets forth the meaning of the Scripture, we believe the article, not on account of Augustine, but on account of the Word of God, and we see that the earlier teachers think the same, although we see that they did not treat this article as fully or as clearly.

## Another Example

Peter, bishop of Alexandria, contends against Meletius that the lapsed are to be received back, and he quotes an old authority. For Epiphanius recites these words: "as the doctrine which has come down to us teaches." Therefore that bishop of Alexandria teaches and reminds us that the lapsed are to be received back. We believe this not on account of that bishop, but because we see that this view is taught in the Word of God, and the testimonies of the ancient church agree with it.

Likewise I say that synods of the church are to be heard which teach and remind us when they discuss the Word of God. But they should be examined, and when they draw right conclusions, we believe because of the Word of God. Thus the synod of Nicaea taught piously and usefully, and admonished all posterity with respect to the Son of God. But we believe this article not because of the synod, but because we see that it is so taught in the Word of God.

Other things which are outside the Scriptures are not to be accepted like that. For example, the Nicene Synod laid down the penitential canons, which are human traditions outside the Scriptures and have been the seeds of many superstitious opinions.

Samson's guests were not able to solve the riddle which was proposed to them at the banquet except by asking his spouse. So Samson said: "If you had not plowed with my heifer, you would not have the answer to my question" [Judges 14:18]. Thus one must look around to see where there is an assembly which has the Word of God, and one must examine which assembly of fathers or synods is purer, that is, having fewer opinions outside the Word of God. The church teaches, reminds, and testifies. But one must see whether the things which it proposes have firm testimonies from the Word of God.

Surely it is proper for pious persons to confess that the fathers who fought with the sharpest contentions and held fast to godly dogmas deserve to be honored by those who come after them. This benefit is not to be considered a small matter. Here belongs the dictum of Augustine: "I would not believe the Gospel if the authority of the church did not move me." Augustine does not think that the authority of the church is greater than the authority of the divine Word, or that the church should abolish articles taught in the Word. But he holds that the church is teacher and witness. We would not believe the Gospel if the church did not teach us and testify that this doctrine was handed down from the apostles.

This dictum is useful also for refuting new dogmas which never were found in the church, for example, as the Manichaeans contrived new idle talk. It is necessary that dogmas necessary for godliness first have existed in the preaching of the apostles. New things, and things entirely unknown to the apostolic church, must be rejected. But there is a fuller discussion of Augustine's dictum elsewhere: he certainly does not grant to the church the authority to establish articles of faith contrary to the Word of God, or to abolish articles taught in the Word of God, or lay down new articles of faith.

## Catalog of Examples

I shall collect a number of examples of synods and fathers in order that it may be seen that dissimilar materials are contained in them, and that not all sayings of all, nor all rites of the ancients, are to be accepted as necessary without discrimination. Certain inept persons so admire antiquity that they want all old human rites restored just as if the Spartans were now to institute all the old rites of their state. Rites thought up by men are often harmful, and even if they are acceptable, they are not appropriate for all times.

The Synod of Neocaesarea forbids priests to attend the banquets at second marriages, lest they appear to approve of them. Such ridiculous decrees are mixed in with many good ones. Therefore a choice must be made, and not all sayings of the ancients are to be rashly applauded.

In the year of our Lord 325[2] the Nicene Synod was called together by Constantine, in which Eustathius, the bishop of Antioch, was chairman. Most serious controversies about dogmas were decided in this synod, and the errors of Paul of Samosata and Arius were rightly condemned, as were those of the Cathari, who denied that the lapsed should be received back and that these received remission of sins.

Afterward certain political matters were ordained about the governing of the churches—that the bishop of Alexandria should be over the churches of the Orient, and the Roman bishop over the churches of neighboring nations, and that bishops should be ordained by neighboring bishops. Although these political matters are useful, they are not intended to be considered articles of faith.

In the third place, they added certain ceremonies—the canons of penitence, as they called them—which in the beginning were less harsh, and perhaps contained fewer superstitions. But later the burden and the superstitions grew, and gratuitous forgiveness was obscured. The fathers were not cautious enough in this matter. And since the outcome afterward showed that

---

[2] Melanchthon dated the synods and councils as follows: Nicaea, 324; Constantinople, 383; Ephesus, 433; Chalcedon, 422; and Fifth Carthage, 438. In the translation, we have corrected these dates to conform to those commonly accepted today.

superstitions are increased by such examples, let us not admire this synod so much in this matter that we would be willing either to approve or to restore those canons. Neither do we for this reason disagree with the ancient church; we retain the articles of this synod about dogmas which properly belong to the church. Other things, which are outside or contrary to the Word of God, do not pertain to the church.

In A.D. 381, the Synod of Constantinople was convoked by Theodosius, in which the bishop of Constantinople presided. A grave controversy about the Holy Spirit was resolved. He is a person proceeding from the Father and from the Son, and is God. Eunomius and others who believed the contrary were rightly condemned. Some matters of polity were also decided, e.g., that bishops should not administer anything in dioceses other than their own.

In the year 431 the Synod of Ephesus was convoked by the younger Theodosius, in which Cyril of Alexandria presided. This synod rightly condemned Nestorius. He denied that in Christ the Word is united with human nature in an essential union. He claimed that the Word was only present and dwelt in the human nature like a guest in a home, and was at work there.

This was a controversy of great importance, for the two natures are truly and essentially united in Christ. Neither is it true that only the human nature is the Christ, and that it is the home of the Word which stands by. From then on the godly urged this form of speaking about the unity of the person, that God had been born, had suffered, etc. Although Nestorius denied that he thought the same as Paul of Samosata, I suspect that he actually thought the same thing, but he proposed the old madness hidden under guise of a cover.

In the year 451 the Synod of Chalcedon was convoked by the Emperor Martianus, in which Eutyches was rightly condemned. He also denied the two natures in Christ, and contended that the nature of the Word had been divinely sent, that Christ had been brought forth through a virgin, and that the two natures are not united. This also seems to have renewed the madness of Paul of Samosata, but put forth under a different guise. This judgment of the synod is to be praised.

In other ways human traditions were already increasing in the church. This synod added some bad regulations, not about dogmas, but about ceremonies and acts of worship outside the Scripture. Nevertheless, these regulations are still more modest than others that were brought forth later. At this synod the regulation was first made which prohibits marriage to monks and virgins who had made vows, and excommunicates them if they contract marriages, although it adds the mitigation that also this could be granted according to the judgment of the bishop.

To be sure, many useful matters of polity were decreed at that time, such as that the bishops themselves should not have the administration of church properties, but that the churches should have stewards; that no one should hold more than one ministry; that no one should be ordained if he did not have a ministry; and that in every province the bishops should meet annually, and hold a synod about current controversies of the church.

Meanwhile there were also other synods, either provincial, or, more frequently in which the bishops of neighboring provinces came together. Such was the Synod of Antioch, convoked against Paul of Samosata, which piously and rightly condemned the wickedness of Paul of Samosata prior to the Nicene Synod. Such was also the Synod of Gangara in Galatia, ancient and pure; it has the very best decrees against superstitions concerning marriage, food, and monasticism. It is evident that this synod was convened on account of Montanus, Marcion, and similar persons who greatly increased those superstitions.

Other later synods followed, such as that of Ancyra, which has this memorable regulation: "If deacons at ordination have not promised that they will live celibate, they are to be retained in their ministries, also if they take wives afterward; but if they promised and nevertheless took wives afterward, they are to be removed from the ministry." It also has other canons about years of pentience that are dangerous and superstitious.

The Synod of Laodicea rightly condemns the Novatians, but errs when it also censures lay people who are married twice; it commands them to be punished before they are admitted to communion, and forbids baptism after two weeks of the forty-day feast. The other decrees about polity are honorable, as when the synod forbids marriage with heretics. This synod came shortly after that of Nicaea.

The Synod of Toledo was under the Emperor Honorius; it contains many useful chapters about doctrine. For it piously recounts the articles about divinity and the natures of Christ, and certain other articles. Afterward it adds on certain matters about polity, and ceremonies about chrism and vows. This synod forbids deacons be to elevated to the office of presbyter if they do not abstain from their legitimate wives. Likewise, it excommunicates parents who embrace with parental affection daughters who are obligated by vows if they marry. Likewise, it does not admit such married women to communion unless they leave their husbands.

The fifth Synod of Carthage, held in the year 418, forbids to bishops, presbyters and deacons intercourse with their lawful spouses. Thus little by little the prohibition was increased. Previously, intercourse with their wives had been granted to deacons as the synod of Ancyra testifies; afterward the prohibition followed. These constitutions about celibacy were later repeated in all synods, and there are added sharper punishments, as a certain Synod of Toledo decreed that the possessions of wives should be auctioned off if they returned to their husbands.

Furthermore this Carthaginian Synod contains also another memorable regulation about the chapels and altars of saints where their bodies are not buried. It commands the bishops to demolish these altars and chapels, or, if they fear tumults, it commands them to warn people in sermons not to go to those places. It seems that some have wanted to prohibit a growing superstition in the worship of saints.

The Carthaginian Synod of the year 457 dealt with the appeal of the bishops. The Roman bishop demanded that appeal be permitted whenever anyone appealed to the Roman bishop, and in order to obtain this he committed fraud. He quoted a newly invented decree which affirmed that the Nicene Synod had published a decree that had this same sense. Afterward the fraud was discovered from examples sought from Constantinople, and the petition of the Roman pontiff was rejected. At this synod Augustine was present.[3] By such tricks the Roman pontiffs constructed themselves a road to the primacy. This example reminds us that we should not admire antiquity so much that we free it from all faults.

The fourth Carthaginian Synod [A.D. 399] contains a decree about prayer and offering for the dead in these words: "If penitents who have diligently observed the canons of penitence accidentally die before communing, let their memory be commended with prayers and offerings." That age did not yet have private Masses, but superstition still grew little by little. This canon does not receive the dead unless they have diligently observed the rites of penitence. Likewise, it adds the custom of offerings.

The Synod of Milan, at which Augustine was present,[4] dealt with a most weighty matter, and rightly defended the correct doctrine of original sin, grace, and justification. It also has certain matters of polity among which these are noteworthy: It forbids appeal to bishops who live beyond the sea. Not even the Roman bishop would now accept this decree. Likewise, it forbids to ask the emperor for judges who are not bishops. That was fitting for those times; now it would be harsh. With respect to divorce, it also decreed that the innocent person should not marry again, and it added that one should petition the emperor to make a law to this effect. This also is too harsh. For at Rome Fabiola married again, as is clear from Jerome.

That synod also confirmed that superstition about vows. It permits virgins to be veiled before the twenty-fifth year, contrary to the old canons. Although it decreed tolerably about doctrine, afterward there came some stubbles and superstitious regulations. Therefore not all decrees of synods are to be approved without exception. Yet one must confess that godly synods deserve

---

[3] Augustine died in A.D. 430.
[4] The Synod of Milan was in A.D. 355, and Augustine was born in A.D. 354.

honor because they preserved some articles of the Christian doctrine, and with respect to these it is profitable to hold fast to the witness of synods and antiquity.

## Regarding the Ancient Ecclesiastical Writers

These also deserve honor, particularly insofar as they are witnesses of the ancient and first church of the apostles. For they strengthen us by their testimony about the Trinity, the natures in Christ, the baptism of infants, the use of the Lord's Supper, the ordination of ministers, the use of indifferent things, and the repentance of the lapsed. Regarding all these articles, noteworthy examples of the apostles are cited which defend us.

As for the rest, some were more diligent in some matters, others in other matters, and, as is human, they often thoughtlessly poured out absurd and false statements which they would without doubt have corrected if they had been admonished. Frequently, although they did not hold to a bad opinion, they were not able to say sufficiently clearly what they wanted to say. Often they defended existing traditions too stubbornly on account of the custom of the times; meanwhile, they also held to some false opinions. Therefore not all writings of the fathers are to be approved of without exception. Often they fought among themselves, and it is not rare that one disagrees with himself. Therefore decisions should be made according to the apostolic Scripture. But I will add examples.

### Origen

Origen, who cites examples and statements of apostles and about ancient churches, is a useful witness for posterity about a number of articles: the Trinity, the two natures in Christ, the baptism of infants, original sin, the use of the Lord's Supper, and certain other articles.

Otherwise, he mixed into his writings many false and absurd statements, some of which even his own contemporaries disapproved. He imagines that before the present world there were more worlds. He imagines that the punishments of the devils and the damned will have an end. Even his own contemporaries reproved these things.

When he treats the proposition in Romans [3:28]: "We are justified by faith, not by works," he understands it according to a synecdoche: "we are just by faith, that is, by perfect faith which embraces all virtues." He explains this by saying that the same could be said about other virtues. We are saved through mercy, namely, perfect mercy that embraces the other virtues. This is saying nothing except that people have forgiveness of sins and are righteous on account of works and virtues. And since he pays no attention to what Paul is saying, what Paul calls faith, what the exclusive phrase: "not of works" means he adds confused and intricate explanations and is not consistent with himself.

Meanwhile he pours out some tolerable teaching, but ruins it soon afterward, such as this on Rom. 4: "The beginning of justification by God is faith, which believes in God who justifies. This faith, when it has been justified, like a root conceived during a shower of rain, clings in the lower part of the mind. When it begins to be worked on through the Law of God, branches sprout in it which bear the fruits of works." Therefore the root of righteousness is not from works. Rather, the fruit of works grows from the root of righteousness. By this root, God accepts righteousness without works.

On Romans 3 [:27]: "Where is your boasting?" Now he seems closer to the meaning of Paul, for he admits the exclusive that men are justified solely by faith, and he cites the thief on the cross and the woman in Luke [8:48]: "Your faith has saved you." But afterward, when he explains these things, he seems to want to say that man in the beginning receives remission of sins solely by faith, but afterward is righteous through other virtues, as he himself says afterward: "Faith is counted for righteousness to him who is converted, but afterward righteousness is counted for righteousness." Moreover, there is a strange variety and confusion in his explanation, although he grants that man in the beginning receives remission solely by faith. Nevertheless, if afterward he imagines that the converted are without sin, that they satisfy the Law and are righteous on account of other virtues, he disagrees with Paul and with the other divine Scriptures, according to the statement: "No man living will be justified in your sight" [Rom.3:20]. Likewise: "If we say that we have no sin . . . " [1 John 1:8].

On Romans 7, Origen says clearly that the saints are speaking for another person when they attribute sin to themselves, as with Daniel [9:18]: "Not because of our righteousnesses, but in your mercy you will hear us." He corrupts such statements and teaches confidence in one's own righteousness or despair. On Romans 3 [:21] he says: "The righteousness of God is manifested without Law" means that the new evangelical laws are taught without the natural law. About "Let not your right hand know what the left hand does" [Mt. 6:3] he says the law previously was ignorant. Likewise: "The Law is spiritual" [Rom. 7:14], he understands only of allegory, that is, ceremonies contain an allegory, and frequently he understands "Spirit" incorrectly, not about the impulses of the Holy Spirit, but only of allegorical interpretation or thinking.

On Romans 8[:3], "What was impossible for the Law, because it was made weak through the flesh," Origen transfers flesh to the Law: The flesh of the Law was infirm, that is, the ceremonies were impossible, useless, etc.

But by "flesh" Paul understands the nature of man: "The Law was made weak through the flesh" [Rom. 8:3], that is, it could not be done by human nature. These passages show that Origen is running off the track and is not paying attention to what Paul is after.

I could collect many less important examples, as when he says that Peter stands higher than the rest because it is said to him in the plural number that "it will be loosed in heaven," while to the entire assembly of apostles it is said in the singular number "it will be loosed in heaven" [Mt. 16:19; 18:18; but this is not true]. But I omit these useless things. As to the rest, it is profitable for the learned and for those who use judgment to read the ancient writings, first on account of the historical testimonies, then because comparing them sharpens and exercises students. Thus the reading of Origen will profit also those who have been rightly instructed beforehand and hold fast to the sum and substance of the Christian doctrine.

## Dionysius

There is one booklet of Dionysius about the ecclesiastical episcopate which is useful on account of the history; the others contain useless speculations. There the ceremonies of the sacraments and the rites of the church are taught, and it is clear that at that time ceremonies were still moderate. Most of all, the ceremonies of the Mass should be considered here in order that it may become apparent that the more recent popes in the church have departed far from the ancient form. Certain psalms and readings from the gospel were recited. Prayers were said for the church and the state. Afterward, the presbyter, standing at the altar, recited the words of Christ about the Lord's Supper. Then the sacrament was distributed to people. The giving of thanks followed. This was the rite of the Mass; from this it is clear that the Mass was only a communion, and that there were no private Masses. Thus it also is a matter of wonder that no mention is made of offering [offering the body of the Lord; see below] and that he relates not even a rite of offering. It is profitable to observe chiefly these things in Dionysius in order that we may oppose antiquity to those who are defending the misuses of the Masses.

He tells about baptism, chrism, communions (as I have said), the ordination of presbyters and of those who made vows, the anointing of the dead, where he tells what were the ceremonies at funerals, when the corpse had been set down in the church. In the presence of the people some readings from the sacred writings about the resurrection were recited. Thereafter the people were commanded to give thanks by means of prayers that this person had departed in a godly manner in the knowledge of the Gospel. There was added the exhortation that everyone should pray for a godly exit from this life for himself. This custom was filled with godliness, and is worthy of praise. For what greater benefits can be thought of than to retain the knowledge of Christ in that great struggle, to be helped by Christ and to be saved? Our more recent age has totally abolished this better ceremony and has retained and heaped up worse ones.

Dionysius adds that after this exhortation the presbyters went away and poured oil on the corpse and prayed that God would forgive him any infirmity which remained in him after his conversion. After that the corpse was laid in the earth. These were the only ceremonies at funerals; no mention was made of the dead in the Mass, and much less was the body of the Lord offered for the dead. This profanation of the sacrament was added by a later age.

So much from Dionysius. Although at times there are in him ceremonies which are less evil, there are nevertheless the beginnings of monasticism, and this deserves to be rebuked earnestly because he does not distinguish between sacraments that are divinely instituted and human traditions. He speaks in the same way about the chrism as he does about baptism, and, so to say, makes unimportant things the equal of works. He also places the ordination of monks above the ordination of ministers, which is to be criticized severely, since the ordination of ministers pertains to the preaching of the Gospel, while the ordination of monks is a matter of superstition and is done only for the sake of a worship that is forbidden according to the passage: ''In vain they worship me with commandments of men'' [Mk 7:7]. Nevertheless, there monasticism is called perfection. Therefore his testimonies are useful so far as the history is concerned so that we may know which rites were customary at that time but not so that dogmas and laws can be made from his descriptions.

## Tertullian

Tertullian rightly refuted Marcion and the other heretics of his faction. He has useful testimonies about the Trinity, reciting not his own view but the ancient view received from the apostles. In the writing against Praxeas there is an excellent testimony about the Word, that is, about the Son of God, that he was a person even before he assumed human nature.

On the other hand, the ancients criticize certain errors of Tertullian, namely, that he condemns second marriages and argues in a ridiculous fashion: ''It is not lawful to marry the wife of a dead brother. Marrying a widow left behind by a Christian, he marries the wife of his dead brother; therefore he does not do right.''

He also plays about the rule of the saints, which they imagined would last for a thousand years in this bodily life before the world burns up, and before the last judgment, some being resurrected gradually, others more quickly than those who are resurrected more slowly. This Jewish foolery must be wholly driven out of the church.

In the booklet *De Corona Militis* he says much about human rites and rants most harshly that custom must be accepted as law. Since these sayings were badly distorted in the church, as happens, great errors were strengthened in all ages because the watchfulness of men is never so great that some evil customs do not creep in.

Tertullian lists the most childish customs, that on the first seven days after baptism one should not go into a bath. Likewise, that milk and honey should be offered to the baptized to taste. There he says we also make offerings for the dead, for birthdays annually. Our adversaries now wickedly twist this to Masses for the dead. Why do they omit birthdays if they ascribe so much authority to Tertullian? But he is not speaking about the Lord's Supper. On birthdays and funerals food was indeed brought into the churches, together with other gifts for the poor. They called these offerings and love feasts. The custom had been taken over from the heathen, but somewhat corrected. For the heathen also held feasts in their temples on birthdays and at funerals, and after the Nicene Synod some also forbade this pomp on birthdays.

Therefore, as has been said about other things, the historical testimonies in Tertullian are profitable where he calls to mind what the earlier church thought. But his reports and discussions should not be accepted as dogmas except to the extent that they agree with the apostolic Scripture.

## Cyprian

Cyprian lived around A.D. 260. He has useful testimonies about the Trinity, the baptism of infants, the use of the Lord's Supper, and the manner of the election of bishops, who, he writes, were elected by the assembly of the church, and that their election was approved with the counsel of a number of neighboring bishops.

But the ancients also criticized Cyprian because he held that persons baptized by heretics should be rebaptized. Meanwhile, as he preaches he pours out absurd statements when he exaggerates with immoderate hyperboles a cause which he has instituted. Thus when he writes too harshly about canonical punishments he says that absolution is of no avail unless these punishments have been completed. It is not difficult to see how much that is improper is contained in that dictum.

He also blusters vehemently about celibacy, although he indeed mitigates this subject. He commands that those who had made vows should enter marriage if they do not keep what they promised. In the booklet about alms he says that sins committed before baptism are remitted on account of the sufferings of Christ, but that after baptism forgiveness must be sought through alms. These things are full of absurdity, which he would without doubt have corrected if they had been called to his attention. Therefore not all his statements are to be taken as dogmas.

About the Lord's Supper, he is accustomed to use the words *offering* and *sacrifice,* as others do, who say variously: "We offer prayers, we offer bread and wine, we offer the body and blood of Christ." This is found also in Cyprian. Our adversaries take testimonies from here for defending the profanation of the Lord's Supper in the private Mass, etc.

The power of custom is great, and persons who follow it often speak improperly. Thus we now use the term *Mass,* although the etymology of the term is not known. Thus the ancients retained the terms *offering* and *sacrifice* without being much concerned about the etymology and the proper significance. And because Augustine saw something unsuitable in these terms, he softened them. He says it is called a sacrifice in remembrance of the sacrifice, and an offering in remembrance of the offering. These are figures of speech, as we say that Passover is a memorial or sign of the crossing. But I do not want to explain in many words or excuse the way of speaking of that time. For that is how the people spoke, at times accepting an improper word.

Irenaeus says clearly that this offering is an act of thanksgiving. Others thought the same thing, as the term *Eucharist* (giving of thanks) testifies. Therefore they felt that it was a ceremony by means of which thanks is given. That contains nothing unsuitable. For we receive it in order that we may be reminded of the benefit given us by Christ, and so we may arouse faith. Thereafter we give thanks for the benefit; from this it does not follow that this work should be done for others, be applied to others, etc. The fathers did not even think of these monstrous things. Therefore, when we read the term *sacrifice* and *offering,* we should understand either a sign of sacrifice and offering, or giving of thanks; we should not invent for it applications for others.

Meanwhile they express with the one word *offering* the whole business which is here being done, namely, prayers and the Lord's Supper. When this is done, prayers may be understood to be offerings.

One also reads in Cyprian certain words about the dead which more recent people distort badly: "We offer sacrifices for them." But he says these things about the martyrs, for mention was made of them in prayers when thanks was given to God because he had helped them. Thus the Greek canon says: "We offer for patriarchs, prophets, apostles," that is, we give thanks that you have chosen, redeemed, sanctified, etc., the church from the beginning until now. In the beginning this was the meaning of these words; it was not a prayer that God should lessen the punishments of the dead. During a later time wrong opinions were added, and the earlier words were partially changed, while the form of the old words was partly retained, but posterity understood something other than what earlier persons had understood. Therefore the testimonies of antiquity offer no defense for more recent abuses, which are partly different from present customs, and if they contain something wrong, they ought not to be opposed to firm testimonies of Scripture, because also other ages had their unsuitable customs. This is my answer very simply and without sophistry with respect to the words *offering* and *sacrifice*.

## Basil

In Basil there are useful testimonies about the Trinity, and about penitence, against Novatus. In a sermon on humility he hands down an outstanding statement about the righteousness of faith which openly favors us. Without any sophistry he takes away justification from good works. He is not speaking about ceremonial matters, but about all virtues; nor is he speaking only about works done before renewal, but about virtues in the renewed. He commands us to believe that we are righteous by confidence alone in the mercy promised because of Christ. His words are these: "The apostle says, 'Whoever boasts, let him boast in the Lord' [1 Cor. 1:31], saying that Christ has been made for us wisdom from God, righteousness, sanctification, and redemption. As it is written: 'Let him that glories glory in the Lord' [2 Cor. 10:17]. For this is the perfect and complete glorying in God: when a person does not even take pride in his own righteousness, but acknowledges that he is without true righteousness and that he is justified solely by faith in Christ. Paul boasts that he scorns his own righteousness, and that he is seeking the righteousness through Christ by faith, which is from God."

These words show sufficiently that Basil understood the righteousness by faith in this way, that one must think that we are righteous on account of Christ, through mercy, that is, that we are accepted, but not on account of our own virtues.

As for the rest, regarding the fact that Basil first instituted groups of monks, that example did harm and contained something evil, although he himself did not hold crass superstitions, and these groups still bore a certain image of teachers. Certain books are also being circulated under his name which contain rules of the monks. Some of these are without doubt forgeries and came into being long after Basil, for they are full of false opinions about celibacy and other acts of worship devised without a command of God, and they contain ridiculous foolery. For instance there is a great mass of punishments or satisfactions which he calls ἐπιτίμια: "If a girl were to laugh in the choir, she should sit for two days in the vestibule," and there are similar nursery lullabies. If one wanted to renew these through admiration of antiquity, he would in truth have lost his reason.

## Gregory of Nazianzus

Gregory of Nazianzus treated the article of the Trinity; on other dogmas he only lightly touches. He writes a life of Cyprian in which he relates that a certain girl was loved by Cyprian before his conversion, who, calling on the Virgin Mary, overcame magical incantations of Cyprian.

This example is cited about the invocation of saints. Although it seems to be a made-up story and was afterward spread under the name of Gregory, nevertheless, even if it had actually happened, it should not be cited for confirming the invocation of the saints. For the errors of the godly must not be opposed to the Word of God, and the godly in the church also have their weaknesses at all times.

They also quote from Basil and Gregory that at the end of sermons about the saints they are accustomed to address them: "O Athanasius, pray for us." Even if these direct addresses can be excused as rhetorical figures, it can still happen that after the manner of their time they then invoked the saints. For the invocation of the saints at that time gradually crept into the church, and the errors of the times draw people, so that they disapprove less of the things they are accustomed to and good people adopt them, just as the force of rivers carries the sailors along. Nevertheless the invocation of saints must not be approved of for this reason. And after the custom has grown and its wickedness has been revealed, it ought to be completely removed from the church. Basil does not say anything about invoking [the saints], but says only that the memory of the saints is celebrated in order that we may imitate their virtues. He calls the saints helpers of our prayers, not because they are to be invoked, but because all the blessed in heaven pray for the church and commend it to God.

Epiphanius writes that certain women were calling on the Virgin Mary and were accustomed to carry around her statue. He condemns this whole business and calls it an idolatrous work. Epiphanius contains refutations of ancient heresies, especially with regard to the Trinity and about a few other matters. I judge that his history should be read most of all.

## Chrysostom

The age of Chrysostom had already accepted many bad customs which he does not reprove as he reports them. Thus, he praises those who go to the sepulchers of the saints. He makes mention of prayers for the dead. He adorns monasticism with immoderate and false praises. In the tractate about penitence, he collects many ways of achieving remission of sins, namely, alms, tears, and other works. However, he makes no mention of faith, about which he should have spoken, and this writing contains many false things, and is confused and involved.

The Greeks greatly praised his commentaries on Paul, where in passages about justification and about faith the course of Paul's argument winds up in this way, that he frequently repeats the statement that we receive remission of sins by faith on account of Christ, not on account of works. Chrysostom says expressly: "By faith not only is God loved, but believers feel that they in turn are loved by God, although they are guilty in many ways."

In harmony with this interpretation he shows that he understands faith not merely as knowledge of history, but as confidence that our sins are forgiven us, and indeed he distinguishes this faith from works, from not stealing, not killing, etc. He also says that this is a higher act of worship. Although his explanation is simpler and less impure than that of Origen, it also is obscure and is not always consistent with itself.

On Romans 7 he runs even farther out of bounds. He says concupiscence and emotions are not sins if they do not bring forth the outward work. Nevertheless, if one reads these commentaries with judgment, he will find testimonies about many articles. Although there was at that time darkness in the church, it is clear that very many retained this common understanding that we are given forgiveness of sins on account of Christ, not on account of works. Therefore, although the ancients at times speak less adequately, one can see in other places what they really wanted to say.

With respect to the Lord's Supper, it is sufficiently clear that there were no private Masses. For he describes the presbyter standing at the altar and calling the people to come forward to the communion.

In the booklet about the dignity of the priesthood he learnedly distinguishes between civil and ecclesiastical power, and denies that the ecclesiastical has the right of compelling by physical power.

### Ambrose

Ambrose touches on many matters, including about the Trinity, against the Novatians, and about justification. Although in his commentaries contradictory statements are at times found, they seem to have been written not so much by himself, as introduced by others. Nevertheless, it is clear from his longer discussions that he thought the same about grace and about justification as we teach.

This is testified in the letter to Irenaeus about the Pauline dictum: "The Law works wrath" [Rom. 4:15] in *Epistola 71*. He speaks thus: " 'By the works of the Law no one will be justified' [Rom. 3:20], that is, through the law sin is known, but the guilt is 'not lessened. Therefore, when the Lord

Jesus came he forgave the sin of all, which no one had been able to avoid, and wiped out our bonds by the shedding of his blood. That is what he says: 'Sin abounded through the Law; grace abounded through Jesus' [Rom. 5:20], as John [1:29] says: 'Behold the Lamb of God who takes away the sin of the world.' Therefore let no one boast of his works, because no one is justified by his deeds. Whoever is righteous has it given to him, because he has been justified through Christ. Therefore, it is faith which sets us free through the blood of Christ, for blessed is he whose sin is remitted and has been given forgiveness'' [ cf. Ps. 32:1].

A number of similar statements are also found in other places of this writer, for example, in *De Vocatione Gentium* (Of the calling of the Gentiles). Likewise to the virgin Demetria, where he says: ''For the commandment has been given for no other purpose except that help might be sought from him who gave the commandment.'' Otherwise there are some preparations for the Mass under his name, and certain foolish things which seem to have been forged.

## Jerome

By his translations Jerome performed a useful work for the church, and although his explanations of the prophets are thin, his explanation of the histories, taken from the ancients, is useful. He writes little about dogmas. Writing against Jovinian, he strongly confirms false and superstitious opinions about human traditions. He maligns marriage and attacks it with a shameful speech which is by no means worthy of a Christian. He collects badly distorted statements of Scripture as though they spoke abusively of marriage, e.g.: ''If you live according to the flesh, you will die'' [Rom. 8:13], and similar passages, and says expressly that anyone marrying after a second marriage is not different from a whore. Likewise, that one should look not at what God allows, but at what he wants, as if God did not want marriage. Finally, after the manner of the heathen, he gathers complaints of the common people against the female sex and against marriage. A Christian ought to think far otherwise about them, because he knows that the cause of the infirmity in each sex is the corruption of nature, and that nevertheless for God's sake honor is to be accorded to the female sex. Since God did not create this sex in vain, this work of God should be acknowledged and the divine ordinance highly regarded. Neither is there less infirmity in the minds of men, in matters which have been committed to men. For God's sake, a Christian bears and mitigates the weakness in the companions divinely joined to men in this life, who are also co-heirs of eternal glory. He also knows that it is the will of God that we should care for them as part of the human race, and should not look down on them in diabolical pride. These things and others in the same sense ought to have been said in a Christian discussion, rather than these scurrilous outcries against a sex and a divine ordinance.

With respect to the distinction of foods, he praises rites instituted without a Word of God as though they constituted worship of God, yes, as if they were perfection. He makes the ridiculous statement: "If you want to be perfect, it is good not to drink wine and not to eat meat." There he badly distorts the statement of Paul, who, when he says: "It is good not to eat meat," adds: "if your example harms your brother" [Rom. 14:21]. Although it is necessary that such superstitions be rebuked in the church—for they give rise to many other errors—one should judge prudently with respect to these statements uttered thoughtlessly.

In the dialog against Pelagius he argues rightly that renewal is accomplished not by the powers of free will, but is a work of the Holy Spirit. He is also right in denying that the saints are without sin, and he sets down the noteworthy statement: "We are righteous when we confess that we are sinners, and that our righteousness does not depend on our own merit but on the mercy of God." But what he says later is not satisfactory. He understands the sins of the saints as actual sins, such as the flames of lust or anger or similar things. He does not understand it of the inner and perpetual doubting, carnal security, and concupiscence. Therefore it is clear that there are many lapses in the writings of Jerome, that are not insignificant.

### Augustine

Augustine treated many necessary controversies. He refuted the Arians, Manichaeans, Donatists, and Pelagians. Philosophical opinions had already crept into the church, which Pelagius strengthened, transforming the Gospel into a philosophy. He argued that there is no such thing as original sin, that men are able to satisfy the Law of God, and that this outward obedience merits forgiveness of sins, makes men righteous, and merits eternal life. He taught nothing about faith in Christ, nothing about the aid of the Holy Spirit. This teaching of Pelagius was not evangelical but philosophical, even as the understanding of the scholastic teachers wants almost the same thing, except that they patch on something of monastic superstitions. And now many are slipping into Pelagian opinions because they are plausible to reason.

Augustine in his time restored the doctrine of the Gospel about grace and faith, which had been almost extinguished, and again revitalized it. For this benefit the church is deeply indebted to him. About the doctrine of original sin he speaks with much greater clarity than all others. He also speaks more clearly and correctly about free will, that people are able to perform the outward works of the Law by the powers of free will, also honorable civil works, but that without the Holy Spirit they are unable to have spiritual impulses, true fear of God, and true patience, that is, the newness which should be found in those who are to be saved.

He teaches a useful distinction between letter and spirit; he teaches about gratuitous remission; he calls to our attention how Paul is to be understood when he says: "By the works of the law no man is justified" [Rom. 3:20], namely, that he takes away justification not only from ceremonies but also from moral works. The church had great need of this reminder. For Origen and many who followed him had spread the false interpretation in the church that justification is taken away only by ceremonies, and had imagined that people satisfy the Law and are righteous on account of their works. Augustine treats this question expressly in the book about the spirit and the letter, and declares that Paul is speaking also about morals as a whole when he denies that we are righteous by the Law. Therefore he denies that people satisfy the Law, Romans 8.

It is most useful to remember this admonition of Augustine and this topic of his. Since reason does not clearly see the magnitude of original sin and of our natural corruption, it easily slips into those opinions. It thinks the Law is unsatisfied and that men are righteous on account of works. Thus the righteousness of faith is directly obscured and lost, and true spiritual exercises are cast out, namely, true prayer, which must rest solely on mercy. Thus we are now being derided by our adversaries, who want to appear to be the more prudent. They loudly shout that we are ineptly exaggerating man's infirmity and are ridiculously taking justification away from works, although reason does not understand righteousness to be anything other except obedience according to the Law.

But the teaching of the Gospel about sin and the righteousness of faith is the hidden and special wisdom of the true church, which also few of the writers knew, and some wiser ones more obscurely, others more clearly. The Scotists and similar teachers completely buried it. Therefore, let us diligently guard the doctrine which has been brought to light after God has again made it known.

Furthermore, why do our adversaries not consider in their turn how absurd it is to say that Christ has set us free only from ceremonies? Likewise, if the liberation pertains only to ceremonial matters, then it did not profit the fathers who were before Moses. We must declare that liberation from the Law pertains to the entire church from the beginning of the world until its end. These things are, as I have said, more fully discussed in the booklet about the spirit and the letter.

Finally, those who understand it only of ceremonies are totally ignorant of what liberation from the Law is. As all men after the fall of Adam are oppressed by sin, by the wrath of God, death, the immense troubles of life, and eternal punishments, so all are burdened by the Law, which rebukes sin, accuses us, and kills us with eternal terror, as Paul says [cf. Rom. 7:7 ff.]. Therefore to be set free from the Law is to be set free from that accusation, so that we are not subject to the wrath of God and to eternal death [Cf. Rom. 8:2]. It is not merely to be set free from rites and outward shows, but much more to be rescued from the Law which terrifies, curses, damns and kills. This is made clear when something else is offered on account of which we are pronounced righteous, namely, the Son of God, who was made the sacrificial victim for us.

In the same way, Adam, Noah, Abraham, and all the elect before Moses were set free from the Law. They were accused by the Law; they were driven by dreadful terrors and by a sense of the wrath of God and the curse. But amid these terrors they were raised up by knowledge of mercy, promised because of the Lord who was to come, and they declared that they were pronounced righteous on account of the coming sacrificial victim, not on account of the Law [cf. Heb. 11:13]. They knew that their sins were not mere outward faults, but an inner uncleanness, horrible doubting about God, anger and indignation against God in adversities, and other evil impulses. They knew that sin itself, the infirmity of our nature, and the wrath of God are not taken away by any Law. But they also knew that they had been snatched out of such great miseries by knowledge of and trust in the promised Savior. Thus they also were set free from the moral Law, insofar as it judges and kills them, and from eternal wrath which the Law proclaims. They knew that the gratuitous remission of sins is not set before us through natural knowledge. Therefore, they sought forgiveness from somewhere else. But if they had thought that they would be righteous when they would be without sin, they would have sunk down with an agonized conscience. But they knew that a Savior had been promised for this reason, that they might declare that they pleased God even though they were unworthy and unclean. Thus they believed that they were righteous not on account of the Law, but on account of the Savior who would come.

Liberation from the Law embraces these great things. Carnally secure persons who do not know what true repentance and calling on God is do not understand these things. Finally, also those who are not exercised by afflictions, who have minds occupied with pleasures, who delight in their own opinions and despise the Word of God, or who bend it to their own imaginations and corrupt it, do not understand these things. Some of our more astute adversaries, although they see that Augustine's and our interpretation is truly the meaning of Paul and of the prophetic and apostolic Scripture, nevertheless thrust on us the opinion of Origen, Jerome, and Chrysostom. They cite the authority of who knows what persons, not because they truly with all their mind approve of them, but only in order to create a smokescreen for the inexperienced, lest they should appear to have been defeated.

For our adversaries do not bring a good conscience to these struggles, neither zeal for seeking the truth. They only bring hatred against us, contempt for the Gospel, and concern for protecting their own authority. They are not concerned about what the people should think about Christ or how the churches should be taught. To some extent they openly practice deceit, as do Cochlaeus, Wicelius, and others. In some respects they are tyrants and the accomplices of tyrants who, on account of their reputation of wisdom or virtue, govern the counsels of popes, kings, and princes, although they are persons who have no God, who think that all religions are fabrications, and are wonderfully pleased with themselves because they dare to break wind against thunderclaps, as the wit in the comedy says. And they will express such opinions at synods about the glory of Christ, whose name they consider as being a fable.

Therefore, I exhort pious readers that they should first consider the kinds of doctrine, whether they set forth the meaning of the prophetic and apostolic Scripture simply and without sophistry. Then, when the fathers are cited, they should consider which sayings of the fathers are in agreement with the divine voice. Finally, as Paul commands to test the spirits [cf. 1 Thess. 5:21; 1 John 4:1], one should look at the will of each father and at the substance of his counsel. Our adversaries do that not in order to emend anything, but in order that they may defend their tyranny in any way they can, and strengthen and defend their power. For this reason kings and popes are against the marriage of priests, because they see that celibacy is more expedient for retaining their power and wealth. Since, in this way, the marks of their impious will are visible in certain manifest articles, it is plain enough that they are not motivated by a good spirit, but that they are enemies of Christ, and that also in other articles they are not seeking the truth. Therefore we shall steadfastly repudiate their judgments.

On Ps. 42 [43] Augustine declares that a regenerate person is not righteous on account of works, but by faith, for he says this: ''Be afraid if you say that you are righteous if you do not hold fast what is said in another Psalm [143:2]: 'Enter not into judgment with your servant.' For if You would apply judgment without mercy, where shall I go? 'Lord, if you should mark iniquities, O Lord, who shall stand?' [Ps. 130:3]. 'Do not enter into judgment with your servant, because in your sight no man living shall be justified [Ps. 143:2]. Therefore if no person living will be justified in your sight, because everyone lives here, woe to him if God should enter into judgment with him. For also in another prophet he scolds the arrogant and proud thus: 'Why do you contend with me in judgment? All of you have forsaken me, says the Lord' [Jer. 2:29]. Therefore do not contend in judgment. Be concerned to be righteous and no matter what kind of person you have been, confess that you are a sinner. Always hope for mercy, and, secure in that humble confession, say to your soul which is troubled and cries out against you: 'Why are you sad, O my soul? Why do you trouble me?' [Ps. 42:5]. You wanted to hope strongly in yourself. Hope in the Lord, not in yourself. For what are you in yourself? What are you of yourself? Let him be your health who received wounds on your account, and says: Hope in the Lord.' "

On Ps. 31 [32] Augustine asks, "Who are the happy ones? Not those in whom he does not find sin, for he finds it in everyone: 'For all have sinned and come short of the glory of God' [Rom. 3:23]. Therefore, if sins are found in everyone, it follows that none are happy except those whose sins are forgiven. The Apostle reminds us of this when he says: 'Abraham believed God, and it was reckoned to him for righteousness' [Rom. 4:3].''

Here Augustine correctly applies the statement about faith, and testifies that he understands by faith not merely the knowledge of history, but confidence. We are confident that sins are forgiven us because of Christ. Indeed, no one is able to understand Paul's meaning unless he understands the term *faith*. Understanding faith only as knowledge of history and not as confidence in the mercy promised because of Christ is truly, as the saying goes, to wander about in the marketplace. It is not surprising that the monks went completely astray in explaining Paul, because on this subject they hallucinated shamefully. And now this darkness is the chief hindrance which prevents them from accepting the doctrine about faith because they do not understand the term *faith* correctly. Why do they not ponder such statements of Augustine's as the one I have just quoted? Here he testifies that Augustine wants this, that Abraham was pronounced righteous because he believed not only about his descendants but about the remission of sins.

Such statements which one meets here and there in Augustine show sufficiently clearly that he thinks the same about grace and about faith as we teach. Thus he also says in *De Spiritu et Litera*: "From the Law we fear God. However, through faith we flee to mercy." Here he learnedly distinguishes the Law from the Gospel.

Although here and there figures of speech occur in writings which are not sufficiently explained or are unsuitable, these must be forgiven to his times, because the custom of the common people had accepted certain figures, such as the term *merit*, and certain others, and the learned were not able to drive them out. Besides, the writers themselves were not sufficiently accustomed to accurate examinations, and one can judge how great the darkness was in the church at that time from the fact that the wicked opinion of Pelagius was received with such great applause that Augustine and a few others were not able to drive it out from the church without great struggles.

If with respect to ceremonies someone opposes to us the age of Augustine, he should know that not even Augustine himself was pleased with all the rites and persuasions of his time. For he complains that many superstitious opinions clung to the church, that human traditions were placed ahead of the commandments of God, and that ceremonies had been so multiplied that the servitude of the Jews was more bearable than that of the church. These are his words to Januarius in *Epistola* 119:[5] "The mercy of God wanted religion itself to be free with very few and very simple sacraments of celebration. But they weigh it down with servile burdens so that the condition of the Jews was more bearable, who however were subject to divine laws, not to human." And first he says about human rites: "This whole class of things has free observances." Then he expressly commands that useless human rites should be abolished. Therefore Augustine does not so approve of the ceremonies of his time that he wanted the church to be set up according to this norm. For many things had become accepted which not even he himself approved; rather, he wanted them reproved and corrected. He observes some according to the custom of that time, even as we all condone many things according to present customs.

At that time sermons about purgatory began to grow greatly in number. He neither refutes nor confirms these; he merely reports them, saying that some people were of the opinion that the souls of the godly are purged after they have departed from the bodies. But in book 9 of his *Confessions* he prays a prayer for his dead mother with these words: "Inspire your servants, Lord, that they may remember my mother and father at the altar. He does not ask more than this. Although he said this modestly, it is now criminally twisted to the offering of the sacrament for the dead, as it was not done at the time of Augustine.

Vows were also customary at that time, and the question occurs whether marriages contracted after a vow ought to be dissolved. There is a statement of Augustine about this matter in *Decretis* 27. q. 1. C. *nuptiarum*. Although Augustine here ascribes more to vows than was fitting, he declares that marriages contracted after a vow should not be dissolved and that they truly are marriages, so that one person should not violate the vow to the injury of another. Neither does the obligation between two persons become invalid when one person previously had a different purpose. He says these things in sum he says in that text. But the error concerning vows was stronger than the mitigation of Augustine. Regulations which followed later tore marriages

---

[5] Melanchthon summarizes chapter 1 of Letter LIV in *The Confessions and Letters of St. Augustine*, ed. Philip Schaff, vol. 1 in A Select Library of the Nicene and Post-Nicene Fathers of the Christian Church (Grand Rapids: Eerdmans, 1956) p. 300.

apart. Augustine saw that this separation was an evil, but he did not sufficiently consider what evil there was in the vows themselves because it was too difficult to see. For he was defeated by the opinions of the people of his age. The custom of making vows had already been accepted. The admiration of many who lived at that time was very great; admiration influences judgment. Therefore, he does not question whether vows are valid, although many errors were involved in them. They were considered acts of worship, as of special merit for righteousness, and as perfection. Likewise, they were impossible to keep for many. If he had refuted these things earlier, he would have been better able to prohibit the dissolution of marriages.

It is certain, therefore, that already at that time many errors clung to the church. Although Augustine was opposed to some of these, he considered others good. After these are uncovered, they ought not to be defended. Although the examples of the ancients were in their time passed over in silence, they certainly should not be used now to confirm greater abuses. The conclusion is by no means valid: Augustine commands that prayer should be made at the altar for his mother, therefore Masses for the dead are to be approved. Or: In Augustine's time some thought that there was a purgatory, therefore Masses, indulgences, and other things done for the dead should be approved. For at the time of Augustine there were not yet the monstrous forms of ungodliness, although the seeds were gradually being sown.

## Gregory

Gregory became pope in the year 590, exactly 157 [160] years after the death of Augustine. Meanwhile, many barbarian tribes had streamed into Italy including Goths, Lombards, and their allies. Not only had the study of literature died down and the churches had become neglected, but also these same barbarian tribes which occupied Italy had brought in with them or easily accepted many superstitious opinions. Therefore in a short time the abuses were greatly increased.

As Italy was thus being cut up it seemed to be a particular happiness to be far removed from the state, to live in some kind of solitude without family, without children, and not to see the destruction of cities and the devastation of the fatherland. For it is a sad thing to say what Aeneas says: "I also was a large part of these things." Therefore moderate men who had families congratulated the monks on account of their quiet life. Thus admiration of the monks increased, and many began to seek and to love solitude.

The barbarian people by nature admire new rites which have a show of outstanding piety, and, as it were, business deals with God. Therefore it is not surprising that the crowd of monks grew at that time, and favorable opinions about that kind of works floated about, and that the light of the Gospel about true faith and true acts of worship was extinguished.

The veneration of the saints was pleasing to the barbarians. After the custom had once been accepted according to the manner of the heathen to honor them with statues and special[6] temples, the custom grew through imitation by the powerful. Little by little there came to it such great ungodliness that the veneration of the saints was not different in the following centuries from the manifest idolatry of the heathen. Anna and George were invoked in no other way than Juno, Mars, or Hercules. People ran to the statues, and bishops confirmed such idol-mania with great authority; teachers praised it. The sum and substance of religion consisted in such acts of worship. Meanwhile, there was great silence about invoking Christ and about faith.

There the beginnings of such great impiety should have been guarded against. Instead, Gregory greatly strengthened them. He instituted the public rite of invocation of the godly dead; he commanded that temples should be dedicated to their bones and dust.

At that time also the opinion crept in that an offering of the body and blood of Christ should be made for the dead. This opinion brought forth a dreadful profanation of the sacrament.

Although even greater darkness followed after the age of Gregory, these errors at that time clung to the church: a false persuasion about monasticism; works contrived without a command of God; the invocation of the saints; and the offering of the body of Christ for the dead. These errors thereafter drew great ruin in their train. Therefore, the age of Gregory cannot be the norm for improving the church. In order that it may be possible to see this more clearly, I shall first list the more evident errors of Gregory, then I shall discuss a few things about the Lord's Supper. In Book 3 of his Epistles, the Epistle to the bishop of Catania in Sicily, Gregory commands: "Subdeacons or deacons are not to use the custom of spouses whom they had married before they were ordained," although the Sicilians had previously followed the Greek custom and had not forbidden the custom of spouses to the married. This lapse is sufficiently clear. For no pious person can approve the separating of a lawful marriage.

He tells that there was a certain Speciosus who preferred to relinquish the office of subdeacon rather than do without the conjugal custom. Whoever this man was, he certainly was gifted with saner judgment than those who broke up such marriages.

The sin of Gregory is increased by the fact that he wanted this custom

---

[6]  The text here has *pericularibus*, a word not found in Latin dictionaries. The context calls for *peculiaribus*, and we have so translated.

to be received in the Sicilian churches, which until that time had, according to the decrees of the old synods, retained marriages in all grades of clergy and had not burdened deacons and others with vows. Why does Gregory take to himself the rule over other churches when he shouts so mournfully that he detests the name of universal bishop? Moreover, why does he separate marriages where deacons had not been burdened with vows? Why does he not here honor the authority of earlier synods? Since this lapse includes manifest ungodliness and tyranny, it is quite clear that the age of Gregory was not without great errors.

Likewise, how unjust he is toward those who as children had been educated in monasteries by order of their parents, and after they had matured, asked for a different kind of life. About these he answers that it is sinful for them to leave the monastic life. This hardness must be rebuked not only because harm has been done to their age, but also because it greatly strengthened superstitious opinions about monastic acts of worship.

I shall add a third error which is not difficult to see. He is influenced by ghosts to approve of offering the sacrament for the dead. He tells about two who after death served in the baths, of whom the one begged that an offering of the sacrament might be made for him, that he might be set free from these punishments. From these ghosts he accepts dogmas in the church contrary to the clear commandment of God. Deut. 18[:11]: "Do not seek truth from the dead." And Is. 8[:19]: "Should a people seek truth for the living from God or from the dead?" Therefore no matter what the condition of souls is after this life, dogmas are not to be taken from ghosts. And who does not see that it is a poetical fancy when he says that after death the godly are made bathmasters? A similar fable has been contrived about the daughters of Danaus who draw water with sieves.

## Conclusion

We have not drawn up this catalog in order to add refutations of the errors, since they are found elsewhere in sufficient number. I only wanted to list the errors to show that those persons are deceived who so greatly admire the fathers as though they had been without error and had never disagreed with the clear divine writings. Although the more learned fathers teach us something, nevertheless one must judge them according to the Word of God.

Refraining from all refutations, I shall briefly add certain things about the offering on behalf of the dead. There is no need to ask whether there is a purgatory; this question has nothing to do with offering. Even if there were a purgatory, it is nevertheless wicked to offer for the dead. There are many firm reasons. First, it is an act of wickedness to institute an act of worship in the church without a command from God. The application of the Lord's Supper to others is done without any divine command or testimony. Therefore this application is without any doubt wicked.

Very many statements confirm the major premise. "You shall not have other gods" [Ex. 20:3; Deut. 5:7]. In this commandment also strange acts of worship are forbidden. Here belongs the statement: "In vain they worship me with commandments of men" [Mark 7:7]. Likewise: "Whatever is not of faith is sin" [Rom. 14:23]. Moreover, acts of worship that are without a command from God cannot be done from faith. The world does not understand how great a sin it is to invent acts of worship without a command from God, to depart from the Word of God. The prophets preach much about this crime and deplore the blindness of men who invent acts of worship and dogmas about the will of God with dreadful boldness, and who do not hold fast to the Word and the worship in which God set forth his will to us. These blind persons seek God in other ways. It is certain that Christ did not give us the Sacrament on behalf of the dead. What mention is there of the dead? He commands that the Supper be celebrated in order that we may remember his death and his benefits [cf. 1 Cor. 11:24 ff.]. Are the dead present, and do they remember it together with us? I shall briefly add other arguments also.

Second, the statement is sure and it cannot be shaken: "The righteous shall live by his faith" [Rom. 1:17]. Therefore it is necessary that we receive remission of sins while we are alive, and it is impossible that anyone should receive remission because of a work or sacrifice of some priest. Obscure and ambiguous matters call for long explanations. However, this error about offering is refuted by such clear and firm arguments that they do not call for a lengthy explanation. The doctrine about the remission of sins is certain and clear. No one receives forgiveness unless he accepts it with his own faith. If anyone takes this understanding away, he commits an insult to Christ. Those persons who imagine that offering merits remission for the dead offer an insult to Christ.

Third, the use of the sacrament profits only those who as they use it remember the death and the benefits of Christ. It is impossible that this work should be of use to the dead, who neither use it nor add the remembrance there. What goes before is clear from the institution of Christ, who commands that this ministry be celebrated in remembrance [cf. 1 Cor. 11:24, 25]. Nothing else is to be added by the imagination to the institution. If anyone adds anything by his own imagination, if he transfers it to the dead, he wickedly defiles the institution of Christ.

Fourth, the Scripture says plainly: "Blessed are the dead who die in the Lord" [Rev. 14:13]. Rom. 8[:10]: "The body is dead because of sin; however, the spirit lives because of justification," that is, those justified with respect to the spirit, as long as they carry about this body to which the remnants of sin cling, are afflicted in various ways in order that faith, the knowledge of God, and spiritual newness may increase in prayer. But when the body has died, the remnants of sin are destroyed. And Paul adds expressly that the spirit lives because of justification. The life of the justified spirit is not fear or a sense of the wrath of God, but it is joy in the Holy Spirit, as Paul says [cf. Rom. 14:17]. Therefore there are no punishments of purgatory.

Christ says to the converted thief: "Today you will be with me in paradise" [Luke 23:43], that is, in a tranquil and blessed life, not in punishments and fears. Therefore the souls of the righteous do not go away to torments, but to spiritual joy and peace. In this life the godly are plagued by dreadful afflictions, because God according to His wonderful counsel wants his church to be subjected to the cross and to taste the afflictions of Christ. Thus Adam, Isaac, Jacob, Joseph, Daniel, Isaiah, Jeremiah, John the Baptizer, and other lights of the church were in difficulties, the magnitude of which no one is able to describe. Therefore Peter says: "Humble yourselves under the mighty hand of God" [1 Pet. 5:6]. Although there are such punishments of the godly while they live in the body, why should it be said that there are such punishments after death? The purpose of these afflictions is that the remnants of sin in the flesh may be acknowledged, and that people may repent. But after death there is no room for repentance, as Paul clearly declares, 2 Cor. 3 [2 Cor. 5:10]: "Everyone will receive the things which he had done in the body." The Psalms also teach this: "The dead do not praise you, Lord" [Ps. 88:10; 115:17]. Likewise: "Because in death there is none who remember you" [Ps. 6:5]. Therefore it cannot be said that some are so plagued by such tortures after death that they repent.

If our adversaries say that these torments are not inflicted in order that repentance may increase, but that they are satisfactions, then this opinion must be disapproved all the more. For the doctrine about satisfactions which the masters of [Lombard's] *Sentences* thought up is false and wicked. And indeed, into those discussions there flow together, as in the bilge of a ship, many lies about purgatory, vows, offering for the dead, and finally many others. Since purgatory, as they call it, cannot be affirmed, it is godless to institute an offering for liberating the dead. However, even if there were a purgatory, the Lord's Supper could not be transferred to the dead.

But why do I argue? The mention of purgatory arose from ghosts, then was strengthened on account of financial gain, and now it is being defended by popes, cardinals, bishops, and canons who are plainly Epicureans and securely despise the judgment of God. They take the things which they read about punishments after death as the fables of the poets about Ixion, Sisyphus,

Tantalus, or similar persons, and laugh at the stupidity of others who declare that God intends eternal punishments for the wicked.

Therefore I omit a discussion for the present. At the Synod of Basel the Greeks brought in a speech about purgatory which is today found in the library at Pforzheim, in which they discuss the passage of Paul in 1 Cor. 3[:15], which a more recent age has twisted to purgatory, although it is certain that passage speaks about repentance: "He will be saved, but only as through fire." Paul wants a fall into sin to be corrected by repentance. He is speaking about this present life in which there is room for repentance. Surely the saying is true: "The speech of truth is simple." Since Paul is speaking about repentance, this passage cannot be twisted to speak about torments after death.

The answer about the passage in Maccabees is also quite plain. A jurist says: "The truth is not vitiated by the wrong things that are done." And Demosthenes, in reproving evil examples, says against Aristocrates: "Do not allow us to say: 'Thus it happened,' but 'It is right to happen.' " The Levitical sacrifices did not wipe away sins before God; none were afterward instituted for the dead. Therefore it was an error to sacrifice for the sins of the dead, even as the Jews frequently accepted other wrong acts of worship. For the nature of men is prone to superstition in every age. Since that example militates against the Scripture, it must not be quoted for confirming superstitions in the church. These are the chief things which are quoted about purgatory. I have inserted this discussion that it may be more apparent that the lapse of Gregory, who confirmed offering for the dead, openly militates against the apostolic Scriptures.

Since this is so, also the canon of the Mass, as it is called, is to be reproved, in which it is said that an offering is for the redemption of the living and the dead. What audacity it was to transfer the sacrament to the dead when the institution speaks so clearly about the living, about a remembrance! Gregory writes that this canon was composed by a certain scholar, as he himself calls him. But no matter who the author was who put together this rhapsody, it cannot be denied that the Latin canon disagrees with both Greek canons, although the Greek canons also do not agree with each other but differ in important places.

Until now I have spoken of Gregory, and I do not want to add the writers of the following ages. For the doctrine degenerated even more afterward. There came to it also the tyranny of the popes, although until this time Gregory repudiates the title of universal bishop and strongly scolds it, as a number of epistles in book 4 testify.

I could add the complaints of ancient writers about the greed and the ignorance of the bishops which, if they tell us nothing else, at least tell us that the church is by no means to be set up according to the example and pattern of that time. But in the Apocalyse of John there are set before us dreadful pictures which without doubt signify the times of the church, and slow that wicked teachers would at once go about in the church and would suppress the truth with tyrannical rule.

Also the histories of the synods show what a fury there was in very many bishops who inflamed rulers and the common people with strange tricks to protect their wickedness, exactly as now popes and bishops attempt with every trick to incite the minds of kings to start civil war.

With what a sad complaint Basil, at the close of his book about the Holy Spirit, deplores the madness and the wickedness of the bishops of his time. He tells that they sought to defend their wicked dogmas with seditions and murders. And to the Italian and Gallic bishops he writes thus:[7] "The true dogmas have been overthrown; pious laws are frustrated; the ambition of people who do not fear God seizes the governance of the churches. There is no way to honor except through godlessness, with the result that whoever is maddest and most audacious in ruining godly and true dogmas is judged most worthy of the honor of bishop. The earnestness befitting priests has departed. Shepherds who will feed the flock of the Lord with learning are lacking."

Thus this man pictures the bishops of his time, to whose vices a more recent age has added the desire to rule and tyrannies.

Since it is certain, therefore, that that age was not without vices, it must be granted to the church that it seek counsel from the Word of God, as the Father in heaven commands that we hear his Son, and David says: "Your Word is a lamp to my feet" [Ps. 119:105].

Although I have passed over many things that were absurdly said, I have not collected these errors of the ancient writers in order to take away anything from their true praises. I believe that there were very many pious and out-standing men among them—some even exceptionally well deserving—but not even they wanted to have their pronouncements placed ahead of the teaching of Christ. Those who now oppose the authority of the ancients to us are greatly misusing their testimonies. Although seeds of errors were scattered in those times, such abominable abuses had not yet found their way into the church. In the beginning there was some mention of the saints. How great an amount of ungodliness came to it later? The speech of Gregory Nazianzus must not be quoted, since his age did not yet know this recent idolatry.

But why do our adversaries appeal to the authority of the church, although they are fighting not about doctrine, not about religion, but about their lusts and possessions? They do not want their tranquillity disturbed. This is the

---

[7] Melanchthon here offers first the Greek text and then a Latin translation. This translation is of the Latin.

one and only reason why they desire to destroy us. For certain dogmas are clearer than the light of noon. And yet, to suppress this, manifest cruelty is exercised. They kill godly priests—learned and good men—on account of marriage. Where can one read about any barbarian land where men are killed on account of honorable marriage? If they approve of the ancient church, why do they not imitate the first times in this? Do they think that Ambrose or Augustine would have approved of these cruel punishments? Truly they would have cursed this inhumanity and would have testified openly that these popes were authors of cruelty, not members of the church, but instruments of the devil, and would without any doubt have undertaken the defense of pious priests, women, and children, and all peoples who are connected with this cause.

I have said which is the true church. It is clear that we faithfully retain and guard the doctrine of the catholic church of Christ taught in the prophetic and apostolic Scriptures, and also in our confessions. It is clear that we think of the catholic church as Christ thinks. I add also this, that the foremost writers—Ambrose, Augustine, and a few others—think the same, if they are properly understood, and a few things are forgiven them which at that time did not come into controversy.

With respect to the liturgy, there is no doubt that there were neither private Masses, nor Masses sold for money, nor funeral Masses before Gregory, nor had the invocation of saints begun to be celebrated much before Gregory.

Also the law about perpetual celibacy is quite recent. It is being defended for no other reason except that celibacy is more suitable for guarding wealth. Those who assert that the marriage of priests militates against divine law do a manifest injury to the Word of God.

The men on our side have said many things more clearly than the ancients about repentance, about the remission of sins and justification (which we say people receive by faith on account of Christ, not on account of works), about satisfaction, about the keys, about human traditions, and about matters of church government. It appears that these are in agreement with the constant opinion of those who were more learned and more experience in spiritual matters. If they had read this explanation and method they would joyfully have approved of them because they were godly persons, as I hear that a famous man, a Parisian theologian, told that he first understood the statement of Augustine about justification more correctly from our explanation.

I know that it is possible to quote many things from the writings of the ancients which fight against our statements. And everyone quotes what seems suitable for his own pleasure, so that from the same flowers the bees gather honey but the spiders poison. But let deceits be far removed from the judgments of the church. I shall not appeal to all writers, but to the better ones—Ambrose, Augustine, and others to the extent that they agree with these. Although they themselves at times said wrong things, they will forgive us if we rebuke certain things as long as we follow the clear and sure meaning of the divine Scriptures, and do not depart from the symbols, and hold what they themselves saw and intended but were not always able to make clear. For it is beyond doubt that the kind of doctrine which we profess is truly the consensus of the catholic church of Christ, as the symbols, the saner synods, and the more learned fathers show. This is how I answer the more moderate persons who oppose the authority of the church or the fathers to us.

A certain new kind of wise men arise who, although they are atheists, want no controversies at all to be carried on about religion. They praise peace and harmony, curse all who in any way sow discords, and judge that these should be taken away as refuse and pestilence of the human race. This is the one and only philosophy of popes, cardinals, kings, canons, and many who want to show that they are statesmen. These persons do not want their leisure to be disturbed or their dignity shaken, and hate a doctrine which it seems will harm their comforts. Finally, each has a different reason. In the council of kings they all say that no change is to be granted, and that the concord of the church and the authority of the ordered power must be preserved.

They also have their own orators who put forth the most vehement speeches in favor of this opinion. There is no need to name all of them since we have the writings of many of them. But from all these, Omphalius recently sewed together a patchquilt. In the beginning, as though he were Solon or an areopagite, he preaches about the dignity of laws. He scolds seditions and tells about contempt for law, and how sweet the harmony of good order which the laws bring about is in the state. Then, although he does not name a certain profession, he shows clearly enough whom he is chiefly seeking out. He declaims against us who have rejected certain tyrannical and wicked laws of the popes. Although I am not of the opinion that he is saying these things *gratis*, nevertheless, since the same things are being said by great and eloquent men, I shall not discuss what he is trying to accomplish.

This whole class of speeches is intended to strengthen the minds of the mighty, lest they give ear to any moderate and godly counsels, but that, inflamed, they may exercise unjust savagery. As David prayed that the counsels of Ahithophel might not prevail [cf. 1 Sam. 15:31], so also we shall pray God that the eloquence of these orators may not suppress the truth and glory of Christ. Since it is written: "Out of the mouths of infants and sucklings you have perfected praise" [Ps. 8:2; Mt. 21:16], we hope that God will not fail to be with us as we refute these slanders and as we proclaim the glory of Christ.

I know that they are speaking plausibly about the dignity of the laws, peace, and the common tranquillity. I am not so ignorant with respect to literature nor so unaquainted with a civil way of life. I also think that in the state those burdens which can be tolerated without impiety must be condoned for the common tranquillity. With respect to such things the statements are valid: "Evil sleeps well if it is not stirred up." Also what Plato says: "As the mad acts of a father, so also the customs of a foolish fatherland must be borne." These things are rightly said in the proper place about civil burdens which can be borne without impiety, but these philosophical judgments should not be transferred destroying the glory of Christ. Errors in doctrine and idolatry should certainly not be hidden, as Christ says: "If anyone shall deny me, I shall confound him" [Mt. 10:33]. The first commandment: "You shall not have other gods" [Ex. 20:3] must be set high over all human things—laws of men, governments, orderly power, peace, fatherland, and concord. Nothing is more venerable than these, but nevertheless the name of God is to be placed above them all.

The prophets and apostles without doubt most dearly loved their fatherland, its tranquillity, and other good things. Nevertheless, they were compelled to rebuke wicked worship and evil opinions. And indeed, Christ professes that he is bringing a kind of doctrine which, like a fire, will kindle great discords. For it is necessary that there be fights about the worship of God, because the devil burns with a dreadful hatred for God, and tries as much as he can to destroy the Word of God. He incites wicked persons against God and draws along with himself the most flourishing governments. It is with these enemies that Christ wages war.

Since it is necessary that the godly reprove and abolish ungodly worship, prophets and apostles cannot avoid being authors of changes. Although political wisdom shrinks back from the very term *change,* also the godly, who certainly are not all dumb or foolish, understand how many difficulties and dangers changes bring with them. Nevertheless, a Christian breast prefers the commandments of God and high mindedly accepts all difficulties. He understands that they are all ruled by Christ, to whom all things have been subjected, as the prophet says [cf. Ps. 110].

I answer with these things briefly, not only to the speech of Omphalius, but also to the arguments of those wise persons who in all councils make speeches about avoiding changes and about concord. Although persons who are without God laugh at this answer, it is useful for the godly to consider these arguments, lest that kind of wisdom deter minds from godliness and from the profession of the truth.

I write these things most of all for the purpose of admonishing the youth. The wicked now capture the minds of many with all kinds of lures—riches and other pleasant things. Then indeed they also hold those that are in their net with these persuasions. Saying that changes are to be avoided because it is proper to favor the common authority in order to guard the present form of the state. No matter how praiseworthy these are, Christians must be admonished not to forget this commandment: "You shall not have other gods" [Ex. 20:3].

I am grieved that some who are gifted with excellent minds are conspiring with the ungodly to incite kings to cruelty and to confirm ungodliness. It is a virtue worthy of great and outstanding men to confer diligence and authority most of all on the glory of God. This aim should be set before all, that each one in his own place should, as much as he can, do something for the preservation of the heavenly doctrine. I shall not speak here about the other little parasites who write dishonest books. They belong to the race of flatterers such as Dionysius the Sicilian nourished, who took the spittle of the tyrant and licked it, proclaiming that it was sweeter than nectar.

I return to those wise persons, some of whom pretend to be religious. After they see that the absurd superstitions of earlier times cannot be excused, they invent less harsh interpretations for rites and decrees in order that they may secretly stabilize impiety by preserving the rites and faulty decrees. Such is the book published at Cologne under the title of *Reformation*. I hear that Cardinal Contarini in Italy is accustomed to say that the Lutherans are inflicting an injury on the most distinguished Romans when they ascribe to them the errors of plebeian writers, such as of legends, *Dormi Secure*, and similar ones. The foremost Romans had never held thus or had approved of those foolish books; thus they now lead the errors away from themselves. I know also that there are everywhere very many people who with this new trick seek to grasp the praise of special wisdom, who are chiefly after this: after they have borrowed from our books many things which have been corrected by us and have carelessly adulterated our pens, they give us an unjust teacher's pay. For they do not cease to exercise cruelty. Moreover, they do not consider that this new sophistry will be the final destruction of the true religion.

If it is permitted to the more audacious intellects to mix in glosses according to their own will, what is going to happen? There is manifest idolatry in the cult of the saints, in Masses for the dead, and glosses are nevertheless coatrived for retaining rites which are themselves faulty. Perhaps a little later they will excuse Egyptian superstitions. Let this godless and pernicious sophistry which vouches for what is contrary to fact be far removed from the church! Worship not instituted by an express Word of God is of itself evil even if you attach to it whatever gloss you wish, because it is not divinely instituted. It is evil also for this reason, that this custom, even if you think differently, gives to the saints honor which belongs to God, as all can hear.

I could cite many examples, but I desist and urge the godly to curse this nefarious sophistry. Hezekiah not only corrected the superstitious opinions about the brazen serpent, but destroyed the statue itself [2 Kings 18:4]. Thus godliness demands that we cast off together with ungodly opinions the rites themselves which are not proper customs of the realm. Thus the Scripture commands that idols be destroyed. It follows that the rites themselves of private Masses, the invocation of saints, the observance of vows, monk's garb, the monastic brotherhoods, the bond of celibacy, the distinction of foods, and similar foolish rites which have their origin from superstitions should be taken away and abolished.

But what am I arguing? Those who paint evil rites with this sophistry do not truly do this in order to remove errors from the church, but in order, under any kind of pretext, to defend their authority and skillfully establish impiety. For wrong opinions easily spring up again if the rites themselves remain. The godly must be vigilant, for the devil fights against the Gospel, not only openly inciting tyrants to savagery, but also slyly constructing ambushes under the pretext of wisdom and pouring out beautiful persuasions. The Holy Spirit often teaches about being wary of these, as Paul says to Timothy that deceitful spirits will come [Cf. 1 Tim. 4:1], and to the Colossians he says that human traditions will have the appearance of wisdom [cf. Col. 2:23]. Not only will manifestly foolish dreams be spread, such as were many ancient and recent ones and as were a little earlier the manifest frauds of the indulgences, but even astute men may skillfully paint false dogmas and wicked rites so that they may be received with great applause, be loved, and held fast. Does not the wickedness of Paul of Samosata have the appearance of wisdom? Is not the error of Pelagius plausible to profane intellects? Thus these things have an appearance of wisdom. It serves peace and tranquillity to retain the customs people are used to. Therefore, the more objectionable opinions may be removed and better-sounding interpretations invented if the rites themselves are retained. This seems to be said splendidly while what is done is far otherwise.

These hypocrisies are revealed in the history of Christ. After they had blindfolded him, they struck his cheeks laughing, commanding him to prophecy by whom he had been struck. So these excusers of impious rites make sport with Christ and the church. After they have thought up some tasteless gloss they think they have now put a blindfold on the eyes of Christ. Then they add blows, that is, they establish their wickedness. They inflame kings to cruelty and institute triumphs as if they had already completely destroyed the truth. They receive applause in their theater. They are praised by the wicked and loved by kings whose lusts they serve. But we must pray to God that he may suppress these types of flatterers.

Nicander says there is a kind of serpent which he calls Hemorrhoidae. They are tiny beasts, one foot in length, but the power of their poison is so great that on a person struck by them bloody sweat breaks out over the entire body, so that blood flows abundantly out of the mouth, nostrils, ears, and bladder, the eyes shed bloody tears, and the entire body burns with an incredible inflammation. When a beast of this kind had in Egypt killed the master of Helen's ship, a heroic woman crushed it with her foot. For this reason, also the descendants of the Hemorrhoidae are said to waver, having lost their sting. Moreover, the outcome shows that this new sophistry of the interpreters of traditions is a poison no different from that of the Hemorrhoidae. Although the unlearned have been made uncertain by us, they still fight with stubborness and hatred, but they do not fight with authority. These Hemorrhoidae are held in admiration because of their opinions about the doctrine, on account of schisms, and, as Paul calls it, on account of the appearance of wisdom [cf. Col. 2:23]. They incite the minds of the mighty to oppress the truth. Inflamed by this poison the princes conceive flames of hatred. They become bloodthirsty and madly cruel. But Christ does not permit the light of the Gospel to be darkened, as it is written: "Whatever is of God will not be abolished" [cf. Mt. 24:35; Mark 13:31; Luke 26:33]. Therefore the church, in which the true doctrine is shining, will finally extract the stings from the Hemorrhoidae. These sophistical interpretations and the astute and cruel counsels of the wicked will not suppress the truth.

Here and there persons desirous of a godly agreement look for papal synods and hope that these will heal the church or correct its faults. But they are greatly deceived. For the popes and their associates and companions will never cease to wage war against Christ. I am not moved to expect this by merely human conjectures, which are many and weighty, but by the examples of all ages. For Christ says that blasphemers—who fight against the truth contrary to their own conscience, defend manifest idol-mania, and defile themselves with the blood of the godly—are not healed. Madness without doubt accompanies blasphemies and parricides, as the histories of Cain, Pharaoh, Saul, and the Jewish people testify. And God threatens blindness to blasphemers, as the Psalm [69:23] says: "Their eyes will be darkened." Therefore the pleas increase daily while the princes bind themselves to wicked alliances. Neither do they only go about openly, but they also build traps against the life of pious princes. Are we to think that they would tolerate moderate or pious counsels? We have experienced already a number of times that many who simulated moderation were really after nothing except to suppress us, catch us in a net, and destroy the entire kind of teaching.

I know that there are a certain few saner persons in the assemblies of the enemies who deplore the stubbornness of the mighty, but their counsels are rejected as counsels of schoolmen. Since these things are so, godly minds and those who think about their own salvation and the glory of Christ must ask which is the true church, in order that they may join it and be a part of this assembly and the flock of Christ, as Christ says: "He that is not with me is against me" [Luke 11:23]. Thereafter he should know that tyrants and persecutors of Christ, and those who either aid savagery or approve of it are by no means the church. About these we hold fast the very sure rule of Paul: "If anyone preaches another Gospel, let him be anathema" [Gal. 1:8]. And when he says: "Let him be anathema," let us not think that he is using a mild or vulgar malediction. When he says "anathema" he indicates that God has cast the enemies of the true doctrine out of the church, that they are to be avoided as gruesome pestilences whom God curses. Good people should know that they are polluted by the society and custom of such people, and that grave punishments will be given for friendship and association with them. The Psalm [109:18] says about people of this kind: "He puts on cursing as a garment, and it enters his inside like water, and as oil into his bones." Contact with this cursing harms others who are joined with those who oppose the truth and exercise savagery against the godly.

Therefore let us not think that it is of little importance that we have this commandment: "If anyone preaches another Gospel, let him be anathema" [Gal. 1:8]. They are not bishops; they are not members of the church, but enemies of Christ who, since they are driven by furies, are not concerned about harmony and peace of the church, but about establishing their tyranny. They are not eager to heal the church, but to set in motion civil wars, the devastation of churches, and murders of pious priests and of pious women. Therefore one must not expect betterment of the churches from them, but everyone should rather try to separate himself from them in thought, mind, and will. Everyone should flee from their idol-madness and should not listen to their abuses of the true doctrine, none should aid or approve of their plans, nor should anyone strengthen their power. "Flee idolatry," Paul says [1 Cor. 10:14]. These are not to be considered light precepts. Therefore let the true church be sought. We know that its prayers are heard; we know that in it are the members of Christ; we know that to it belong the promises of the Gospel. The promises do not belong to the enemies of the Gospel, even as they do not belong to the Jews or to the Mohammedans, as God frequently testifies and as Christ, the high priest, says in Ps. 16[:4]: "Their libations of blood I will not pour out or take their names upon my lips." Who would not be moved by this sad threat to flee the assembly of those who are adversaries of the true church?

Finally, the divine Scripture in both its parts is full of such speeches which command us to flee the enemies of the true doctrine and the true church, and to embrace the true doctrine, to love, aid, and adorn the true church. Let us not think that the church is merely a Platonic state. The true church is the assembly in which the pure doctrine of the Gospel shines forth and in which the divinely delivered sacraments are rightly administered. In such an assembly there are bound to be some living members of the church who render God true worship, who repent, call on God in true faith, show zeal and labor for spreading the Gospel, show their confession, serve their calling, and perform the pious duties commanded by God. They are exercised by dangers of every kind in which they practice calling on God and other good works. This I declare to be the true church, to which the godly everywhere on earth should be joined in belief, will and confession. And I consider our churches to be like that by the grace of God, since they profess the pure doctrine of the Gospel, which is without any doubt in agreement with the understanding of the catholic church of Christ.

Would that good minds might consider how important it is not to be in the camp of the enemies of the church, but to be a citizen of the true church of Christ for the sake of which God wanted to become known. For the sake of the true church he created everything. He has sanctified it with the blood of his own Son. In the true church he has revealed himself with wonderful works through the fathers, Noah, Abraham, Joseph, Moses, David, Elijah, Elisha, the apostles, and other lights of the church who ultimately will have eternal life and glory, and will enjoy association with God and the good angels. What glory and bliss it is to be an associate in this assembly, to be seen in the battle-line with Christ as the leader, around which the good angels fly, in which there are the chief men Adam, Noah, Abraham, Moses, Elijah, and other men endowed with outstanding gifts. In this battle-line you will already certainly have a place if you do not aid, approve of the wickedness and cruelty of the enemies of the church, but embrace the true doctrine, confess it, and adorn it with godly customs. The Psalm [122:6] says: "Pray for the peace of Jerusalem; blessed are those who love her." What a lovely and sweet statement! It urges all to aid every kind of office of the church to guard the purity and consensus of the church, to do good to teachers so they may commend the common safety to God in prayers and vows, and may keep wicked teachers and tyrants away from it.

I wish with all my mind that the men in government, which should and are able to help the church, would consider the magnitude of these duties. They should have regard for those who will come after us, to whom they wish to leave the state well organized. They ought much more to hand down to them the true knowledge of God, uncorrupted religion, the pure Gospel, and rightly constituted churches, as Paul commands Timothy faithfully to guard what has been entrusted to him in order that it may come uncontaminated to those who come after us [cf. 1 Tim. 6:20]. We see that this care does not trouble popes, cardinals, and canons at all. They fight about their wealth, not about the doctrine. Therefore others should assume this care in the schools and in the government of states. This sacrifice in particular God demands of all, as Peter says that we have been called so that we should show forth the good deeds of God [1 Pet. 2:9]. This foremost purpose of all counsels and actions should be set before the wise in order that they may serve the glory of Christ. God promises very great rewards for this service in this verse: "Blessed will be those who love the church" [cf. Ps. 122:6]. He promises defense, successes, and perpetual salvation to those who love the true church. With these words the godly should arouse their minds to care for the service of the church, and should not only strengthen themselves against the threats of tyrants, but should also fortify themselves against the sophistry of those who falsely cite testimonies of antiquity and the church for the defense of their ungodly dogmas. It was my desire to instruct students to some extent for the purpose of refuting these.

# Chapter 15

**1–2. We who are strong ought to bear with the failings of the weak**

Now he turns to the stronger, and in doing so repeats the second of the above propositions. For although he had previously spoken to both sides, he now teaches that side from which more prudence and fairness is demanded—the more learned. For he demands that they should show their strength more in tolerating than in disturbing the weak. He writes the same to the Corinthians, admonishing the learned that they should keep in mind the unlearned when he says: "Knowledge puffs up; love edifies" [1 Cor. 8:1].

For it seems that the more learned showed their learning in the use of liberty, as happens also in our time. But Paul commands that the opposite should be done, that the learned should provide a model for the unlearned, and by their pleasing behavior should invite the weak to the Gospel, and lift them up and strengthen them. Since we ought to use our powers not for harming, but for aiding others, as each one has greater gifts, so he ought all the more to strive to benefit others.

He adds the phrase: "Let each of us please his neighbor for his good, to edify him." Here he teaches that the use of liberty should be somewhat moderated, and what offenses we ought to avoid. There are two kinds of offense. Some people call the first kind offense that is taken. We call it Pharisaical offense when not brothers but enemies of the Gospel are irritated, when either the sound doctrine is taught or their wicked doctrine is rebuked, or some good and necessary work is done where the hypocrites think the example harms them, as the Pharisees in the Gospel were offended when Christ healed the sick on the Sabbath.

When Paul says that we should please others for good and for edification, he does not want the wickedness of the hypocrites strengthened by our hypocracy, but that the necessary doctrine be taught even to the unwilling and that the works commanded by God should be done. Such examples are to be found everywhere in the Scriptures. When kingdoms and states undergo change, there is always some offense and evil. Nevertheless, it was necessary that Moses should obey the commandment of God. The apostles had to preach the Gospel although the high priests forbade it and it was quite clear that it would bring the greatest change to the whole state.

This statement fortifies our consciences against these offenses: "We must obey God more than men'' [Acts 5:29]. And in general, one should think thus about the doctrine, both with the enemies of the Gospel and with those who want to be considered brethren, the doctrine must not[1] be hidden on account of the offenses.

## Faith Is to Be Placed Ahead of Love

The second kind of offense is called offense given, by which brethren are offended. For it is either bad doctrine or a bad example which harms others, or which others imitate, or because the glory of God or the church is harmed. For not only the enemies of the Gospel but also weak brethren are influenced by bad examples so that they speak evil of the church and the Gospel, and of Christ himself.

To this kind of offense belongs also a work that is in itself an indifferent thing but is done at the wrong time, where the example harms others. An example is the use of liberty among the common crowd which may be carried away by freedom, and with the weak who, since they do not understand the causes of freedom, are turned away from the Gospel and judge the kind of doctrine to be unholy, or imitate the examples of freedom with a doubting conscience.

About this kind of offense Paul teaches us correctly in this passage. He commands us to yield to the brethren for good and for edification he commands that we should invite others to the Gospel by our kindness, and raise up the weak by every service, so that they may be able to grow and make progress in the knowledge of Christ. If they appear to be scared away from the Gospel by the use of liberty, we should refrain from the use of our liberty until they have been better instructed. Moreover, these are brethren, not hypocrites or Epicureans who suppress the sound doctrine or kill those who teach godly things. Rather, these brethren permit themselves to be taught.

But in the case of the enemies of the Gospel, it is a matter of confession to show an example of liberty, as Paul writes to the Galatians [cf. Gal. 5] that he had done. And Christ excuses the apostles for violating the pharisaical tradition in Matthew 15. For it also is a pharisaical offense when enemies of the Gospel are offended by examples of liberty which are testimonies to the doctrine. Christ does not want us to be troubled by such offenses when he says: "Let them alone; they are blind, and leaders of the blind" [Mt. 15:14]. Because the Pharisees insist on their traditions with their ungodly opinions, they can justly be omitted, as has been said above.

But since there are some enemies who can be healed, moderation also

---

[1] The *CR* text omits the particle *non*, which is in our 1540 edition. The context suggests that the particle should be included.

pleases me. I love the teaching of the school of Aristotle which in all outward duties and in this custom of life praises moderation. We should be moderate in the use of liberty so that humaneness is not lacking in us, and so we may not rashly incite tumults.

Isocrates, a very wise man, says: "Since it is very difficult to reach the medium itself, it is better to err on that side where we risk less than is necessary, rather than on the other, where there is more boldness." If only this were taken into consideration in this business, which is full of danger! I shall quote his words since perhaps someone will love this precept more on account of the authority of so great a man: "It is best to reach the right point in time, since people find it hard to learn how to do without something they have, and hard and not to have an abundance. The moderate are better able to slim down in times of need than in times of plenty." But if virtue really is a certain middle road (according to a geometrical proportion, as Aristotle thinks), nature itself teaches us that a lack agrees better with moderation than overabundance. For in a geometrical proportion the middle number is closer to the least than to the greater as far as the total is concerned, as 2.4.8. Who does not see that the number four is farther removed from the number eight than from the number two?

### 3–4. For Christ did not please himself

To the precept he adds a reason taken from the example of Christ, which is quite clear. Afterward he commends to us the divine Scriptures and teaches a precept which is very beneficial with respect to the use of the Scriptures. He commands that we should hold fast our hope through patience and comfort of the Scriptures. This precept has great power if we test it in trials.

For its meaning is that no other revelations, no other illuminations are to be sought or looked for from heaven. When we are in anguish, we must look to this Word, which we hear or read, written beforehand in the sacred books. And we are to think that the promises set before believers in general are truly meant also for us. By this Word, faith and hope ought to be raised up, and we should know that this promise is a comfort also for us, and that God works through this Word.

Certain fanatics loudly shout that we are attributing a certain magical power to the words of Scripture. They command us to lay aside the Scriptures and to seek the will of God in certain other cogitations. But this shows that they do not know what faith is. For God wants to be sought in his Word, not outside of the Word in human imaginings. We do not attribute to words any magical powers, but hold that the will of God cannot be known except through the Word. Therefore we must run to the Word of God in all afflictions, as also Paul teaches in the epistle to the Ephesians [cf. Eph. 6:17]. For faith is knowledge of the will of God, since it is trust in the mercy and benevolence of God. Moreover, nothing is more deceitful than human imaginings outside the Word. When this has been lost sight of, the mind is oppressed by reasonings which command men to despair. Both Jews and Greeks have thoughts about God, and indeed say that he is good and merciful. But in a struggle of conscience they are overwhelmed by arguments which command them to despair, because they do not lay hold of the firm and sure promise in which God promises that he wants to forgive sins *gratis*.

The fanatics boast about their Spirit, and imagine that great impulses of the Spirit are brought about in minds without the Word of God. But Paul openly says the opposite: "Faith comes from hearing; hearing from the Word of God" [Rom. 10:17]. Therefore the Holy Spirit works through the Word. But those who hold the opposite and philosophize with idle minds do not consider how consciences are to be lifted up and comforted in true struggles.

Paul connects faith and hope in order to show what the difference is between philosophical and Christian patience. Let us distinguish them clearly and simply. Philosophical patience is without faith or hope of divine help. And if someone has any philosophical patience, it is shattered and overcome in the judgment of God, since it feels the eternal wrath of God. Perhaps in other calamities against men it may help a little. Since it is obedience by which we steadfastly obey right reason, lest, broken by grief, we do something that is against honor. But Christian patience is made up of two things: obedience toward God, and faith which awaits and hopes for divine help.

### 5–6. May the God of patience

This is a votum or prayer, which is a preparation for the close of this topic about the use of ceremonies. We pray that we may be given zeal for both peace and concord. He calls God a God of patience, as if he said: "God of the patient," that is, a God who regards and comforts those who suffer, as the Scripture frequently says elsewhere: Ps. 34[:18]: "The Lord is near to the brokenhearted, and saves the poor in spirit"; Ps. 10[:14]: "The poor man commits himself to you; you are the helper of the fatherless"; Ps. 12[:5]: 'Because of the misery of the poor and the groan of the needy, I will now arise,' says the Lord." Ps. 145[:14]: "The Lord upholds all who are falling, and raises up all who are bowed down"; Ps. 49[50:15]: "Call upon me in the day of trouble; I will deliver you." Let us fix these and similar statements firmly in our minds and declare that they are meant for us. With such promises let us arouse faith in ourselves, and nourish and strengthen it, for faith is nourished and made strong by this kind of exercise.

## 7–13. Therefore receive one another as also Christ has received us

This is the conclusion of the entire topic about the use of ceremonies. He exhorts Jews and Gentiles to concord and quotes the example of Christ which he set before them above. Although Christ is the Son of God, he most lovely embraced us who are poor and unworthy redeemed us by his death, and preserves us by his favor. Paul commands us to imitate this example and not to permit the tranquillity and concord of the church to be shaken on account of having different of rites.

Because this controversy about rites was then chiefly between Gentiles and Jews, he again inculcates in the Jews the testimonies which show that the Gospel belongs also to the Gentiles. Therefore, the Jews should not despise the Gentiles but embrace them as brothers and truly people of God. At the same time, he strengthens the Gentiles with these testimonies, lest they doubt that the benefits of Christ are meant also for them.

He cites among other passages a statement taken from Isaiah [Is. 11:10] which he quotes according to the translators of the Septuagint, as he usually does. However, the meaning of the Greek reading is not in disagreement with the Hebrew; it does not even differ much in the matter of the words. The Hebrews read thus: "In that day there will be a root of Jesse, which will stand that it may be a sign to the peoples. The nations will seek him, and his death[2] shall be glorious." What is read here: "he will stand that he may be a sign to the peoples," the Greeks translated: "he will be raised up that he may rule over the nations." The Hebrew word which we here translate as "sign" signifies banners, trophies, and similar memorials. He understands that Christ will be a leader and victor, under whose banner we will be safe, and by whose protection we will be shielded and defended against the greatest evils, which are sin, the wrath of God, hell, and the power of the devil. What the Hebrew has: "the people shall seek him," is the same as what the Greek says: "the nations shall hope in him." Those who expect help and salvation from someone hope and wait—they run and flee to him. The Hebrew says this with "they shall seek him." Therefore, if a person interprets the Greek reading skillfully, he will see that the meaning agrees wholly with the Hebrew reading.

This statement beautifully depicts the resurrection and reign of Christ. When he says "his death will be glorious," he indicates that he will not perish in death like other kings who lose their kingdoms when they die. But

---

[2] The Latin text has *erit mors eius gloriosa*, "his death shall be glorious." The next paragraph of Melanchthon's commentary also has this reading. The Masoretic text has *menuhato*, "his resting place." Either Melanchthon understood "his resting place" to mean "his grave," or he had a Hebrew text with the second and third consonants missing: *mtw*, which could be vocalized *moto*, "his death." The LXX has "resting place."

this king will occupy his kingdom through death, and after his death he will reign truly and gloriously. For also after his death he will be a sign to the peoples. Gentiles will run to him, expecting help and salvation from him. Therefore he will return to life after death. He will not be idle, but will defend, govern, and save those who flee to him.

The prophets are accustomed to hint at the resurrection of Christ in this way, because they testify that people will adore him forever, as in Ps. 72[:5]: "And they will fear him as long as the sun and moon endure." Likewise: "You are a priest forever" [Ps. 110:4; Heb. 7:21]. It was necessary for Christ to rise from the dead because he was to reign forever. For in this mortal life no king lives or rules forever.

Therefore this also signifies that the reign of Christ will not be a worldly reign, but a heavenly one in which things are done in a heavenly way, and in which the will of God will be brought to us.

Furthermore, the meaning would be a sad one if it described a kingdom in which only threats of God's judgment against men were set before us. The kingdom of Christ is described very differently here. A very great comfort is set forth in the most pleasing manner in these words. "The peoples shall hope in him." The reign of Christ will not be a reign of death and perdition, but a kingdom of hope and salvation. Christ came not in order to condemn, not to destroy, but that he might save and restore us already now before those damned and condemned to death.

This new kingdom has been established to be more powerful than the kingdom of sin and the Law. Since the Law had been given earlier, in which the wrath of God against sin had been shown, Christ did not come in order to bring a Law in which He would again condemn us. He brings a promise and comfort against that condemnation. Although our sins terrify us, we should know that Christ has been given us in order that we should hope for salvation. Through this high priest we have a gracious God. This leader shields us against the devil, death, and the savagery of the world. Therefore let us look to this verse in all afflictions: "The people will hope in him." Let us acknowledge that help and salvation must be sought and expected from Christ.

This phrase means the same thing: "He will stand as a sign to the peoples." This means he will reign, and people will look and flee to him as to the banner of a victor, and they will be defended by this leader and victor.

This also indicates what the nature of the kingdom of Christ will be. When he says "They will hope," it signifies that we will be upheld by this hope. Meanwhile, we are afflicted in this world and suffer harsh treatment. Nevertheless, we are defended and snatched out of our difficulties through Christ. But this tiny verse embraces so many things that it is difficult to enumerate them all; I am simply not confident that I could explain it.

Yet this explanation also must be added: in the kingdom of Christ, the highest worship is to hope in him. This is an outstanding proclamation about faith. God wants to be worshiped chiefly by this hope and trust in mercy. It also contains great comfort; since it calls for this hope against wrath, it surely hates and forbids despair.

Furthermore, this little verse ascribes to Christ divine power. It commands us to call on Christ, who is not reigning visibly. It commands us to hope in him. This certainly is ascribing to him divine power to hear prayer, and work in us, even though he does not dwell with us visibly and in the way mortals do. But I am not able to unwrap all things which this passage in Isaiah contains.

I have said these things in order that I might call this outstanding phrase to the attention of the reader, and that I might, as it were, set it in a more prominent place, because it teaches us that the kingdom of Christ is not a kingdom of death and perdition, but a kingdom of hope and salvation.

### 14–24. I am certain, my brethren

Now that he has finished this whole topic about the use of ceremonies, it might seem that he has scolded too vehemently, and certainly he has pointed out those who were abusing their liberty, grumblers, and those who because of their superstition were too unfair and too harsh toward good persons who were using their liberty. So Paul adds a reprieve by which he again calms the entire assembly of that church. For this reprieve of liberty, according to my judgment, properly belongs to the topic of the use of ceremonies. Although Paul speaks briefly, if one will observe the weight of the words, he will feel that Paul castigates both sides harshly: both the boisterous ones who want all things everywhere to be permitted to them, and the Timons[3] who demand that certain superstitious and Jewish ceremonies be diligently observed. If Paul has offended someone, he again placates him politely in the following way.

Since he wants to gain their good will, he expresses an opinion that does them honor in the matter at hand. He gives them first of all the praise that they are good and learned. Then he shows that he is led by his office not so much to teach them as to remind the learned. For the word *remind* carries less offense. When he mentions his office, he reminds them in passing how widely he had spread the Gospel. In order that they may have confidence in his teaching, he quotes also the miracles which vouch for the truth of his teaching. We should remember these miracles in order that we may know that we can safely give assent to the teaching of Paul as the Word of God, and may know for certain that the teaching of Paul has the approval of God.

---

3 Timon (d. ca. 230 B.C.) was a celebrated misanthrope of Athens.

Besides, he here again alludes to the topic of sacrifice when he mentions the sacrifices, the Gospel, etc. I have said that sacrifice is a work we render to God in order to bestow honor on him and confess that he is truly a God who hears our prayers, etc. However, when the New Testament demands true knowledge of God and righteousness of the heart—for together with eternal life it brings wisdom and eternal righteousness—it has sacrifices. These sacrifices are not dead animals, but living and abiding things: hearts which offer knowledge of God, fear, faith, prayer, proclamation of the Gospel and the benefits of God, giving of thanks, confession, patience and similar impulses which obey the Law of God. These things were signified in the Levitical ceremonies.

Because the New Testament does not contain shadows but wisdom and righteousness of the heart, it does not have ceremonies which are to be sacrifices *ex opere operato.* Under the law the Levites prepared the sacrificial victims and slaughtered cattle; however, the priests did the sacrificing. Thus in the New Testament the ministers of the Gospel both offer themselves and prepare other sacrifices. When they teach the Gospel and proclaim the mercy of God, when they call on God and give thanks, they are truly sacrificing and offering praise to God. They confess that he truly is God and Savior, as is written to the Hebrews [13:15]: "Through him let us always offer the sacrifice of praise to God," that is, the fruit of the lips which confess his name.

When they teach, they are also preparing other sacrifices. For those who believe the Gospel also become sacrifices. They are killed, that is, they become terrified through the knowledge of sin, and are made more alive, raised up by confidence in the mercy of God, and they acknowledge God. Therefore they offer him prayer, thanksgiving, confession, patience, and similar virtues. These sacrifices are acceptable to God on account of Christ, the high Priest, whom they accept as mediator when they hear the Gospel.

From this one can easily understand why this figure was chosen, ἱερουργοῦντα τὸ εὐαγγέλιον, "sacrificing the Gospel." For he wanted us to remember which are the true sacrifices of the New Testament. When he adds "so the offering up of the Gentiles might be acceptable," although it seems to be said ambiguously the statements are related to each other. Paul intends that the Gentiles offered by himself that is, prepared as sacrifices, may be acceptable, or that what the Gentiles are now offering, that is, that they are believing and calling on God, may be acceptable. For also the Gentiles themselves, have been prepared and, so to speak, consecrated and they offer their sacrifices. Thus the result of the matter is the same. In sum, he says that he spreads the Gospel everywhere in order that the Gentiles may come to know God, and become the people of God and sacrifices, and may call upon God and glorify him.

When he says "sanctified in the Holy Spirit," he teaches again that in the New Testament the outward duties are not sacrifices, nor do they please God *ex opere operato*. For he says the offering of the Gentiles is acceptable in this way—if it has been sanctified by the Holy Spirit, that is, if the Gentiles offer spiritual impulses, fear of God, and trust in the mercy of God.

Let us here observe the most honorable praises of the ministry of the Word. The preaching of the Gospel, explaining it, and treating it are the necessary sacrifices of the New Testament. This ought to comfort both those who teach and those who learn the Gospel amid so many difficulties which must be endured by both. The teachers should know that this worship of God is necessary. They should know it must be rendered for the sake of the glory of God. They should know that it pleases God, although some people hear the Gospel negligently, others despise it, and still others even persecute it. Also those who are learning the Gospel should remember that zeal for learning the Gospel is an act of worshiping of God which God both demands and approves. For we see how earnestly God commands this when he says about the Son: "Hear him" [Mark 9:7]. Therefore it is necessary to offer to God this duty, this act of worship.

Although we may be engaged in other occupations, as, for example, tillers of the soil are commended in the Law to consecrate the firstfruits of their labor to God, so let us also consecrate part of our labor and study to God. Although those persons who become moderately versed in humane letters and other common disciplines and then give themselves wholly to the study of the sacred books are greatly despised and hated, they also should comfort themselves with the argument that this kind of study is a necessary act of worship of God. It pertains to the glory of God, if only it is carried on in godly fashion. If they will consider this, they will easily scorn the judgments of those who flee far from Christian teaching as though it were defilement, and those who ridicule all who do not totally forsake sacred letters either from contempt of religion or because other professions bring in more money.

### 25–33. Now I am setting out for Jerusalem to serve the saints

Since he was speaking of his office, he mentioned in passing his travels. He adds that at some time he would also go to Rome after he returned from Jerusalem, where he says he is now going to deliver the money which had been collected everywhere for aiding the Christians in Judaea who had lost all their possessions on account of the profession of the Gospel. Under the Emperor Claudius, during whose time this epistle of Paul was written, a great famine was endured in the whole world, most of all in the Orient. At that time the Christians in Judaea most of all needed foreign aid because they had been robbed of their possessions.

Paul distinguishes from other alms the money collected for those who had first taught the Gospel. For this is a truer reward owed to teachers. He says: "They are their debtors. For if the Gentiles enjoy their spiritual good things, they ought in turn to supply carnal good things to them." Paul in this passage reminds us what we owe to teachers of the Gospel, a matter about which he speaks frequently and more fully in his other epistles.

Since we are at present living in a harsh age, in which those who teach and govern churches are treated most cruelly, I concluded that here the readers should be admonished that they should consider what they owe to those who govern the churches. Let them learn likewise what grave punishments God has threatened to those who despise the priests and teachers of the church and do not aid them proportionately. When Christ says that a laborer is worthy of his reward [Lk 10:7], he shows that a reward is owed to priests. Since this service is owed, more is required of us than in regard to the other alms, which are given *gratis*. And in another place Christ adds the glorious promise: "Whoever gives a cup of fresh water to drink to one of the least of these because he is a disciple, truly I say to you, he will not lose his reward" [Mt. 10:42; cf. Mark 9:41]. If we believe Christ, let us here show our faith and in this hope treat priests more humanely and generously, expecting that without doubt Christ will return thanks to us in greater measure.

This kind of service deserves many and great rewards, both spiritual and corporal: public peace, increases of our possessions, and defense, as Paul teaches in 2 Cor. 9. Conversely, the neglect of this duty is punished with the most severe punishments, as is written in Haggai, where God says that crops had been ruined and that other calamities besides had happened because the people were neglecting the temple and the priests. These are his words: "While my house is being neglected, each of you looks after his own house. On this account the heavens above you are forbidden to give dew and the earth is forbidden to give its produce [Hag. 1:9–10].

But what is happening now? In some places priests are cut down with more than Scythian cruelty. In other places they are all but compelled to perish from hunger, together with their poor wives and little children. The people not only give nothing of their own to them but also shamefully rob them of the payments which were donated to the churches by the generosity of our ancestors for the support of teachers and students of the sacred writings. In this matter there is a twofold evil: the present priests are killed by hunger, and because none are supported by the public to study sacred letters, there will be no men capable to teach the churches in the future. This threatens the destruction of the Christian religion everywhere. For how can religion be preserved without the study of literature, without capable teachers? Those irreligious persons are not only cruel toward present priests, but they also attempt to destroy the entire Christian religion as much as they can.

The laws of ancient rulers establish the most dreadful punishments for robbing temples. This is not, as the unlearned judge, because of some superstition, as though God wanted to be placated and worshiped with gold, but because the wisest rulers understood that the resources of the churches must be employed for preserving studies of the Christian doctrine. It is good for the state not only that food be provided for the present priests, but also so that the Christian doctrine will be propagated to those who come after us. This can be done in no other way except if good intellects who are destined for the study of sacred letters are publicly supported so that there may be some left who are able to teach rightly for those who come after us. It is necessary that these should be publicly nourished like soldiers, because while they bestow their labor on this matter they are not able to learn other skills which bring in money. Paul says most earnestly both about those who teach and of those who learn, comparing this order with the military: "No one fights as a soldier at his own expense" [1 Cor. 9:7]. For he shows that those who serve the church must be nourished at public expense.

But we shout these things in vain in these most miserable times, in which the Christian religion lies oppressed by manifold tyranny. However, the good are to be admonished all the more, lest they be led by these examples not to think reverently enough about priests. For we see how greatly these examples harm the common people. Therefore let us frequently remind ourselves of these things; let us inculcate them frequently in the people. We shall earn great rewards if we treat priests well. We will help them if we are concerned that the doctrine of Christ be faithfully propagated to those who come after us, and if we care that dreadful but just punishments will be given by God to those who are cruel to priests, who refuse to aid the study of the Christian doctrine.

On the other hand, also let priests remember their duty to teach rightly, to heal wavering consciences, and to adorn the Gospel with fitting morals. Those Epicureans—who not only do not teach the Gospel, but heartily laugh at all religions and consider sacred things as a source of gain—do not deserve to be called priests.

# Chapter 16

Almost this entire chapter is taken up with greetings. It is profitable to remember this example against certain hypocrites who take away all humane duties from the saints, since this act of friendliness indeed has significance for Christian love and is appropriate for teachers in particular.

In the end he admonishes them not to permit evil teachers, or those who sow teachings which militate against the Gospel, to come in or listen to them. When a physician has shown the remedies, he commands also to avoid the things which seem to be harmful. So after the apostle taught the chief topic of the Christian doctrine above, he urges them to be circumspect and watch lest some godless teachers sneak in on them.

So they may be able more easily to shun them, he indicates the tricks by which these impostors get around the inexperienced. They deceive, he says [v. 18], by eloquent speeches and praises.

Eloquent speeches without doubt mean flattering sermons. For there are flatteries both in the customs of those who teach and in the kind of teaching itself. As far as customs are concerned, these hypcrites know how to put on the complete appearance of friendliness, kindness, and patience. They know how to play skillfully on the feelings of those with whom they are dealing. Examples of this can easily be found among the monks. While the Anabaptists know they teach many things which are not totally false, they also teach absurdities and things that are against the entire nature of men. Nevertheless, they capture the minds of people with the prodigious simulation of patience and modesty. Here their doctrine also has its attractions. In a sense it flatters people, as when the common people are suddenly relieved of burdensome traditions and ingenious persons are freed from the bonds of heavenly dogmas which seem absurd to reason.

Ἐυλογίαι in Greek mean "praises," but Paul, after the Hebrew manner of speaking, calls εὐλογίας benedictions, that is, prayers for good things and glorious promises. These things easily make fools of minds occupied with hope, fear, and other emotions, as when riches are promised to the worshipers of Anna, when monks promise eternal life for their rites, and when they promise success in all undertakings for the sacrifice of a Mass. It is necessary that minds be fortified against all snares of this kind by sure and firm knowledge of the Word of God. As Peter says in 2 Pet. 1[:19]: "You will do well to pay attention to the prophetic message as to a lamp shining in a dark place until the day dawns and the morning star rises in your hearts.''

May God govern our hearts with his Holy Spirit for the sake of our Lord Jesus Christ, that we may hold fast the Gospel taught from heaven and go forward in knowledge and trust in Christ. May we adorn the glory of the Gospel with all godly duties, and may God again grant a godly and lasting concord to the church. Amen.

Thanks be to God!

# PERSON INDEX

# SCRIPTURE INDEX

www.ingramcontent.com/pod-product-compliance
Lightning Source LLC
Chambersburg PA
CBHW030257100426
42812CB00002B/474

*Black Silent Majority: The Rockefeller Drug Laws and the Politics of Punishment* (Cambridge, MA: Harvard University Press, 2015), 245–46; Richard Norton Smith, *On His Own Terms: A Life of Nelson Rockefeller* (New York: Random House, 2014), 574; Heather Ann Thompson, *Blood in the Water: The Attica Prison Uprising of 1971 and Its Legacy* (New York: Knopf, 2016), 19; Kohler-Hausmann, *Getting Tough*, 87.

4. Jennifer Mittelstadt, *From Welfare to Workfare: The Unintended Consequences of Liberal Reform, 1945-1965* (Chapel Hill: University of North Carolina Press, 2005), 113–19; Naomi Murakawa, *The First Civil Right: How Liberals Built Prison America* (New York: Oxford University Press, 2014); Elizabeth Hinton, *From the War on Poverty to the War on Crime* (Cambridge, MA: Harvard University Press, 2017).

5. Jarrod Shanahan, *Captives: How Rikers Island Took New York City Hostage* (London: Verso, 2022), 92–99.

6. Morrow to Rockefeller, memo, November 10, 1971.

7. Robert O. Self, *All in the Family: The Realignment of American Democracy Since the 1960s* (New York: Hill and Wang, 2012), 17–46.

8. See Marisa Chappell, *The War on Welfare: Family, Poverty, and Politics in Modern America* (Philadelphia: University of Pennsylvania Press, 2010), 21–64.

9. Pete Hamill, "The Revolt of the White Lower Middle Class," *New York Magazine*, April 14, 1969.

10. Claus Offe, "Legitimacy Versus Efficiency," in *Contradictions of the Welfare State*, ed. John Keane (Cambridge, MA: MIT Press, 1984), 143–44.

11. Interview of Harry O'Donnell by Hugh Morrow, August 9, 1980, p. 2, RG 4, series Q.2, box 3, folder 36, Rockefeller Papers.

12. Marsha E. Barrett, "Nelson Rockefeller, Racial Politics, and the Undoing of Moderate Republicanism" (PhD diss., Rutgers University, 2014), 287. See also Joshua M. Mound, "Inflated Hopes, Taxing Times: Fiscal Crisis, the Pocketbook Squeeze, and the Roots of the Tax Revolt" (PhD diss., University of Michigan, 2015).

13. Smith, *On His Own Terms*, 393; John D. Williams, "Rocky, the Bond Salesman," *Wall Street Journal*, November 3, 1967, p. 30; Sydney H. Schanberg, "Pay as Who Goes?," *New York Times*, January 20, 1968, p. 23.

14. Schanberg, "Pay as Who Goes?"

15. Nelson A. Rockefeller, "Message to the Legislature" [January 3, 1968], in *Public Papers of Nelson A. Rockefeller* (Albany: State of New York, 1968), 10.

16. Andrew Johns, *Vietnam's Second Front: Domestic Politics, the Republican Party, and the War* (Lexington: University of Kentucky Press, 2004), 203–4; Julilly Kohler-Hausmann, "Guns and Butter: The Welfare State, the Carceral State, and the Politics of Exclusion in the Postwar United States," *Journal of American History* 102, no. 1 (June 1, 2015): 87–99; Melinda Cooper, *Family Values: Between Neoliberalism and the New Social Conservatism* (Cambridge, MA: Zone Books, 2017), 25–67.

17. Quoted in Chesly Manly, "U.S. in Fiscal Crisis Because of LBJ, Rocky Charges," *Chicago Tribune*, February 20, 1968, p. 4.

18. Richard Ablin, "New York City's Perpetual Fiscal Crisis," *Wall Street Journal*, October 30, 1967, p. 18.

19. Richard Cloward and Frances Fox Piven, *Poor People's Movements: Why They Succeed, How They Fail* (New York: Pantheon, 1977), 264–362; Kornbluh, *The Battle for Welfare Rights*;

Annelise Orleck, *Storming Caesars Palace: How Black Mothers Fought Their Own War on Poverty* (Boston: Beacon Press, 2005); Premilla Nadasen, *Welfare Warriors: The Welfare Rights Movement in the United States* (New York: Routledge, 2005).

20. Kim Phillips-Fein, *Fear City: New York's Fiscal Crisis and the Rise of Austerity Politics* (New York: Henry Holt, 2017), 35–37.

21. Jon Shelton, *Teacher Strike!: Public Education and the Making of a New American Political Order* (Urbana: University of Illinois Press, 2017), 36; Joshua B. Freeman, *In Transit: Transport Workers Union in NYC, 1933–1966* (New York: Oxford University Press, 2001), 427 n. 53; Smith, *On His Own Terms*, 502.

22. Clarence Taylor, "Race, Rights, Empowerment," in *Summer in the City: John Lindsay, New York, and the American Dream*, ed. Joseph P. Viteritti (Baltimore: Johns Hopkins University Press, 2014), 71.

23. Joshua M. Zeitz, *White Ethnic New York: Jews, Catholics, and the Shaping of Postwar Politics* (Chapel Hill: University of North Carolina Press 2007), 181–84; Themis Chronopoulos, "The Lindsay Administration and the Sanitation Crisis of New York City, 1966–1973," *Journal of Urban History* 40, no. 6 (November 1, 2014): 1142–44.

24. Maria C. Lizzi, "'My Heart is as Black as Yours': White Backlash, Racial Identity, and Italian American Stereotypes in New York City's 1969 Mayoral Campaign," *Journal of American Ethnic History* 27, no. 3 (Spring 2008): 50.

25. "A Moral Issue of Garbage," *Life*, February 23, 1968, 63.

26. Typed notes on the strike, [ca. February 1968], RG 15, series 10.4, box 18, folder 168, Rockefeller Papers; "Statement by Nelson Rockefeller," February 8, 1968, and "Statement by Nelson Rockefeller," February 12, 1968, RG 15, series 10.4, box 18, folder 168, Rockefeller Papers; Vincent J. Cannato, *The Ungovernable City: John Lindsay and His Struggle to Save New York* (New York: Basic Books, 2001), 199–200.

27. "A Moral Issue of Garbage," 66.

28. Joseph A. McCartin, "'Fire the Hell out of Them': Sanitation Workers' Struggles and the Normalization of the Striker Replacement Strategy in the 1970s," *Labor: Studies in Working-Class History of the Americas* 2, no. 3 (September 1, 2005): 73–74.

29. Cannato, *The Ungovernable City*, 201–4.

30. Interview with T. Norman Hurd by Hugh Morrow, January 10, 1980, RG 4, Series Q.2, box 3, folder 15, Rockefeller Papers.

31. Michael A. Cohen, *American Maelstrom: The 1968 Election and the Politics of Division* (New York: Oxford University Press, 2016), 196–217; Matthew Lassiter, *The Silent Majority: Suburban Politics in the Sunbelt South* (Princeton, NJ: Princeton University Press, 2006), 232–33.

32. Quoted in "Rocky Says Role in Strike Cost Him GOP Nomination," *Washington Post*, October 28, 1969, p. 4.

33. A. H. Raskin, "Why New York is 'Strike City,'" *New York Times*, December 22, 1968, p. SM7.

34. See John D. Skrentny and Thomas J. Sugrue, "The White Ethnic Strategy," in *Rightward Bound: Making America Conservative in the 1970s*, ed. Bruce Schulman and Julian Zelizer (Cambridge, MA: Harvard University Press, 2008), 171–79; Self, *All in the Family*, 41; Timothy J. Lombardo, *Blue-Collar Conservatism: Frank Rizzo's Philadelphia and Populist Politics* (Philadelphia: University of Pennsylvania Press, 2018), 5–17; Kenneth D. Durr, *Behind the Backlash: White Working-Class Politics in Baltimore, 1940–1980* (Chapel Hill: University of North Carolina Press, 2003), 147–49; Jefferson Cowie, *Stayin' Alive: The 1970s and the Last Days of the Working Class* (New York: New Press, 2010), 80–81.

35. Peter Kihss, "Teamsters Score Rise in Welfare," *New York Times*, June 14, 1968, p. 35.

36. Quoted in Peter Kihss, "Welfare Grants to Rise in State," *New York Times*, June 27, 1968, p. 31; "'Living Wage,'" *New York Times*, September 24, 1968, p. 46.

37. Kornbluh, *Battle for Welfare Rights*, 94, 104–11.

38. Interview of William Pfeifer by Hugh Morrow and Thomas Stephens, April 5, 1980, pp. 42–43, RG 4, series Q.2, box 3, folder 44, Rockefeller Papers.

39. "Unbalanced State Budget," *New York Times*, December 24, 1968, p. 22.

40. Interview of Edward Kresky by Hugh Morrow, August 24, 1979, p. 45, RG 4, Series Q.2, box 3, folder 47, Rockefeller Papers.

41. Quoted in Sydney H. Schanberg, "Rockefeller Hints at Sales Tax Rise," *New York Times*, December 11, 1968, p. 1.

42. Quoted in William Fulton, "Report from New York," *Chicago Tribune*, December 24, 1968, p. 11.

43. "Social-Aid Pleas in State Rise 50%," *New York Times*, December 29, 1968, p. 43.

44. Quoted in "Social-Aid Pleas in State Rise 50%."

45. John A. Hamilton, "The Welfare Muddle," *New York Times*, December 29, 1968, p. E2. Between 1966 and 1968, Mississippi payments per person rose only a mere fifty cents, whereas New York's grew by another thirteen dollars. "Program and Operating Statistics: Public Assistance in September 1968," *Welfare in Review* 6 (January-February 1969): 47.

46. "Social-Aid Pleas in State Rise 50%." See also, William D. Berry, Richard C. Fording and Russell L. Hanson, "Reassessing the 'Race to the Bottom' in State Welfare Policy," *Journal of Politics* 65, no. 2 (May 1, 2003): 327–49.

47. Karen Tani, *States of Dependency: Welfare, Rights, and American Governance, 1935–1972* (New York: Cambridge University Press, 2016), 7.

48. See Stephen Amberg, "Constructing Industrial Order in the Center of the American Economy: How Electoral Competition and Social Collaboration Evolved in Twentieth-Century New York," *Studies in American Political Development* 31, no. 1 (April 1, 2017): 108–129.

49. Clyde Woods, *Development Arrested: The Blues and Plantation Power in the Mississippi Delta* (London, Verso 2017), 196–200.

50. Cathy Kunzinger Urwin, *Agenda for Reform: Winthrop Rockefeller as Governor of Arkansas, 1967–71* (Fayetteville: University of Arkansas Press, 1991), 88–89, 196.

51. "Nixon's Response to Inquiries About His Economic Policies," *New York Times*, October 27, 1968, p. F14.

52. Nelson A. Rockefeller, *The Future of Federalism* (Cambridge, MA: Harvard University Press, 2013 [1962]), 44

53. David S. Broder, "Rocky Urges Federalizing of Welfare," *Washington Post*, December 6, 1968, p. A1.

54. David S. Broder, "Retention of Bliss Indicated," *Washington Post*, December 8, 1968, p. A1.

55. Quoted in Broder, "Rocky Urges Federalizing of Welfare."

56. Kohler-Hausman, *Getting Tough*, 141–46.

57. "Excerpts from Rockefeller's Message to the Legislature Asking a Trimmed Budget," *New York Times*, January 22, 1969, p. 30.

58. "Memo for Richard M. Nixon," January 30, 1969, box 39, folder "Rockefeller, Nelson (Gov.) 1/1/69–12/31/69," White House Central Files, Alphabetical Name Files, Nixon Papers.

59. Rockefeller admitted beforehand that he was only "moderately optimistic" about the White House's response to his proposals. The governor worried that Nixon might well choose to

follow the lead of the Johnson administration and continue waging war in Vietnam instead of shifting resources to state and local governments. Leroy F. Aarons, "Revenue-Sharing Plan to Be Urged by Rocky," *Washington Post*, February 12, 1969, p. A2; James Reston, "Nelson Rockefeller on the Fiscal Crisis," *New York Times*, January 10, 1969, p. 46.

60. Smith, *On His Own Terms*, 546–47.

61. Daniel P. Moynihan, *The Politics of a Guaranteed Income: The Nixon Administration and the Family Assistance Plan* (New York: Vintage, 1973), 97.

62. Moynihan, *The Politics of a Guaranteed Income*, 97.

63. Ellen Reese, *Backlash Against Welfare Mothers: Past and Present* (Berkeley: University of California Press, 2005), 101.

64. Chappell, *The War on Welfare*, 70.

65. Moynihan, *The Politics of a Guaranteed Income*, 97.

66. Richard Nixon, "Address to the Nation on Domestic Programs" [August 8, 1969], *The American Presidency Project*, https://www.presidency.ucsb.edu/node/239998.

67. Brian Steensland, *The Failed Welfare Revolution: America's Struggle over Guaranteed Income Policy* (Princeton, NJ: Princeton University Press, 2008), 14, 61; Robert L. Allen, *Black Awakening in Capitalist America: An Analytical History* (Trenton, NJ: Africa World Press, 1992 [1969]), 239–40; Chappell, *The War on Welfare*, 65–105.

68. Steensland, *The Failed Welfare Revolution*, 61.

69. Quoted in "State Chiefs Praise Nixon Welfare Plan," *Chicago Tribune*, August 10, 1969, p. 8.

70. Quoted in William Russell Coil, "'New Deal Republican': James A. Rhodes and the Transformation of the Republican Party, 1933–1983" (PhD diss., Ohio State University, 2005), 281.

71. "The Governors' Views on Federal-State and State-Local Relations," *Public Administration Review* 30 (January-February 1970): 40; Taylor Pensoneau, *Governor Richard Ogilvie: In the Interest of the State* (Carbondale: Southern Illinois University Press, 1997).

72. Nixon, "Address to the Nation on Domestic Programs."

73. Richard A. Hogarty, *Massachusetts Politics and Public Policy: Studies in Power and Leadership* (Amherst: University of Massachusetts Press, 2002), 76–77.

74. Diane Lund and Toby Sherwood, "Welfare Law," in *1971 Annual Survey of Massachusetts Law* (Boston: Little and Brown, 1972), 22.

75. Quoted in "Sargent Welfare," *Bay State Banner*, December 11, 1969, p. 9.

76. Nadasen, *Welfare Warriors*, 95.

77. Quoted in "Sargent Governor Signs Welfare Bill over Recipients' Protest," *Bay State Banner*, September 4, 1969, p. 1.

78. Cloward and Piven, *Poor People's Movements*, 306–7.

79. The governor's staff estimated that the FAP still left New York State on the hook for some $80 million in welfare costs, a figure projected to reach $275 million by 1975. Mary McAniff to Nelson Rockefeller, memo, July 30, 1969, RG 15, series 34, box 36, folder 909, Rockefeller Papers. In response to Rockefeller's concerns, the administration outlined a series of stipulations that would require states to spend federal money in the "general area of public assistance." John R. Price to Daniel P. Moynihan, memo, August 4, 1969, box 39, folder "Rockefeller, Nelson (Gov.) 1/1/69–12/31/69," White House Central Files, Alphabetical Name Files, Nixon Library.

80. US Congress, House of Representatives, Committee on Ways and Means, *Social Security and Welfare Proposals*, 91 Cong., 1 sess., October 31, 1969, pp. 1290.

81. Herbert Stein, *Presidential Economics: The Making of Economic Policy from Roosevelt to Clinton* (Washington, DC: American Enterprise Institute, 1994), 136–37.

82. That said, NAM still demanded the phased elimination of food stamps and cutting off benefits for anyone on strike. Jill Quadagno, "Race, Class, and Gender in the U.S. Welfare State: Nixon's Failed Family Assistance Plan," *American Sociological Review* 55, no. 1 (February 1, 1990): 19–20.

83. Steensland, *The Failed Welfare Revolution*, 101.

84. Quoted in Tom Herman, "Welfare Reform: The Southern View," *Wall Street Journal*, December 15, 1970, p. 22.

85. Bruce J. Schulman, *From Cotton Belt to Sunbelt: Federal Policy, Economic Development, and the Transformation of the South, 1938–1980* (New York: Oxford University Press, 1991), 198; Thomas A. Lyson, *Two Sides to the Sunbelt: The Growing Divergence Between the Rural and Urban South* (New York: Praeger, 1989), 134; Lassiter, *The Silent Majority*, 11.

86. Quadagno, "Race, Class, and Gender in the U.S. Welfare State," 21–22; Joseph Hower, "Jerry Wurf, the Rise Of AFSME, and the Fate of Labor Liberalism, 1947–1981" (PhD diss., Georgetown University, 2013), 278–79.

87. Steensland, *The Failed Welfare Revolution*, 153–54; Self, *All in the Family*, 40; Chappell, *The War on Welfare*, 89–90.

88. Interview with Johnnie Tillmon, January 16, 1994, Henry Hampton Collection, Department of Special Collections, Washington University in St. Louis Libraries.

89. Eva C. Bertram, "The Institutional Origins of 'Workfarist' Social Policy," *Studies in American Political Development* 21, no. 2 (Fall 2007): 203–29.

90. Peter Siskind, "Shades of Black and Green: The Making of Racial and Environmental Liberalism in Nelson Rockefeller's New York," *Journal of Urban History* 34, no. 2 (January 1, 2008): 245.

91. Jason Epstein, "The Last Days of New York," in *The Fiscal Crisis of American Cities: Essays on the Political Economy of Urban America with Special Reference to New York*, ed. Roger E. Alcaly and David Mermelstein (New York: Vintage, 1977), 66. See also John H. Mollenkopf, *The Contested City* (Princeton, NJ: Princeton University Press, 1983), 3–4, 25.

92. Smith, *On His Own Terms*, 287; Joshua Freeman, *Working-Class New York: Life and Labor Since World War Two* (New York: Free Press, 2000), 102–3.

93. Jack Newfield, "The Case Against Nelson Rockefeller," *New York Magazine*, March 9, 1970, pp. 26, 28–29.

94. Joshua B. Freeman, "Hardhats: Construction Workers, Manliness, and the 1970 Pro-War Demonstrations," *Journal of Social Science History* 26, no. 4 (Summer 1993): 733–34.

95. See, for example, Brian Purnell, "'The Revolution Has Come to Brooklyn': Construction Trades Protests and the Negro Revolt of 1963," in *Black Power at Work: Community Control, Affirmative Action, and the Construction Industry*, ed. David A. Goldberg and Trevor Griffey (Ithaca, NY: Cornell University Press, 2010), 23–47.

96. For the Buffalo protestors, effective affirmative action required the immediate establishment of a state "construction school" and a hiring hall operated by the State Commission on Human Rights. "Action Groups Demand Rocky Arrange Jobs for Negroes on UB Project," clipping, February 7, 1969, RG 15, series 8, box 1, folder 11, Rockefeller Papers.

97. Committee for Efficiency in Government, "Official Lawlessness in New York State: Construction Employment, Government Inaction, and the $275 Million Annual Cost," [November 1969], pp. 2, 57, RG 15, series 21.1, box 24, folder 251, Rockefeller Papers.

98. "Statement by Governor Nelson A. Rockefeller," press release, February 13, 1970, pp. 1–5, "Affirmative Action Program Proposed by Bricklayers Local 45 New York, Carpenters District Council of Buffalo and Vicinity, Ironworkers Local No. 6, Laborers Local 210, and Teamsters Local 499," [ca. February 1970], and "Affirmative Action Program Proposed by the Building and Construction Trades Council of Buffalo and Vicinity and Construction Industry to Provide Equal Employment Opportunity," [February 1970], RG 15, series 8, box 1, folder 1, Rockefeller Papers. See also "Governor Bars Negro Job Quota; Hails Union Plan," New York Times, July 26, 1963, p. 1; Purnell, "'The Revolution Has Come to Brooklyn,'" 43–44; Dale Wright to Alexander Aldrich, September 27, 1963, RG 15, series 21.1, box 23, folder 241, Rockefeller Papers; "Transcript of News Conference of Governor Nelson A. Rockefeller," January 5, 1964, RG 15, series 21.1, box 23, folder 241, Rockefeller Papers.

99. Quoted in "'Racist Unions' Set Plan for State, Gaiter Says," Buffalo Evening News, February 13, 1970, RG 15, series 8, box 1, folder 11, Rockefeller Papers.

100. "Asks Nixon for 'Philly Plan' For Jobs in Buffalo," Jet, March 5, 1970, p. 4.

101. Dean J. Kotlowski, Nixon's Civil Rights: Politics, Principle, and Policy (Cambridge, MA: Harvard University Press, 2001), 111.

102. Jospeh Mattina, et al. to Alton Marshall and Anthony G. Adinolfi, memo, [ca. April 1970], RG 15, series 8, box 1, folder 12, Rockefeller Papers; "Rocky Aides to Resume Minority Hiring Talks," Courier Express, March 25, 1970; "Talks Collapse in State Bid for Minority Accord," Buffalo News, March 25, 1970; "Minority Rejects Move for Accord," Courier Express, March 26, 1970, RG 15, series 8, box 1, folder 11, Rockefeller Papers; Nelson Rockefeller to James T. Hemphill, June 6, 1970, RG 15, series 8, box 1, folder 12, Rockefeller Papers.

103. Edmund F. Wehrle, "'Partisan for the Hard Hats': Charles Colson, George Meany, and the Failed Blue-Collar Strategy," Labor: Studies in Working-Class History of the Americas 5, no. 3 (Fall 2008): 54–56.

104. "Hard Hats, Students, and GOP Moderates," Ripon Forum, September 1970, p. 8. Founded in 1962, the Ripon Society (named after one of the founding sites of the Republican Party) became a key advocacy and research group pushing against right-wing mobilization within the GOP. See Geoffrey Kabaservice, Rule and Ruin: The Downfall of Moderation and the Destruction of the Republican Party, from Eisenhower to the Tea Party (New York: Oxford University Press, 2012), 72–96.

105. Taylor, "Race, Rights, Empowerment," 70–71; Diana Lurie, "Underneath the Hard Hats: A Political Symposium," New York Magazine, November 2, 1970, p. 30.

106. Smith, On His Own Terms, 565–66.

107. Quoted in "Rockefeller Carefully Testing Political Winds," New York Times, October 11, 1970, p. 175.

108. To quote Reagan: "I didn't leave the Democratic Party. The Democratic Party left me." Rick Perlstein, The Invisible Bridge: The Fall of Nixon and the Rise of Reagan (New York: Simon & Schuster, 2014), 403.

109. Harry O'Donnnell to Burdell Bixby, Hugh Morrow, and Tom Losee, memo, June 9, 1970, RG 15, series 21.1, box 11, folder 125, Rockefeller Papers.

110. David Stebenne, Arthur J. Goldberg: New Deal Liberal (New York: Oxford University Press, 1996), 378.

111. "Rockefeller for Governor," October 31, 1970, RG 15, series 21.6, box 106, folder 1284, Rockefeller Papers.

112. Nelson Rockefeller, "Remarks to New York State Building and Construction Trades Convention," August 6, 1970, p. 1, RG 15, series 33, box 77, folder 3114, Rockefeller Papers.

113. Victor Riesel, "Rockefeller-Labor Alliance Neutralizing Lindsay, Kennedy," *Human Events*, July 4, 1970.

114. Stebenne, *Arthur J. Goldberg*, 375.

115. Quoted in Emanuel Perlmutter, "Teamsters Break Custom and Back Rockefeller," *New York Times*, June 2, 1970, p. 1.

116. See Philip F. Rubio, *There's Always Work at the Post Office: African American Postal Workers and the Fight for Jobs, Justice, and Equality* (Chapel Hill: University of North Carolina Press, 2010), 233–61.

117. Stephen A. Hopkins to Joseph Persico, August 20, 1970, RG 15, series 33, box 78, folder 3152, Rockefeller Papers; Damon Stetson, "Delegates Welcome Governor at A.F.L.-C.I.O. Parley," *New York Times*, September 4, 1970, p. 1.

118. Victor Borella to Nelson Rockefeller, memo, September 14, 1970, RG 15, series 21.3, box 73, folder 802, Rockefeller Papers.

119. Quoted in Emanuel Perlmutter, "Gotbaum Assails Labor 'Rightists,'" *New York Times*, September 28, 1970, p. 11.

120. Lurie, "Underneath the Hard Hats," 30, 33.

121. The Rockefeller campaign identified twenty-nine New York City assembly districts (accounting for some 45 percent of the city's entire electorate) as being working-class "white ethnic" bastions. "Report of the 1970 New York City Republican Campaign," pp. 2–3, RG 15, series 21.5, box 104, folder 1248, Rockefeller Papers.

122. Kevin Phillips, "Voting Patterns in New York City (1952–1966)," typescript, February 1967, pp. 1–3, RG 15, series 21.2, box 77, folder 847, Rockefeller Papers. See also Cowie, *Stayin' Alive*, 130–31.

123. Ripon Society, *Lessons of Victory* (New York: Dial Press, 1969), 148.

124. Hugh Morrow to Nelson Rockefeller, memo, July 23, 1970, RG 15, series 21.3, box 72, folder 798, Rockefeller Papers.

125. "Report of the 1970 New York City Republican Campaign," p. 19.

126. Interview of Joseph W. Canzeri by Hugh Morrow, August 21 and 23, 1979, p. 37, RG 4, series Q.2, box 1, folder 3, Rockefeller Papers.

127. Rockefeller's share of the Black vote fell by ten points since 1966, dropping from 36 percent to about 20 percent four years later. "Report of the 1970 New York City Republican Campaign," pp. 10, 19–20.

128. Phillips, "Voting Patterns in New York City (1952–1966)," pp. 9–10.

129. Raymond Brown, "Campaigning with the Gov.," *New York Amsterdam News*, October 31, 1970, p. 40.

130. Interview of Fiorvante (Fred) Perrotta by Hugh Morrow, March 11, 1980, p. 24, RG 4, Series Q.2, box 3, folder 46, Rockefeller Papers.

131. George T. Bell to John D. Ehrlichman, memo, December 21, 1971, box 39, folder "1/1/72–[8/1/74] (1)," White House Central Files, Alphabetical Name Files, Nixon Papers.

132. Robert Mason, "'I Was Going to Build a New Republican Party and a New Majority': Richard Nixon as Party Leader, 1969–73," *Journal of American Studies* 39, no. 3 (December 1, 2005): 469–70.

133. "A Republican Majority?," *Wall Street Journal*, April 27, 1970, p. 18.

134. Quoted in "Unions Aim for the Blue-Collar Vote," *Business Week*, September 1970, p. 48.

135. Richard J. Levine, "Strikes Ahead?," *Wall Street Journal*, January 27, 1970, p. 1.

136. "Memo to President Nixon," [ca. January 1970], box 5-P, folder "Declassified Romney HUD Papers," Romney Papers; Cowie, *Stayin' Alive*, 133–34.

137. Cowie, *Stayin' Alive*, 141–42.

138. "Nixon and Labor," *New York Times*, September 13, 1970, p. E3.

139. Duncan Foley, "The Balance Sheet: Foley's Law," *Ripon Forum*, April 1970, p. 26.

140. Quoted in Cowie, *Stayin' Alive*, 143.

141. "Detroit Stalemate: A Blow for Economic Recovery," *Business Week*, September 19, 1970, p. 30.

142. Quoted in Byron E. Calame, "Jobs and Votes," *Wall Street Journal*, October 21, 1970, p. 1.

143. Quoted in Rowland Evans and Richard Novak, "Will Strike by GM Doom GOP Hopes in the Midwest?," *Philadelphia Inquirer*, October 26, 1970, p. 9.

144. Mason, "'I Was Going to Build a New Republican Party and a New Majority,'" 472–73.

145. "Northrup Study on Aid to Striking Workers," in *Hearings, Reports and Prints of the House Committee on Interstate and Foreign Commerce* (Washington, DC: US Government Printing Office, 1971), p. 520.

146. Albert J. Thieblot Jr. and Ronald M. Cowin, *Welfare and Strikes: The Use of Public Funds to Support Strikers* (Philadelphia: Industrial Relations Unit, Wharton School, 1972), 105, 108–9.

147. "The Family-Assistance Plan: A Chronology," *Social Service Review* 46 (December 1, 1972): 605.

148. "Rockefeller for Governor," press release, October 31, 1970, RG 15, series 21.6, box 106, folder 1284, Rockefeller Papers; Kohler-Hausmann, *Getting Tough*, 69–70.

149. "Campaigning with the Gov.," p. 40.

150. Jackie Robinson to Nelson Rockefeller, memo, March 18, 1971, RG 15, series 10.3, box 59, folder 655, Rockefeller Papers.

151. Stephen A. Hopkins to Robert R. Douglass, March 19, 1971, RG 15, series 10.3, box 59, folder 655, Rockefeller Papers.

152. New York State Department of Social Services, press release, March 12, 1971, RG 15, series 10.3, box 59, folder 655, Rockefeller Papers.

153. Louis J. Lefkowitz to Nelson Rockefeller, memo, March 18, 1971, RG 15, series 10.3, box 59, folder 655, Rockefeller Papers.

154. "Governor Rockefeller's Special Message to the Legislature," press release, March 28, 1971, RG 15, series 10.3, box 59, folder 655, Rockefeller Papers.

155. Barry Van Lare to Robert Douglass, memo, June 15, 1971, RG 15, series 10.3, box 59, folder 657, Rockefeller Papers.

156. Louis Levine to Nelson Rockefeller, September 23, 1971, RG 15, series 10.3, box 51, folder 682, Rockefeller Papers.

157. Peter Kihss, "2 Welfare Plans Backed by H.E.W," *New York Times*, November 25, 1971, p. 38.

158. C. Gerald Fraser, "Plan on Welfare is Criticized Here," *New York Times*, December 5, 1971, p. 15; "Workers, Clients Against Join Welfare Plan," *New York Amsterdam News*, November 20, 1971, p. A14; "Local Opposition Mounts to Rocky's Welfare Plan," *New York Amsterdam News*, November 6, 1971, p. C9.

159. Ken Cole to Jonathan Moore, memo, April 26, 1971, box 39, folder "1/1/71-12/31/71," White House Central Files, Alphabetical Name Files, Nixon Papers.

160. Kohler-Hausmann, *Getting Tough*, 145–46.

161. Richard Wiebe to Nelson Rockefeller, memo, November 11, 1971, RG 15, series 10.3, box 51, folder 584, Rockefeller Papers.

162. Christopher Baylor, *First to the Party: The Group Origins of Political Transformation* (Philadelphia: University of Pennsylvania Press, 2017), 120–41; Daniel Schlozman, *When Movements Anchor Parties: Electoral Alignments in American History* (Princeton, NJ: Princeton University Press, 2015), 101–7; Daniel K. Williams, *God's Own Party: The Making of the Christian Right* (New York: Oxford University Press, 2010), 113.

163. Donald T. Critchlow, *Intended Consequences: Birth Control, Abortion, and the Federal Government in Modern America* (New York: Oxford University Press, 1999), 79–81.

164. Quoted in Melanie K. Welch, "Not Women's Rights: Birth Control as Poverty Control in Arkansas," *Arkansas Historical Quarterly* 69, no. 3 (Autumn 2010): 221.

165. "Report of the Governor's Commission Appointed to Review New York State's Abortion Law," March 1968, pp. 16–17, 34–35, RG 15, series 10.3, box 23, folder 219, Rockefeller Papers.

166. Stacie Taranto, *Kitchen Table Politics: Conservative Women and Family Values in New York* (Philadelphia: University of Pennsylvania Press, 2017), 63–69.

167. Quoted in Self, *All in the Family*, 146. See also the interview of Nelson Rockefeller by Barry Gary, April 10, 1970, RG 15, series 21.2, box 1, folder 1, Rockefeller Papers.

168. Daniel K. Williams, *Defenders of the Unborn: The Pro-life Movement Before Roe V. Wade* (New York: Oxford University Press, 2010), 101.

169. Taranto, *Kitchen Table Politics*, 69.

170. Taranto, *Kitchen Table Politics*, 77–82.

171. That compromise laid the basis for the congressional Hyde Amendment barring the use of federal funding for abortions. Taranto, *Kitchen Table Politics*, 75.

172. "City Sues State Over Order That Limits Abortion Payments," *New York Times*, April 13, 1971, p. 43.

173. Quoted in "Plan to Ban Abortion Medicaid Expected to Increase City's Cost," *New York Times*, April 3, 1971, p. 26.

174. Quoted in "Rockefeller Chided About Abortion Plan," *New York Amsterdam News*, May 8, 1971, p. 24.

175. Angela Y. Davis, *Women, Race, & Class* (Boston: Pantheon, 1983), 204.

176. Ron Maiorana to Hugh Morrow, memo, March 9, 1972, RG 15, series 21.2, box 1, folder 1, Rockefeller Papers.

177. Lloyd A. Free and Charles W. Roll to Nelson Rockefeller, memo, [ca. March 1972], RG 15, series 21.5, box 104, folder 1244, Rockefeller Papers.

178. Leslie J. Reagan, *When Abortion Was a Crime: Women, Medicine, and Law in the United States, 1867-1973* (Berkeley: University of California Press, 1998), 241–42.

179. J. Edward Mayer III to Nelson Rockefeller, May 10, 1972, RG 15, series 21.2, box 1, folder 1, Rockefeller Papers.

180. "Editorial delivered by WBBM Radio, Chicago," [ca. May 1972], RG 15, series 21.2, box 1, folder 1, Rockefeller Papers.

181. Taranto, *Kitchen Table Politics*, 82–87.

182. "New York State Abortion Education Program, Election Analysis," December 13, 1972, RG 15, series 10.4, box 39, folder 407, Rockefeller Papers.

183. Beatrice Blair to Nelson Rockefeller, December 1, 1972, RG 15, series 10.4, box 39, folder 407, Rockefeller Papers.

184. Taranto, *Kitchen Table Politics*, 91.

185. "Memorandum on Conference with Governor Rockefeller," December 20, 1972, RG 15, series 10.4, box 39, folder 407, Rockefeller Papers.

186. Taranto, *Kitchen Table Politics*, 89.

187. Michael Whiteman to Nelson Rockefeller, February 19, 1973, memo, RG 15, series 10.4, box 39, folder 407, Rockefeller Papers.

188. Hugh Morrow to Nelson Rockefeller, memo, February 2, 1973, RG 15, series 21.2, box 1, folder 1, Rockefeller Papers.

189. Interview of Kresky by Morrow, August 24, 1979.

190. Paul Vitello, "Edward M. Kresky, Who Calmed Fiscal Panic, Dies at 88," *New York Times*, January 30, 2013, p. A21.

191. Cowie, *Stayin' Alive*, 152–56.

192. Cowie, *Stayin' Alive*, 149–50.

193. See Cooper, *Family Values*.

194. Paul Frymer, "Acting When Elected Officials Won't: Federal Courts and Civil Rights Enforcement in US Labor Unions, 1935–85," *American Political Science Review* 97, no. 3 (August 1, 2003): 494–95; Nancy MacLean, *Freedom is Not Enough: The Opening of the American Workplace* (Cambridge, MA: Harvard University Press, 2006), 275–76.

195. Mark Erlich, and Jeff Grabelsky, "Standing at a Crossroads: The Building Trades in the Twenty-First Century," *Labor History* 46, no. 4 (November 2005): 424.

196. Priya Kandaswamy, *Domestic Contradictions: Race and Gendered Citizenship from Reconstruction to Welfare Reform* (Durham, NC: Duke University Press, 2021), 162.

197. Mason B. Williams, "How the Rockefeller Laws Hit the Streets: Drug Policing and the Politics of State Competence in New York City, 1973–1989," *Modern American History* 4, no. 1 (March 1, 2021): 67–90; Julilly Kohler-Hausmann, "'The Attila the Hun Law': New York's Rockefeller Drug Laws and the Making of a Punitive State," *Journal of Social History* 44, no. 1 (October 1, 2010): 71–95; Donna Murch, "Who's to Blame for Mass Incarceration?," *Boston Review*, October 2015. Cf. Fortner, *Black Silent Majority*.

198. Cooper, *Family Values*.

199. See Andrew Elrod, "The Burglaries Were Never the Story," *N+1*, July 13, 2022.

200. Judith Stein, *Pivotal Decade: How the United States Traded Factories for Finance in the Seventies* (New Haven, CT: Yale University Press, 2010), 112–115; Smith, *On His Own Terms*, 653–57.

### Epilogue

1. President's Commission for a National Agenda for the Eighties, *Urban America in the Eighties: Perspectives and Prospects, Report of Panel V of the President's Commission for a National Agenda for the Eighties*, October 23, 1980; series 5, subseries 13, box 153, Scranton Papers; Robert Pear, "Panel on National Goals Proposes U.S. Aid for Migration to Sun Belt," *New York Times*, December 27, 1980, p. 1; William W. Scranton to Daniel P. Moynihan, January 29, 1981, series 5, subseries 13, box 153, Scranton Papers.

2. *Urban America in the Eighties: Perspectives and Prospects, Report of Panel V*.

3. See, for example, "American Slavonic League Mailing," February 1960, series 2, box 2, file 9, Scranton Papers.

4. Office of Senator Hugh Scott, press release, October 22, 1960, and Bernie Blier to William W. Scranton, March 8, 1960, series 2, box 20, file 20, Scranton Papers; Hugh Scott to William W. Scranton, March 25, 1960, series 2, box 4 file 23, Scranton Papers.

5. Hugh Scott to William W. Scranton, March 25, 1960, series 2, box 4 file 23, Scranton Papers; James Van Zandt to William W. Scranton, May 6, 1960, series 2, box 4, file 24, Scranton Papers; William W. Scranton to Hugh Scott, et al., May 17, 1960, series 2, box 4, file 24, Scranton Papers.

6. "The 'Scranton Plan' Works!," flyer, [November 1959], series 2, box 2, file 1, Scranton Papers.

7. Gregory S. Wilson, *Communities Left Behind: The Area Redevelopment Administration, 1945-1965* (Knoxville: University of Tennessee Press, 2009), 87-88; William W. Scranton to Lawrence F. O'Brien, February 26, 1962, series 2, box 2, file 24, Scranton Papers.

8. Kim Phillips-Fein, "American Counterrevolutionary: Lemuel Ricketts Boulware and General Electric, 1950-1960," in *American Capitalism: Social Thought and Political Economy in the Twentieth Century*, ed. Nelson Lichtenstein (Philadelphia: University of Pennsylvania Press, 2007), 249-270.

9. "Comparison of Scranton Bill with Other Legislation Introduced for Aid to Depressed Areas," typescript, [ca. 1961], series 2, box 4, file 20, Scranton Papers.

10. Thomas D. Morris to Daniel J. Flood, February 28, 1962, series 2, box 2, file 24, Scranton Papers. Another of Scranton's colleagues from Pennsylvania's Republican congressional delegation also lamented that he too heard "the same old story that nothing could be done" from the Department of Defense about the closing of a Curtiss-Wright plant in his district. James Van Zandt to William W. Scranton, February 15, 1962, series 2, box 2, file 24, Scranton Papers.

11. Wilson, *Communities Left Behind*, 88.

12. See Adam Hilton, *True Blues: The Contentious Transformation of the Democratic Party* (Philadelphia: University of Pennsylvania Press, 2021).

13. Brent Cebul, *Illusions of Progress: Business, Poverty, and Liberalism in the American Century* (Philadelphia: University of Pennsylvania Press, 2023), 255.

14. Jimmy Carter, "President's Commission for a National Agenda for the Eighties Statement on Receiving the Commission's Final Report" [January 16, 1981], *The American Presidency Project*, https://www.presidency.ucsb.edu/node/250751; Tim Barker, "Other People's Blood," *N+1*, Spring 2019; Gabriel Winant, "'Hard Times Make for Hard Arteries and Hard Livers': Deindustrialization, Biopolitics, and the Making of a New Working Class," *Journal of Social History* 53, no. 1 (Fall 2019): 107-32.

15. Stuart Hall, "The Great Moving Right Show," in *Selected Political Writings: The Great Moving Right Show and Other Essays*, ed. Sally Davidson et al. (Durham, NC: Duke University Press, 2017), 185.

16. Hall, "The Great Moving Right Show," 171-72.

17. Mike Davis, *Prisoners of the American Dream: Politics and Economy in the History of the US Working Class* (London: Verso, 1986), 246.

18. *Socialism and Black Liberation: A Statement by a Black Revolutionary from the League of Revolutionary Workers* (Detroit: Revolutionary Workers League, 1981), 2-3.

19. James Boggs, *The American Revolution: Pages from a Negro Worker's Notebook* (New York: Monthly Review Press, 1963), 50.

20. See Ruth Wilson Gilmore, "Globalisation and U.S. Prison Growth: From Military Keynesianism to Post-Keynesian Militarism," *Race & Class* 40, nos. 2-3 (1999 March): 171-88;

Jason Hackworth, *Manufacturing Decline: How Racism and the Conservative Movement Crush the American Rust Belt* (New York: Columbia University Press, 2019).

21. Lily Geismer, *Left Behind: The Democrats' Failed Attempt to Solve Inequality* (New York: Public Affairs, 2022).

22. Stephanie L. Mudge, *Leftism Reinvented: Western Parties from Socialism to Neoliberalism* (Cambridge, MA: Harvard University Press, 2018), 260–303; Melinda Cooper, *Family Values: Between Neoliberalism and the New Social Conservatism* (Cambridge, MA: Zone Books, 2017), 25–66. See also Wolfgang Streeck, *Buying Time: The Delayed Crisis of Democratic Capitalism* (London: Verso, 2014), 47–63.

23. Namara Smith, "Send in the Clowns: Centrists, Leftists, Andrew Yang Fans," *N+1*, Spring 2020.

24. Kristoffer Smemo, "Managing a Regime in Crisis: The Twilight of Neoliberalism and the Politics of Economic Recovery During the First Year of the Obama Administration," in *Looking Back on President Barack Obama's Legacy: Hope and Change*, ed. Wilbur C. Rich (New York: Palgrave MacMillan, 2019), 47–68.

25. Republican National Committee, *Growth and Opportunity Project Report* (Washington, DC: RNC, 2013), pp. 5, 9.

26. Daniel Martinez HoSang and Joseph E. Lowndes *Producers, Parasites, Patriots: Race and the New Right-Wing Politics of Precarity* (Minneapolis: University of Minnesota Press, 2019), 52, 70.

27. Turnout for the 2016 presidential election looked like the inverse of 2012 as the key Democratic constituencies that twice carried Obama to victory failed to come out for Hillary Clinton while the same proportion of Romney voters came out solidly for Trump. On top of reclaiming the White House, the GOP won new majorities in Congress and thirty-four state houses. Mike Davis, "Election 2016," *New Left Review* 103 (January-February 2017).

# INDEX

# ACKNOWLEDGMENTS

This book has been a long time in the making. I owe so much to so many people who helped, encouraged, and taught me along the way. My deepest gratitude, of course, comes with the caveat that all errors and omissions found here are mine alone.

The whole thing began with a suggestion Bruce Laurie made while I worked on my master's thesis at the University of Massachusetts, Amherst. On top of giving me the idea to explore how the mass upheavals and struggles of the Depression years forced a reckoning in the Republican Party, I learned how to think and write about the intertwined, and inextricable, histories of work, protest, and politics from a pioneer in the field. I also benefited enormously from Bruce's keen editorial pen and always enjoyed our pints together at the Moan and Dove.

Bruce helped change my life again by introducing me to Nelson Lichtenstein and sending me on my way to Santa Barbara for my PhD. I know I'm not alone when I say that no one could ask for a better advisor and mentor than Nelson. At every step, Nelson's teaching, boundless enthusiasm, intellectual generosity, and unflagging advocacy for my work helped shape a lot of rough ideas and loose threads into a book. He is a comrade and friend. Thank you also to Eileen Boris. I learned so much from Eileen's Marxist Feminism course as well as from the experiences she shared with me from her time at the Massachusetts Commission Against Discrimination. Both Nelson and Eileen welcomed me to California, not to mention making it possible for me to meet my partner, Heather.

I am deeply indebted to my dissertation committee for giving me the foundation on which to build a book. Thank you to Alice O'Connor, who always pushed me to refine my arguments, think more carefully, and above all write better. In her classes and in our many conversations, I learned critically important lessons about the fraught relationship between the production of research knowledge and its impact on policymaking. Her scholarship stands as an example that I tried my best to emulate in these pages. I began this book in earnest in Laura Kalman's research seminars. Laura's expertise and insights and her excitement for this project from the beginning, gave me the confidence to push on. I always looked forward to my meetings with the late M. Stephen Weatherford. Not only did he offer incisive comments on many drafts of many different chapters, but his good cheer kept me focused on the big questions about how ideas, interests, and institutions shape our political world. Stephen's sudden passing leaves me saddened that I could not show him the final product.

I count myself very lucky to have made so many great friends and comrades during my (many) years in graduate school. Much love to the people who made Santa Barbara home, especially Sasha Coles, Andrew Elrod, Joe Figulo-Rosswurm, Jesse Halvorsen, Sarah Johnson, Kurt Newman, Tim Paulson, Samir Sonti, Cody Stephens, Brian Tyrell, and Morag and Will Murphey. Even though Jill Jensen finished just as I arrived, she set me up with an apartment and helped me land jobs over the years. Thank you, Jill! I first met Richard Anderson back in Amherst, and while he continued his graduate studies on the other side of the country, he remained another great friend and ally on the long march through the dissertation and the book project. Over the years I spent wrestling with this book, I especially want to thank Richard, Samir, Joe, and Andrew for graciously reading and commenting on drafts right up until the end.

Whether in classrooms, on conference panels, in writing groups, answering email queries, sharing documents, or their own work in progress, I am indebted to a wide-ranging community of scholars, including Seth Ackerman, Marsha Barrett, Kevin Boyle, Tony Chen, Darren Dochuk, Alice Echols, David Engstrom, Leon Fink, Joshua Freeman, Paul Frymer, Mary O. Furner, Ian Gavigan, Lily Geismer, Joe Hower, Mike Koncewicz, Kevin Kruse, Steve Lilienthal, Joe Peschek, Leah Wright Rigueur, Sam Rosenfeld, Steve Rosswurm, Kara Schlichting, Daniel Schlozman, Andy Seal, David Stebenne, David Stein, the late Judith Stein, Kristin M. Szylvian, Rick Valelly, Mason Williams, and Gabe Winant. I want to also express my appreciation to the many interlocutors, editors, and reviewers who helped me develop my ideas at formative stages of the project. Thanks to Mike Koncewicz for inviting me to present work in progress at the Tamiment Library, and to Kara Schlichting for thoughtful commentary that helped me get through an especially tricky chapter. Thanks, too, to Richard Anderson for including me in the 1968/2018: Cities on the Edge series at Princeton University. Parts of Chapter 1 appeared previously as "A 'New

Dealized' Grand Old Party: Labor and the Emergence of Liberal Republicanism in Minneapolis, 1937–1939," *Labor: Studies in Working-Class History* 11,
no. 2 (Summer 2014): 39–59. Portions of Chapter 2 were first published as
"The Little People's Century: Industrial Pluralism, Economic Development,
and the Emergence of Liberal Republicanism in California, 1942–1946," *Journal of American History* 104, no. 4 (March 2015): 1166–89.

Starting a new life in a new city just as a global pandemic disrupted the
most basic routines would have been impossible without the incredible community we met in St. Louis. Many, many thanks to Peter Kastor who brought
me into the History Department at Washington University and for his efforts
in securing the resources that helped me finish up the book. Thank you as
well to Rebecca Wanzo for everything she has done to help me get settled at
WashU. I've been so fortunate to have such great colleagues as Corinna Treitel
in History, Joe Lowenstein at the Interdisciplinary Project for the Humanities,
and Paige McGinley, Noah Cohan, and Karen Skinner in American Culture
Studies. I so appreciate Dean Erin McGlothlin's good cheer and support as I
wrapped up the book. It's been a pleasure and a privilege to work with such
wonderful students who do so much to keep me curious (and hopeful) about
the past and present. And thanks to so many new friends as well, including Fannie Bialek, Marc Blanc, Rachel Brown, Andrea Friedman, Sid Issar,
Kavi Issar-Brown, Ted Mathys, Lucy Mathys-Smith, Trevor Sangrey, Rachel
Greenwald Smith (whose book *On Compromise* offered up the best possible
definition of the word), and Anika Walke.

No historian can work without all the tireless labor of archivists. I am
grateful for all those who helped me at the Minnesota Historical Society;
California State Archive; Bancroft Library at the University of California,
Berkeley; the Alfred Young Special Collections at UCLA; San Francisco State
University Labor Archive; Eisenhower Presidential Library; Rare Books and
Special Collections at the Rush Rhees Library, University of Rochester; Bent-
ley Historical Library at the University of Michigan; Special Collections and
University Archives at the University of Oregon; Rockefeller Archive Center;
Special Collections and University Archives at the State University of New
York, Stony Brook; University Archives and Special Collections at the Uni-
versity of Southern Indiana; the New Jersey State Library; Special Collections
Library at Pennsylvania State University; the Southern California Library
for Social Studies and Research; the Donald R. & Beverly J. Gerth Archives
& Special Collections at the CSU-Dominguez Hills University Library; and
Olin Library at Washington University in St. Louis. Many institutions also

generously supported this research. I want to thank the Eisenhower Presidential Foundation, the Bentley Library at the University of Michigan, the UCSB Graduate Division of Social Sciences and Humanities, the UCSB Department of History, UCSB History Associates, the Regents of the University of California, the Rockefeller Archive Center, and the Special Collections Library at Pennsylvania State University.

A number of archivists and librarians warrant special mention too. Jennifer Greene of the University of Southern Indiana went above and beyond by digitizing and sending along large chunks of the Charles LaFollette papers. Melinda Windsor of the University of Rochester and Robert Heym and Deborah Mercer of the New Jersey State Library also graciously scanned and shared key documents. At the Rockefeller Archive Center, Amy Fitch offered me great guidance and assistance during my time in Tarrytown and after. Thank you to Jim Quigel, Julie Porterfield, and Athena Jackson for bringing me to State College. I also appreciate the work of Elizabeth Clemens and Mary Wallace at the Reuther Library, Angela Cox of the Richmond, California Public Library, Jenny McElroy of the Minnesota Historical Society, and Sarah McLusky and Diana Bachman at the Bentley Library at the University of Michigan who made possible photo reproductions and permissions.

I've been so lucky to have had the opportunity to publish with Penn Press. My editor, Bob Lockhart, was a steadfast (and most patient) backer of this book through the long process of finishing this project. Bob's positivity, good cheer, and vision for the book always kept me focused, especially through tough times of revising and rethinking big parts of the project. I couldn't ask for a better editor. I owe many, many thanks to the anonymous reviewers who gave this manuscript such close and careful readings. Sarah Watkins provided invaluable copy editing at a crucial stage in the writing and revision. I also want to thank everyone at Penn Press who helped bring this book to a conclusion, especially Lachlan Brooks, Alex Gupta, and Lily Palladino.

As I strained my eyes in front of a computer screen, music always accompanied me during the many hours I spent hunched over a laptop, typing away at this book. These recordings always seemed to help me break through the toughest mental blocks anyone writing a book encounters: Bedhead, *WhatFunLifeWas*, Ash Ra Tempel, *Ash Ra Tempel*, Alex Chilton, *Like Flies on Sherbet*, Alice Coltrane, *Journey in Satchidananda*, and lots and lots of Grateful Dead bootlegs, especially those from June 4, 1970, March 28, 1973, June 23, 1974, August 28, 1981, August 10, 1982, and October 14, 1983. Many thanks to the musicians who made the music that kept me going, and much appreciation to the intrepid and meticulous tapers—archivists in their own right—who captured the Dead on stage.

Family and friends, including those who are no longer here, supported me in so many ways. Old friends Lily Langerud, Nik Haug, Mat Elfring—who first saw me off to graduate school so many years ago now—always welcomed me back home and always made me feel like I never left. Here's to Paul Anderson and the Anderson family, the Berningers (Beth, Dieter, Andrea, and Paul), Kristina DeName, Heidi James, Elliott Sharp, Alli Katz, Al Bernardo, and Colleen Deel, too. My parents Ken Smemo and Nancy O'Brien Smemo, sister Molly Smemo, her partner Abby Kaufman and their little ones Ella and Ruth, and my late grandparents Ken and Beryl O'Brien were always a source of comfort. Margi Waller welcomed me into her home and made me feel like a part of the family on our many stays in the redwoods and the mountains. Thank you as well to Michael and Arlene Spiegler for all their love and support (and a special thanks to Michael for all the music recommendations that helped me finish up the book). My deepest debt is to my parents. From my dad I learned to love trying to uncover the past. From my mom I learned to love everything about reading and writing. Together, they opened whole new worlds for me to explore and experience. For that, I can never thank them enough. I'm thrilled to show this to my mom. I really wish my dad could have lived to see this book.

When all is said and done, I simply could not have finished this—nor could I even imagine having undertaken such an involved project—without Heather Berg's support, guidance, and love. We met in grad school and every day since then has been the happiest of my life. Heather read every word I wrote, more than once, and kept reading. She talked me through plenty of ideas, and out of plenty of bad ones too. I look forward to all our conversations, not to mention all the laughter that animates our days together. Heather's influence on my prose and politics is on every page. I cherish our partnership and feel beyond lucky to share my life with her. I really cannot express how grateful I am for all that she's done and sacrificed to make it possible for me to see this project through to the end. Whenever I lost faith in myself, she never did. Not once. Thank you just isn't enough for her. I'm also excited to one day share this with our child Leif, who arrived just as I wrapped this thing up. Now that this is all done, we can all finally take Gus, a most patient guy, for a long walk.

www.ingramcontent.com/pod-product-compliance
Lightning Source LLC
Chambersburg PA
CBHW030257100426
42812CB00002B/475